STAR WARS REBELS

Based on the series Star Wars Rebels created by

Dave Filoni & Simon Kinberg & Carrie Beck

Based on Star Wars created by

George Lucas

Art by

Mitsuru Aoki

2

CONTENTS

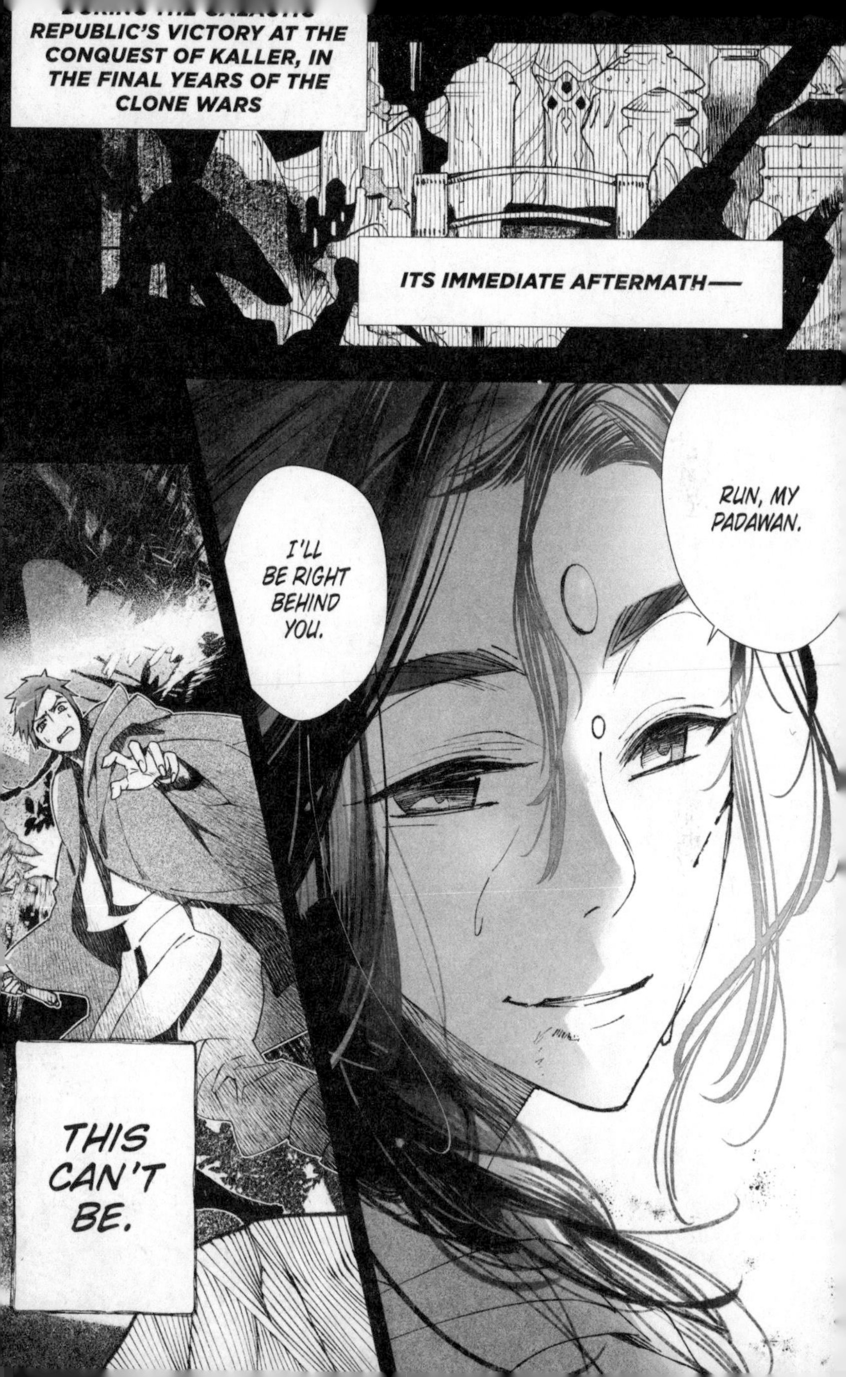
REPUBLIC'S VICTORY AT THE CONQUEST OF KALLER, IN THE FINAL YEARS OF THE CLONE WARS
ITS IMMEDIATE AFTERMATH—
RUN, MY PADAWAN.
I'LL BE RIGHT BEHIND YOU.
THIS CAN'T BE.

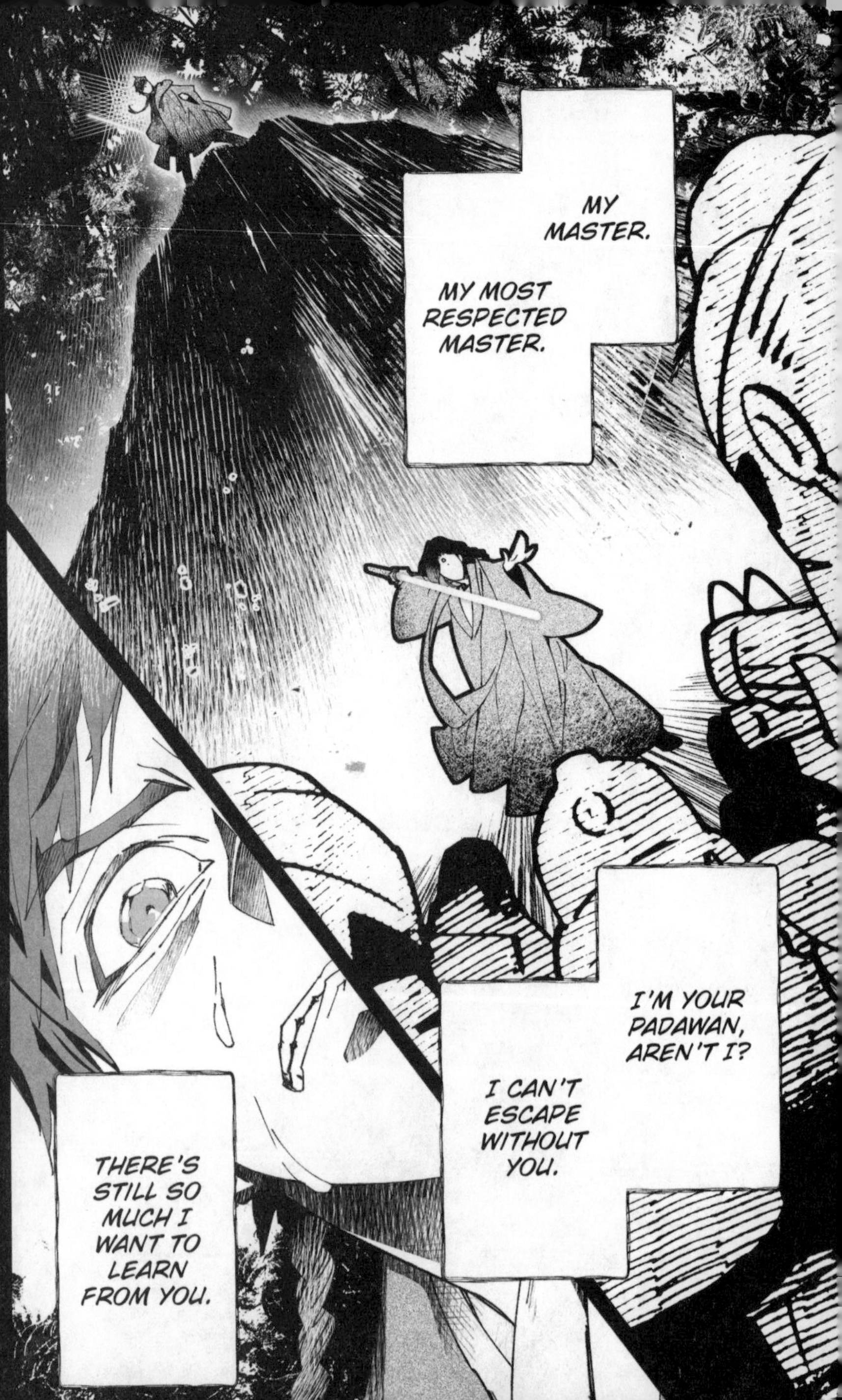
MY MASTER.
MY MOST RESPECTED MASTER.
I'M YOUR PADAWAN, AREN'T I?
I CAN'T ESCAPE WITHOUT YOU.
THERE'S STILL SO MUCH I WANT TO LEARN FROM YOU.

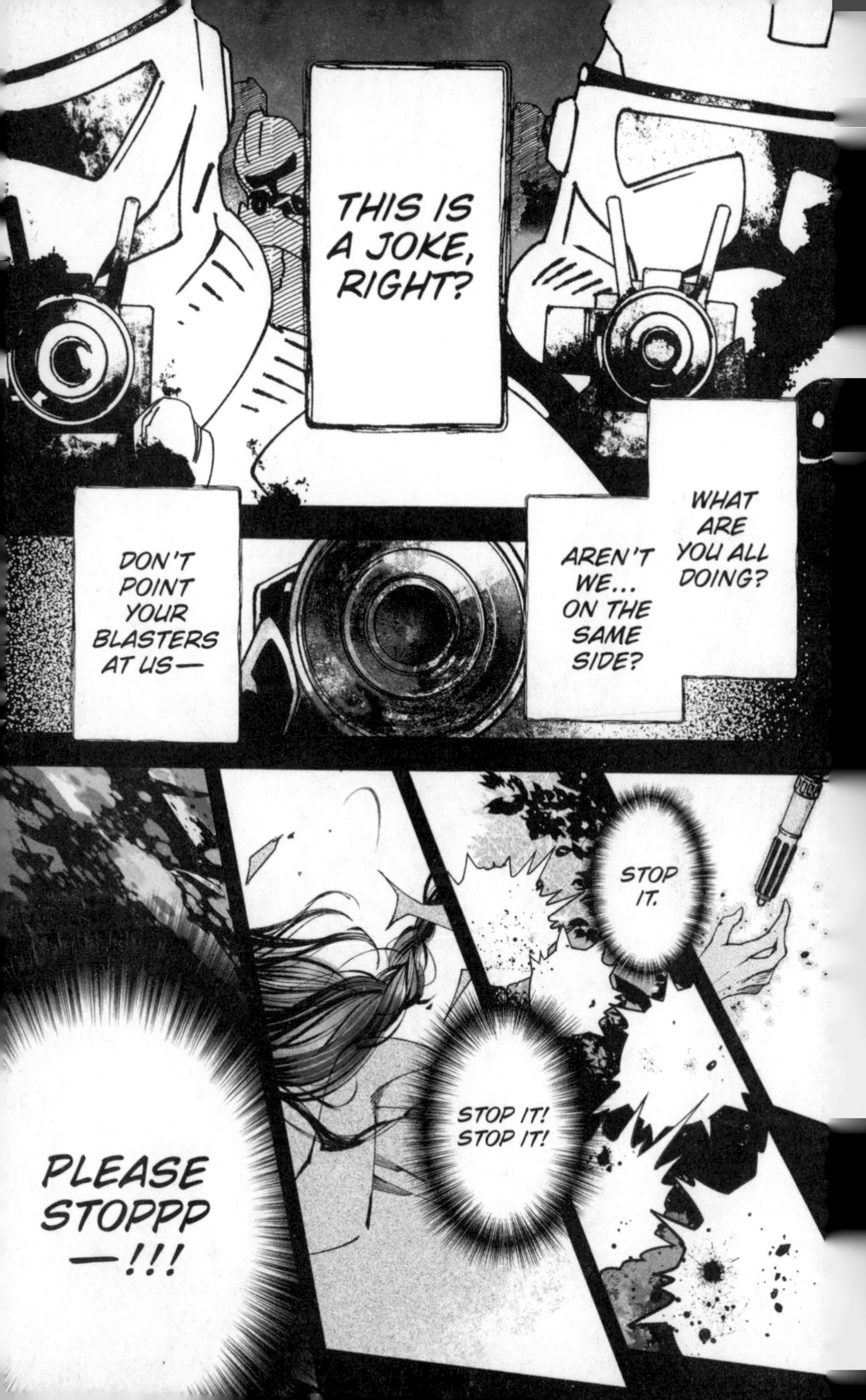
THIS IS A JOKE, RIGHT?
WHAT ARE YOU ALL DOING?
AREN'T WE... ON THE SAME SIDE?
DON'T POINT YOUR BLASTERS AT US—
STOP IT.
STOP IT! STOP IT!
PLEASE STOPPP—!!!

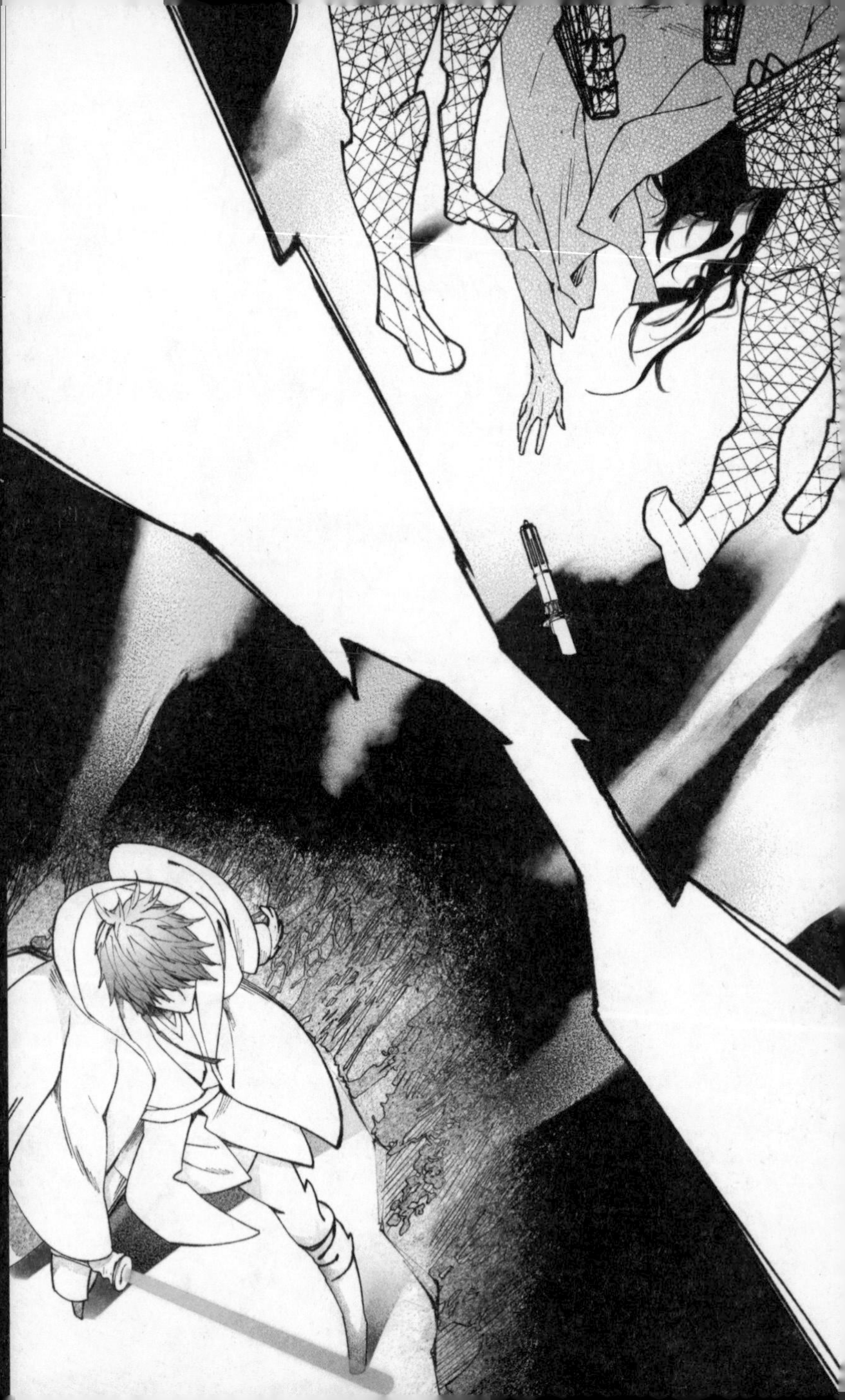

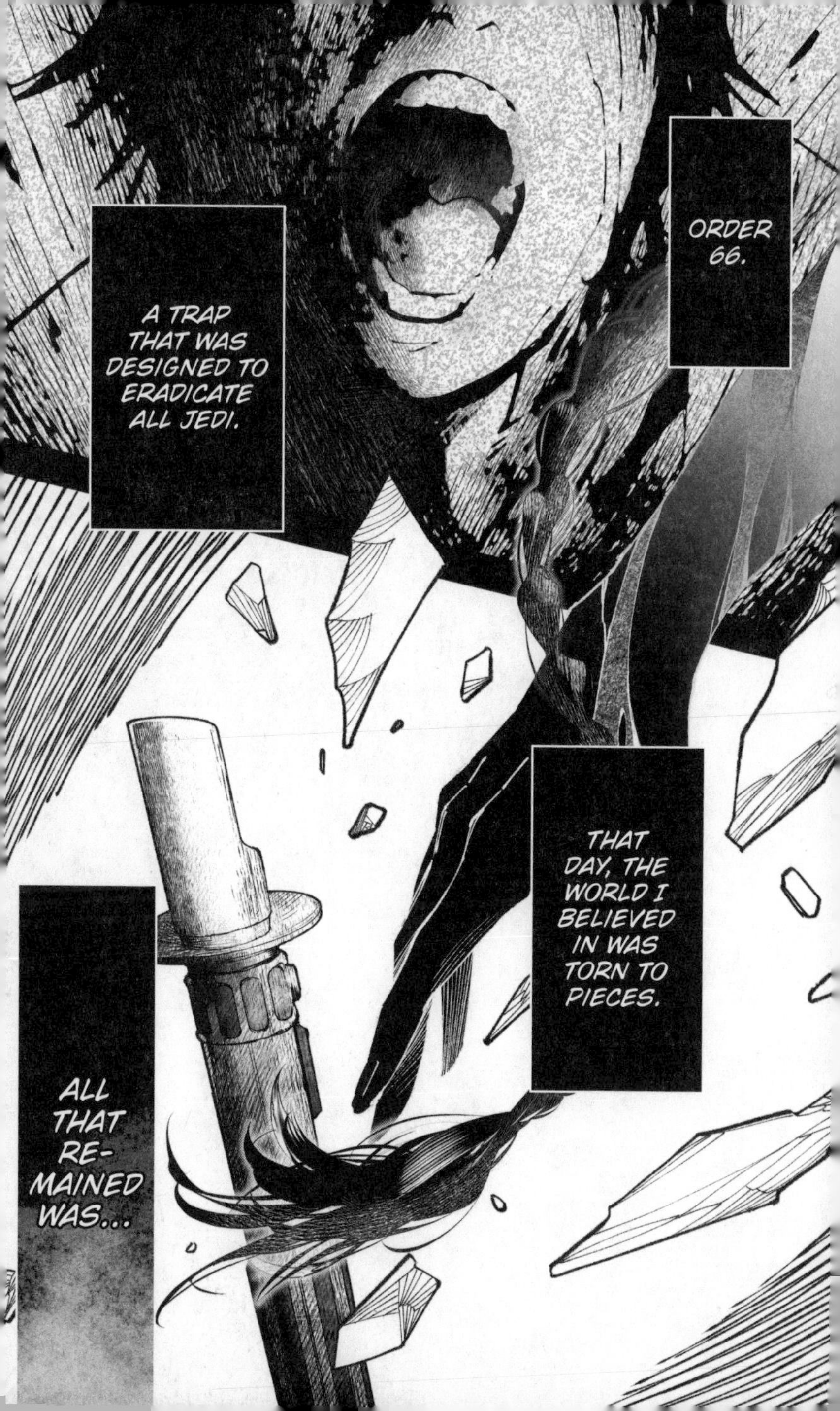
ORDER 66.
A TRAP THAT WAS DESIGNED TO ERADICATE ALL JEDI.
THAT DAY, THE WORLD I BELIEVED IN WAS TORN TO PIECES.
ALL THAT RE-MAINED WAS...

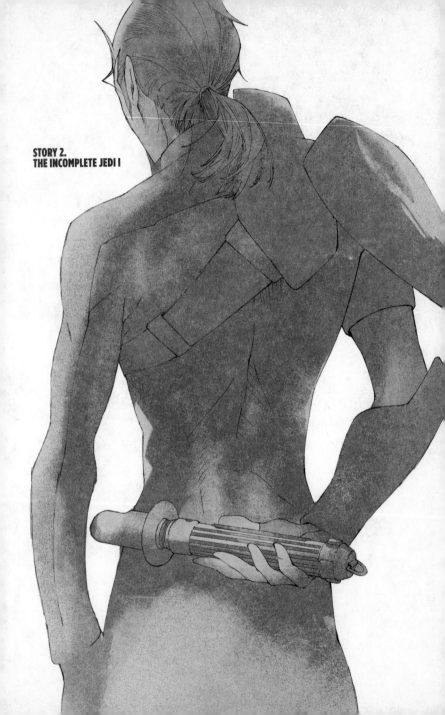

STORY 2.
THE INCOMPLETE JEDI I

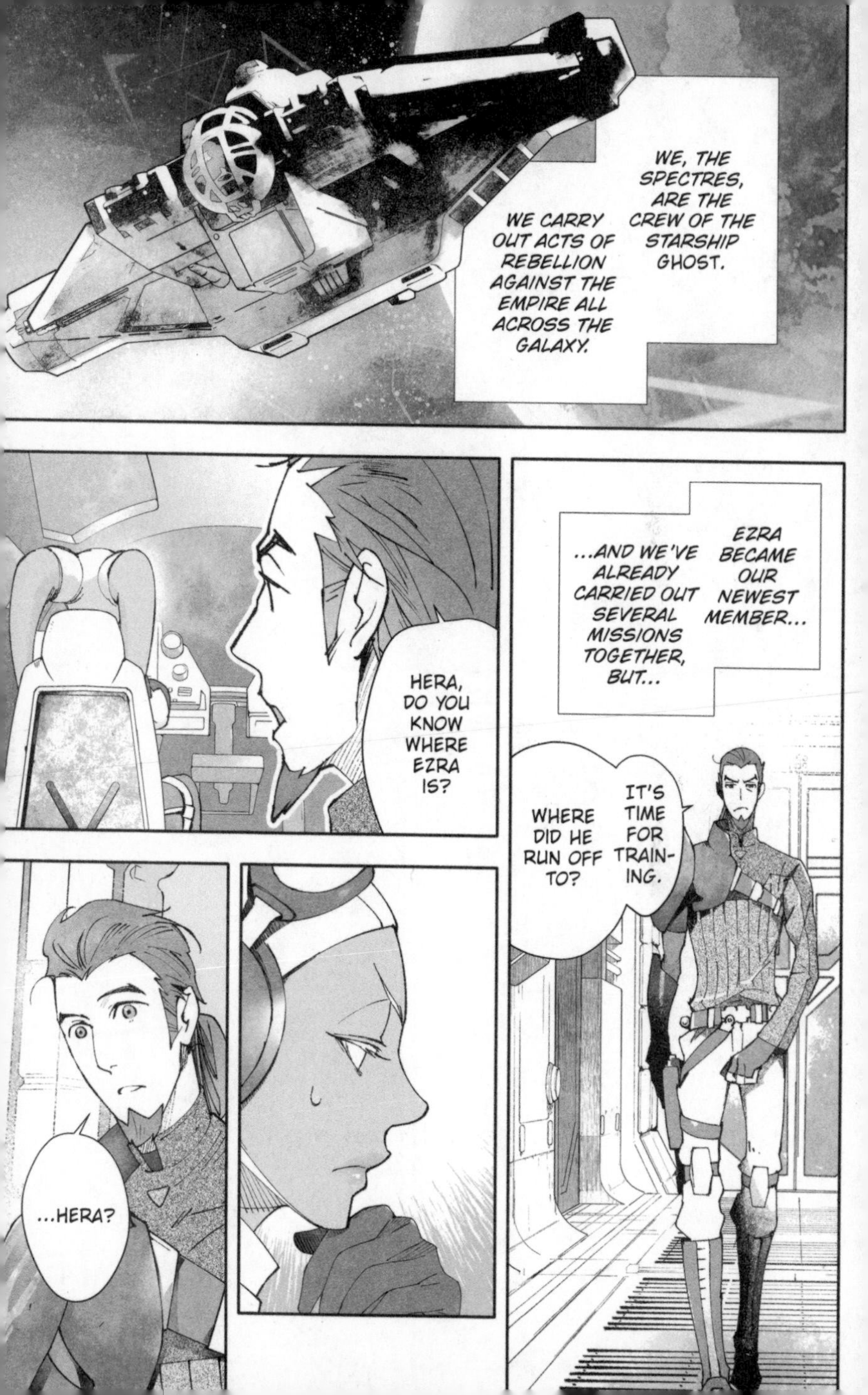
WE, THE SPECTRES, ARE THE CREW OF THE STARSHIP GHOST.
WE CARRY OUT ACTS OF REBELLION AGAINST THE EMPIRE ALL ACROSS THE GALAXY.
EZRA BECAME OUR NEWEST MEMBER...
...AND WE'VE ALREADY CARRIED OUT SEVERAL MISSIONS TOGETHER, BUT...
IT'S TIME FOR TRAIN-ING.
WHERE DID HE RUN OFF TO?
HERA, DO YOU KNOW WHERE EZRA IS?
...HERA?

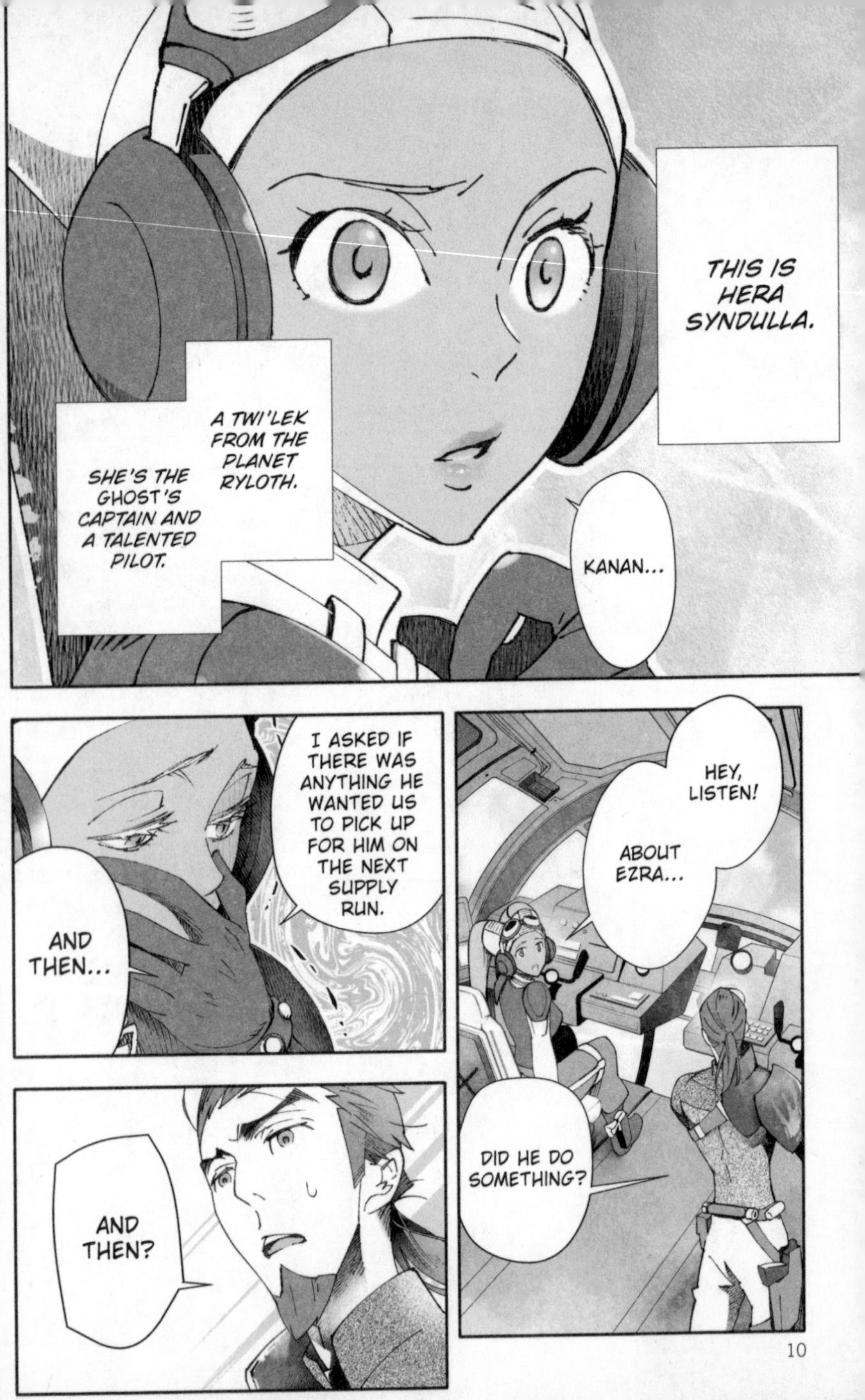
THIS IS HERA SYNDULLA.
A TWI'LEK FROM THE PLANET RYLOTH.
SHE'S THE GHOST'S CAPTAIN AND A TALENTED PILOT.
KANAN...
HEY, LISTEN!
ABOUT EZRA...
DID HE DO SOMETHING?
I ASKED IF THERE WAS ANYTHING HE WANTED US TO PICK UP FOR HIM ON THE NEXT SUPPLY RUN.
AND THEN...
AND THEN?

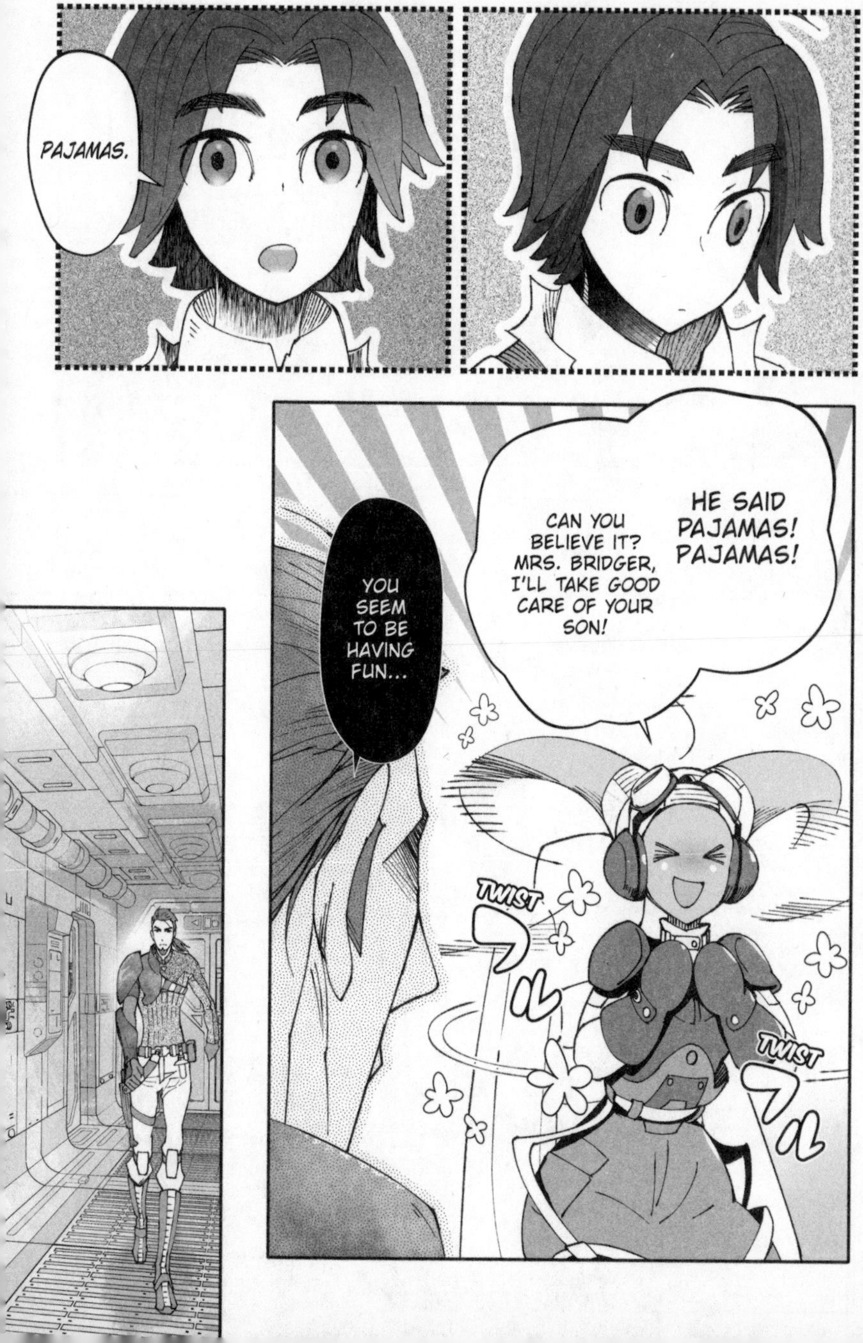
PAJAMAS.
HE SAID PAJAMAS! PAJAMAS!
CAN YOU BELIEVE IT? MRS. BRIDGER, I'LL TAKE GOOD CARE OF YOUR SON!
TWIST
TWIST
YOU SEEM TO BE HAVING FUN...

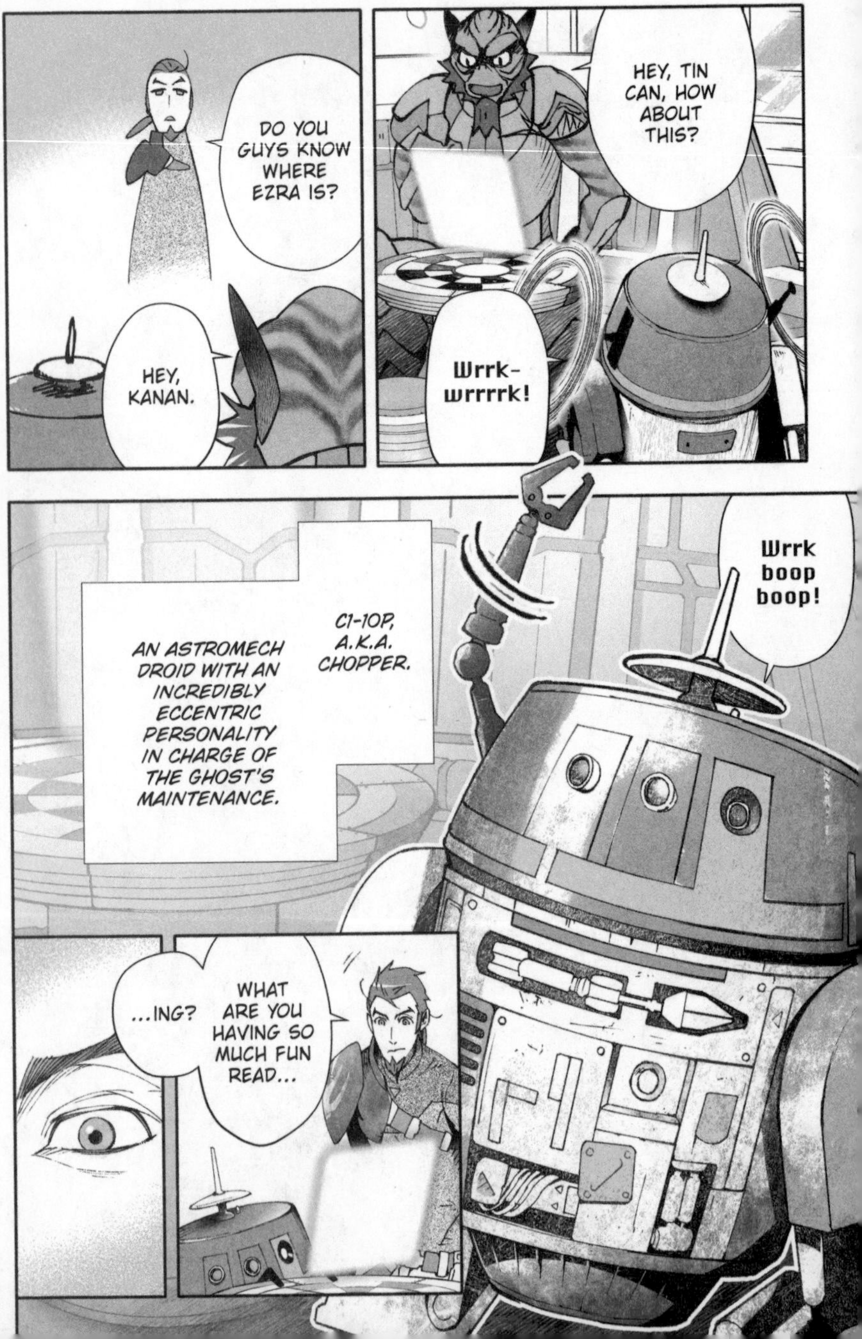
HEY, TIN CAN, HOW ABOUT THIS?
Wrrk-wrrrrk!
DO YOU GUYS KNOW WHERE EZRA IS?
HEY, KANAN.
Wrrk boop boop!
C1-10P, A.K.A. CHOPPER.
AN ASTROMECH DROID WITH AN INCREDIBLY ECCENTRIC PERSONALITY IN CHARGE OF THE GHOST'S MAINTENANCE.
WHAT ARE YOU HAVING SO MUCH FUN READ...
...ING?

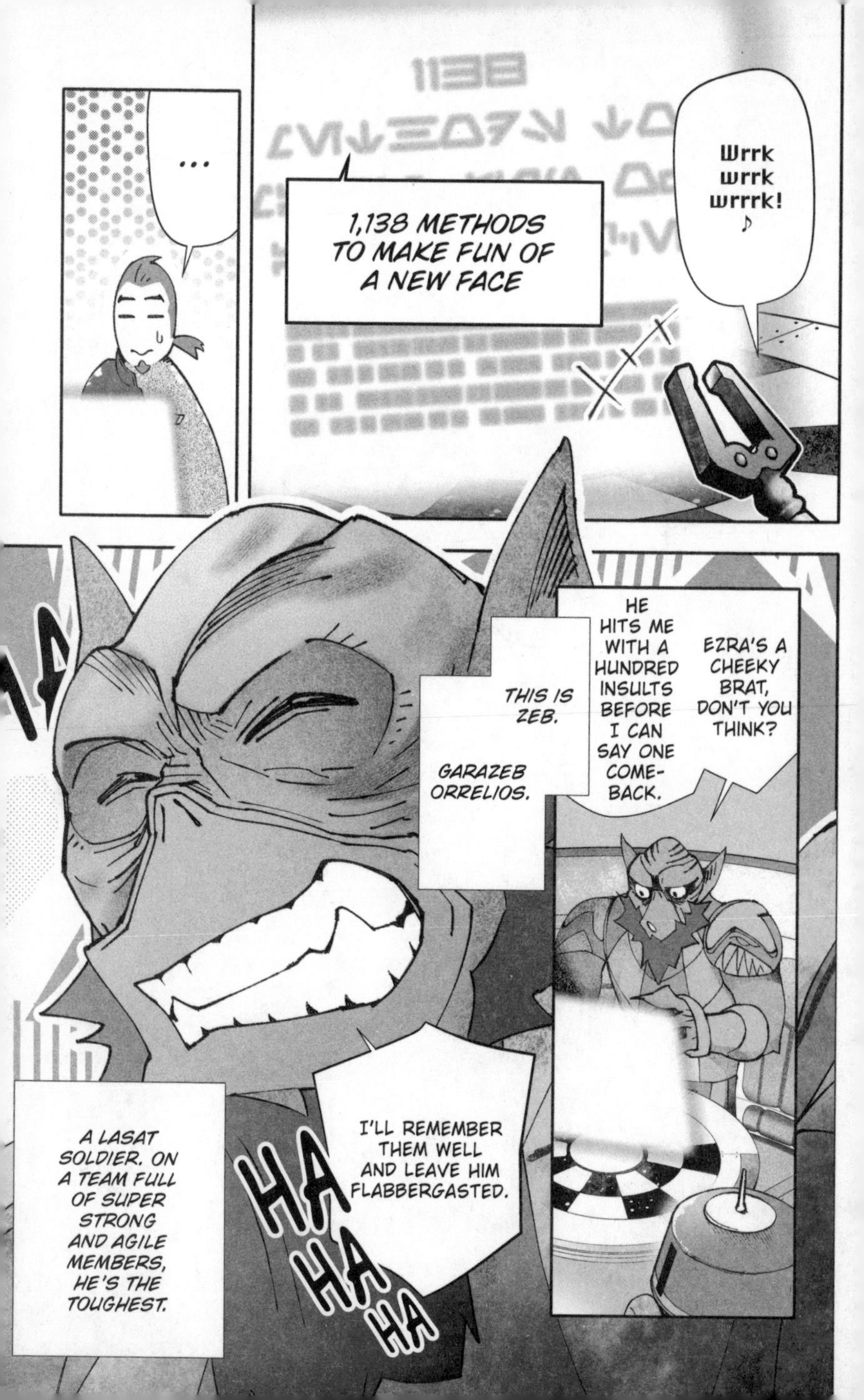
Wrrk wrrk wrrrk! ♪
1,138 METHODS TO MAKE FUN OF A NEW FACE
...
EZRA'S A CHEEKY BRAT, DON'T YOU THINK?
HE HITS ME WITH A HUNDRED INSULTS BEFORE I CAN SAY ONE COME-BACK.
THIS IS ZEB.
GARAZEB ORRELIOS.
I'LL REMEMBER THEM WELL AND LEAVE HIM FLABBERGASTED.
HA HA HA HA
A LASAT SOLDIER. ON A TEAM FULL OF SUPER STRONG AND AGILE MEMBERS, HE'S THE TOUGHEST.

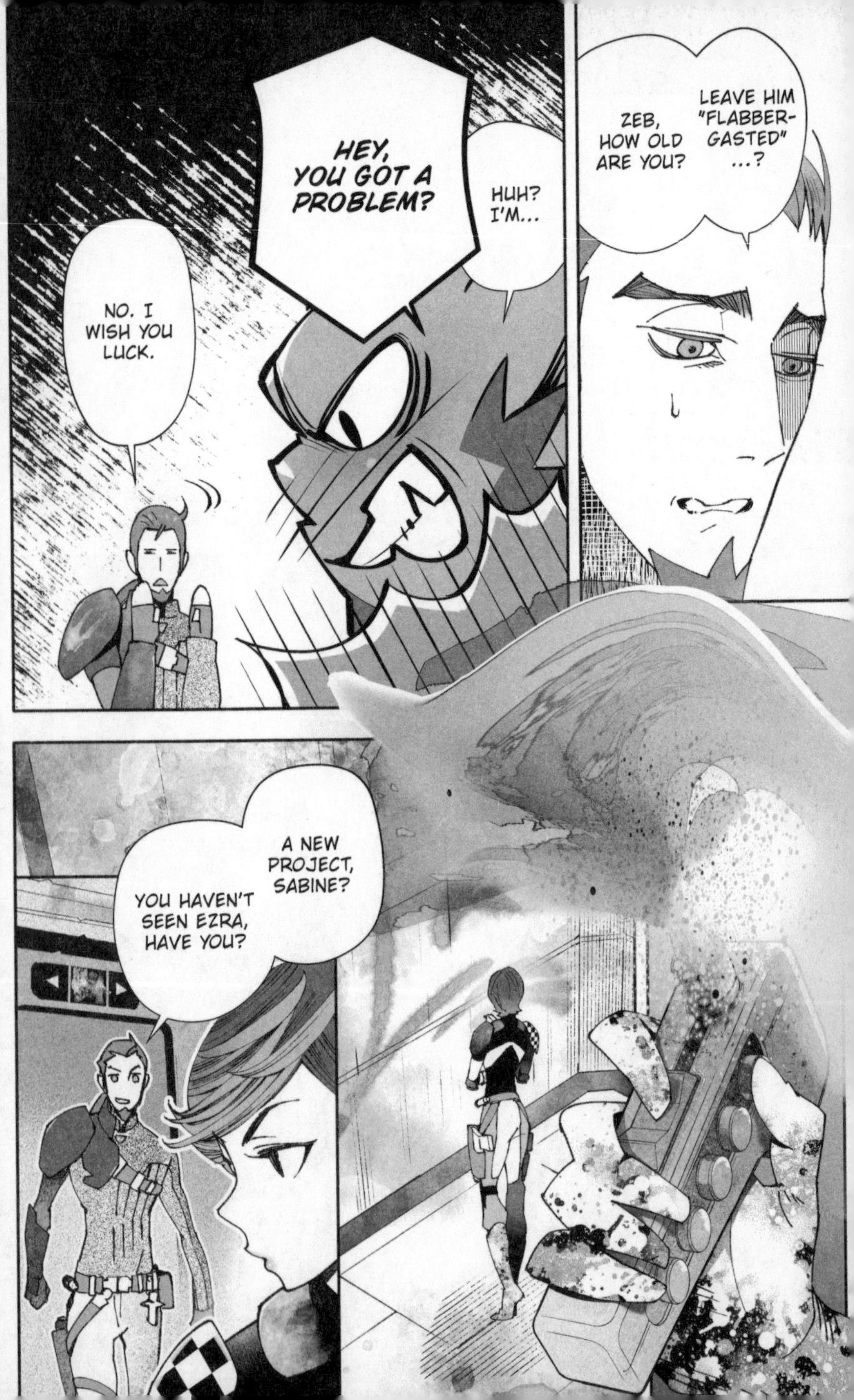
LEAVE HIM "FLABBER-GASTED" ...?
ZEB, HOW OLD ARE YOU?
HUH? I'M...
HEY, YOU GOT A PROBLEM?
NO. I WISH YOU LUCK.
A NEW PROJECT, SABINE?
YOU HAVEN'T SEEN EZRA, HAVE YOU?

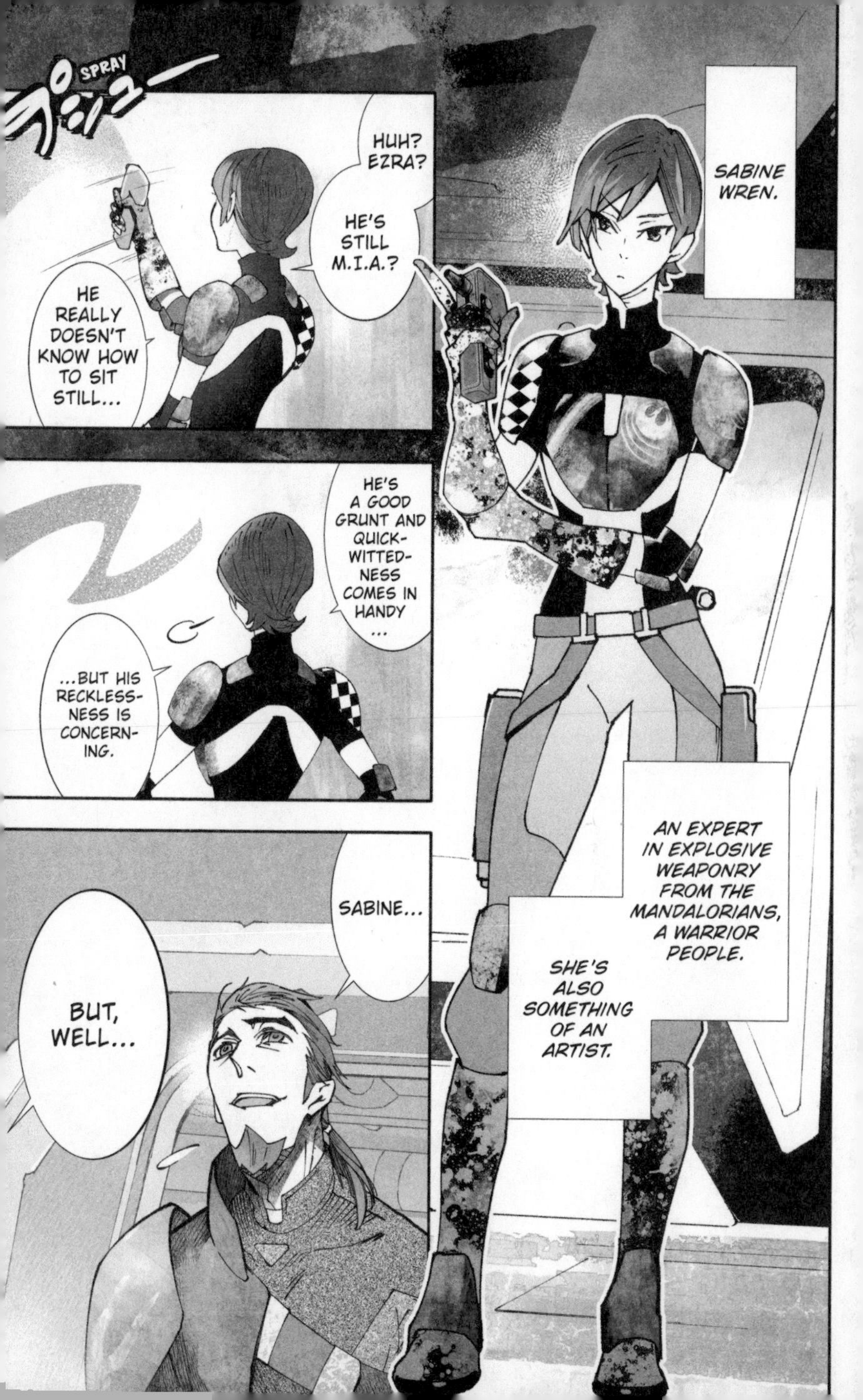
SABINE WREN.
AN EXPERT IN EXPLOSIVE WEAPONRY FROM THE MANDALORIANS, A WARRIOR PEOPLE.
SHE'S ALSO SOMETHING OF AN ARTIST.
SPRAY
HUH? EZRA?
HE'S STILL M.I.A.?
HE REALLY DOESN'T KNOW HOW TO SIT STILL...
HE'S A GOOD GRUNT AND QUICK-WITTED-NESS COMES IN HANDY...
...BUT HIS RECKLESS-NESS IS CONCERN-ING.
SABINE...
BUT, WELL...

WHAAAT?

ぼそっ

...KIND OF CUTE.

...IT'S ALSO...

HEY, KANAN. I FOUND HIM.

A YOUNG BOY WITH A STRONG FORCE SENSITIVITY WHO WE MET ON LOTHAL.

EZRA BRIDGER.

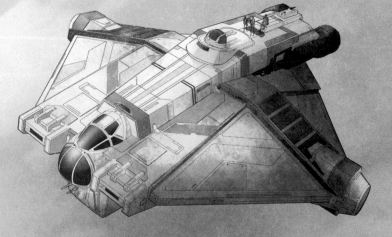

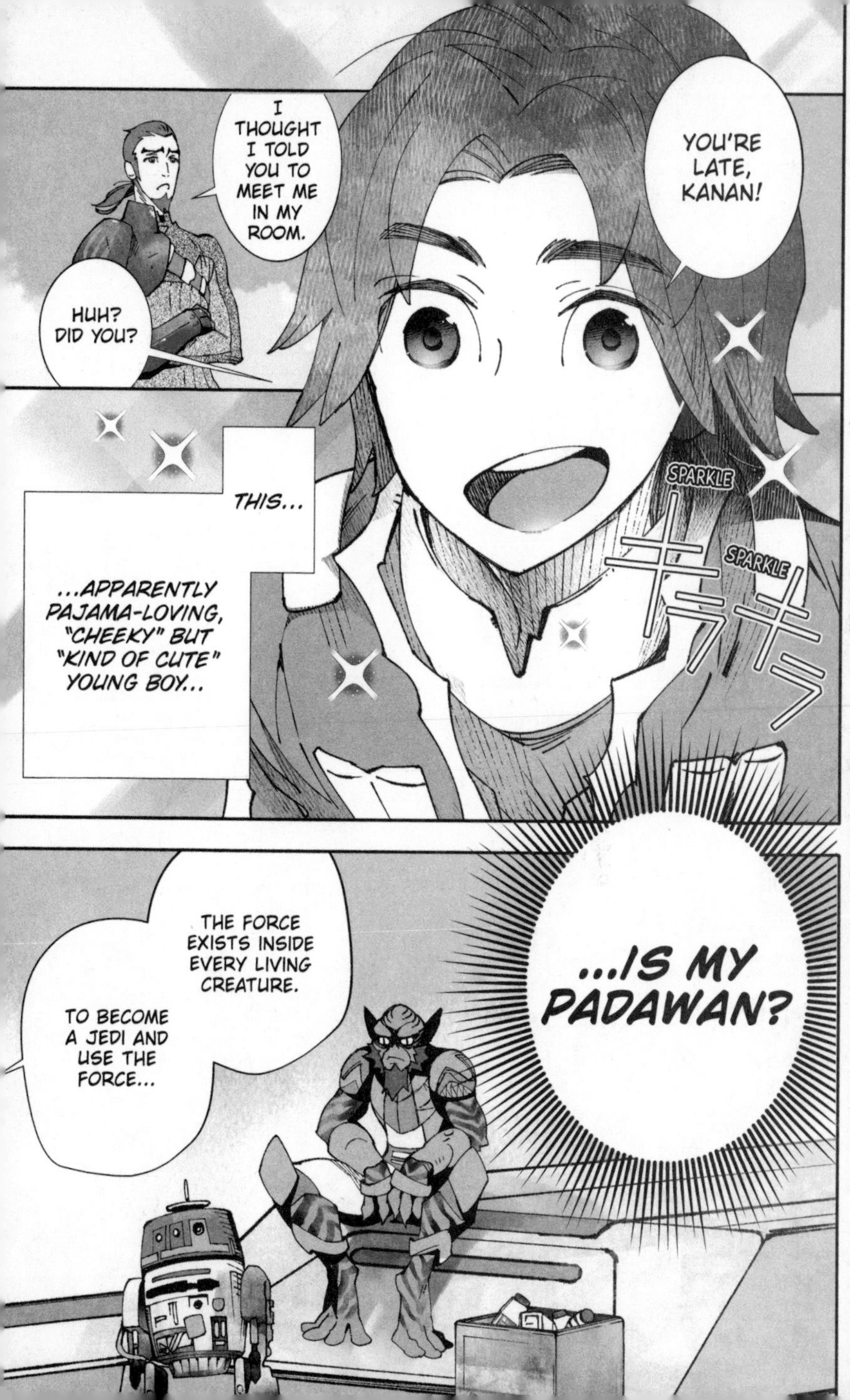
YOU'RE LATE, KANAN!
I THOUGHT I TOLD YOU TO MEET ME IN MY ROOM.
HUH? DID YOU?
SPARKLE
SPARKLE
キラキラ
THIS...
...APPARENTLY PAJAMA-LOVING, "CHEEKY" BUT "KIND OF CUTE" YOUNG BOY...
...IS MY PADAWAN?
THE FORCE EXISTS INSIDE EVERY LIVING CREATURE.
TO BECOME A JEDI AND USE THE FORCE...

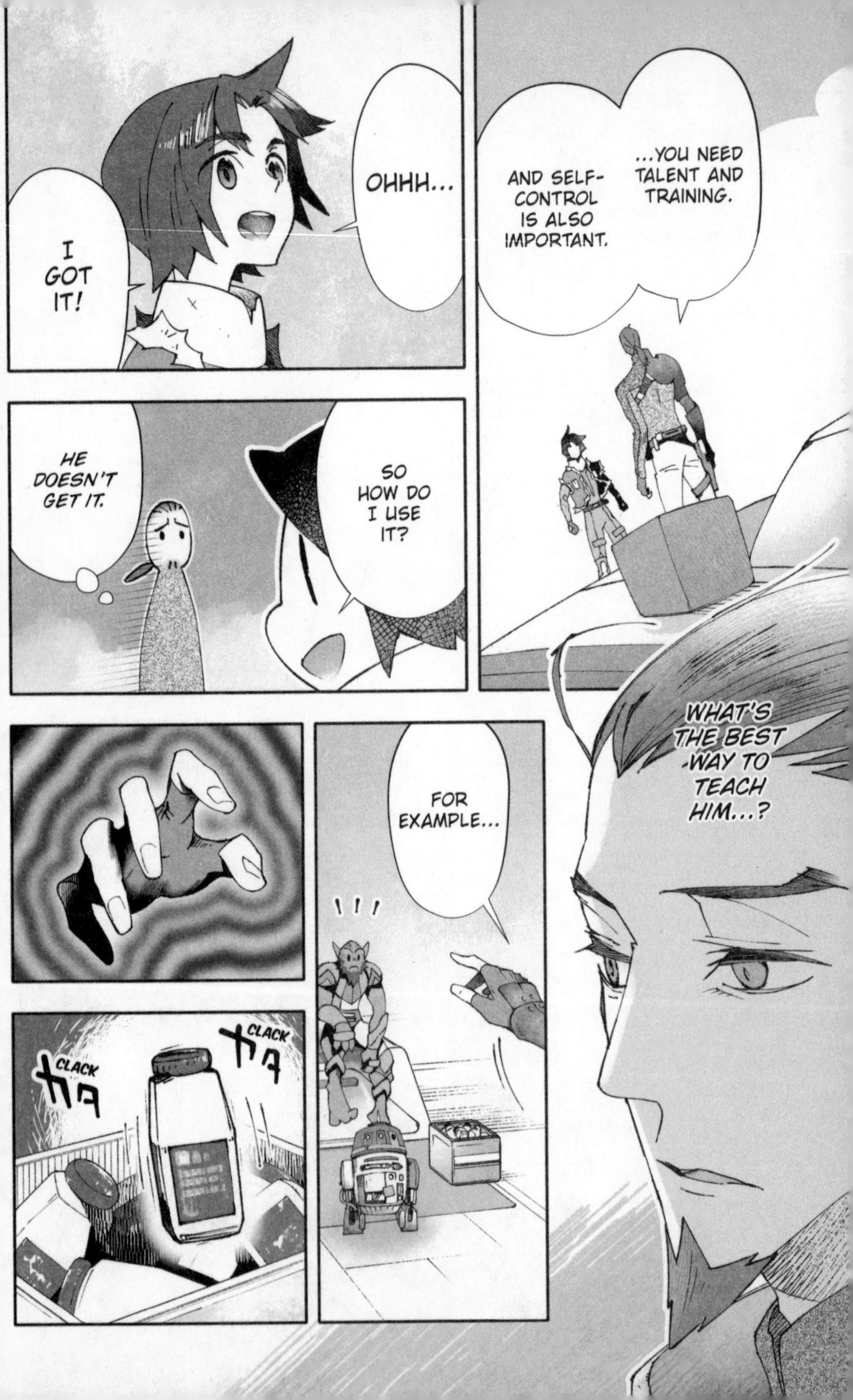
...YOU NEED TALENT AND TRAINING.
AND SELF-CONTROL IS ALSO IMPORTANT.
OHHH...
I GOT IT!
SO HOW DO I USE IT?
HE DOESN'T GET IT.
WHAT'S THE BEST WAY TO TEACH HIM...?
FOR EXAMPLE...
CLACK
CLACK

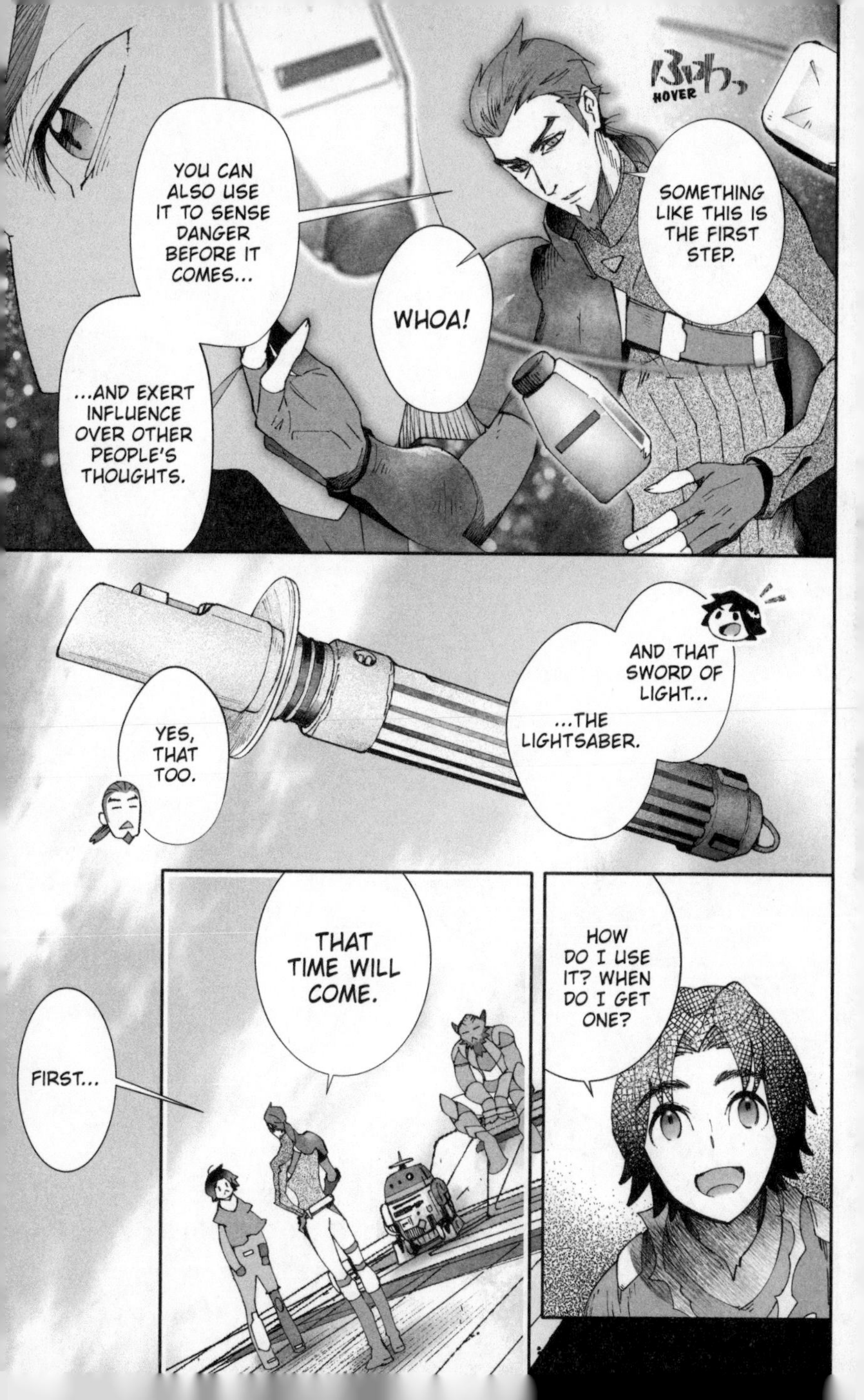
ふわっ
HOVER
SOMETHING LIKE THIS IS THE FIRST STEP.
WHOA!
YOU CAN ALSO USE IT TO SENSE DANGER BEFORE IT COMES...
...AND EXERT INFLUENCE OVER OTHER PEOPLE'S THOUGHTS.
AND THAT SWORD OF LIGHT...
...THE LIGHTSABER.
YES, THAT TOO.
HOW DO I USE IT? WHEN DO I GET ONE?
THAT TIME WILL COME.
FIRST...

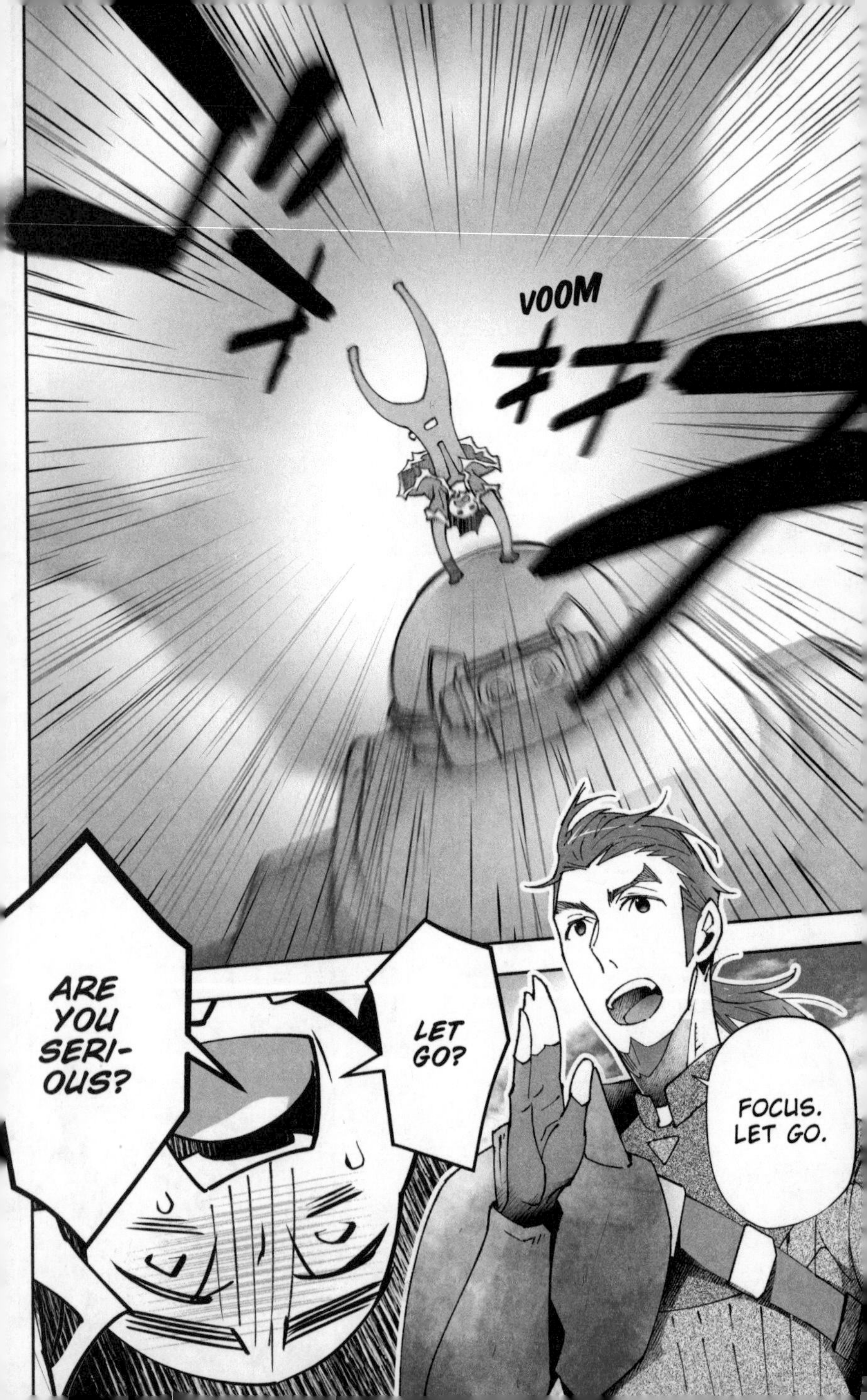
VOOM
FOCUS. LET GO.
LET GO?
ARE YOU SERI-OUS?

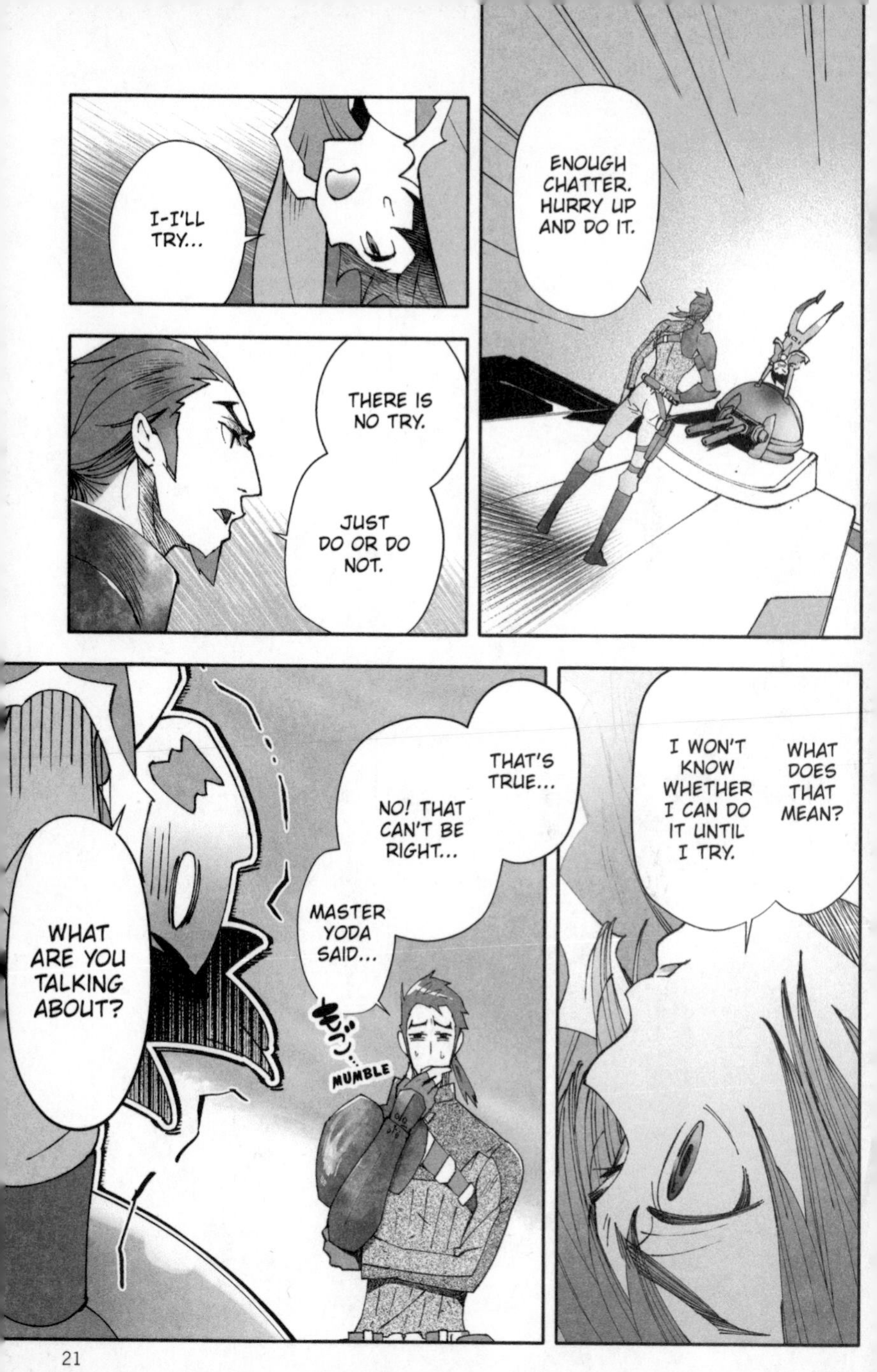
ENOUGH CHATTER. HURRY UP AND DO IT.
I-I'LL TRY...
THERE IS NO TRY.
JUST DO OR DO NOT.
WHAT DOES THAT MEAN?
I WON'T KNOW WHETHER I CAN DO IT UNTIL I TRY.
THAT'S TRUE...
NO! THAT CAN'T BE RIGHT...
MASTER YODA SAID...
MUMBLE
WHAT ARE YOU TALKING ABOUT?

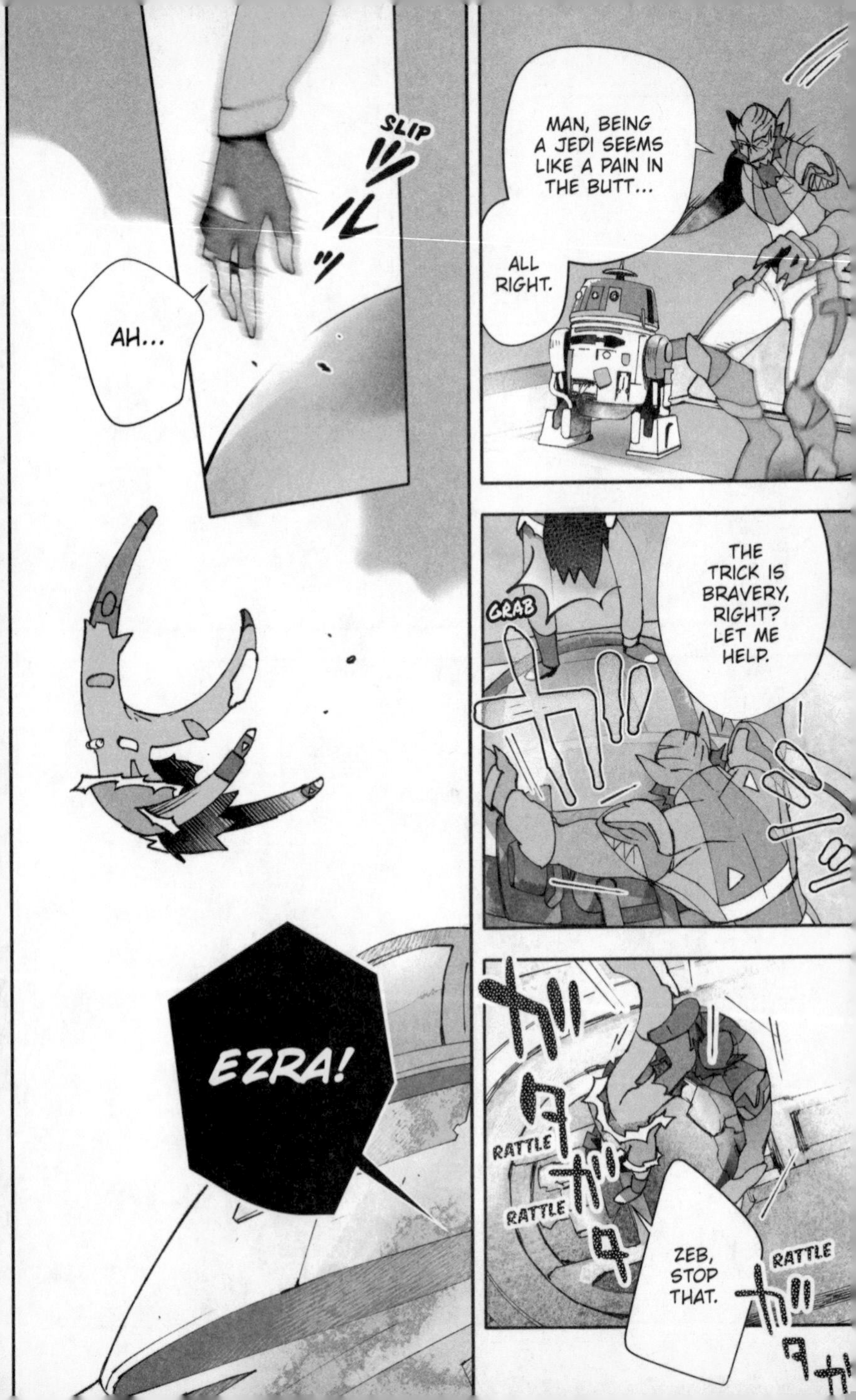
MAN, BEING A JEDI SEEMS LIKE A PAIN IN THE BUTT...
ALL RIGHT.
GRAB
THE TRICK IS BRAVERY, RIGHT? LET ME HELP.
RATTLE
RATTLE
ZEB, STOP THAT.
RATTLE
SLIP
AH...
EZRA!

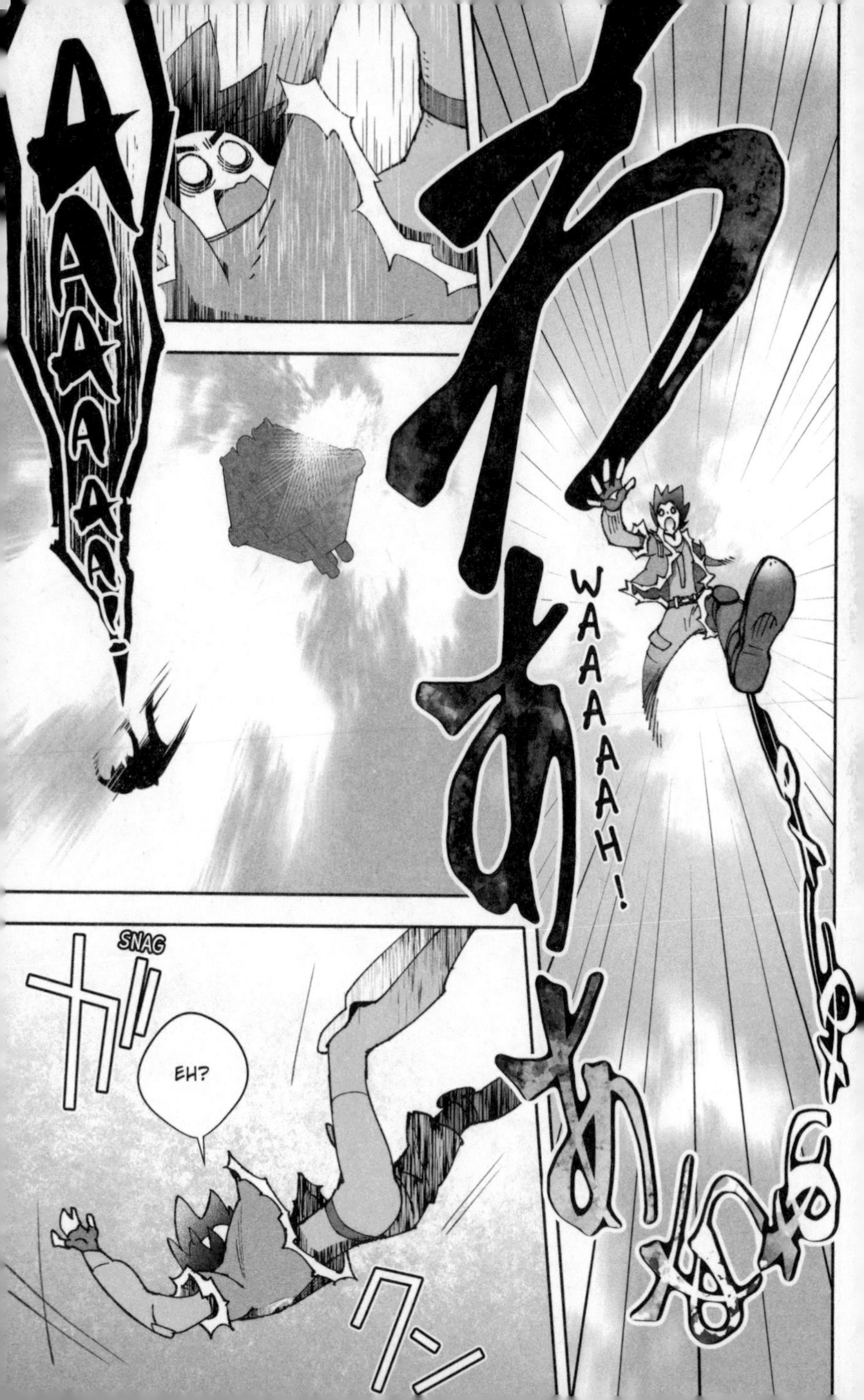
WAAAAAAAH!
AAAAAAAA!
SNAG
EH?

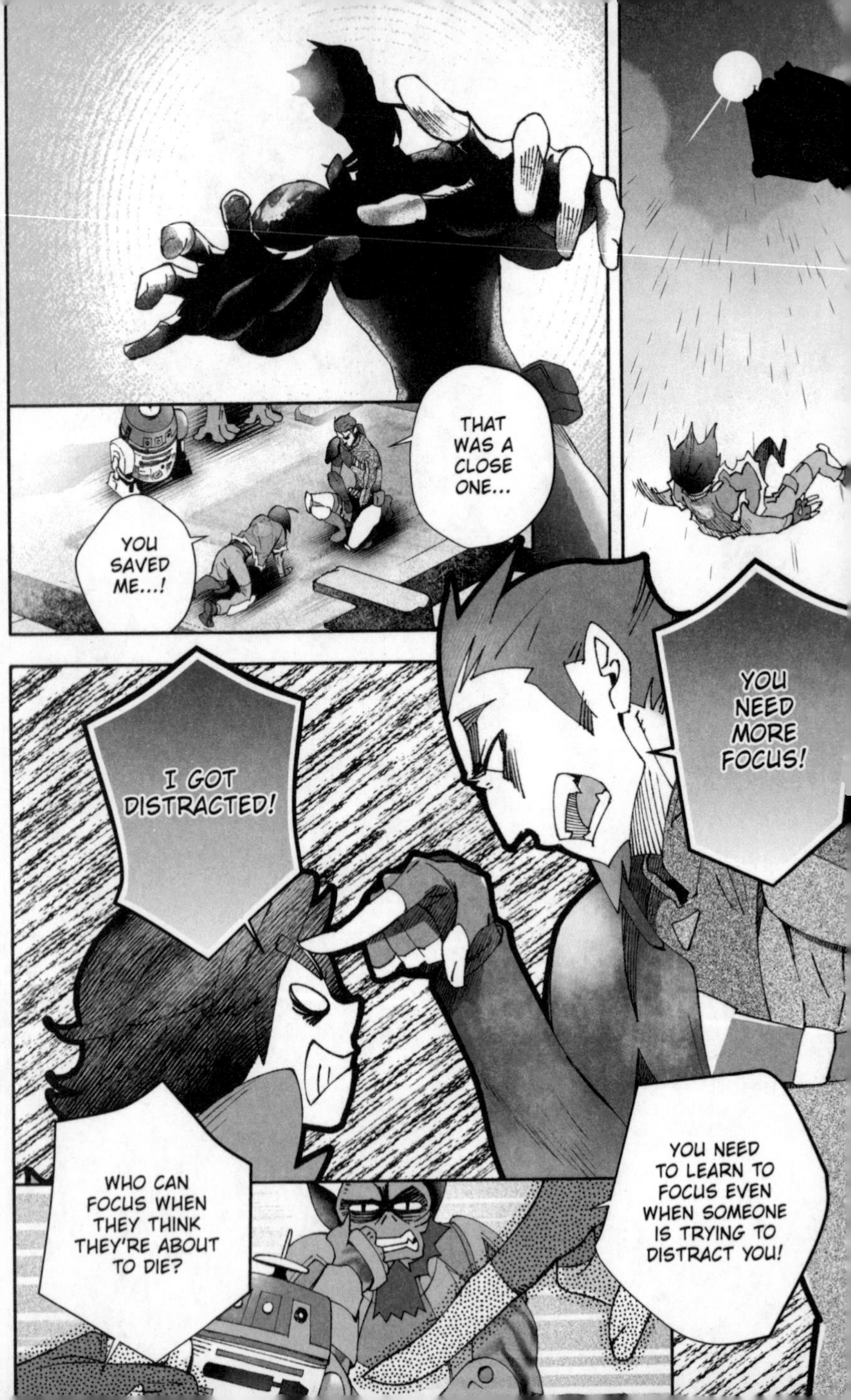
THAT WAS A CLOSE ONE...
YOU SAVED ME...!
YOU NEED MORE FOCUS!
I GOT DISTRACTED!
YOU NEED TO LEARN TO FOCUS EVEN WHEN SOMEONE IS TRYING TO DISTRACT YOU!
WHO CAN FOCUS WHEN THEY THINK THEY'RE ABOUT TO DIE?

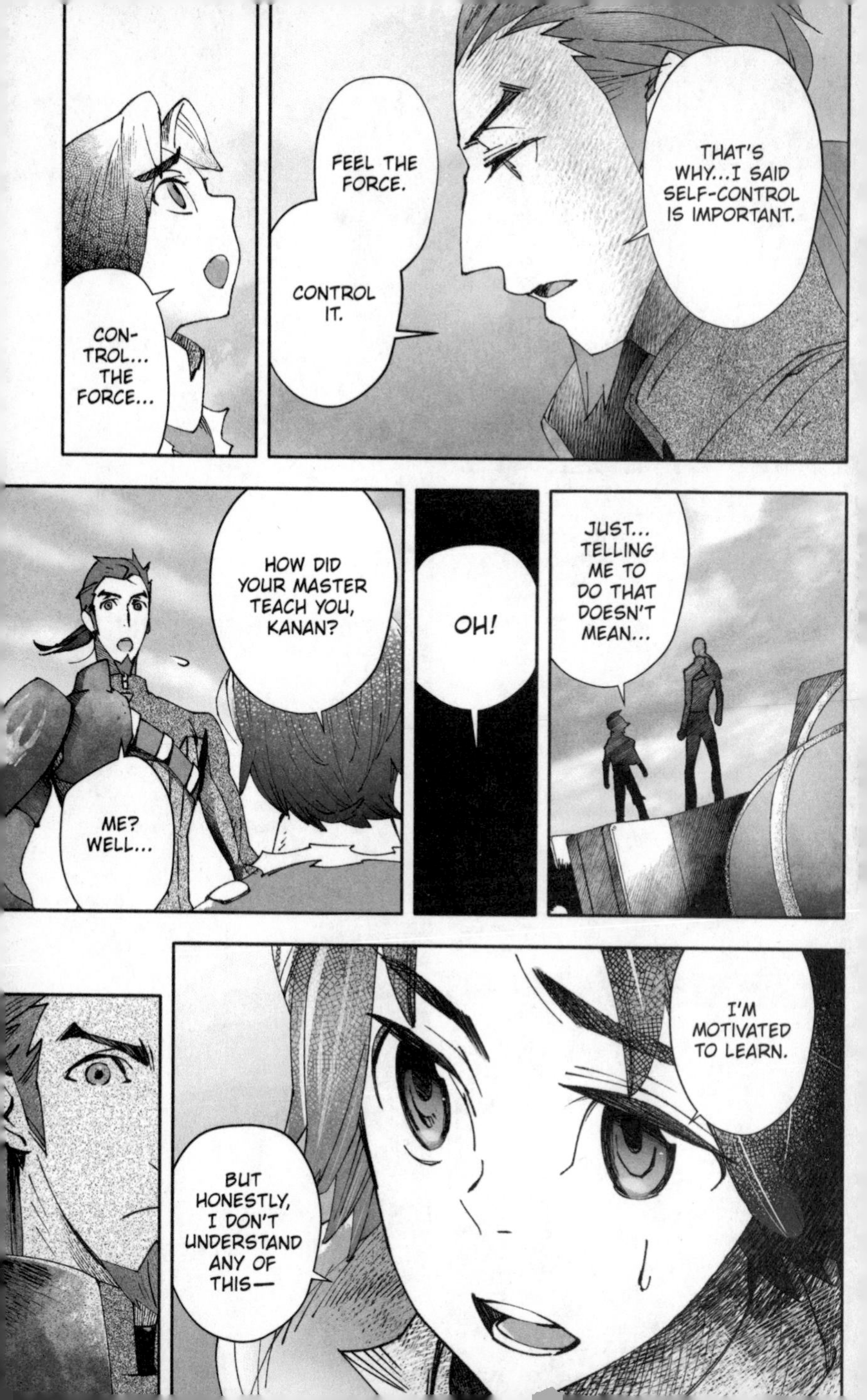
THAT'S WHY...I SAID SELF-CONTROL IS IMPORTANT.
FEEL THE FORCE.
CONTROL IT.
CON-TROL... THE FORCE...
JUST... TELLING ME TO DO THAT DOESN'T MEAN...
OH!
HOW DID YOUR MASTER TEACH YOU, KANAN?
ME? WELL...
I'M MOTIVATED TO LEARN.
BUT HONESTLY, I DON'T UNDERSTAND ANY OF THIS—

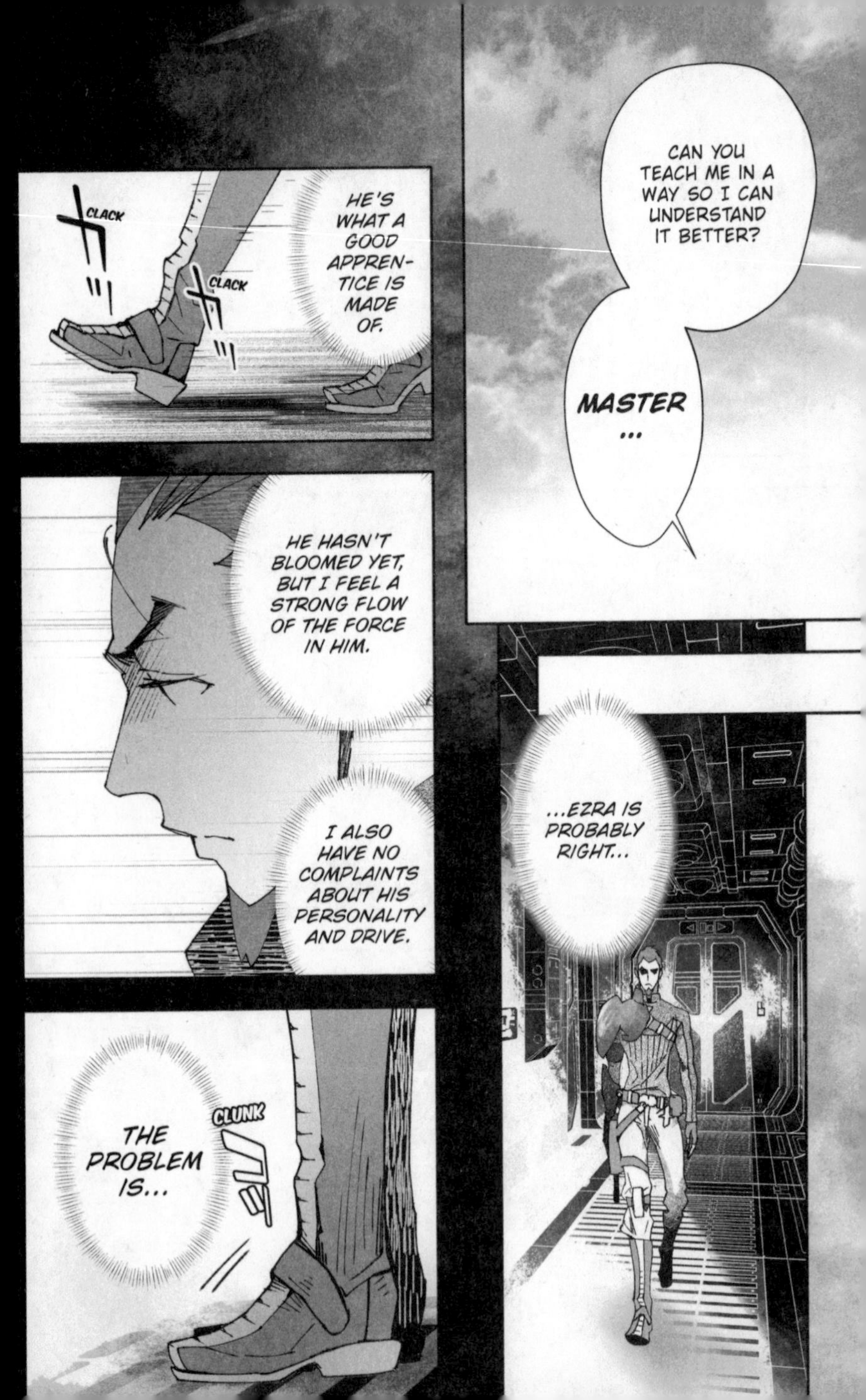
CAN YOU TEACH ME IN A WAY SO I CAN UNDERSTAND IT BETTER?
MASTER ...
...EZRA IS PROBABLY RIGHT...
HE'S WHAT A GOOD APPRENTICE IS MADE OF.
CLACK
CLACK
HE HASN'T BLOOMED YET, BUT I FEEL A STRONG FLOW OF THE FORCE IN HIM.
I ALSO HAVE NO COMPLAINTS ABOUT HIS PERSONALITY AND DRIVE.
CLUNK
THE PROBLEM IS...

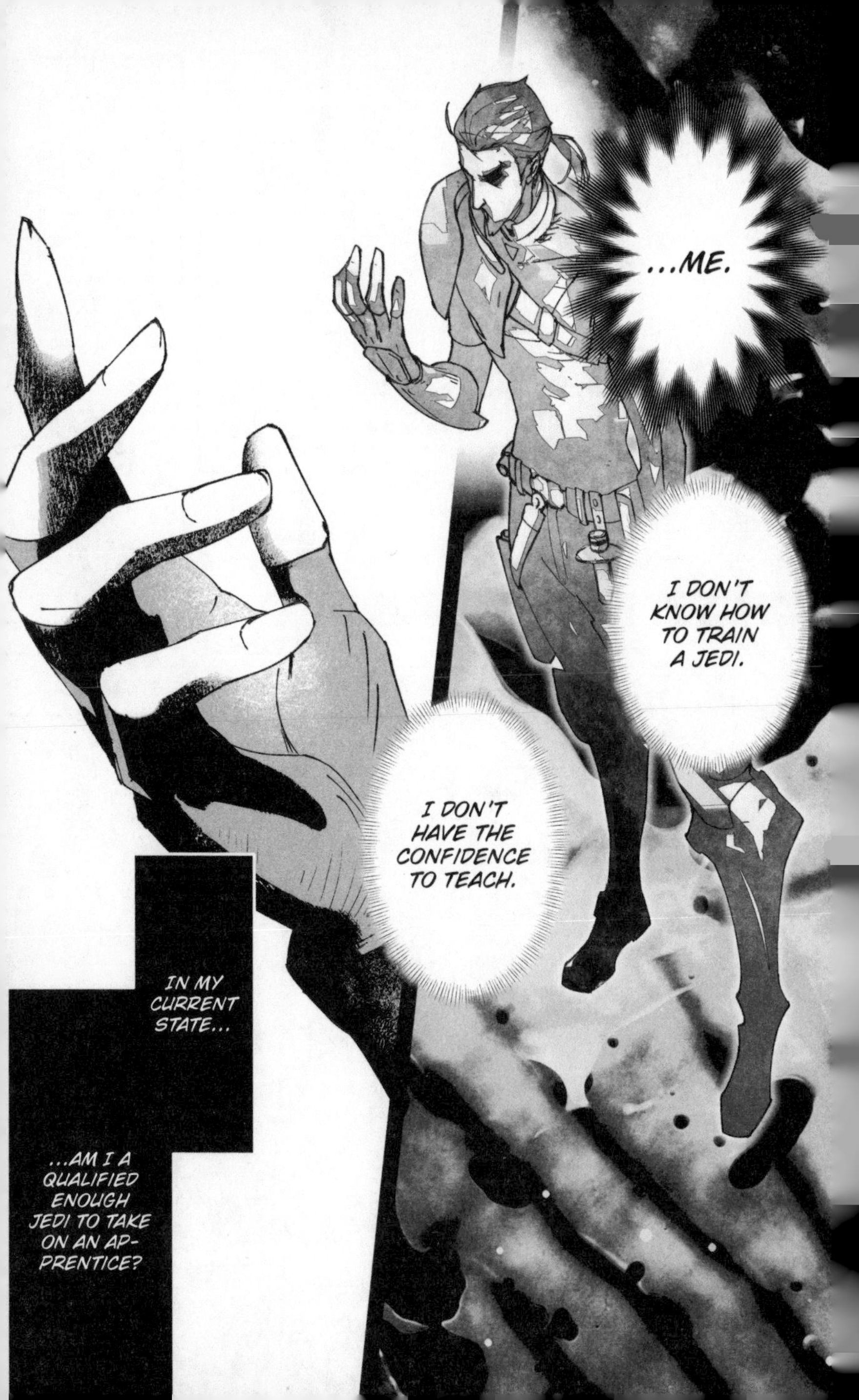
...ME.
I DON'T KNOW HOW TO TRAIN A JEDI.
I DON'T HAVE THE CONFIDENCE TO TEACH.
IN MY CURRENT STATE...
...AM I A QUALIFIED ENOUGH JEDI TO TAKE ON AN AP-PRENTICE?

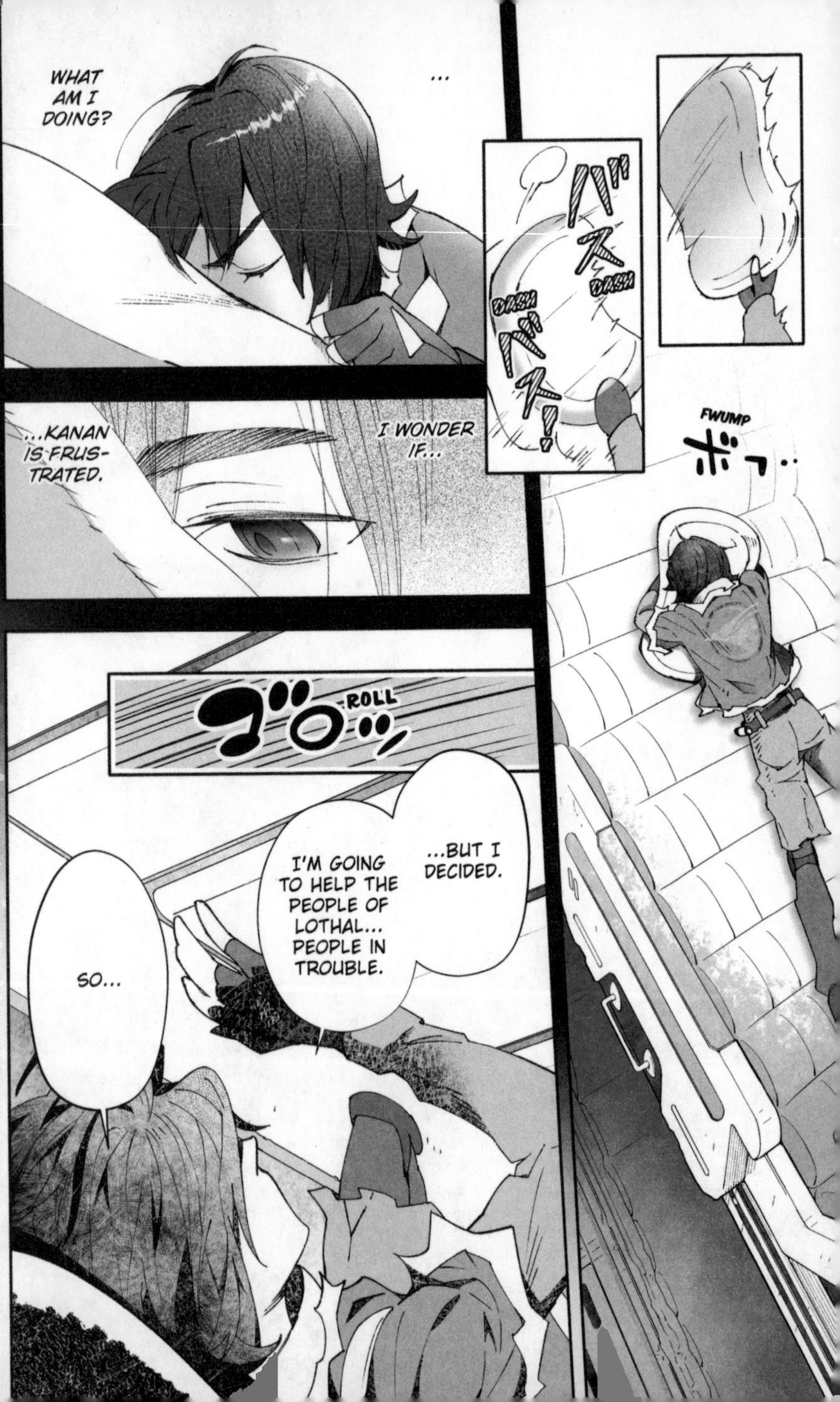
バス DASH
ドスッ! DASH
...
WHAT AM I DOING?
FWUMP
ボフ..
I WONDER IF...
...KANAN IS FRUS-TRATED.
ゴロッ ROLL
...BUT I DECIDED.
I'M GOING TO HELP THE PEOPLE OF LOTHAL... PEOPLE IN TROUBLE.
SO...

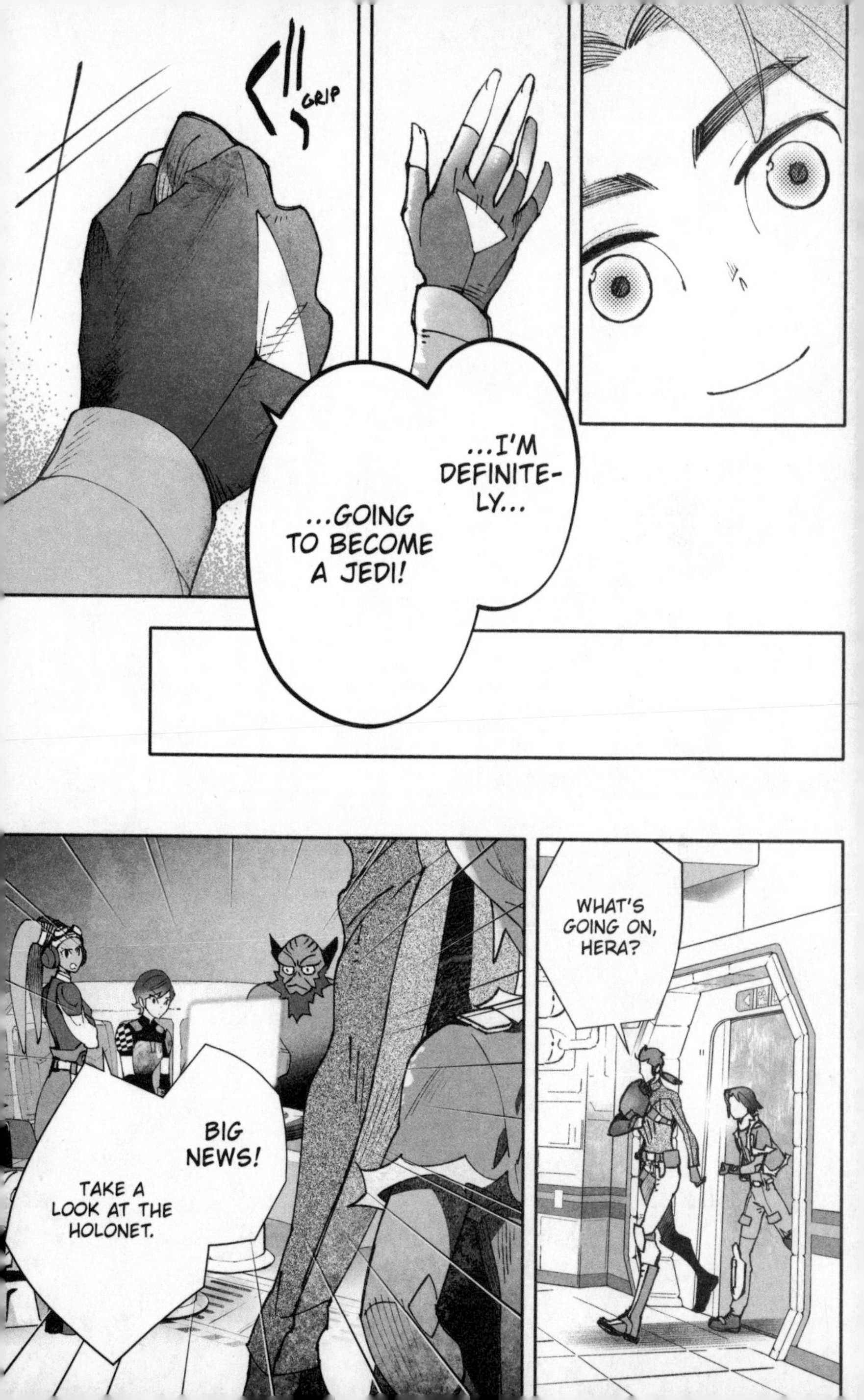
GRIP
...I'M DEFINITELY...
...GOING TO BECOME A JEDI!
WHAT'S GOING ON, HERA?
BIG NEWS!
TAKE A LOOK AT THE HOLONET.

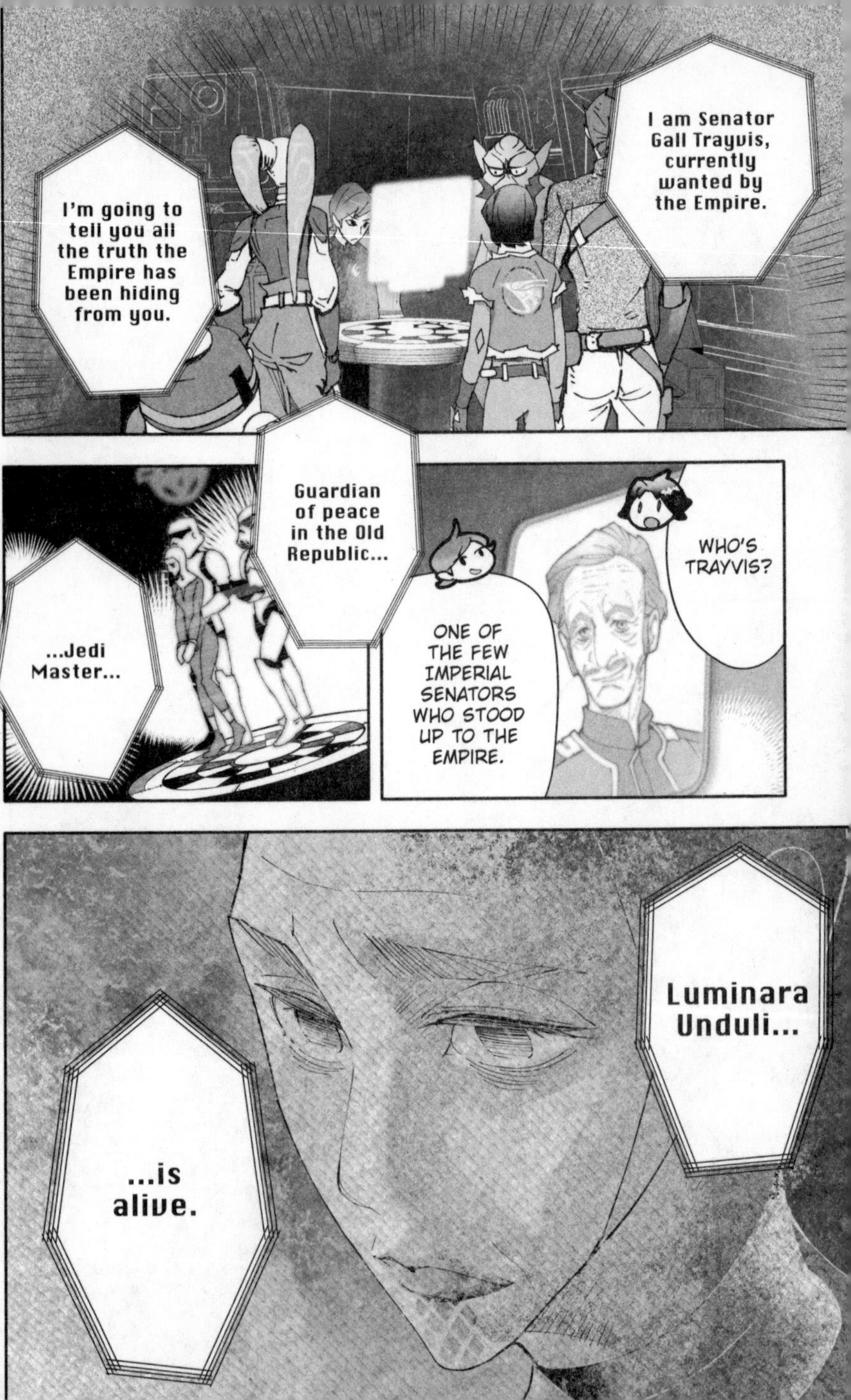
I am Senator Gall Trayvis, currently wanted by the Empire.
I'm going to tell you all the truth the Empire has been hiding from you.
WHO'S TRAYVIS?
ONE OF THE FEW IMPERIAL SENATORS WHO STOOD UP TO THE EMPIRE.
Guardian of peace in the Old Republic...
...Jedi Master...
Luminara Unduli...
...is alive.

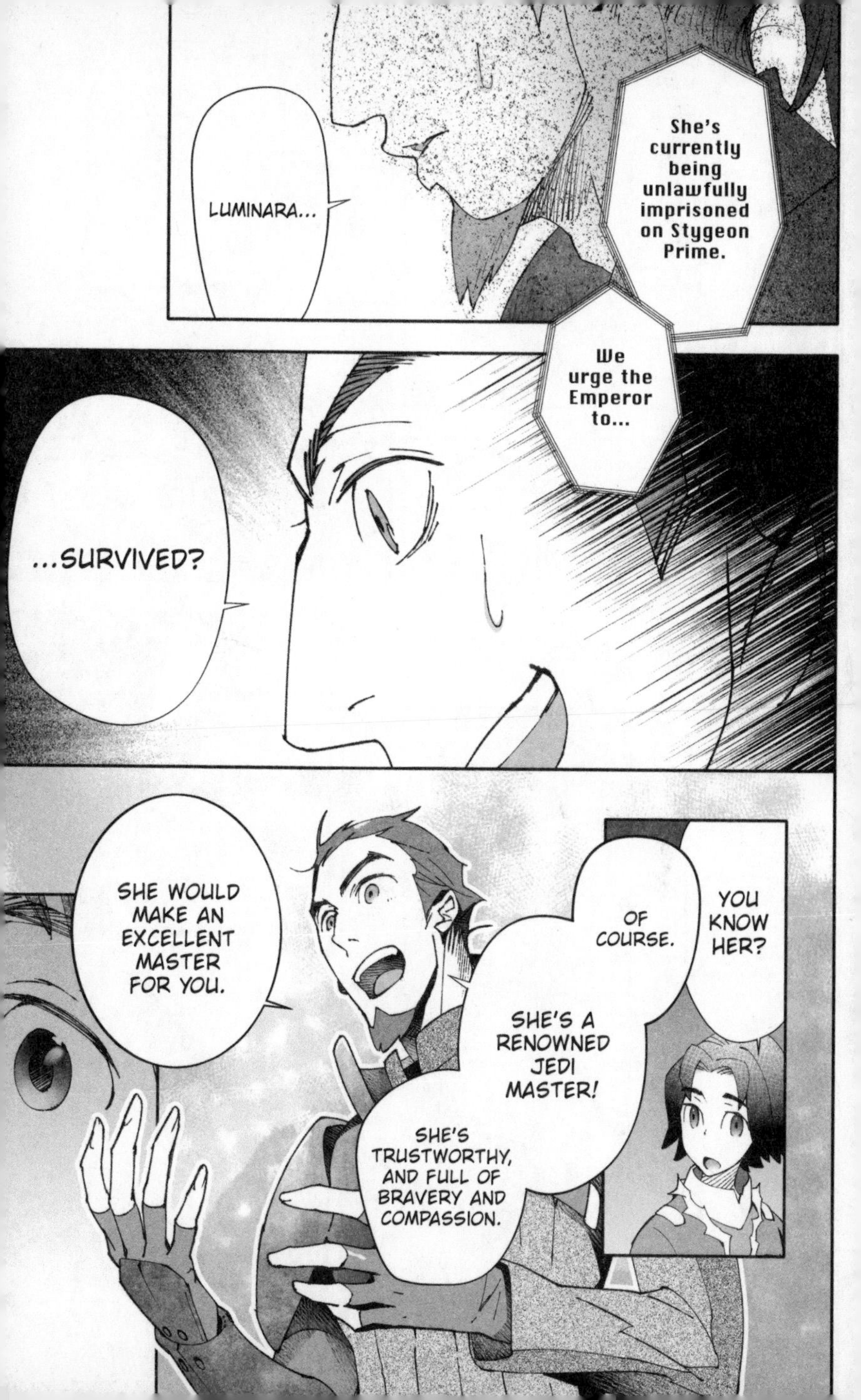

She's currently being unlawfully imprisoned on Stygeon Prime.
LUMINARA...
We urge the Emperor to...
...SURVIVED?
YOU KNOW HER?
OF COURSE.
SHE'S A RENOWNED JEDI MASTER!
SHE'S TRUSTWORTHY, AND FULL OF BRAVERY AND COMPASSION.
SHE WOULD MAKE AN EXCELLENT MASTER FOR YOU.

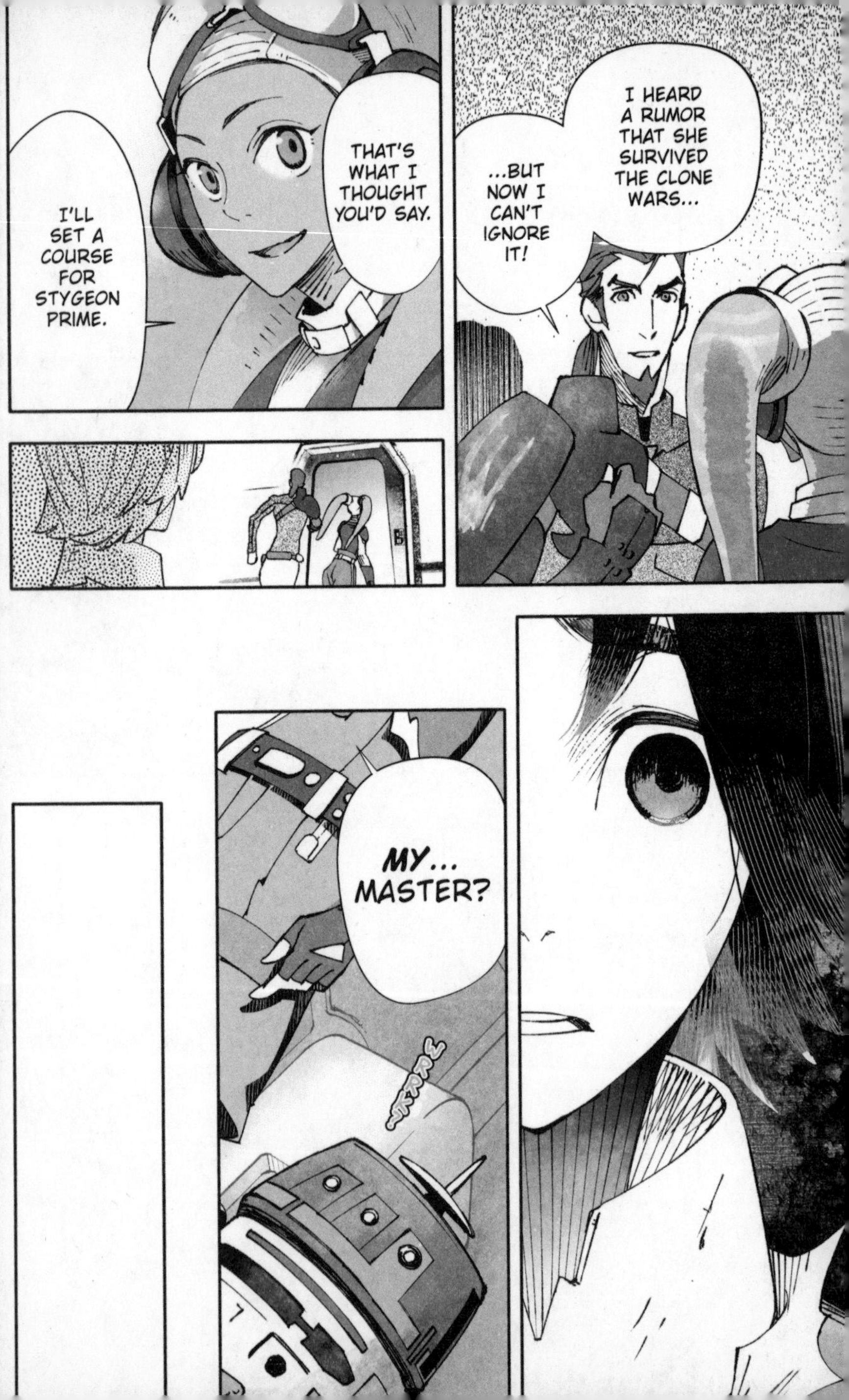
I HEARD A RUMOR THAT SHE SURVIVED THE CLONE WARS...
...BUT NOW I CAN'T IGNORE IT!
THAT'S WHAT I THOUGHT YOU'D SAY.
I'LL SET A COURSE FOR STYGEON PRIME.
MY... MASTER?
WRRK?

STAR WARS
REBELS

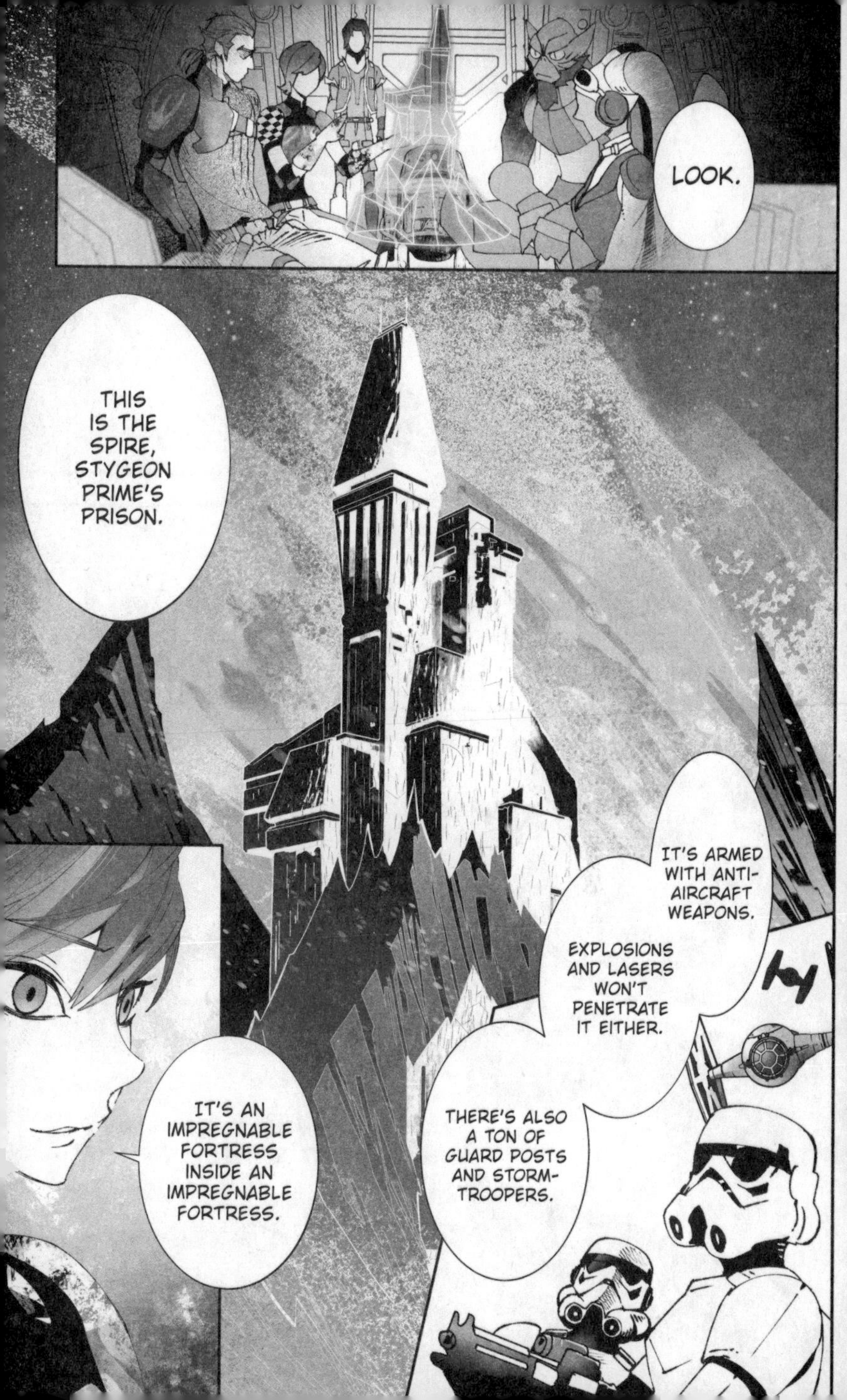
LOOK.
THIS IS THE SPIRE, STYGEON PRIME'S PRISON.
IT'S ARMED WITH ANTI-AIRCRAFT WEAPONS.
EXPLOSIONS AND LASERS WON'T PENETRATE IT EITHER.
THERE'S ALSO A TON OF GUARD POSTS AND STORM-TROOPERS.
IT'S AN IMPREGNABLE FORTRESS INSIDE AN IMPREGNABLE FORTRESS.

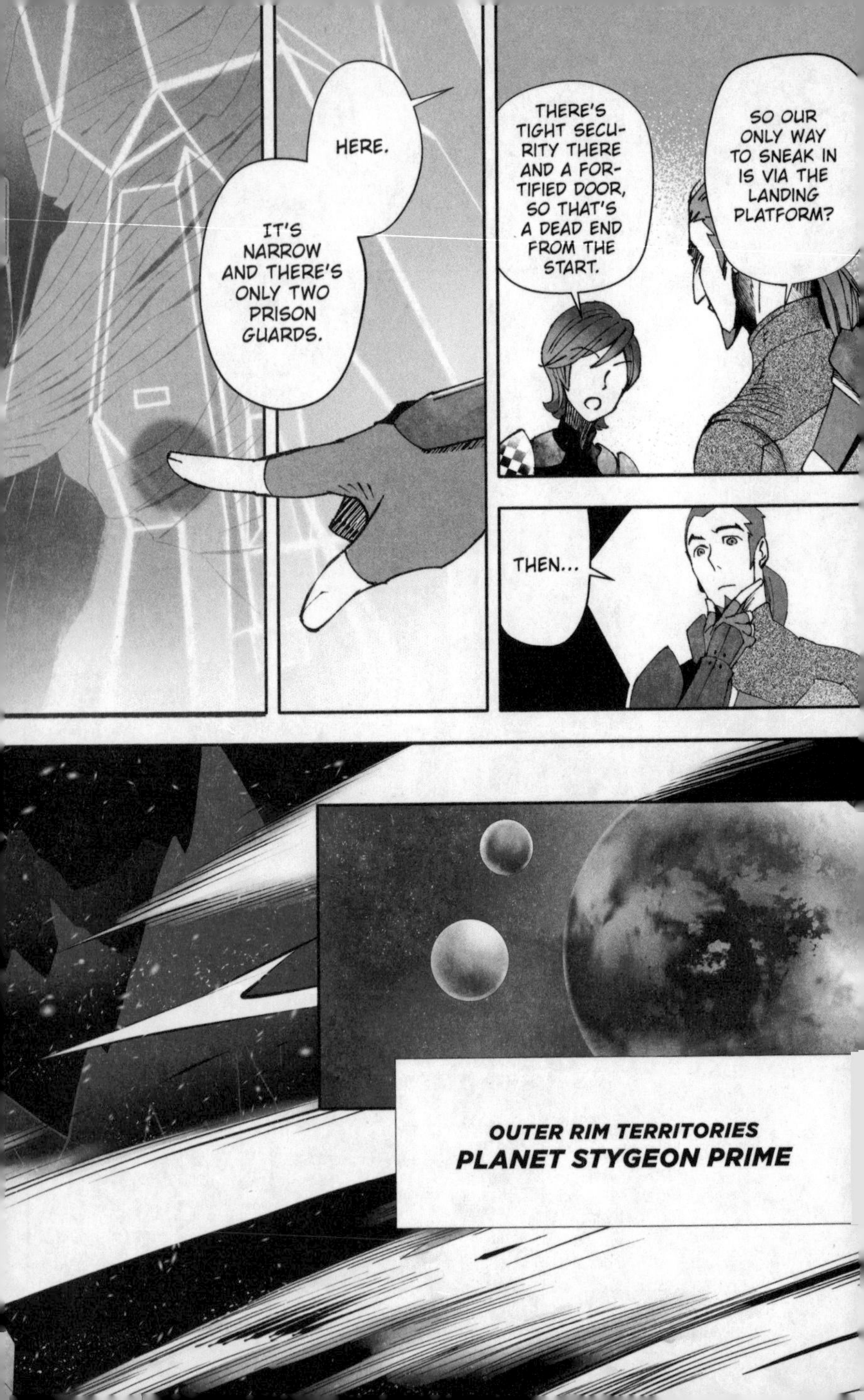
SO OUR ONLY WAY TO SNEAK IN IS VIA THE LANDING PLATFORM?
THERE'S TIGHT SECURITY THERE AND A FORTIFIED DOOR, SO THAT'S A DEAD END FROM THE START.
THEN...
HERE.
IT'S NARROW AND THERE'S ONLY TWO PRISON GUARDS.
OUTER RIM TERRITORIES
PLANET STYGEON PRIME

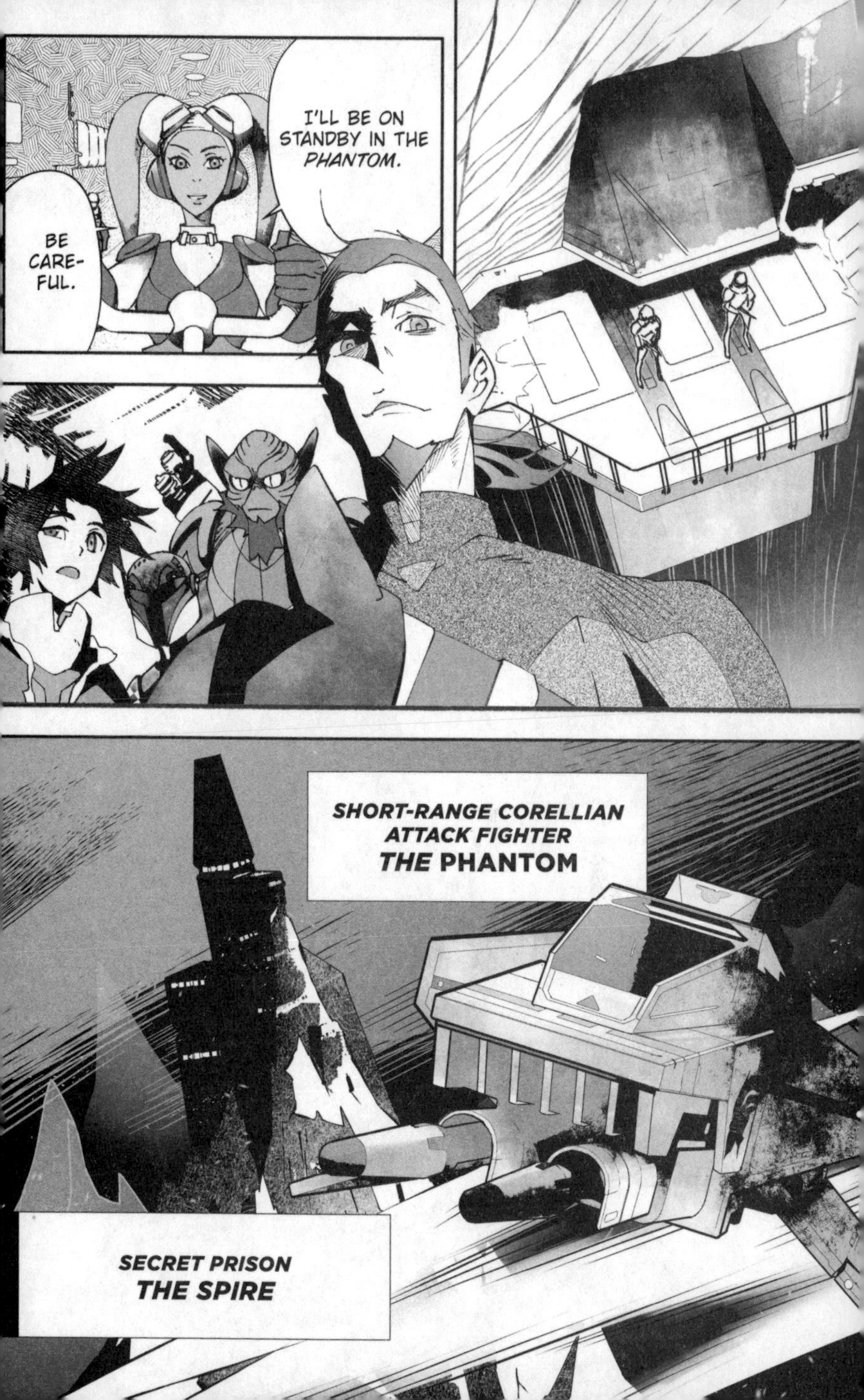
I'LL BE ON STANDBY IN THE *PHANTOM*.
BE CARE-FUL.
SHORT-RANGE CORELLIAN ATTACK FIGHTER **THE PHANTOM**
SECRET PRISON **THE SPIRE**

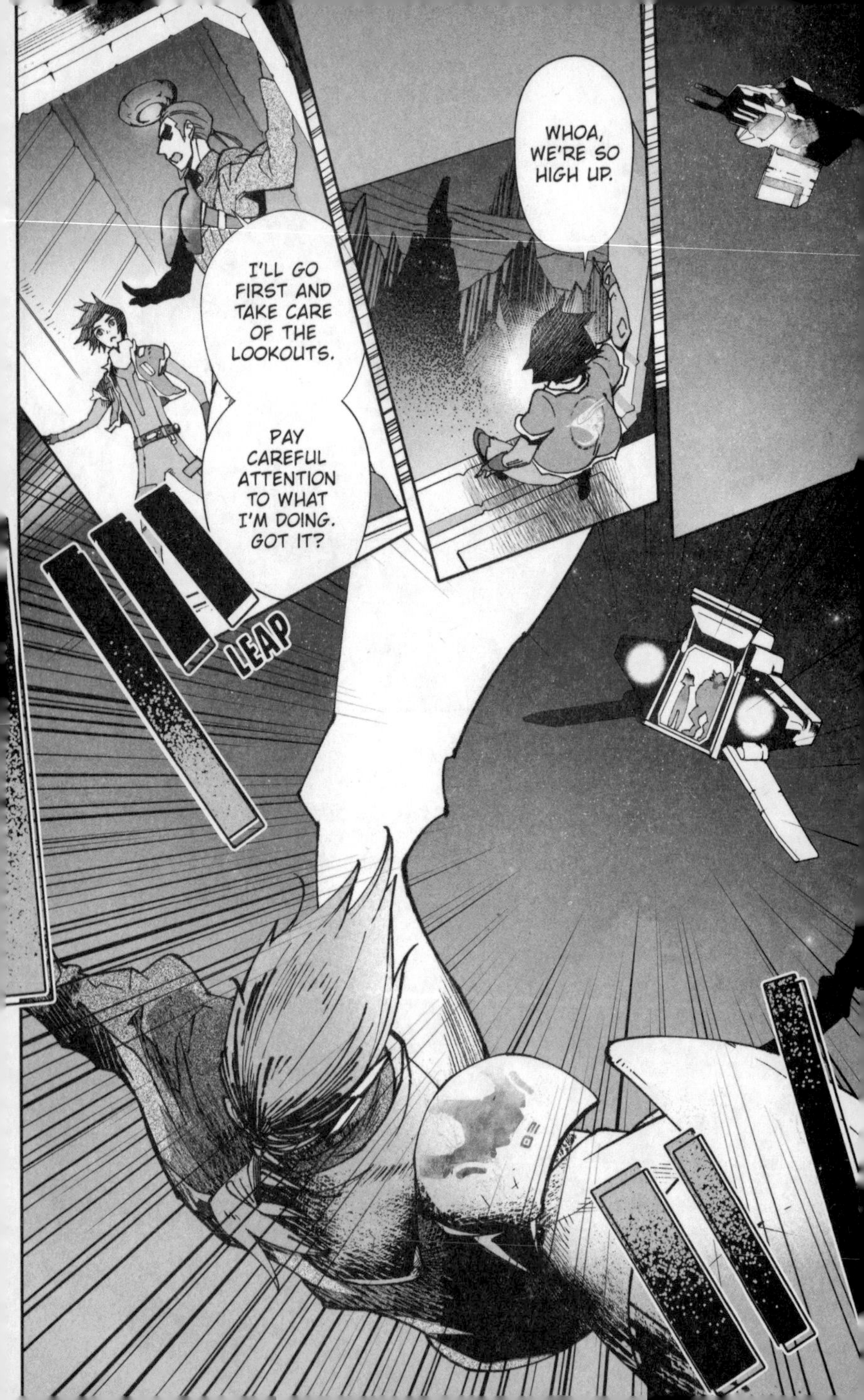
WHOA, WE'RE SO HIGH UP.
I'LL GO FIRST AND TAKE CARE OF THE LOOKOUTS.
PAY CAREFUL ATTENTION TO WHAT I'M DOING. GOT IT?
LEAP

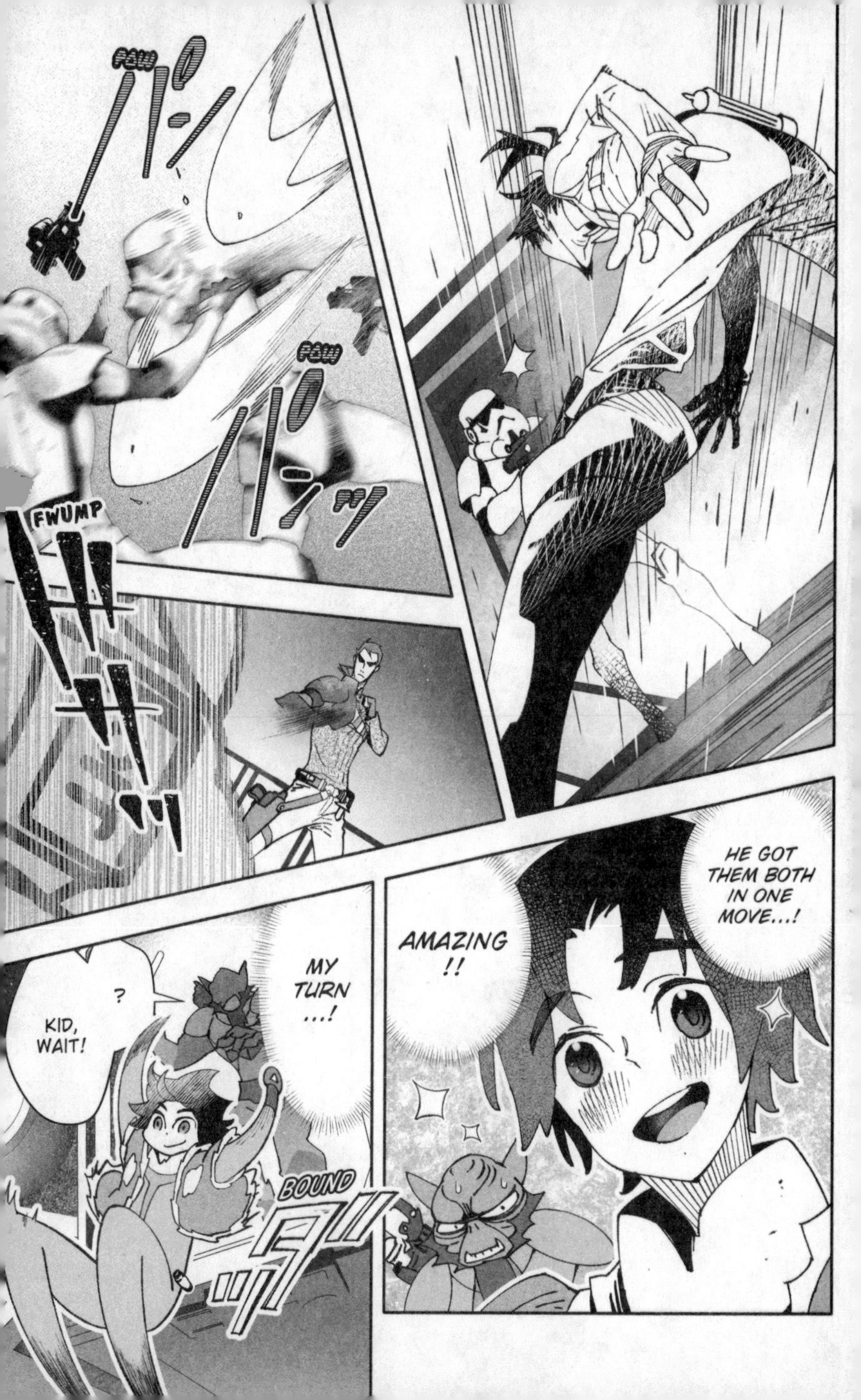
PAW
PAW
FWUMP
HE GOT THEM BOTH IN ONE MOVE...!
AMAZING!!
MY TURN...!
?
KID, WAIT!
BOUND

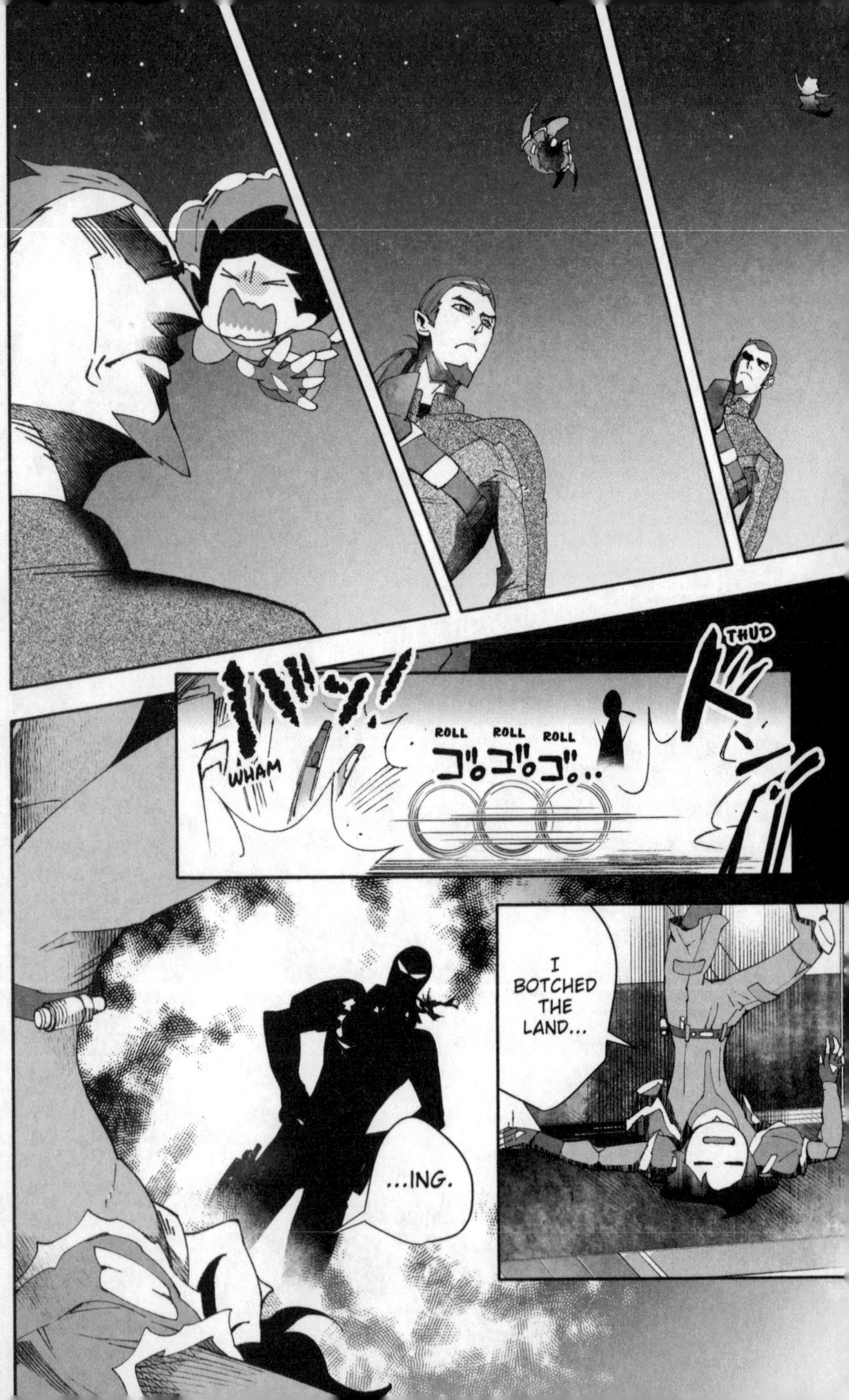
THUD
ROLL
ROLL
ROLL
WHAM
I BOTCHED THE LAND...
...ING.

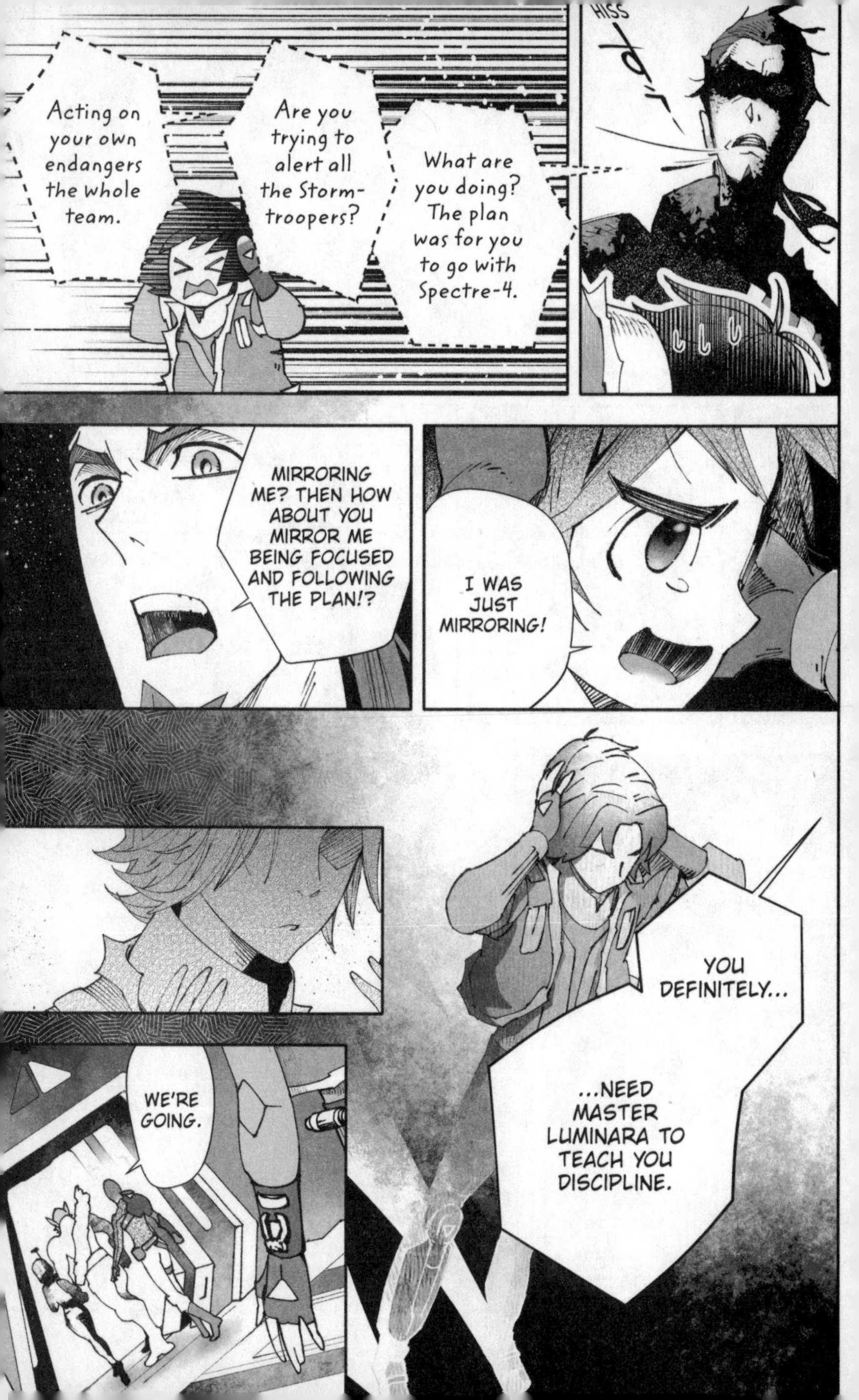
HISS
What are you doing? The plan was for you to go with Spectre-4.
Are you trying to alert all the Storm-troopers?
Acting on your own endangers the whole team.
I WAS JUST MIRRORING!
MIRRORING ME? THEN HOW ABOUT YOU MIRROR ME BEING FOCUSED AND FOLLOWING THE PLAN!?
YOU DEFINITELY...
...NEED MASTER LUMINARA TO TEACH YOU DISCIPLINE.
WE'RE GOING.

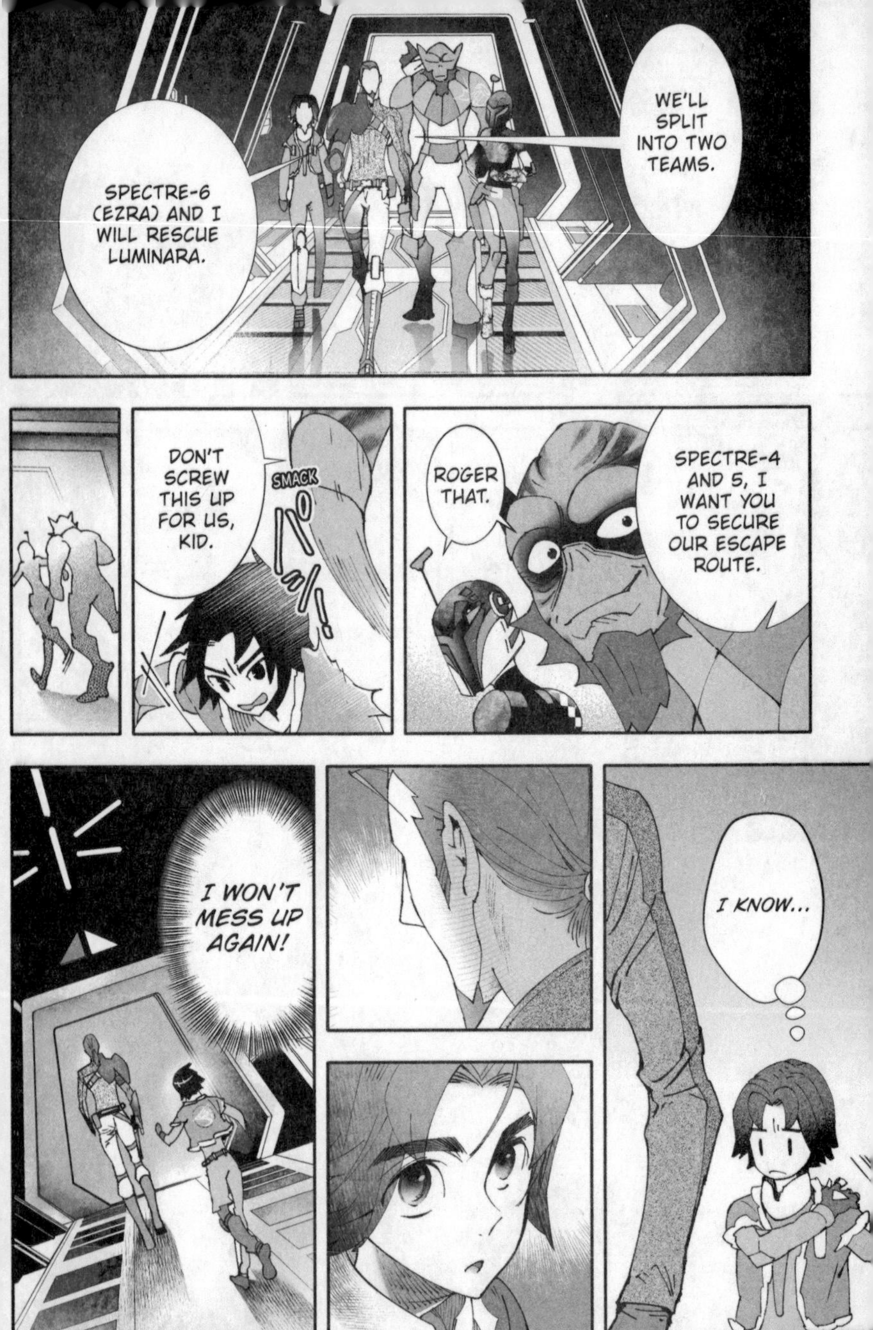
WE'LL SPLIT INTO TWO TEAMS.
SPECTRE-6 (EZRA) AND I WILL RESCUE LUMINARA.
SPECTRE-4 AND 5, I WANT YOU TO SECURE OUR ESCAPE ROUTE.
ROGER THAT.
DON'T SCREW THIS UP FOR US, KID.
SMACK
I KNOW...
I WON'T MESS UP AGAIN!

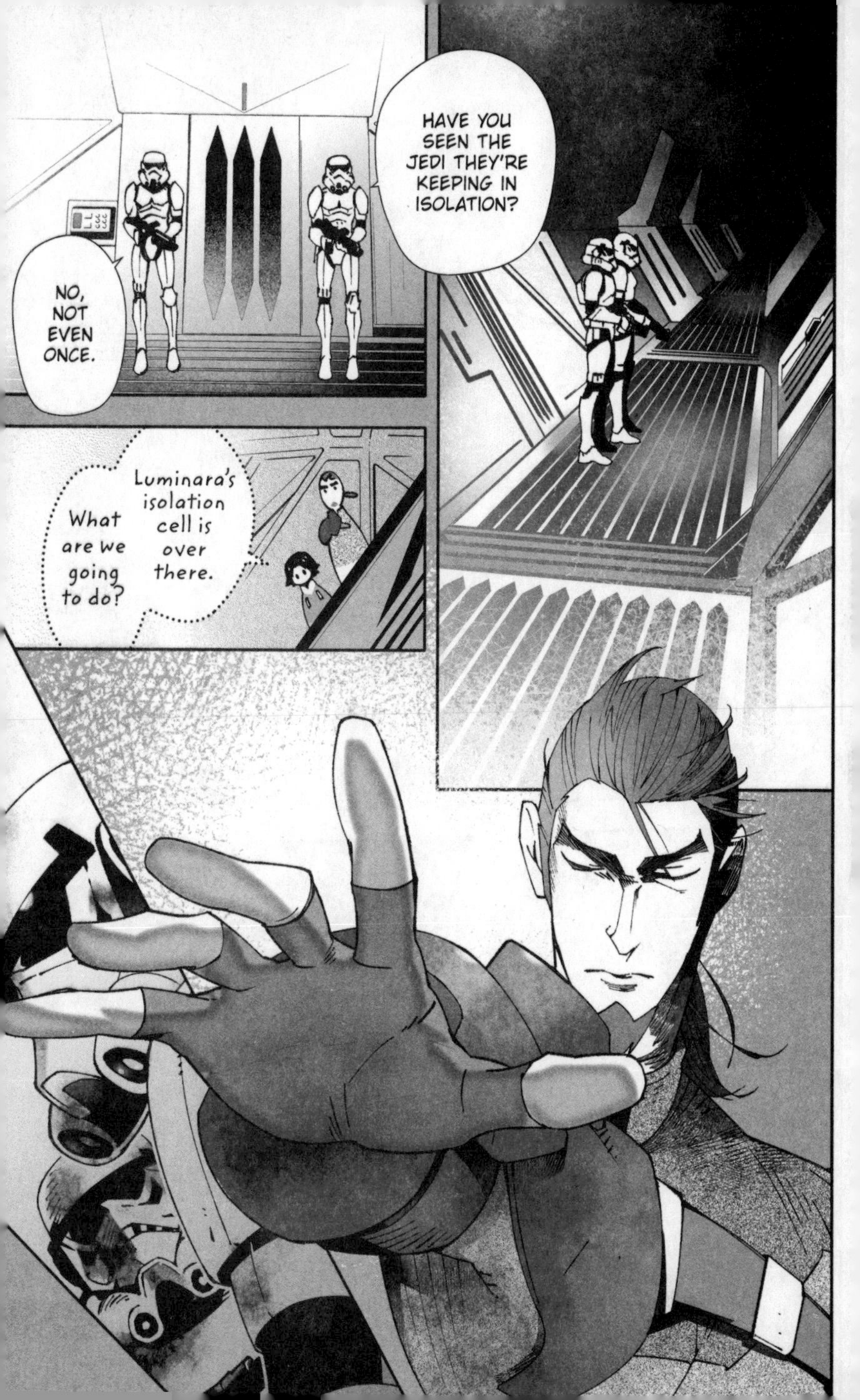
HAVE YOU SEEN THE JEDI THEY'RE KEEPING IN ISOLATION?
NO, NOT EVEN ONCE.
Luminara's isolation cell is over there.
What are we going to do?

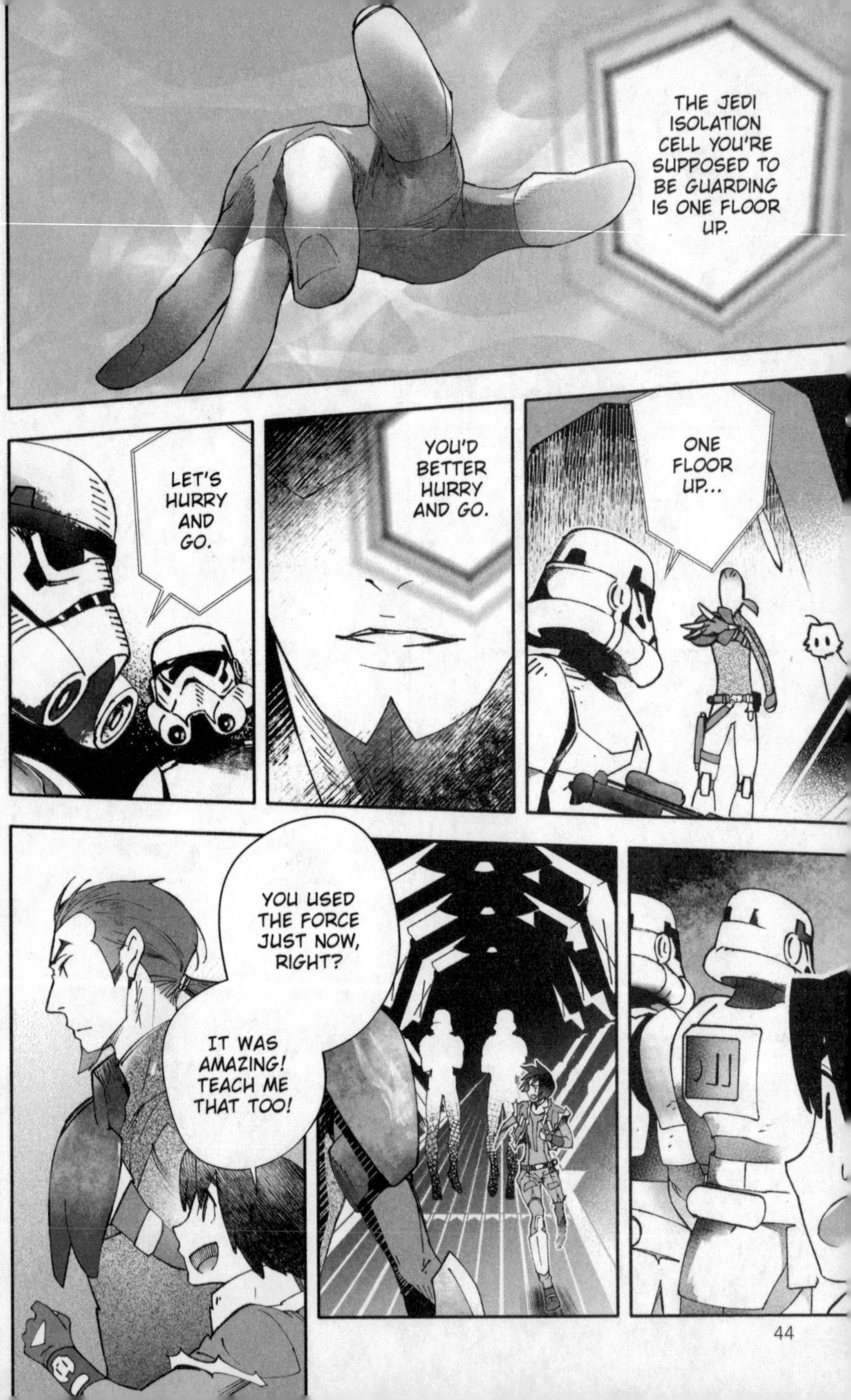
THE JEDI ISOLATION CELL YOU'RE SUPPOSED TO BE GUARDING IS ONE FLOOR UP.
ONE FLOOR UP...
YOU'D BETTER HURRY AND GO.
LET'S HURRY AND GO.
YOU USED THE FORCE JUST NOW, RIGHT?
IT WAS AMAZING! TEACH ME THAT TOO!

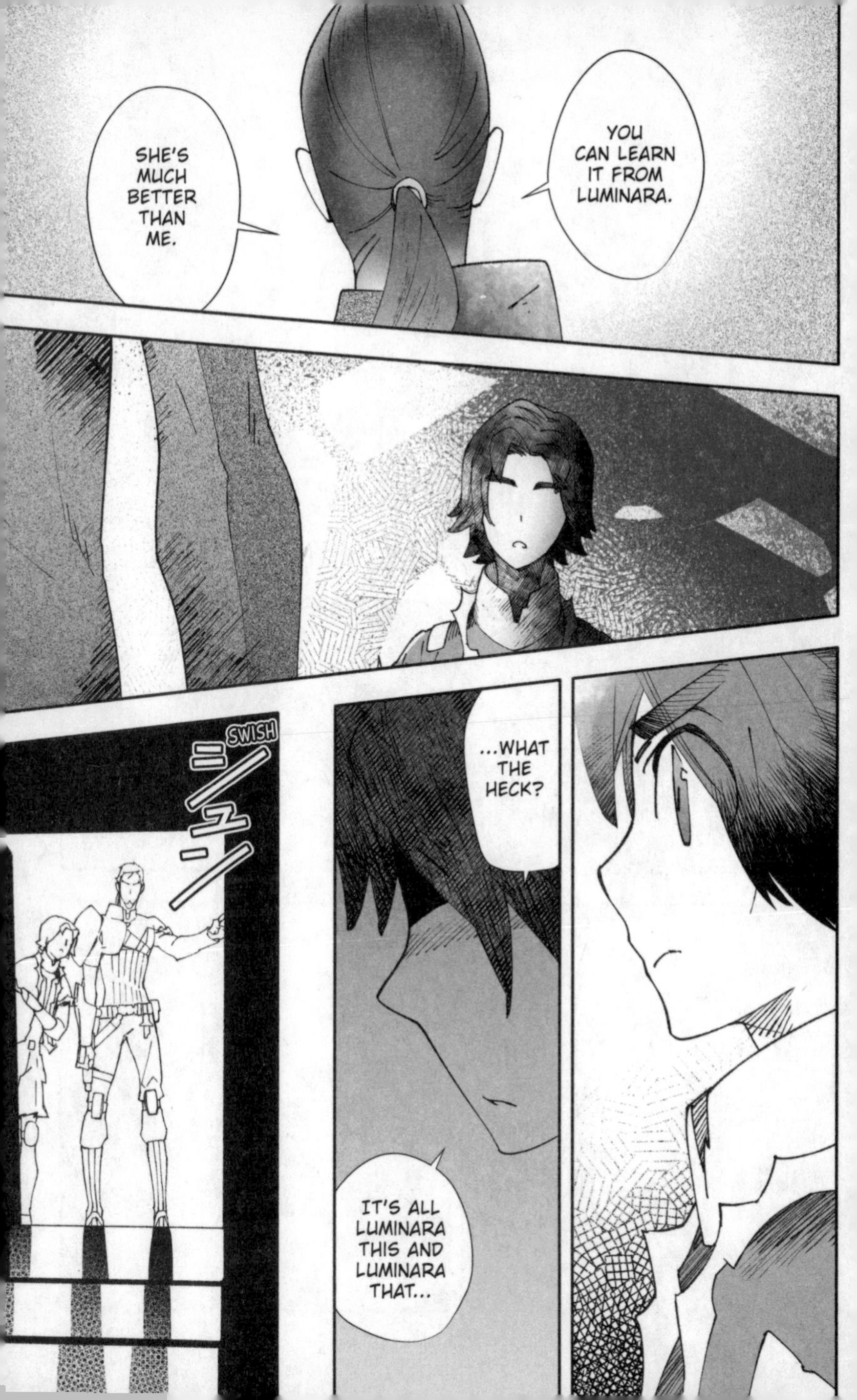
YOU CAN LEARN IT FROM LUMINARA.
SHE'S MUCH BETTER THAN ME.
...WHAT THE HECK?
IT'S ALL LUMINARA THIS AND LUMINARA THAT...
SWISH

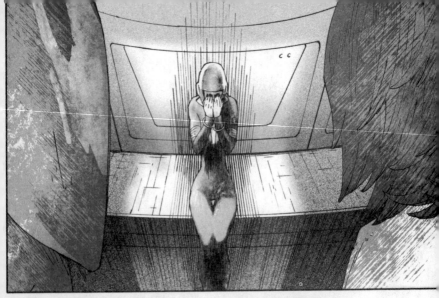

YOU'RE ALIVE... ARE YOU INJURED?

MASTER!

LUMI-NARA?

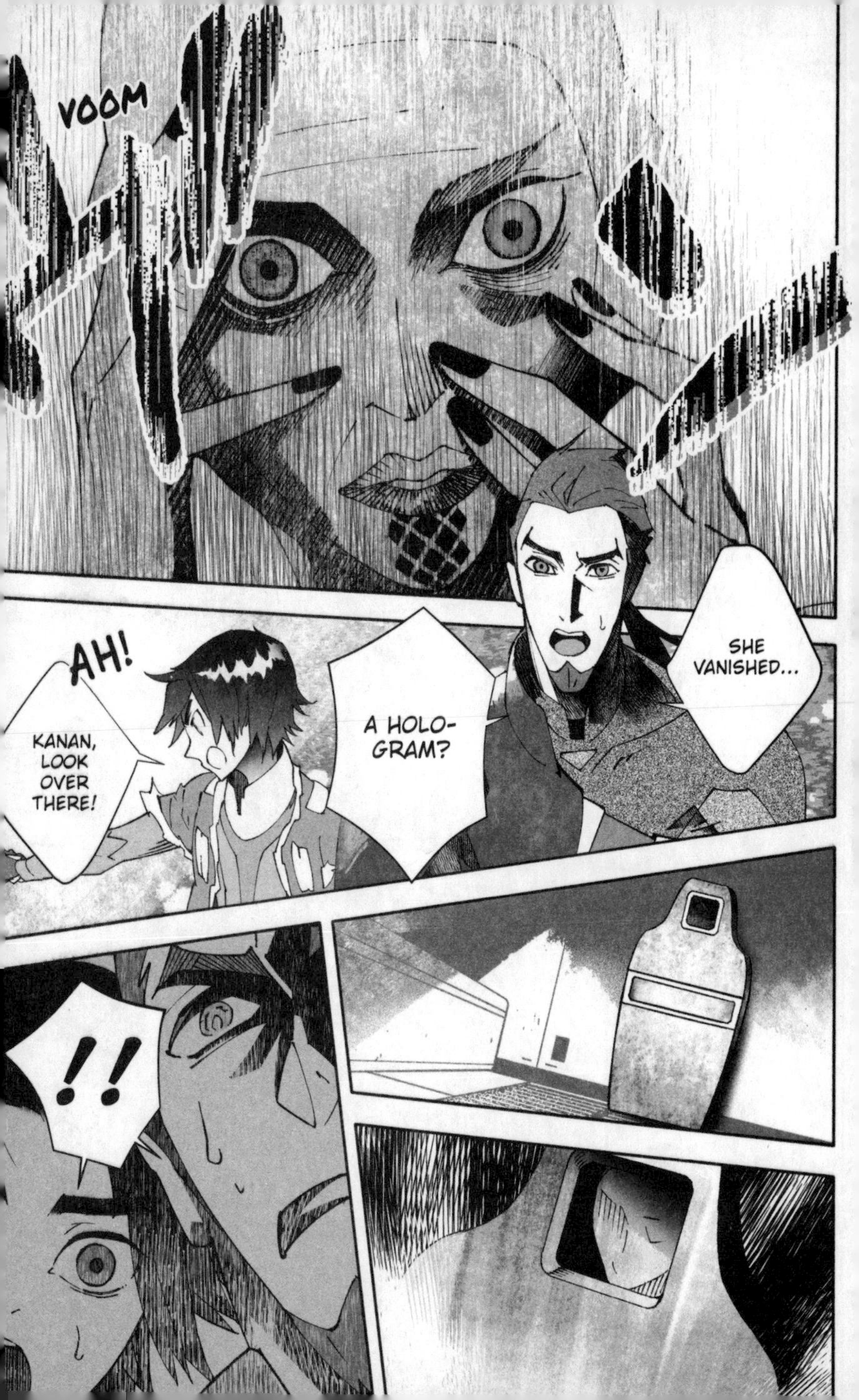
VOOM
SHE VANISHED...
A HOLO-GRAM?
AH!
KANAN, LOOK OVER THERE!
!!

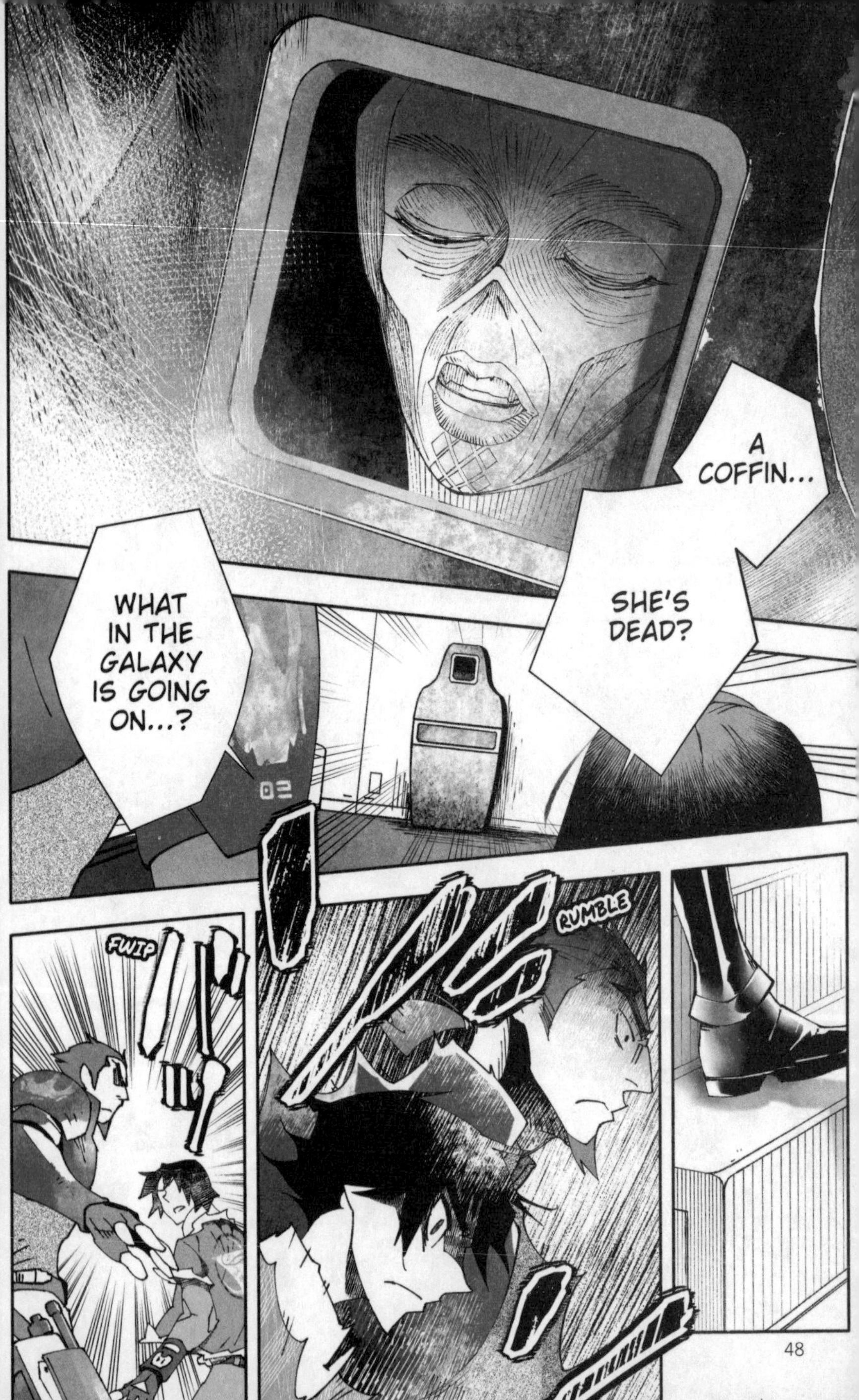
A COFFIN...
SHE'S DEAD?
WHAT IN THE GALAXY IS GOING ON...?
RUMBLE
FWIP

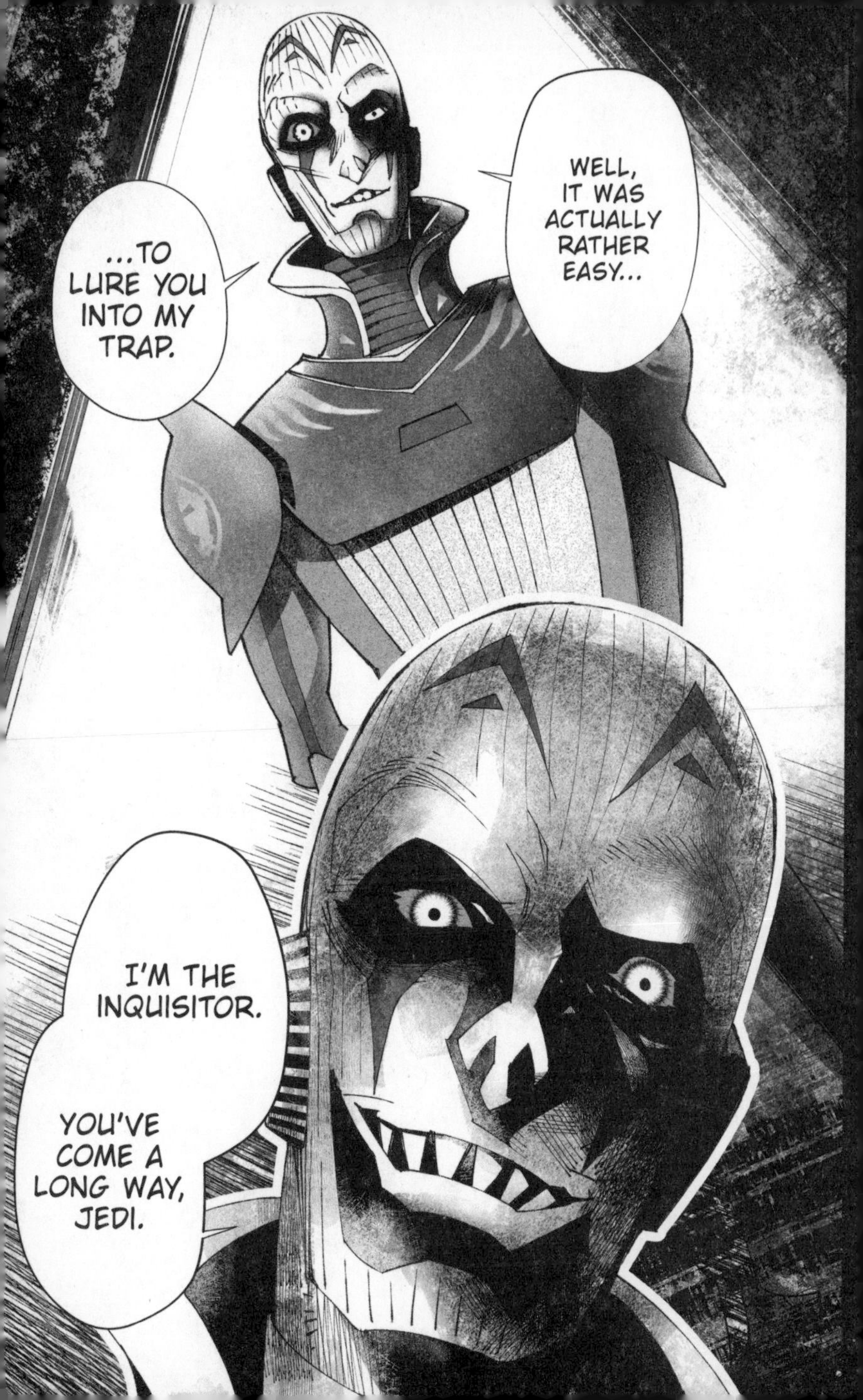
WELL, IT WAS ACTUALLY RATHER EASY...
...TO LURE YOU INTO MY TRAP.
I'M THE INQUISITOR.
YOU'VE COME A LONG WAY, JEDI.

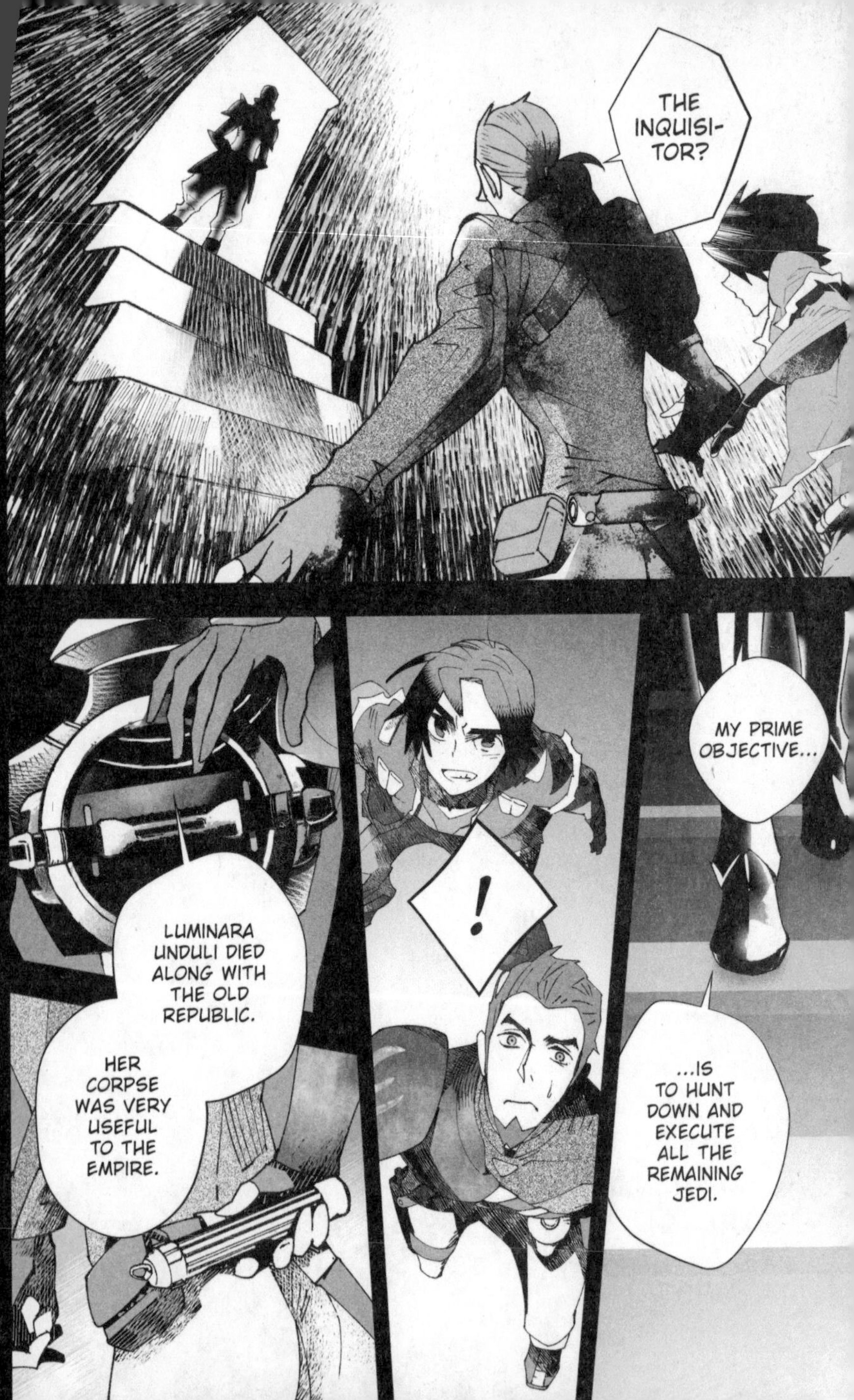
THE INQUISI-TOR?
MY PRIME OBJECTIVE...
...IS TO HUNT DOWN AND EXECUTE ALL THE REMAINING JEDI.
!
LUMINARA UNDULI DIED ALONG WITH THE OLD REPUBLIC.
HER CORPSE WAS VERY USEFUL TO THE EMPIRE.

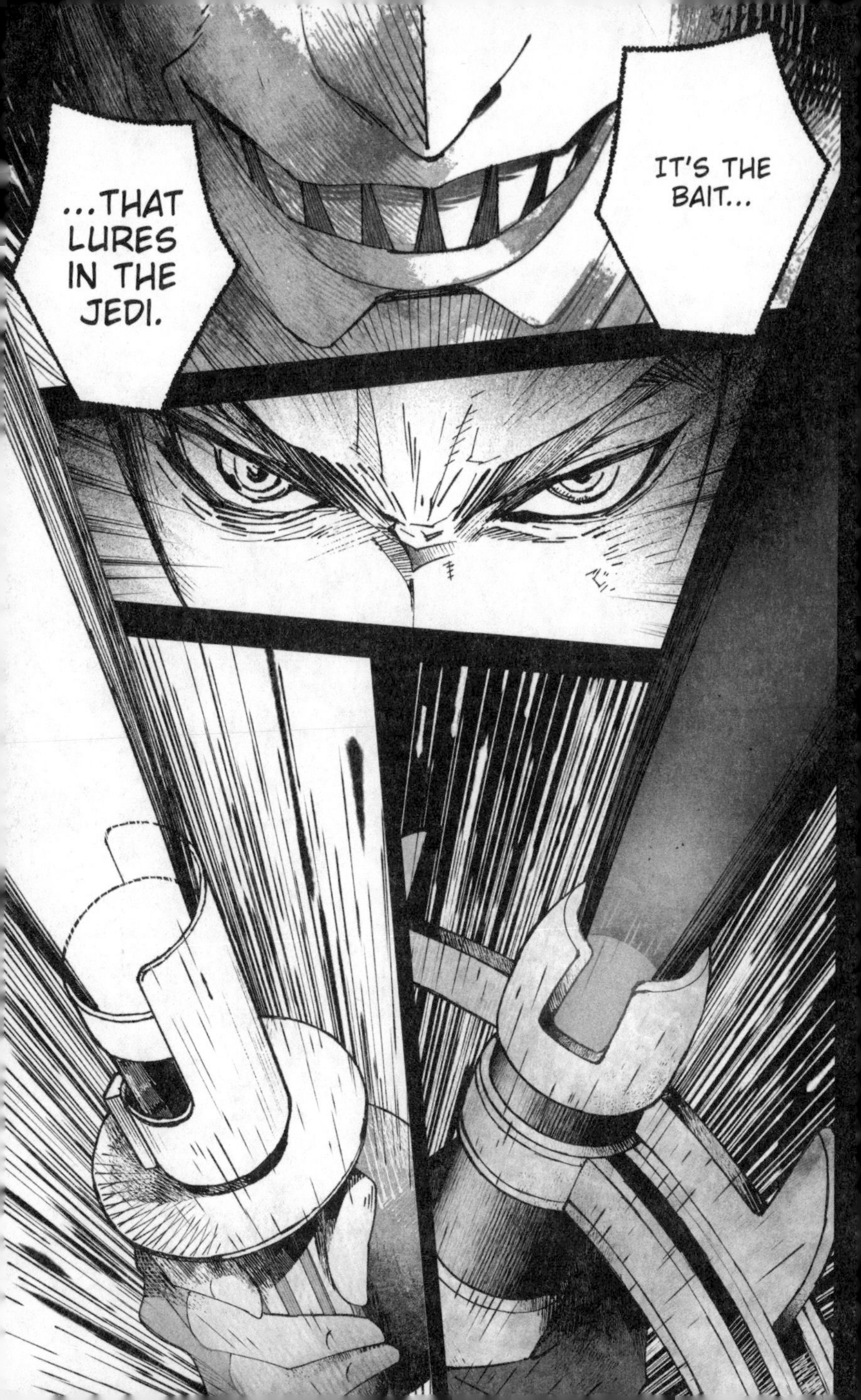
IT'S THE BAIT...
...THAT LURES IN THE JEDI.

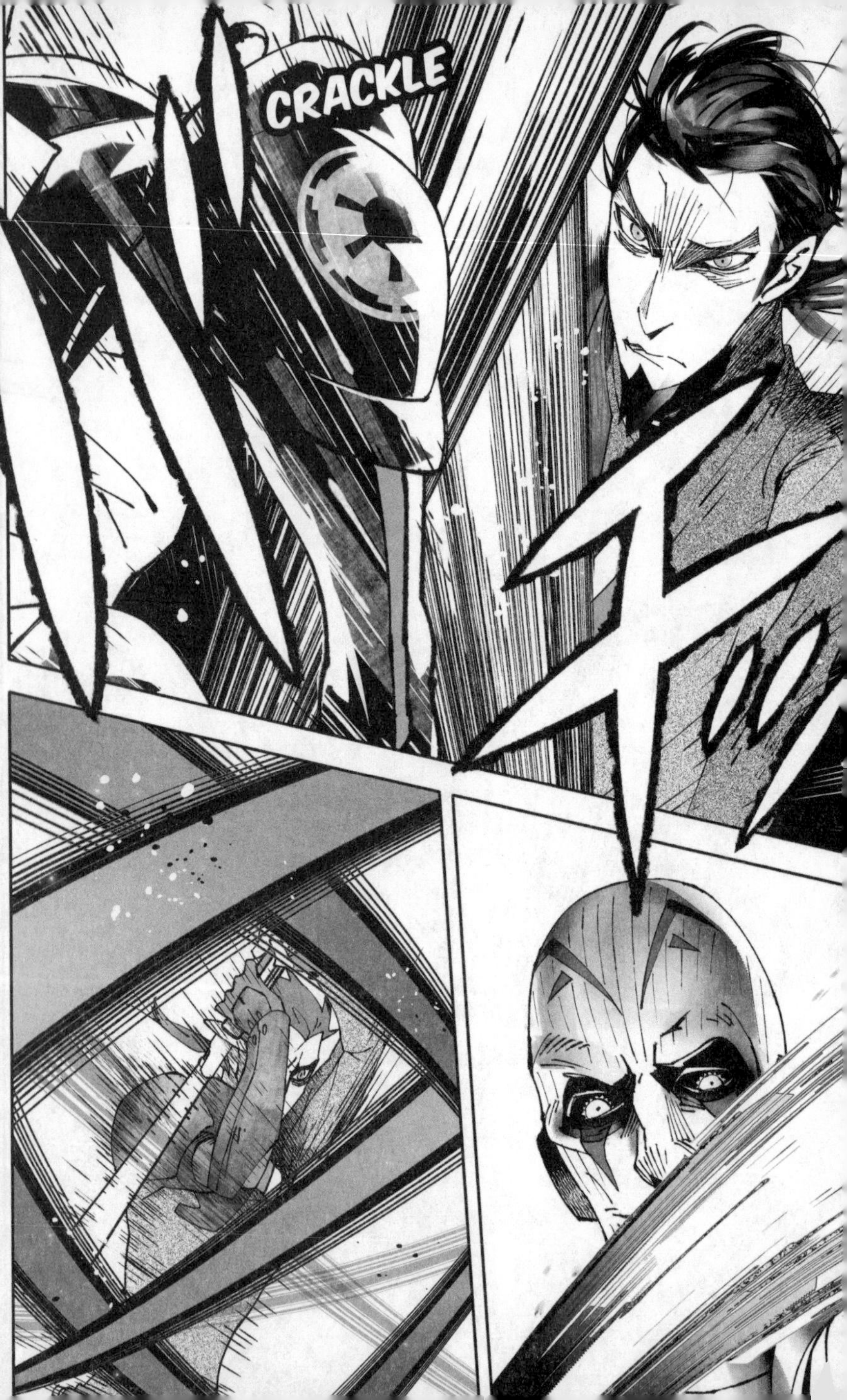
CRACKLE

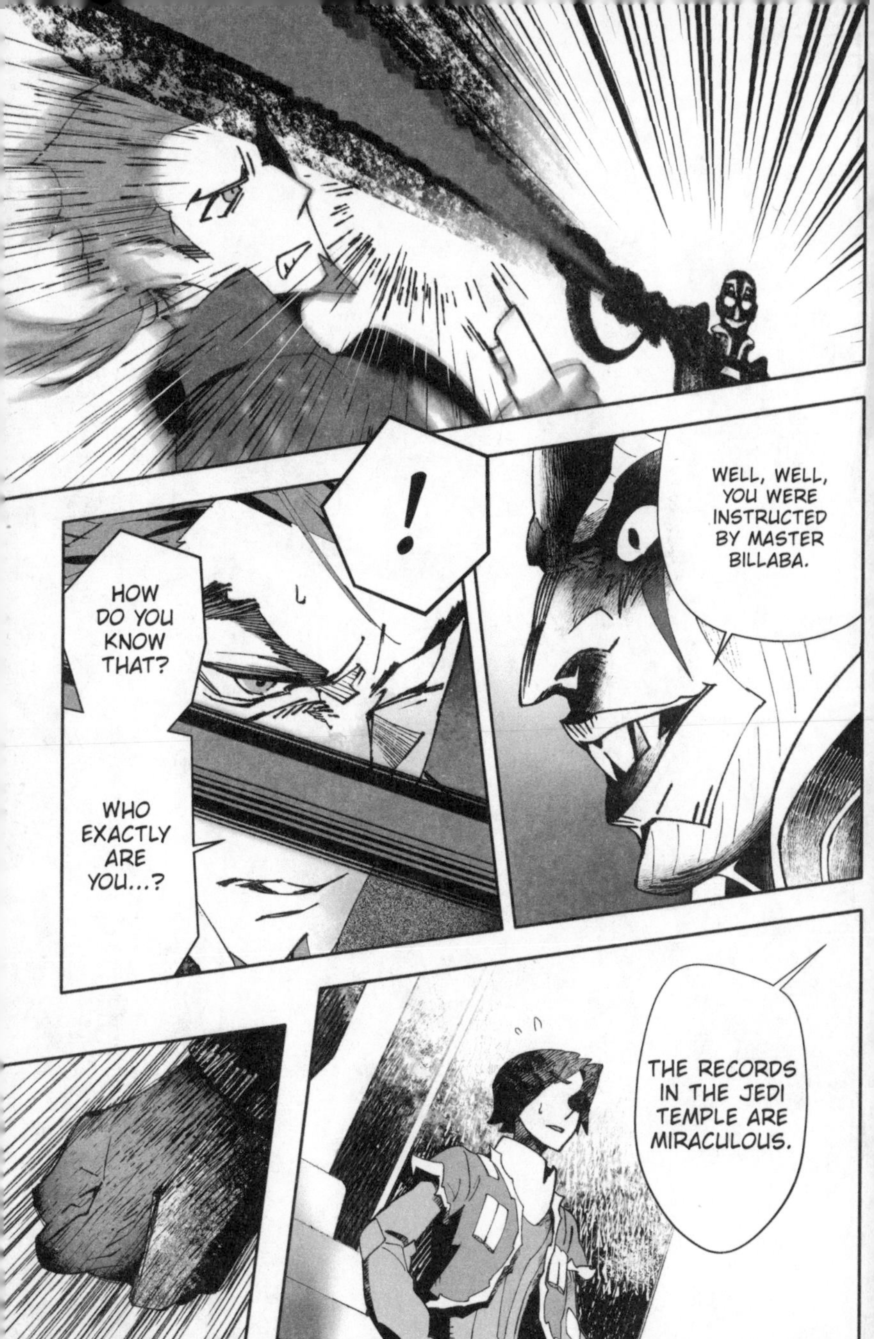
WELL, WELL, YOU WERE INSTRUCTED BY MASTER BILLABA.
!
HOW DO YOU KNOW THAT?
WHO EXACTLY ARE YOU...?
THE RECORDS IN THE JEDI TEMPLE ARE MIRACULOUS.

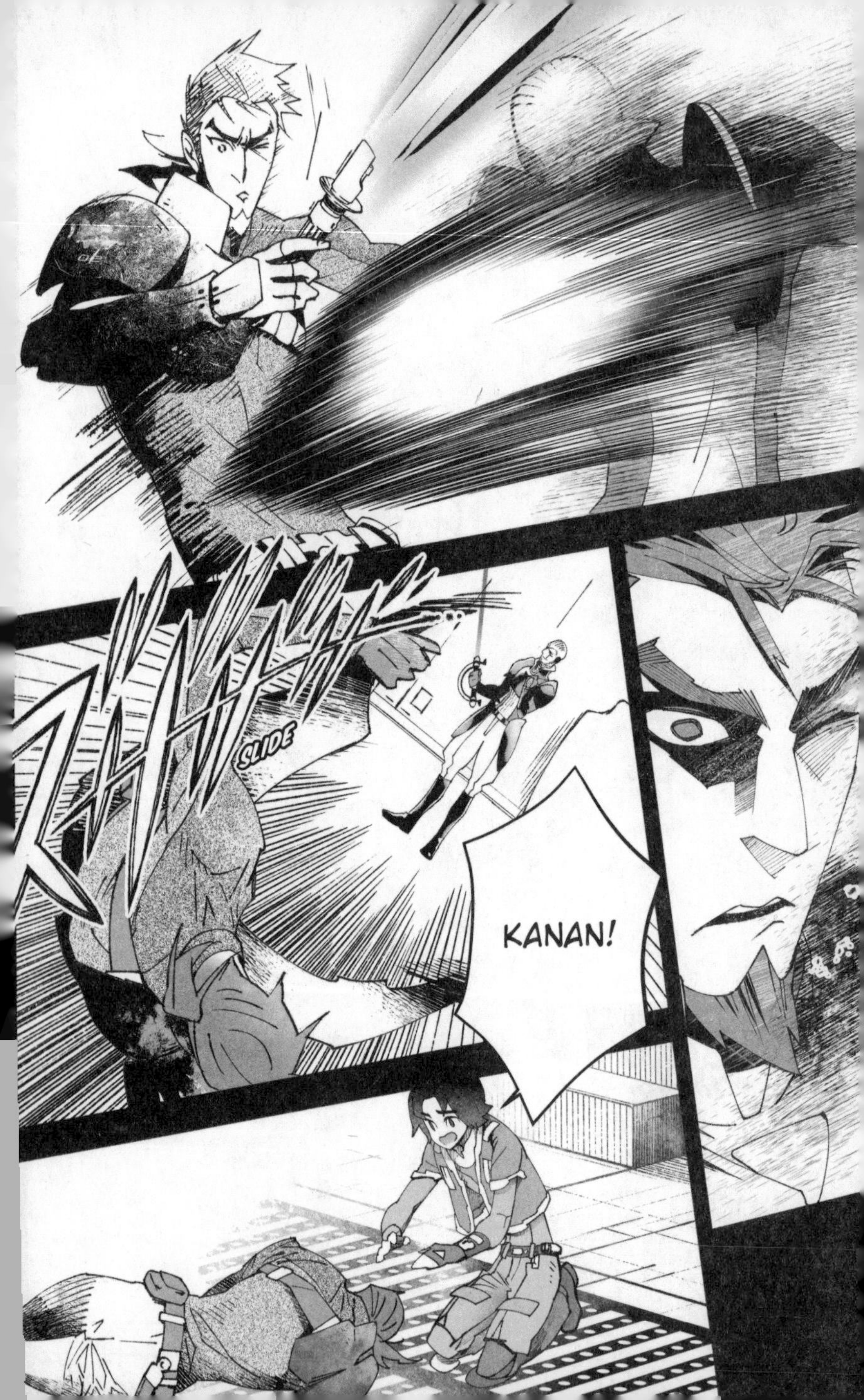
SLIDE
KANAN!

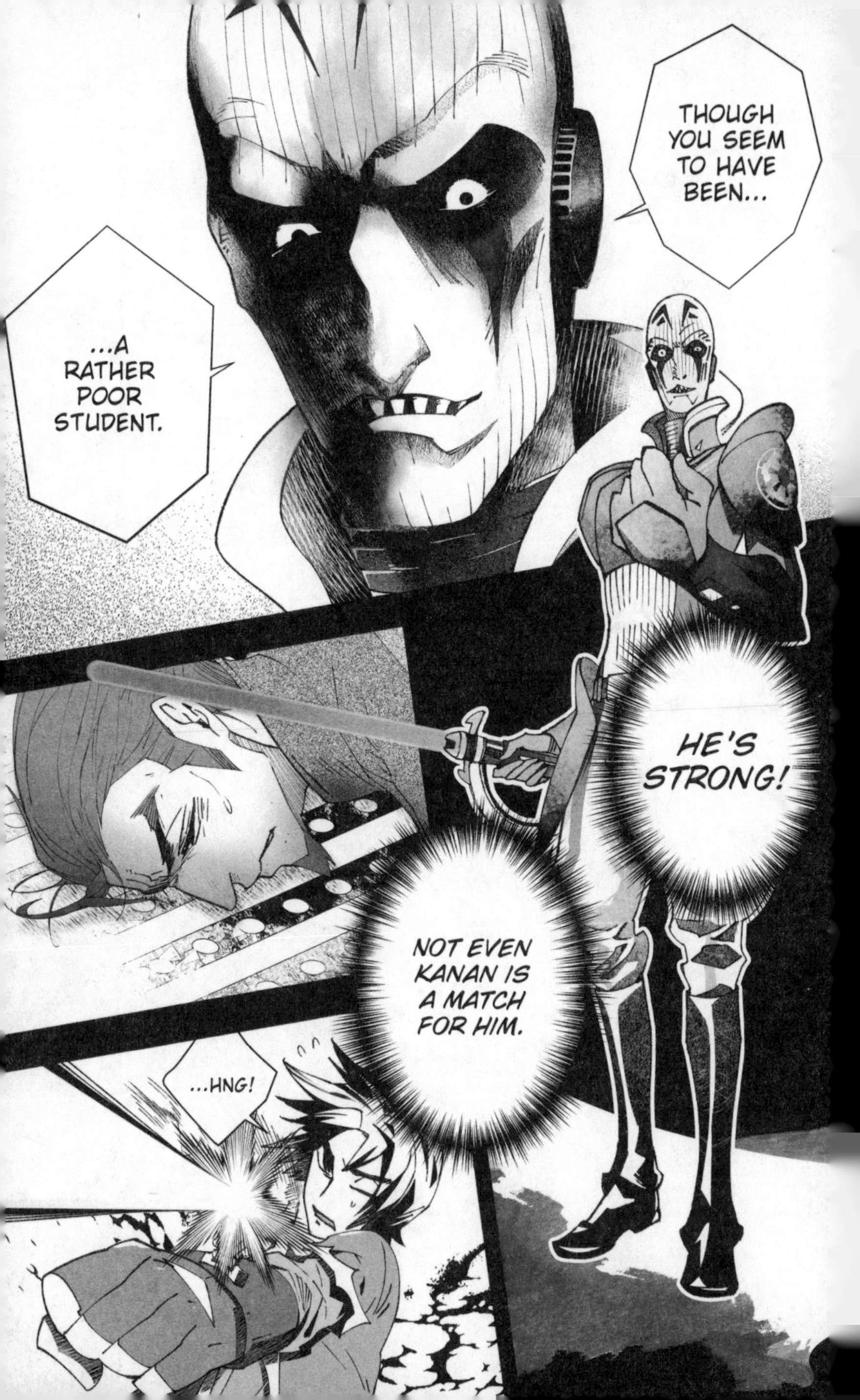
THOUGH YOU SEEM TO HAVE BEEN...
...A RATHER POOR STUDENT.
HE'S STRONG!
NOT EVEN KANAN IS A MATCH FOR HIM.
...HNG!

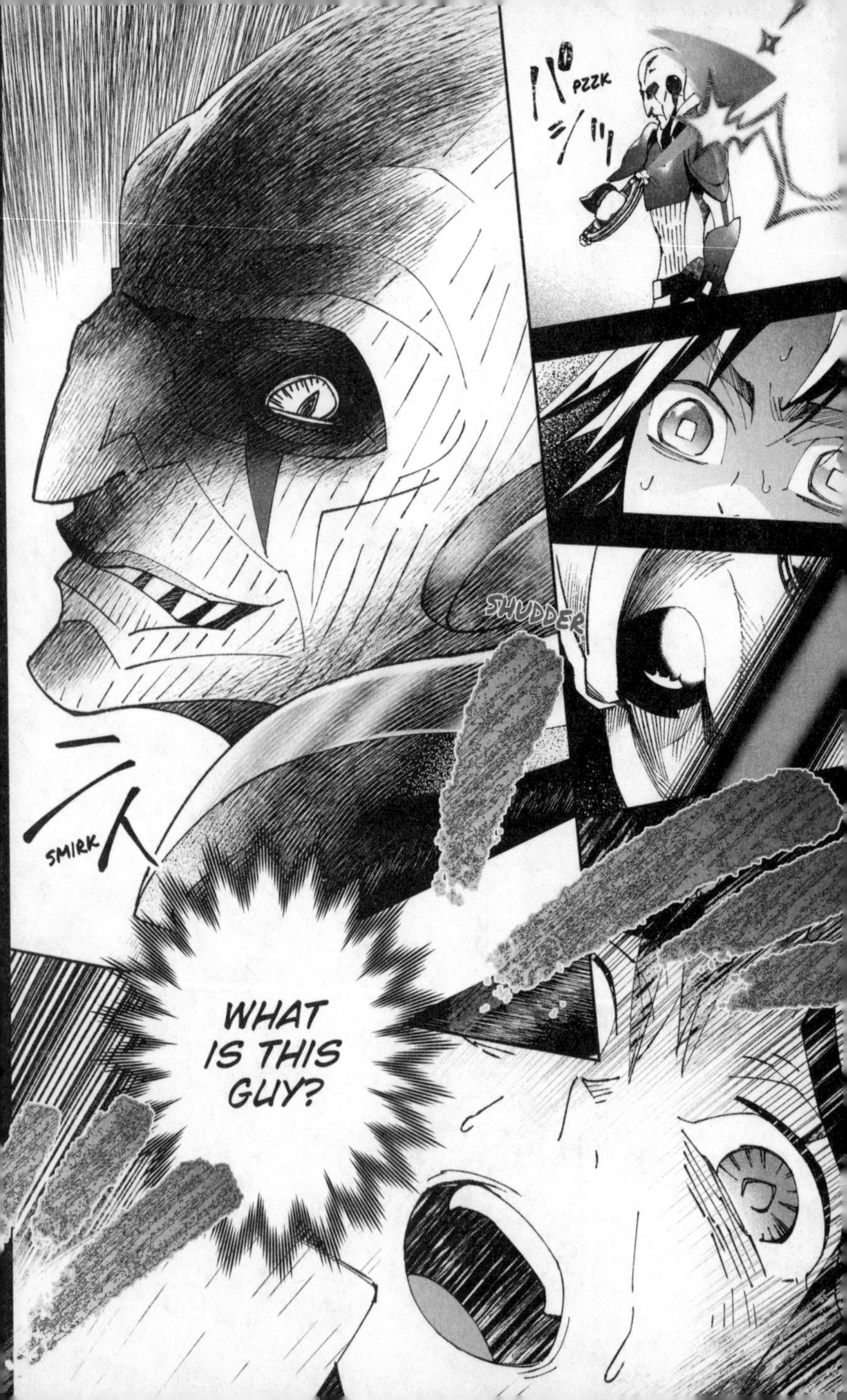
PZZK
SHUDDER
SMIRK
WHAT IS THIS GUY?

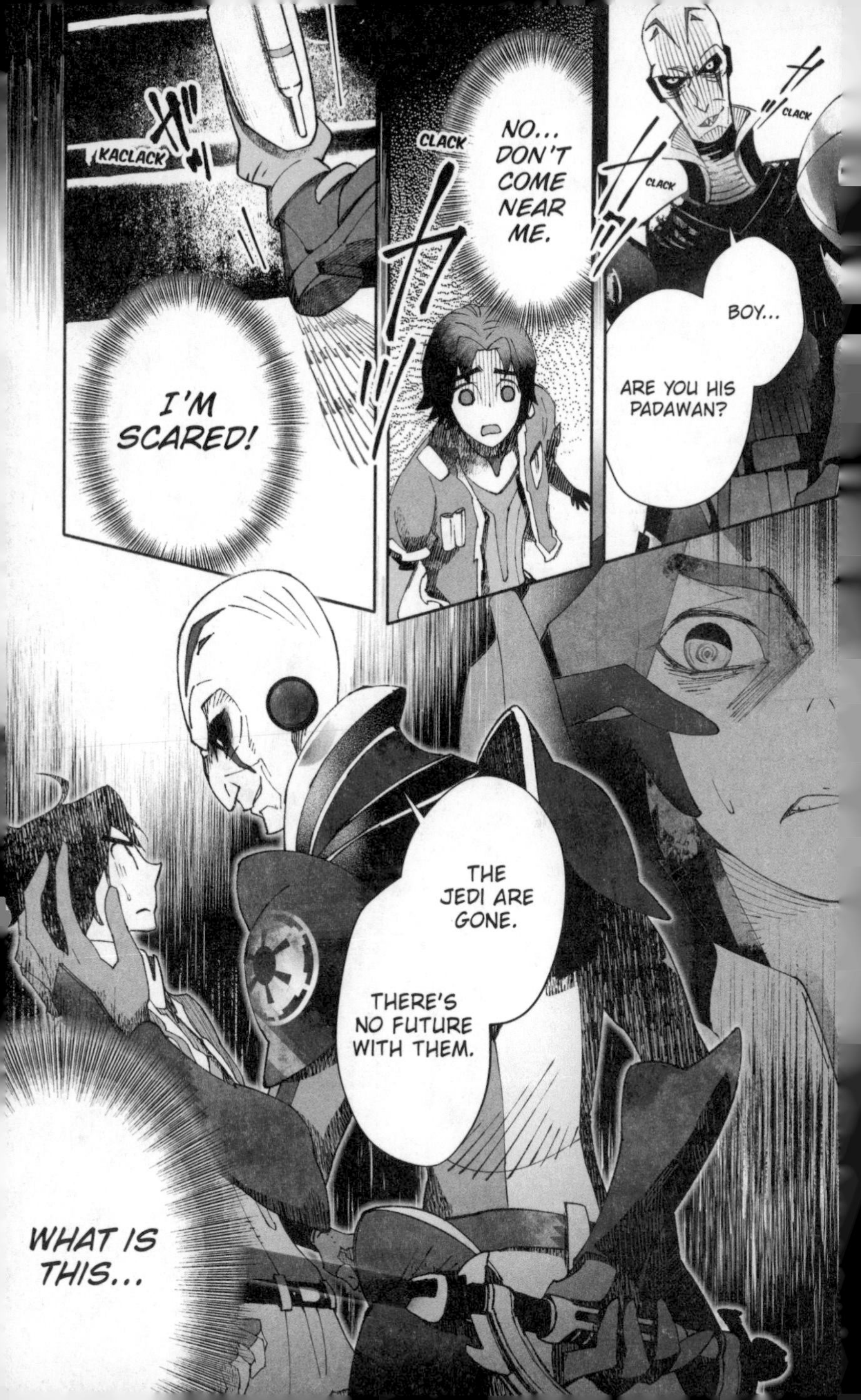
CLACK
CLACK
BOY...
ARE YOU HIS PADAWAN?
CLACK
NO... DON'T COME NEAR ME.
KACLACK
I'M SCARED!
THE JEDI ARE GONE.
THERE'S NO FUTURE WITH THEM.
WHAT IS THIS...

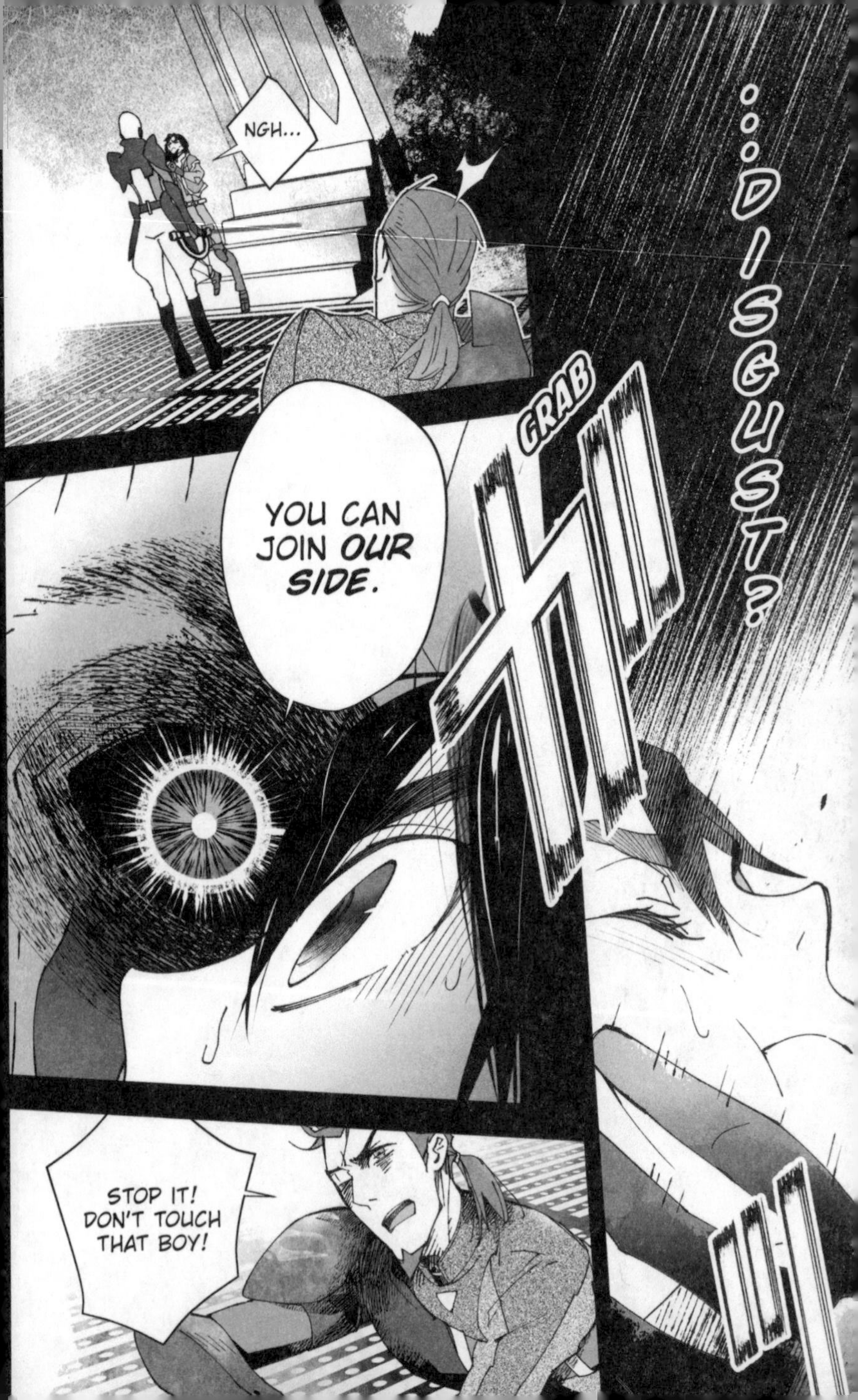
...DISGUST?
GRAB
NGH...
YOU CAN JOIN OUR SIDE.
STOP IT! DON'T TOUCH THAT BOY!

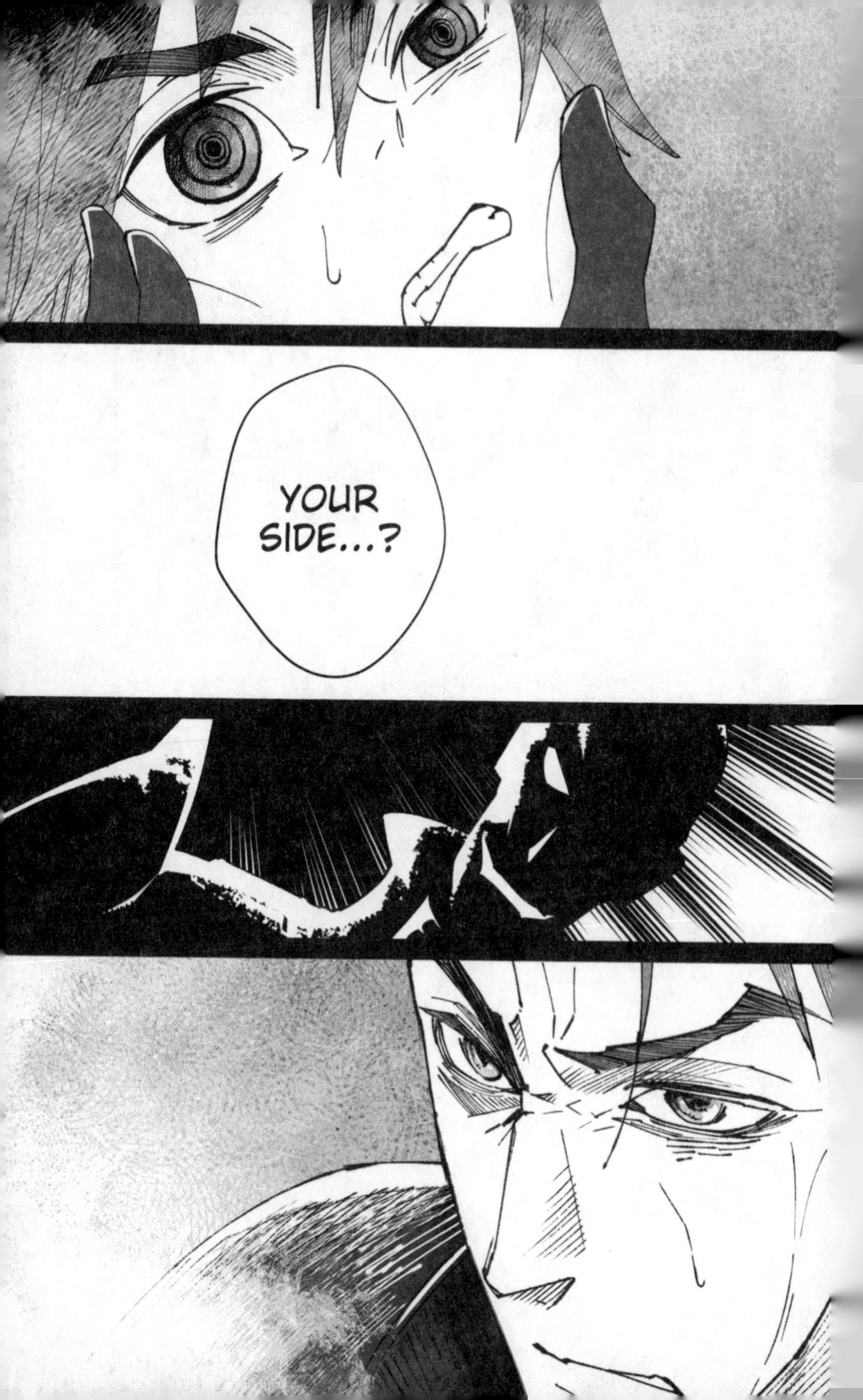
YOUR SIDE...?

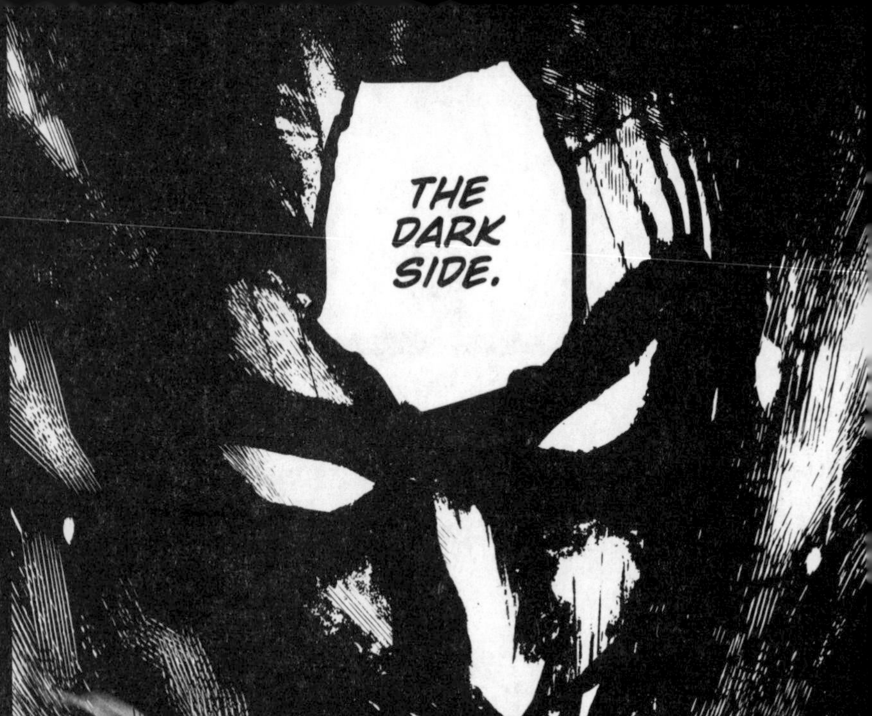
THE DARK SIDE.
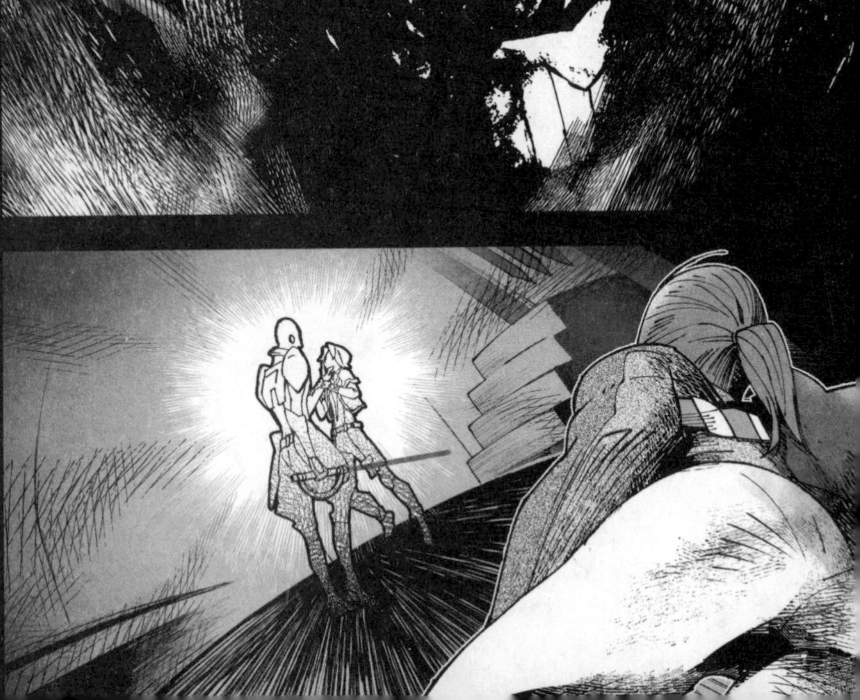

STAR WARS
REBELS

STORY 2. THE INCOMPLETE JEDI II

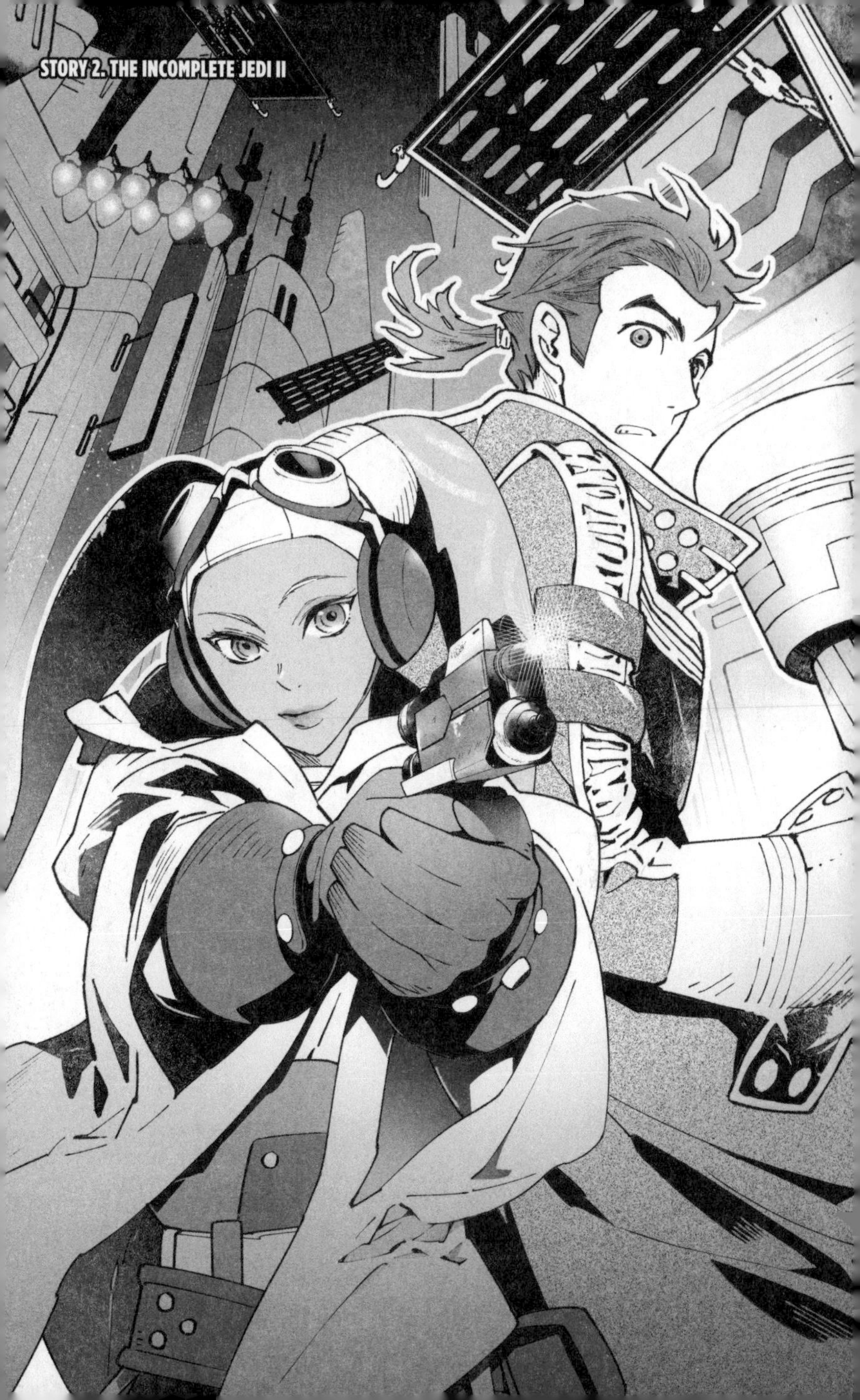

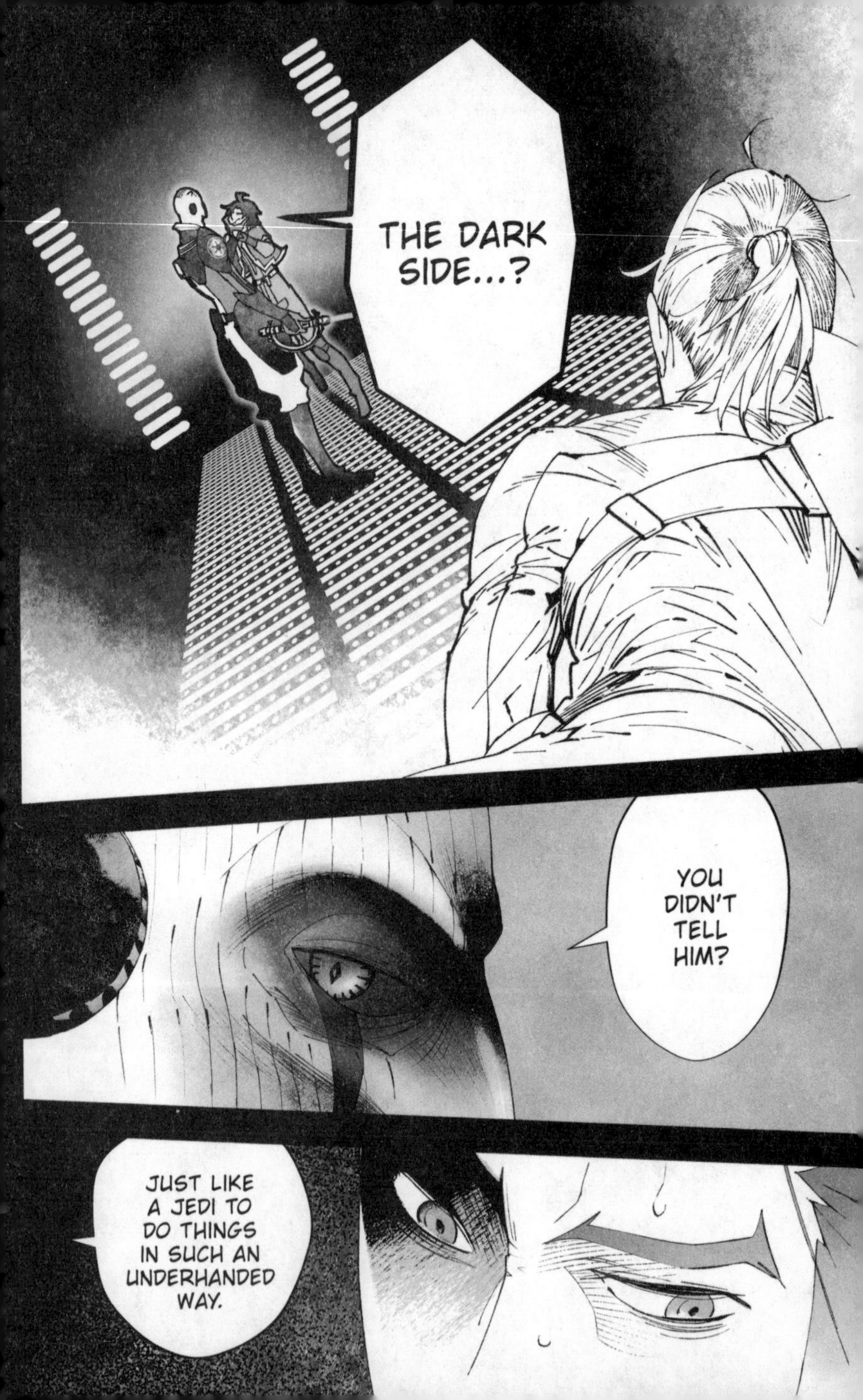
THE DARK SIDE...?
YOU DIDN'T TELL HIM?
JUST LIKE A JEDI TO DO THINGS IN SUCH AN UNDERHANDED WAY.

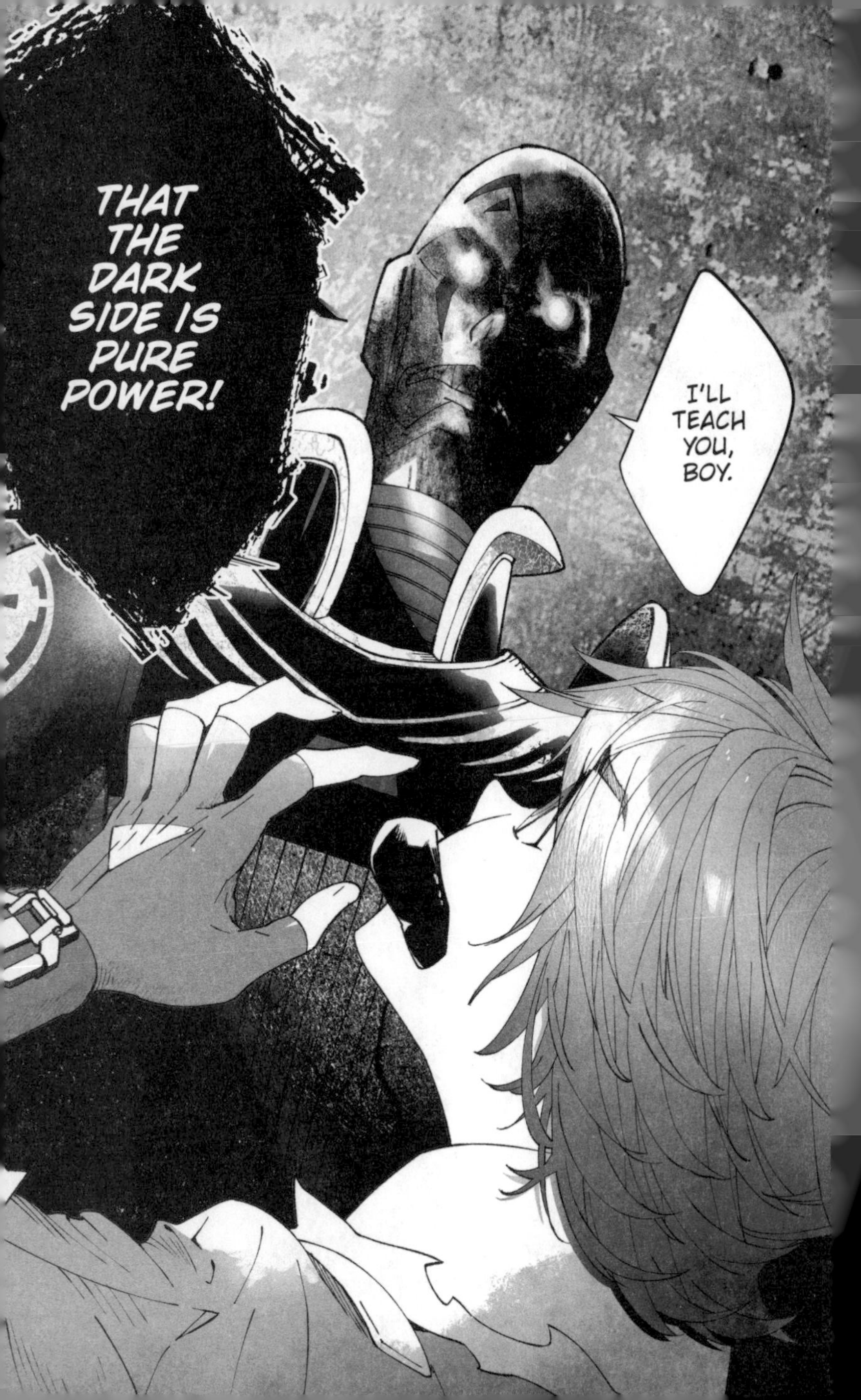
I'LL TEACH YOU, BOY.
THAT THE DARK SIDE IS PURE POWER!

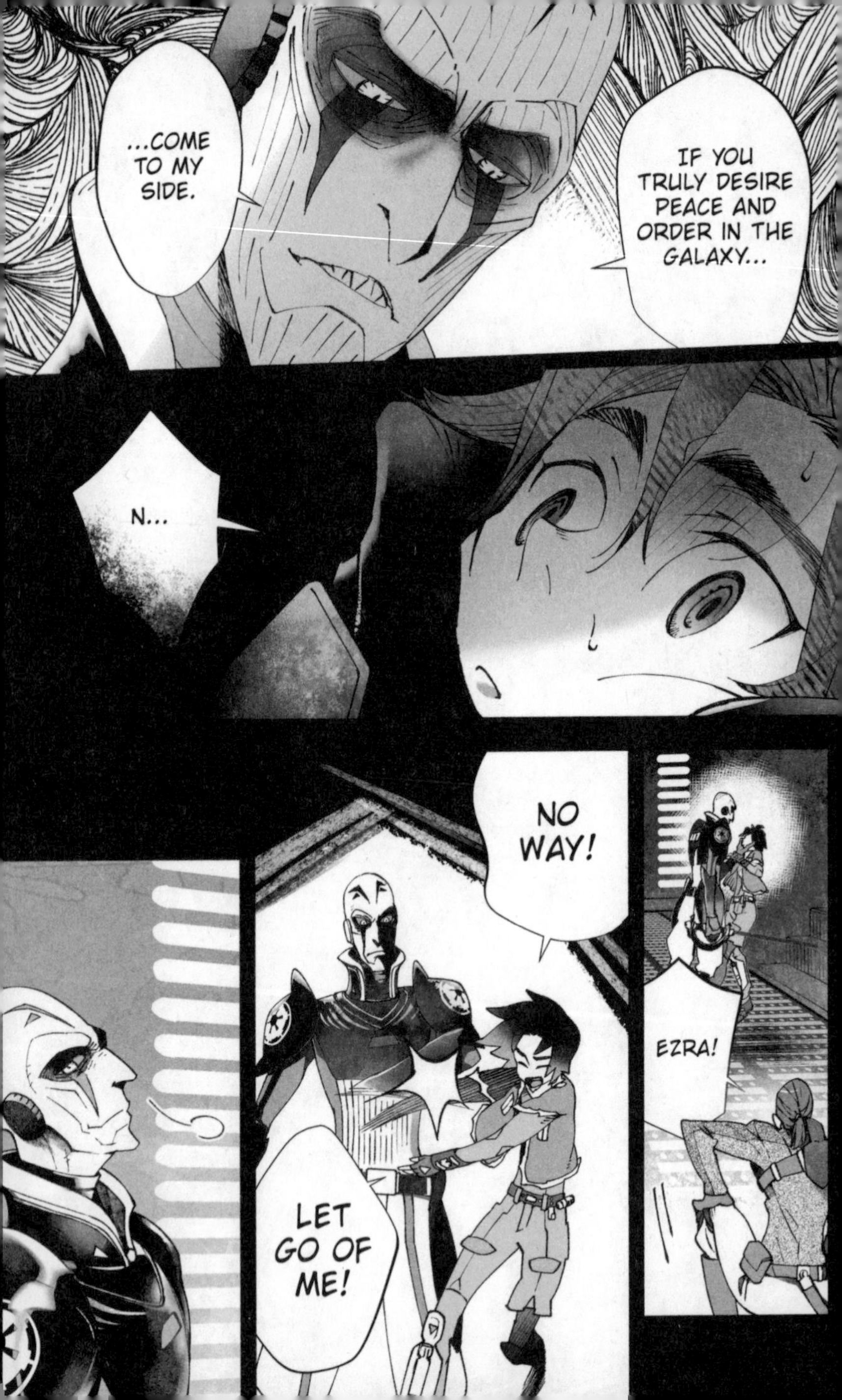
IF YOU TRULY DESIRE PEACE AND ORDER IN THE GALAXY...
...COME TO MY SIDE.
N...
EZRA!
NO WAY!
LET GO OF ME!

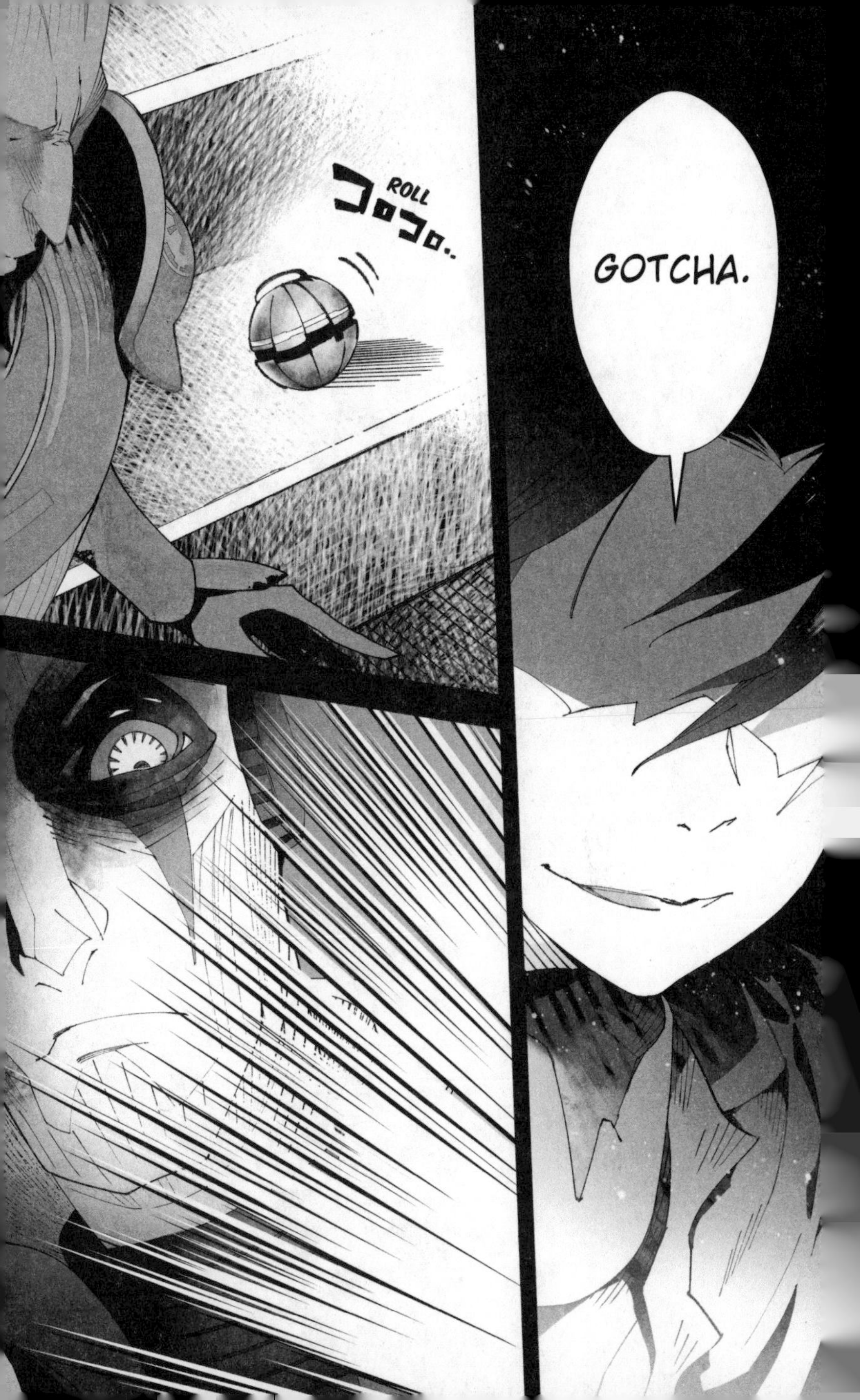
GOTCHA.
ROLL
コロコロ..

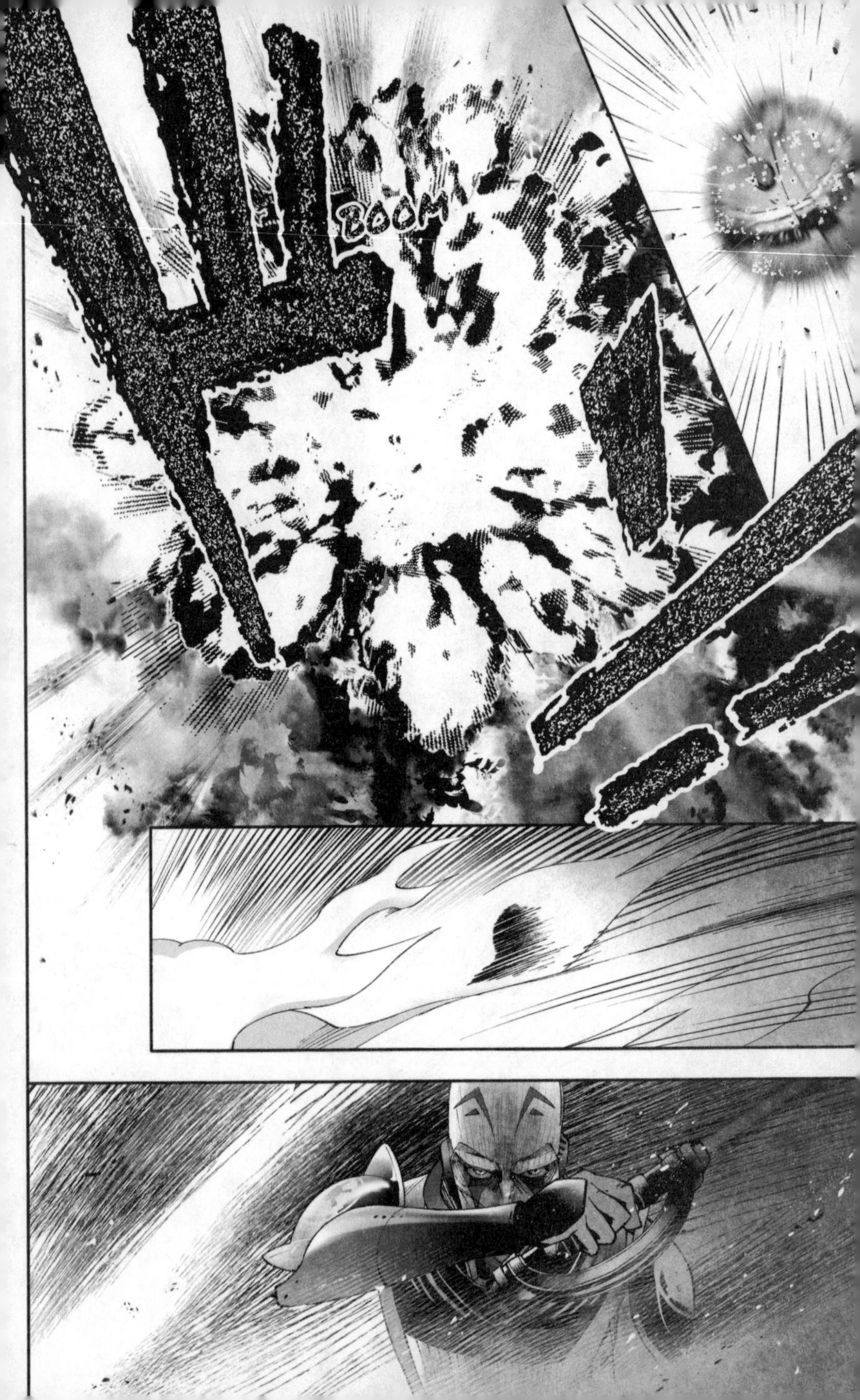
BOOM

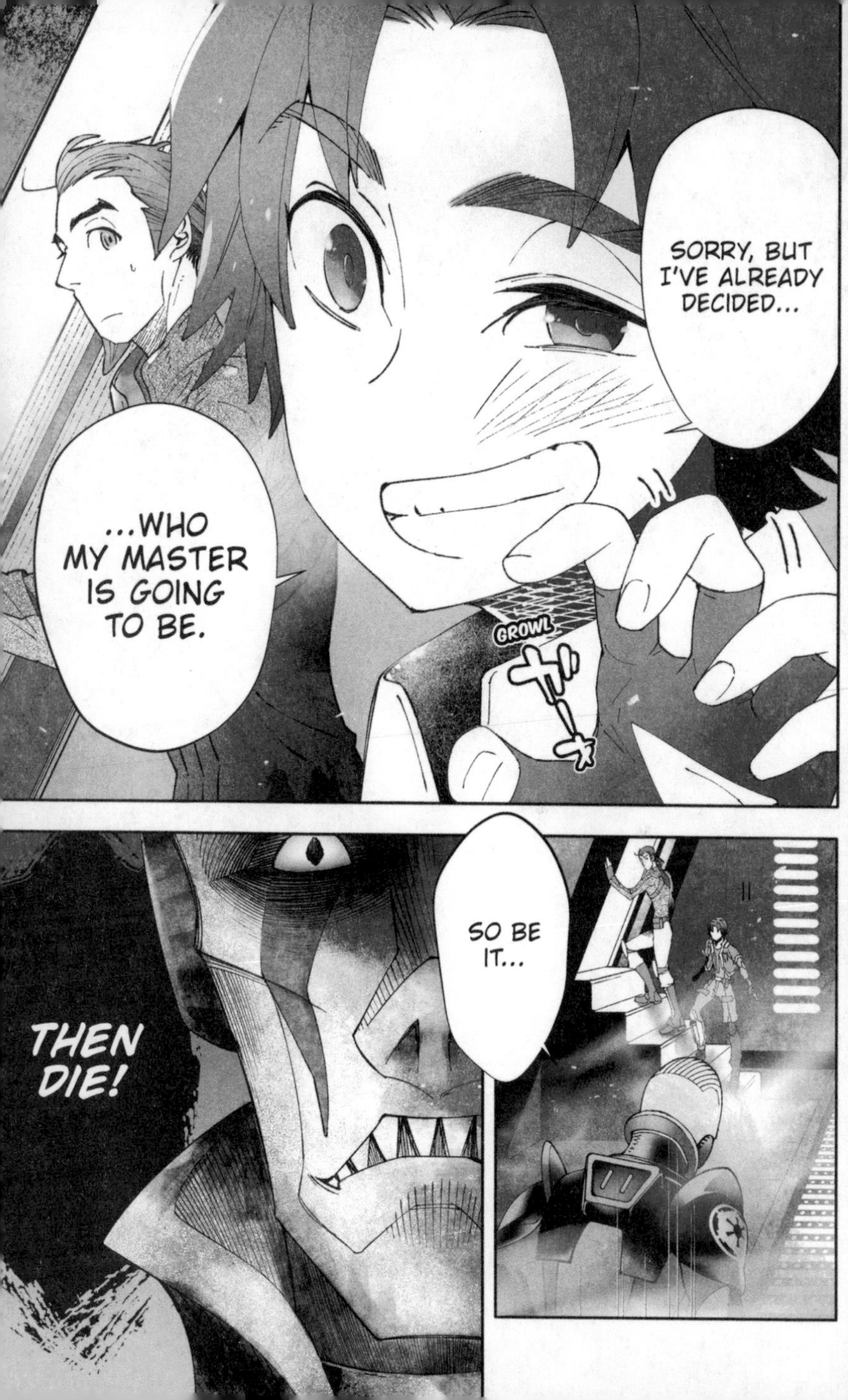
SORRY, BUT I'VE ALREADY DECIDED...
...WHO MY MASTER IS GOING TO BE.
GROWL
SO BE IT...
THEN DIE!

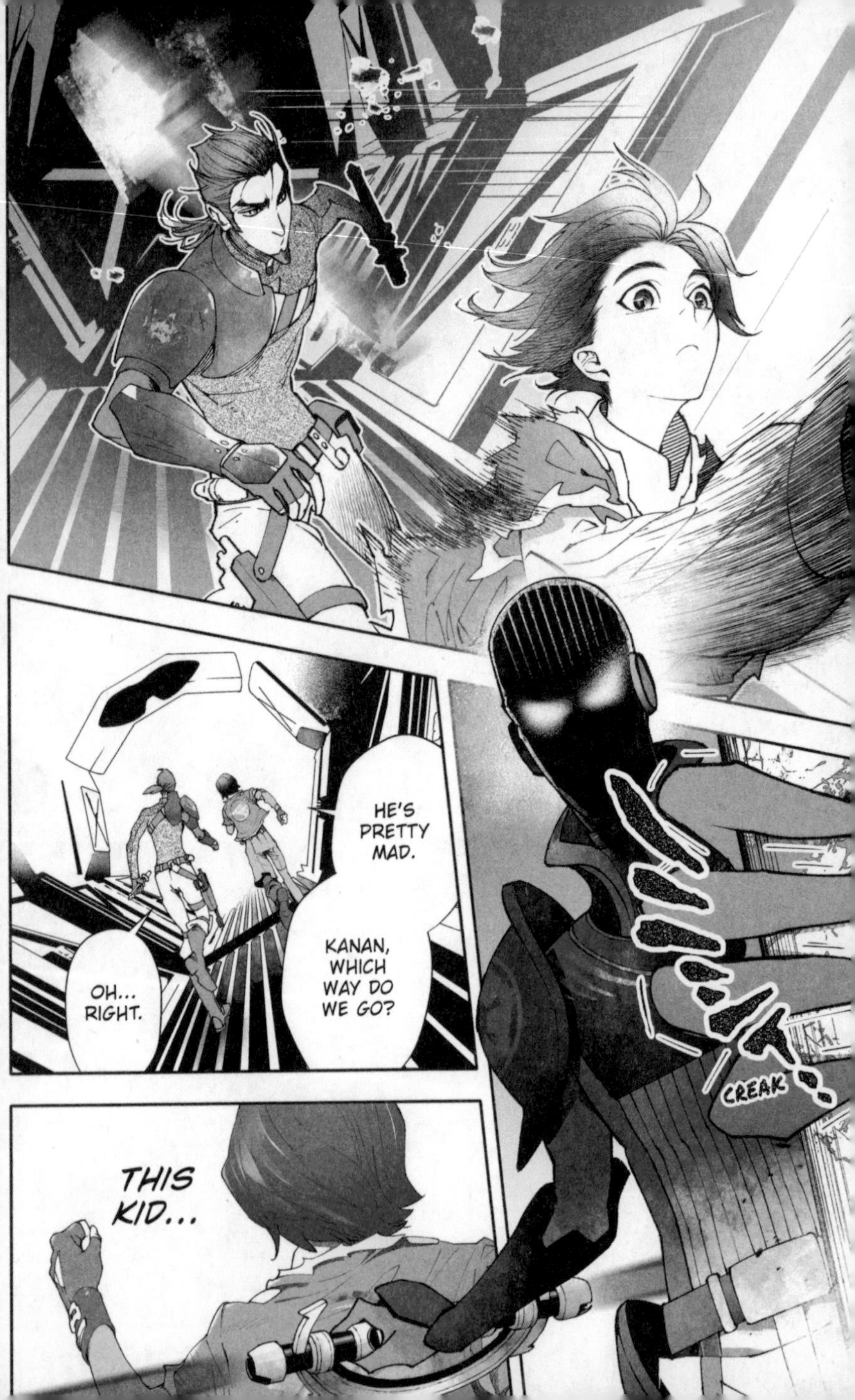
CREAK
HE'S PRETTY MAD.
KANAN, WHICH WAY DO WE GO?
OH... RIGHT.
THIS KID...

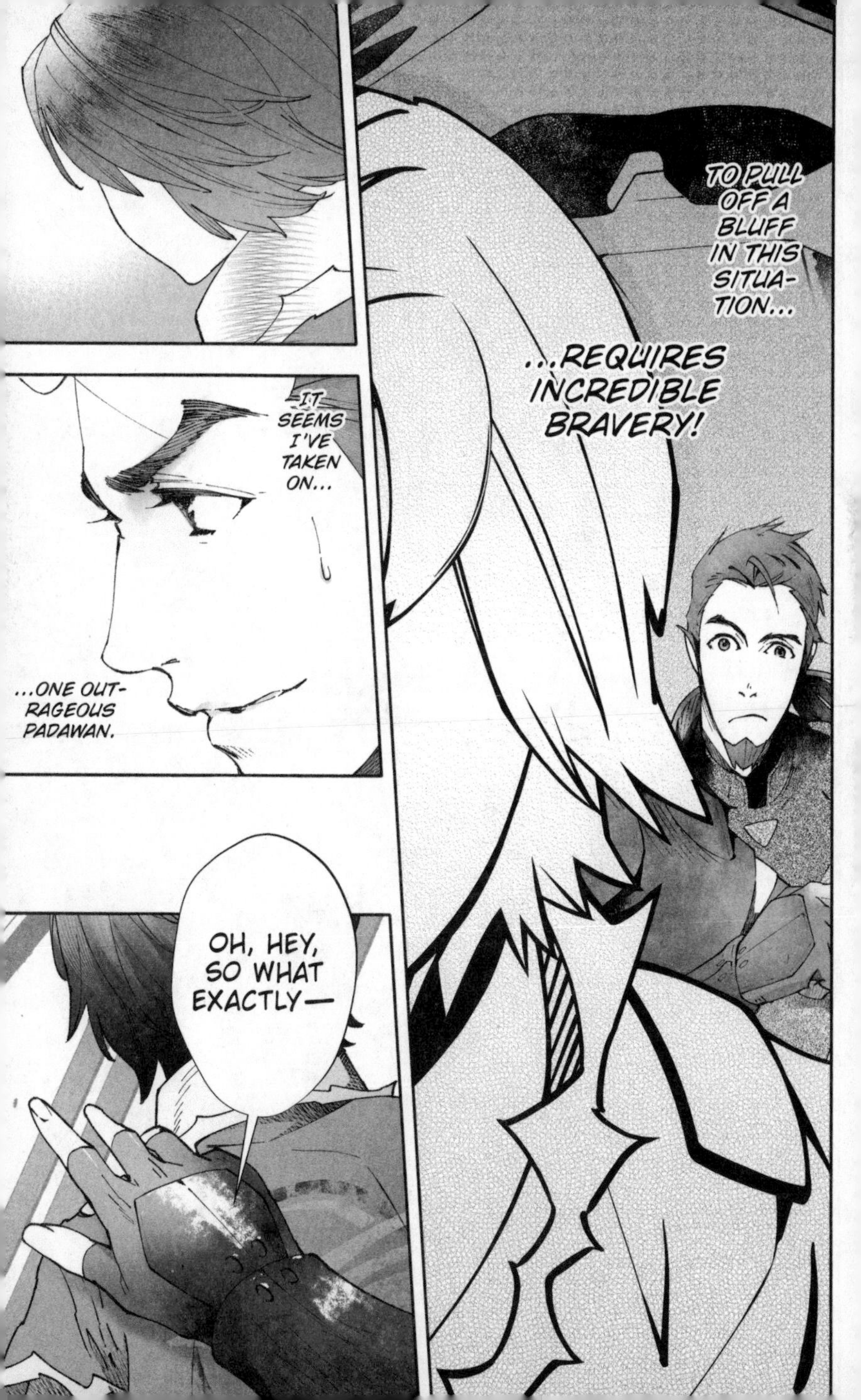
TO PULL OFF A BLUFF IN THIS SITUATION...
...REQUIRES INCREDIBLE BRAVERY!
IT SEEMS I'VE TAKEN ON...
...ONE OUTRAGEOUS PADAWAN.
OH, HEY, SO WHAT EXACTLY—

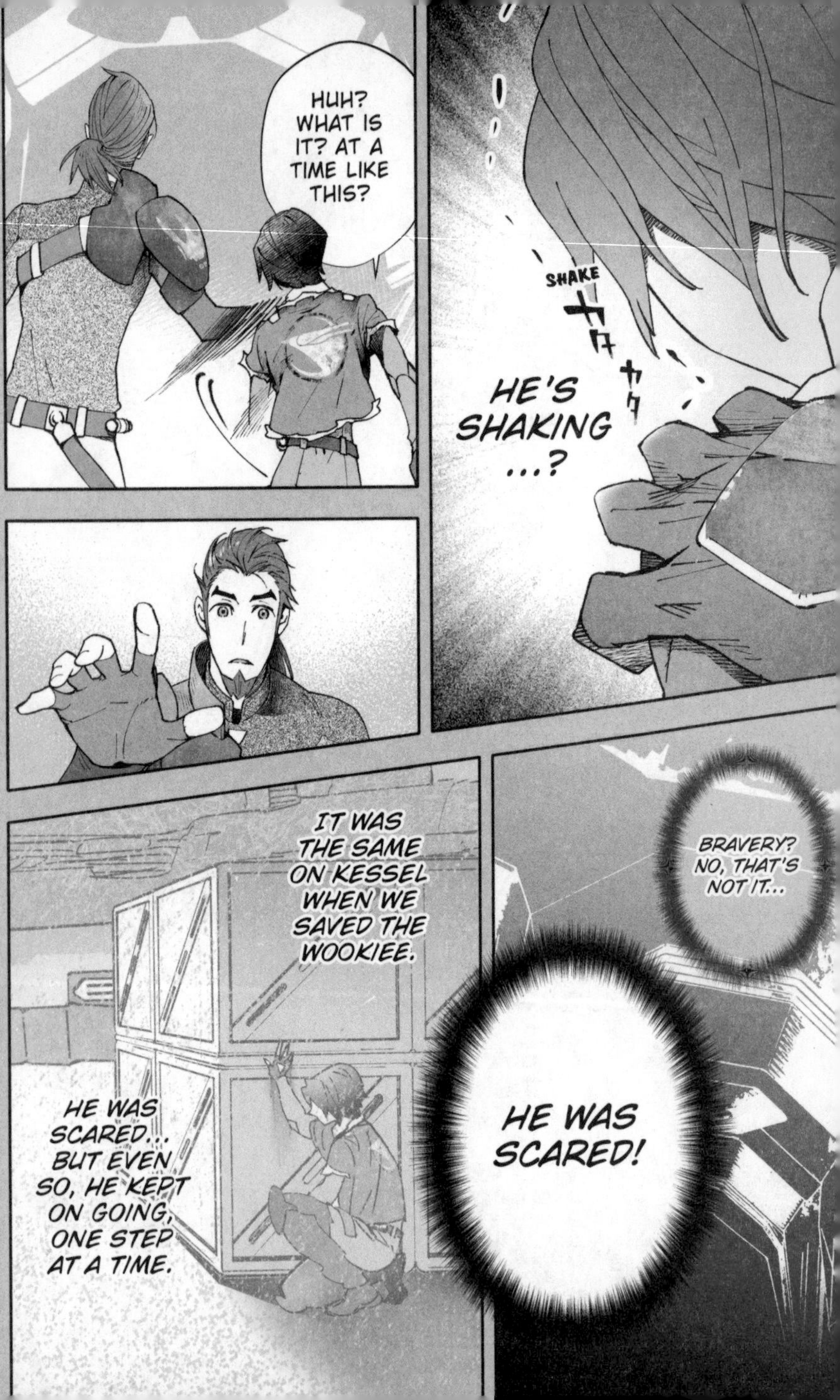
SHAKE
HE'S SHAKING ...?
HUH? WHAT IS IT? AT A TIME LIKE THIS?
BRAVERY? NO, THAT'S NOT IT...
HE WAS SCARED!
IT WAS THE SAME ON KESSEL WHEN WE SAVED THE WOOKIEE.
HE WAS SCARED... BUT EVEN SO, HE KEPT ON GOING, ONE STEP AT A TIME.

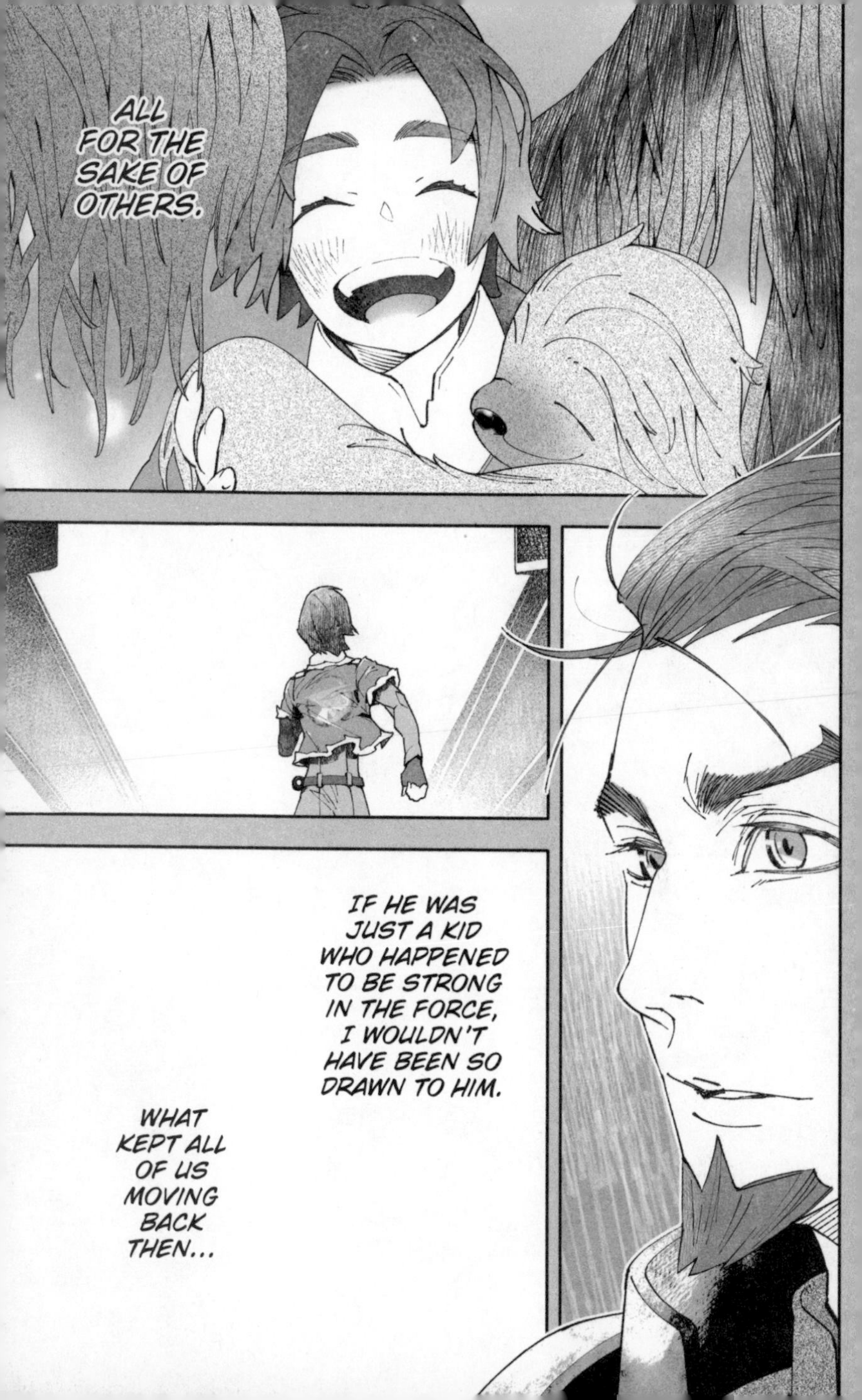
ALL FOR THE SAKE OF OTHERS.
IF HE WAS JUST A KID WHO HAPPENED TO BE STRONG IN THE FORCE, I WOULDN'T HAVE BEEN SO DRAWN TO HIM.
WHAT KEPT ALL OF US MOVING BACK THEN...

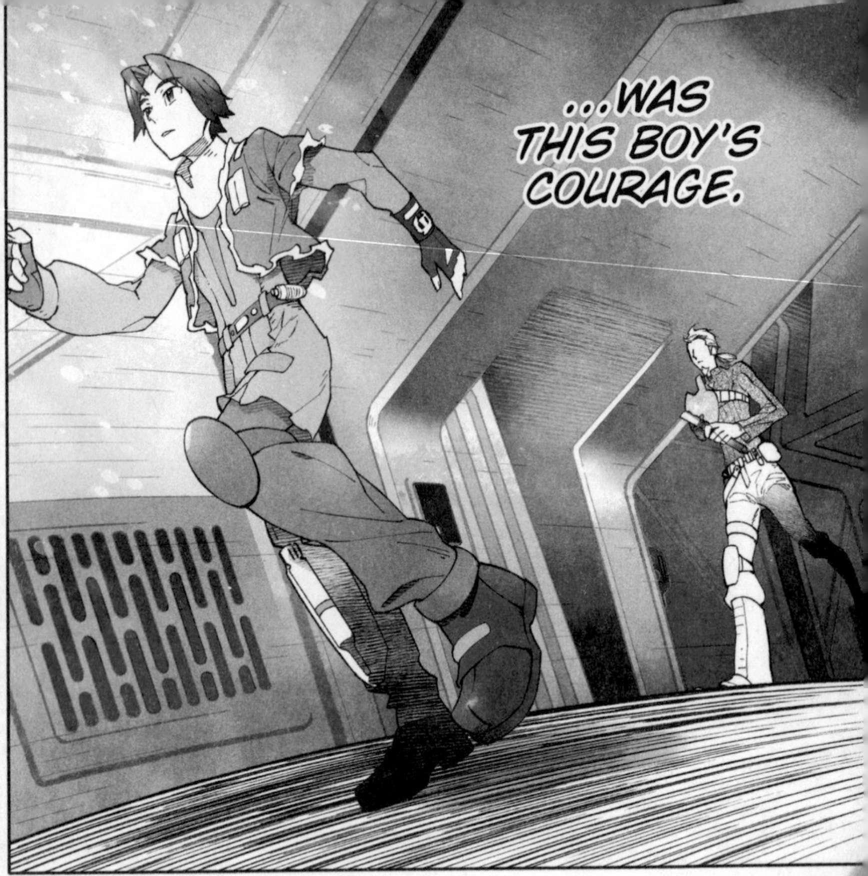
...WAS
THIS BOY'S
COURAGE.
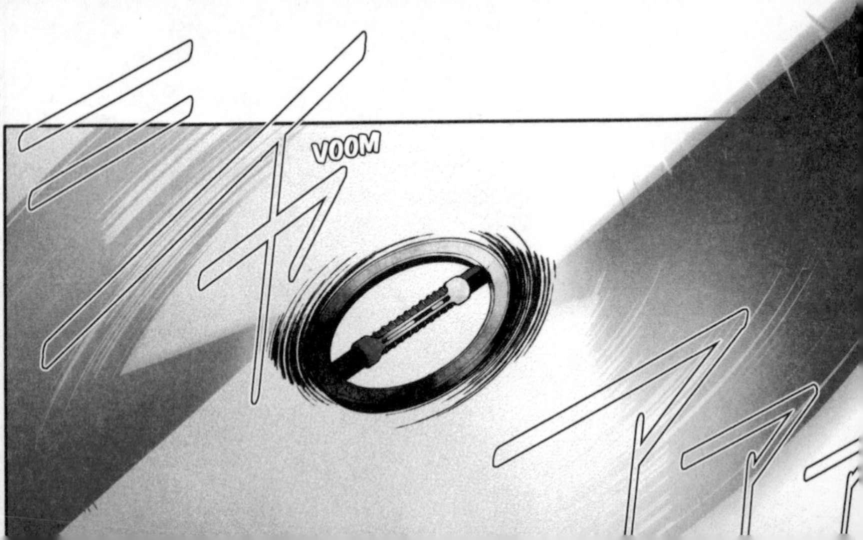
VOOM

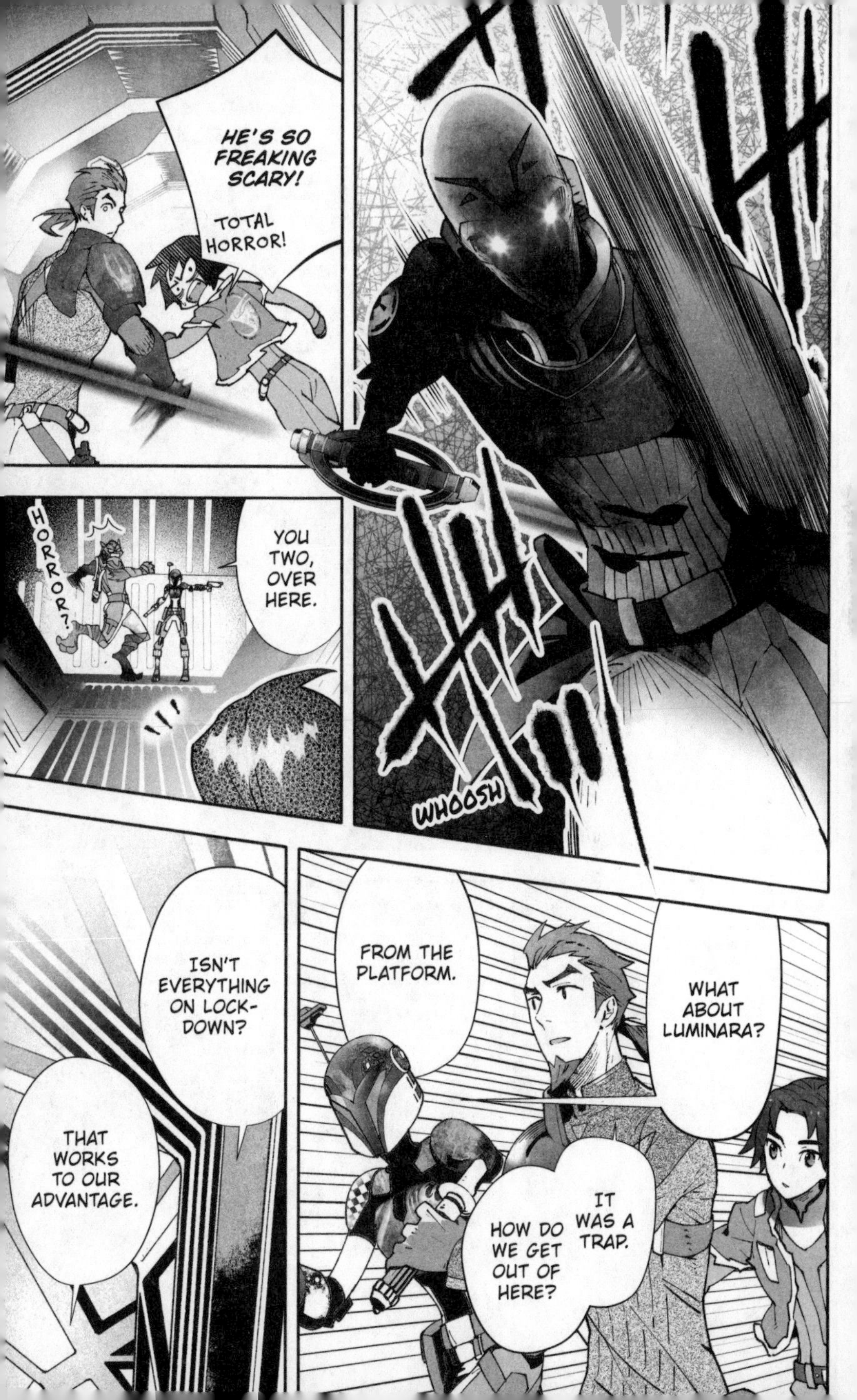
WHOOSH
HE'S SO FREAKING SCARY!
TOTAL HORROR!
YOU TWO, OVER HERE.
HORROR?
WHAT ABOUT LUMINARA?
FROM THE PLATFORM.
IT WAS A TRAP.
HOW DO WE GET OUT OF HERE?
ISN'T EVERYTHING ON LOCK-DOWN?
THAT WORKS TO OUR ADVANTAGE.

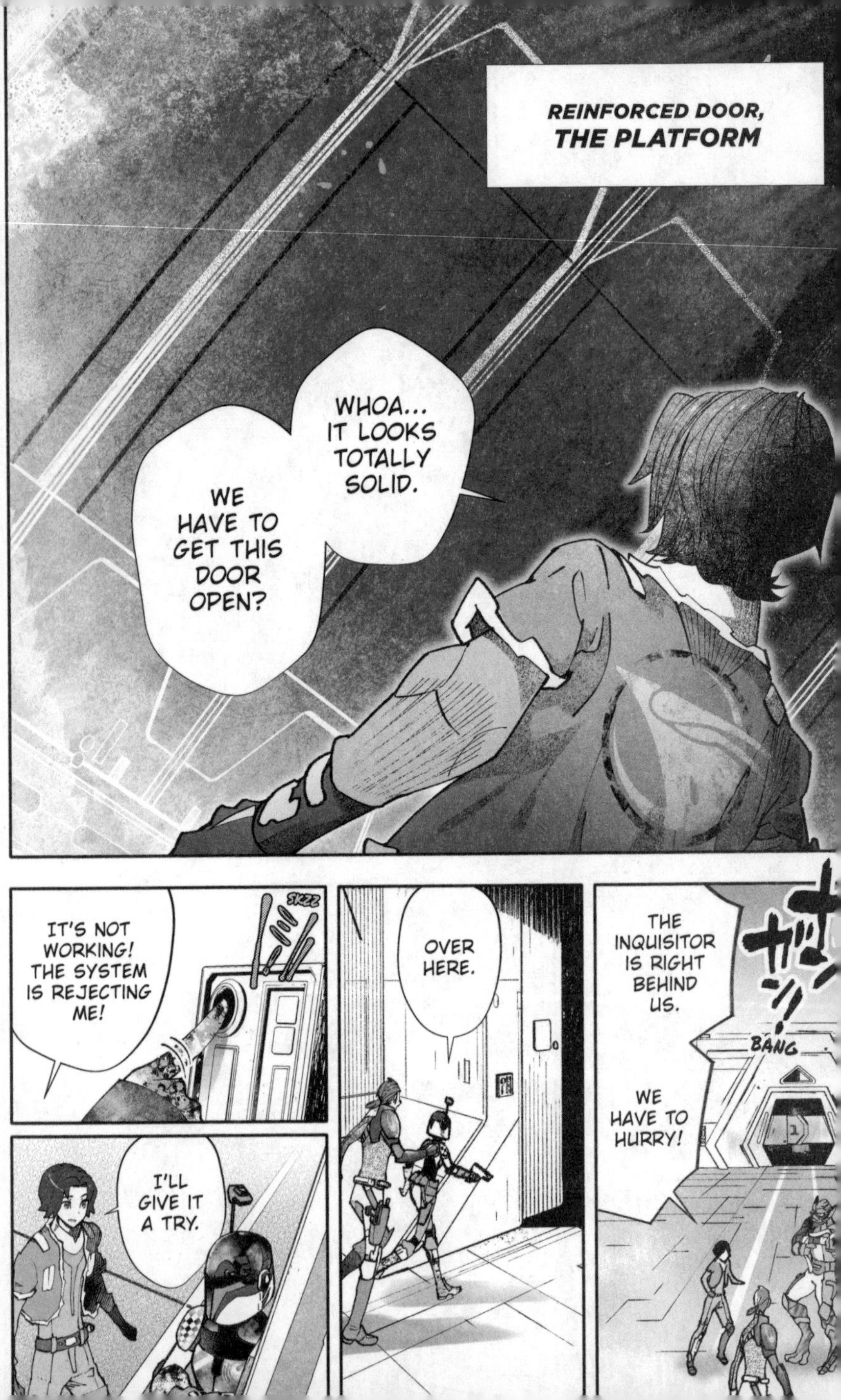
REINFORCED DOOR, THE PLATFORM
WHOA... IT LOOKS TOTALLY SOLID.
WE HAVE TO GET THIS DOOR OPEN?
THE INQUISITOR IS RIGHT BEHIND US.
BANG
WE HAVE TO HURRY!
OVER HERE.
SKZZ
IT'S NOT WORKING! THE SYSTEM IS REJECTING ME!
I'LL GIVE IT A TRY.

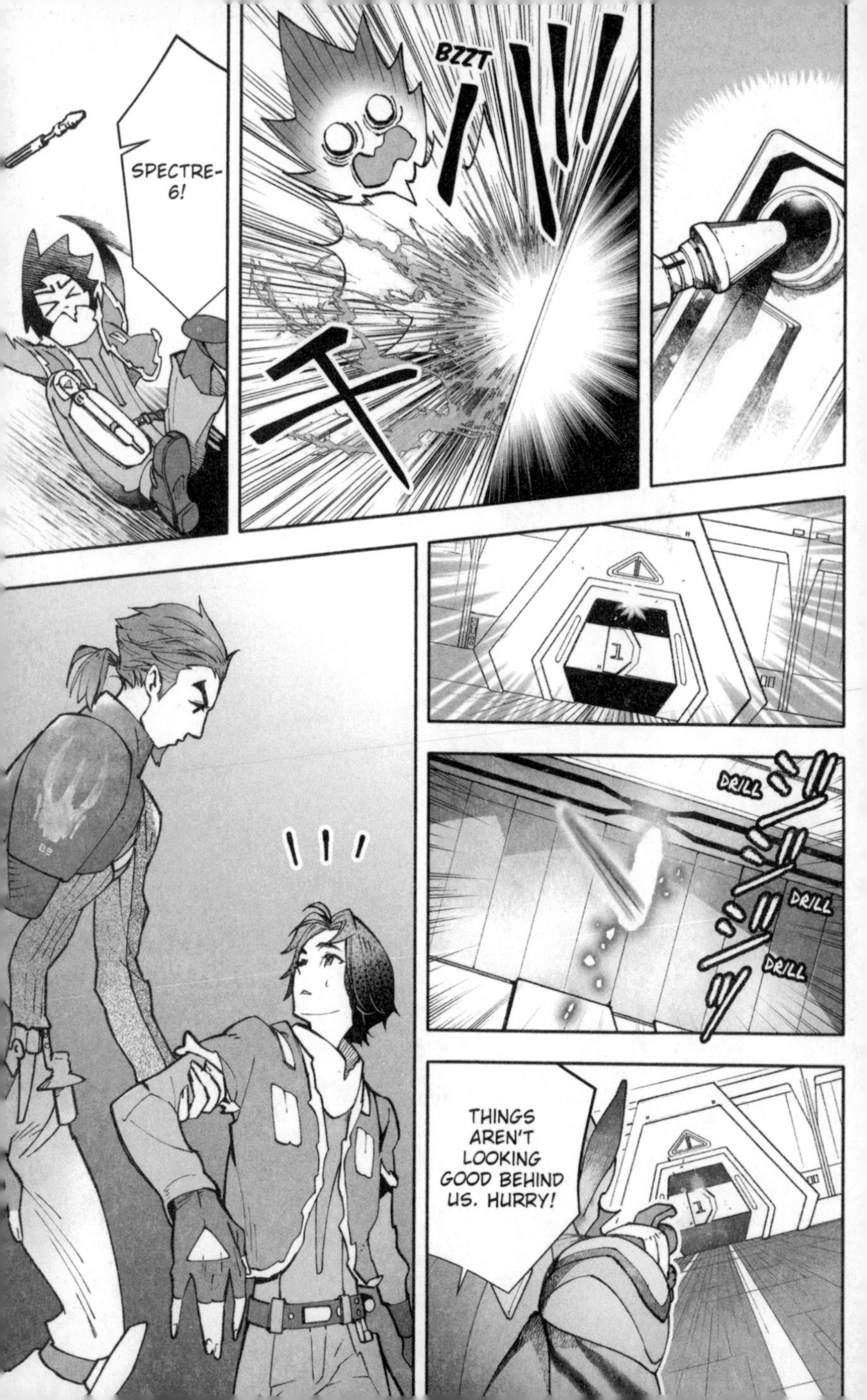
BZZT
SPECTRE-6!
DRILL
DRILL
DRILL
THINGS AREN'T LOOKING GOOD BEHIND US. HURRY!

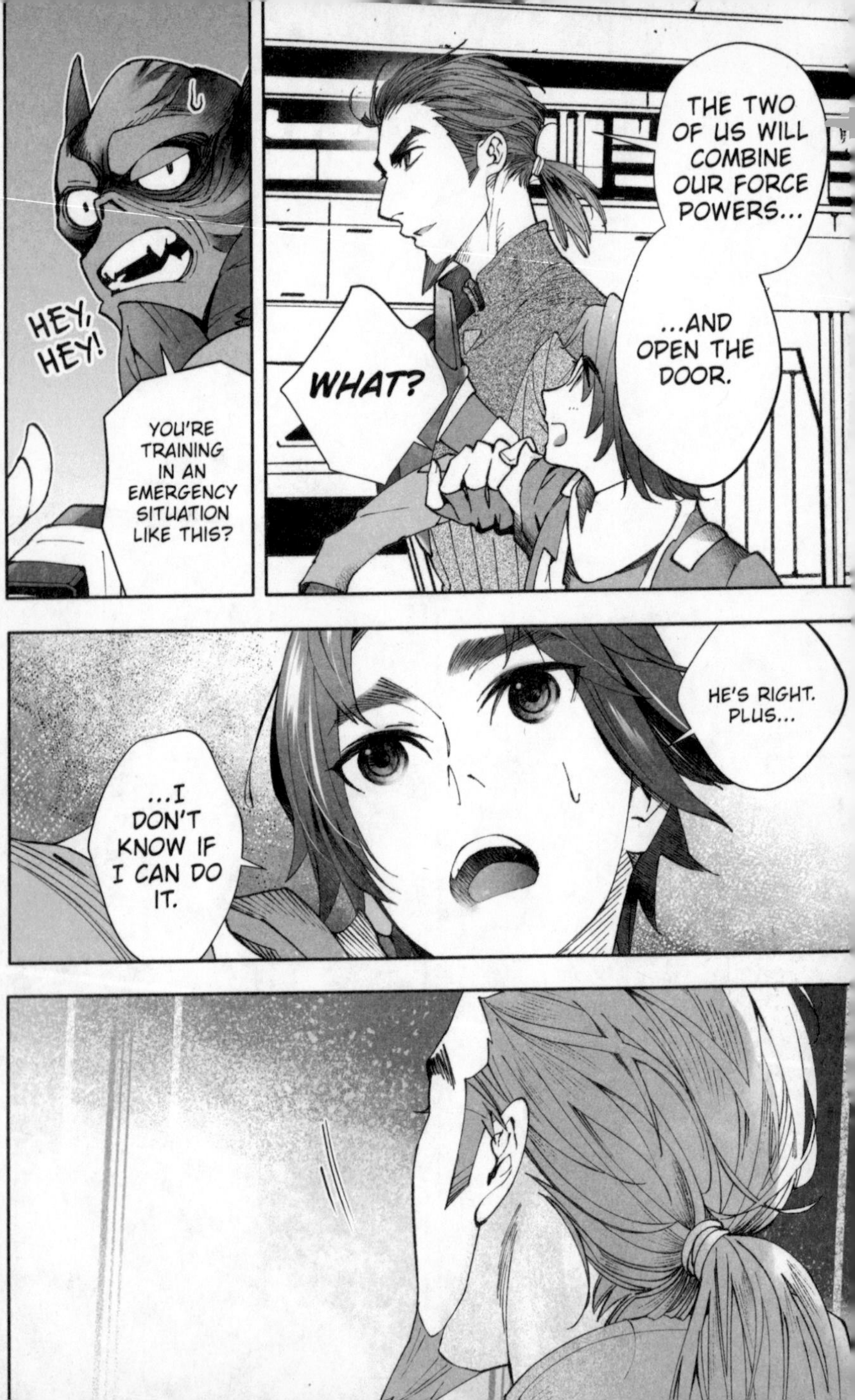
THE TWO OF US WILL COMBINE OUR FORCE POWERS...
...AND OPEN THE DOOR.
WHAT?
HEY, HEY!
YOU'RE TRAINING IN AN EMERGENCY SITUATION LIKE THIS?
HE'S RIGHT. PLUS...
...I DON'T KNOW IF I CAN DO IT.

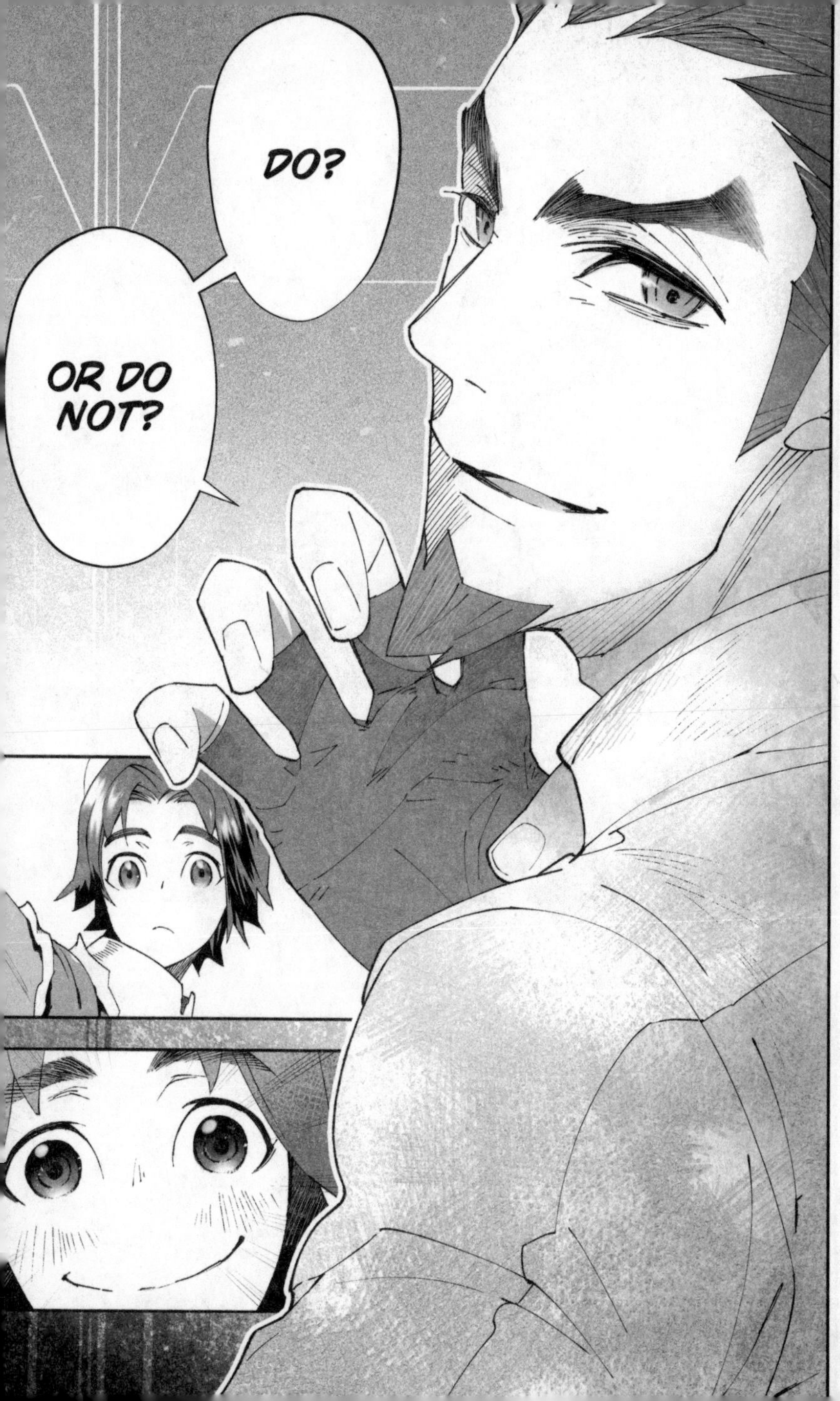
DO?
OR DO NOT?

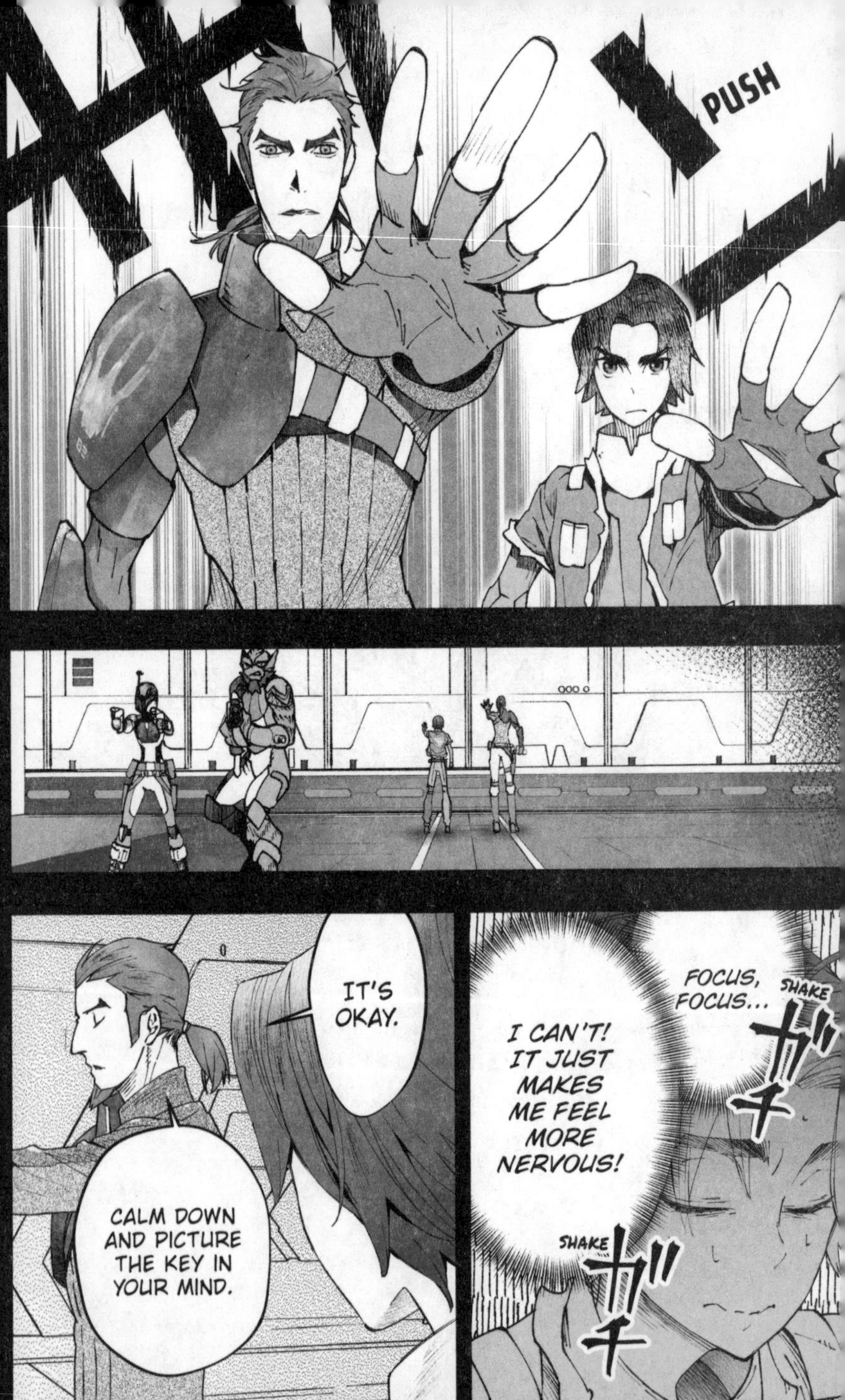
PUSH
FOCUS, FOCUS...
SHAKE
I CAN'T! IT JUST MAKES ME FEEL MORE NERVOUS!
SHAKE
IT'S OKAY.
CALM DOWN AND PICTURE THE KEY IN YOUR MIND.

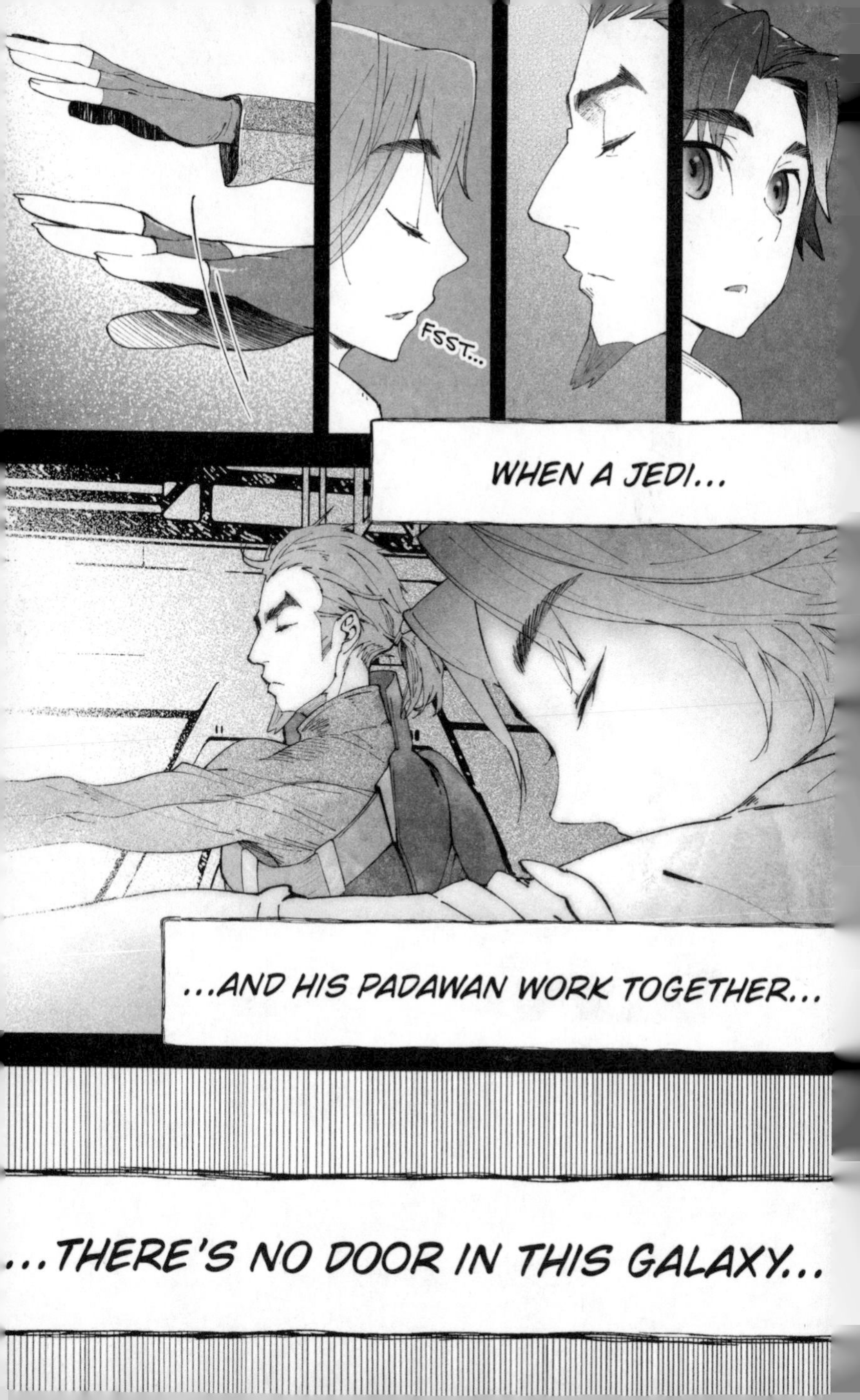
FSST...
WHEN A JEDI...
...AND HIS PADAWAN WORK TOGETHER...
...THERE'S NO DOOR IN THIS GALAXY...

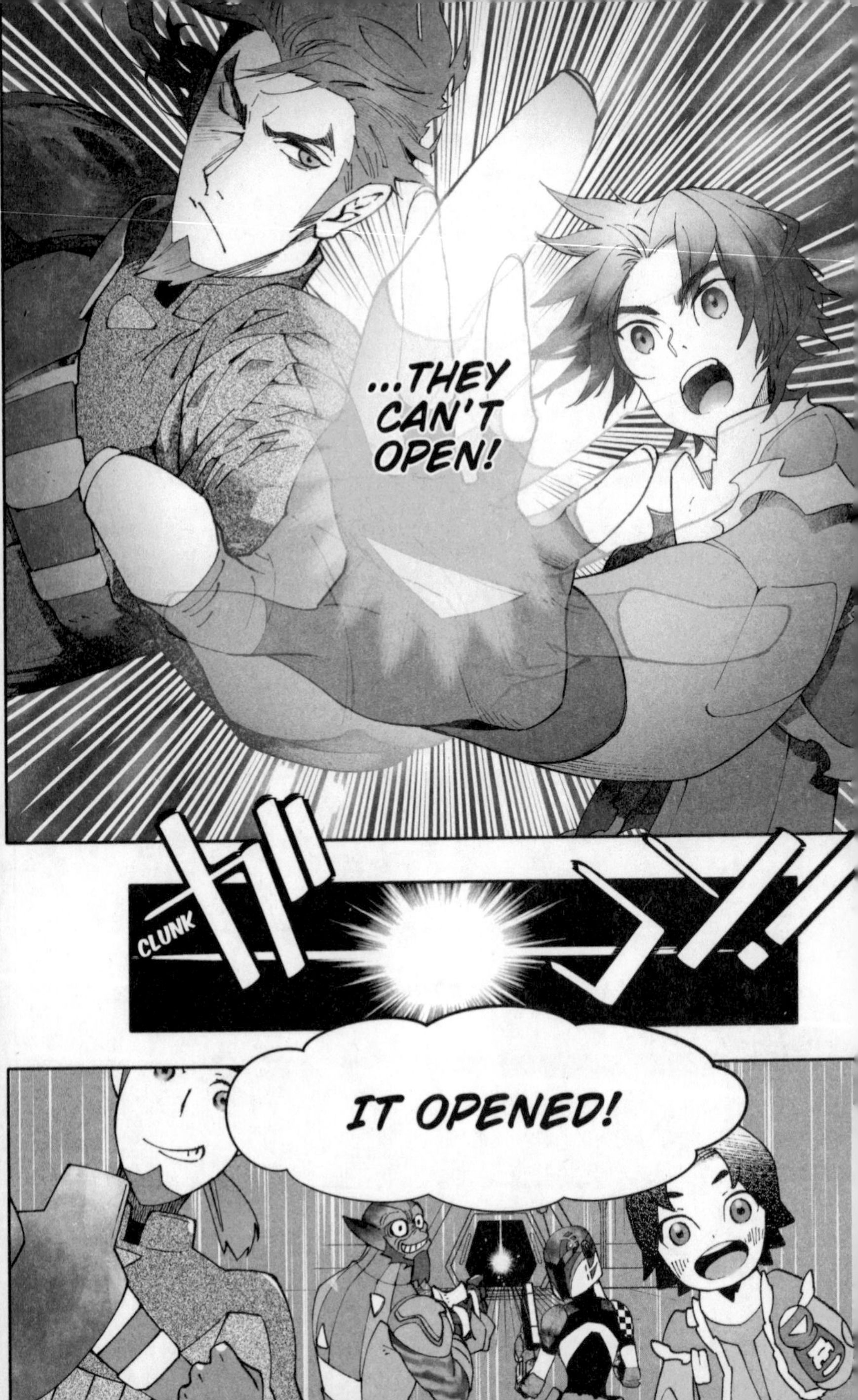
...THEY CAN'T OPEN!
CLUNK
IT OPENED!

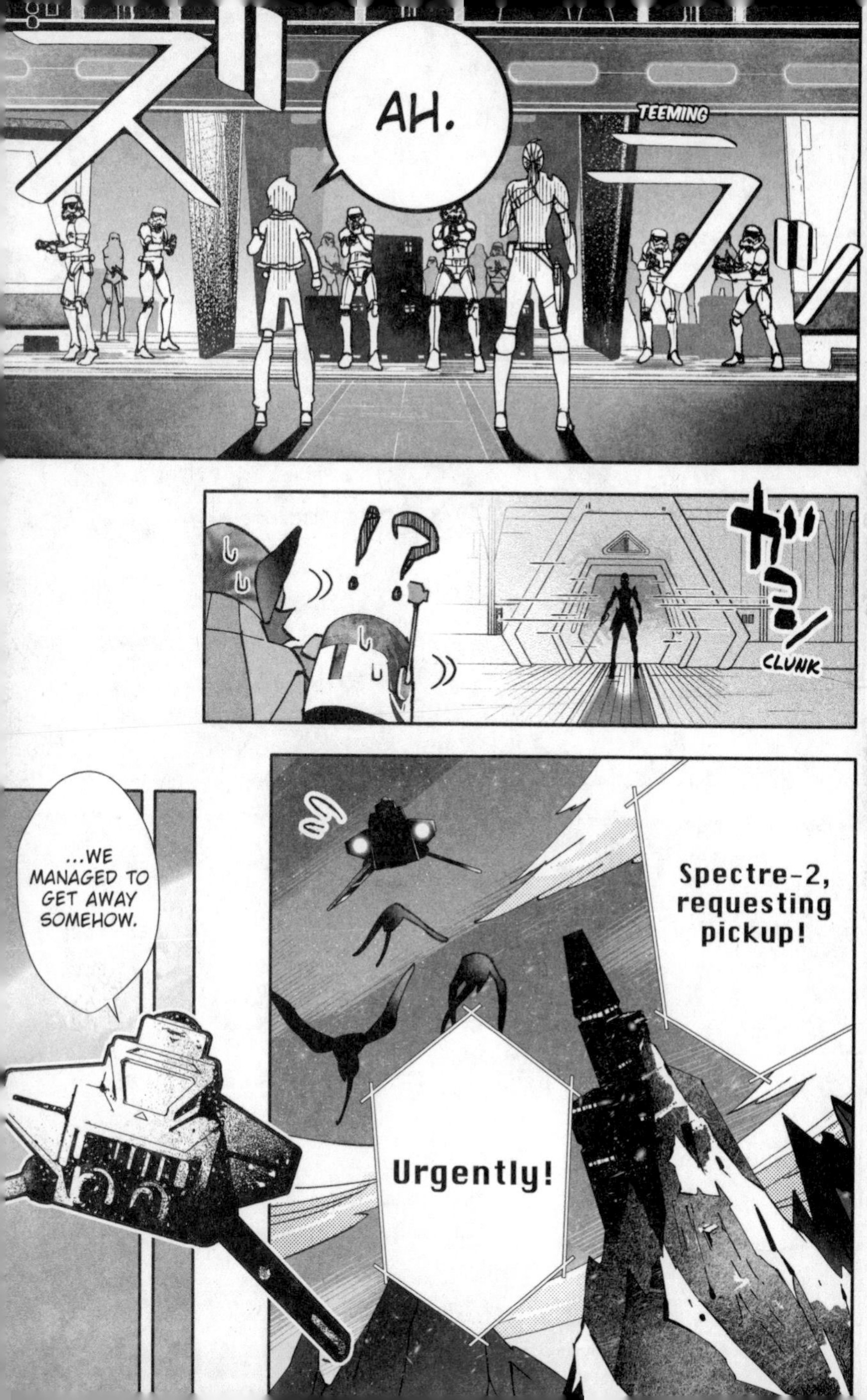
AH.
TEEMING
CLUNK
Spectre-2, requesting pickup!
Urgently!
...WE MANAGED TO GET AWAY SOMEHOW.

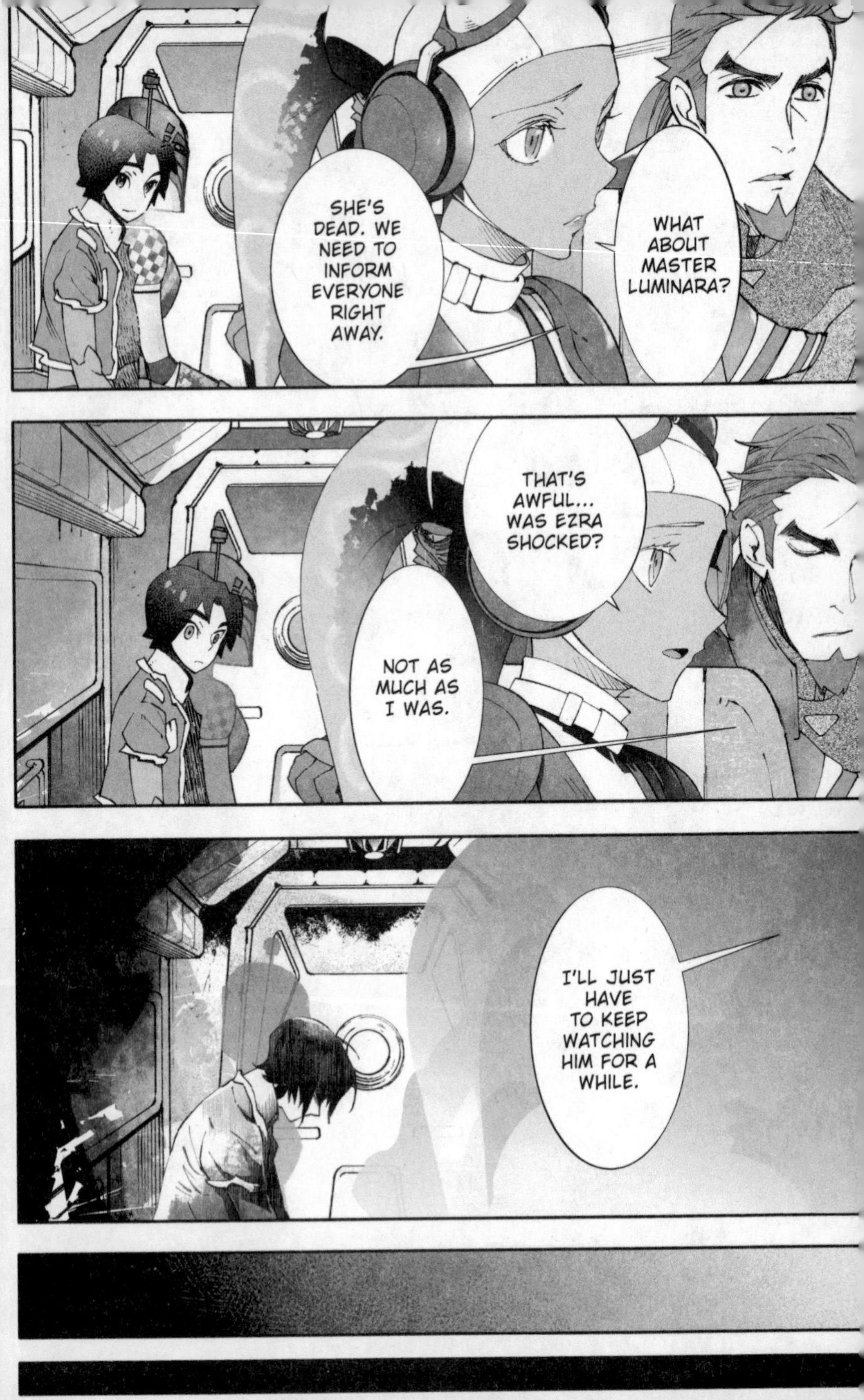
WHAT ABOUT MASTER LUMINARA?
SHE'S DEAD. WE NEED TO INFORM EVERYONE RIGHT AWAY.
THAT'S AWFUL... WAS EZRA SHOCKED?
NOT AS MUCH AS I WAS.
I'LL JUST HAVE TO KEEP WATCHING HIM FOR A WHILE.

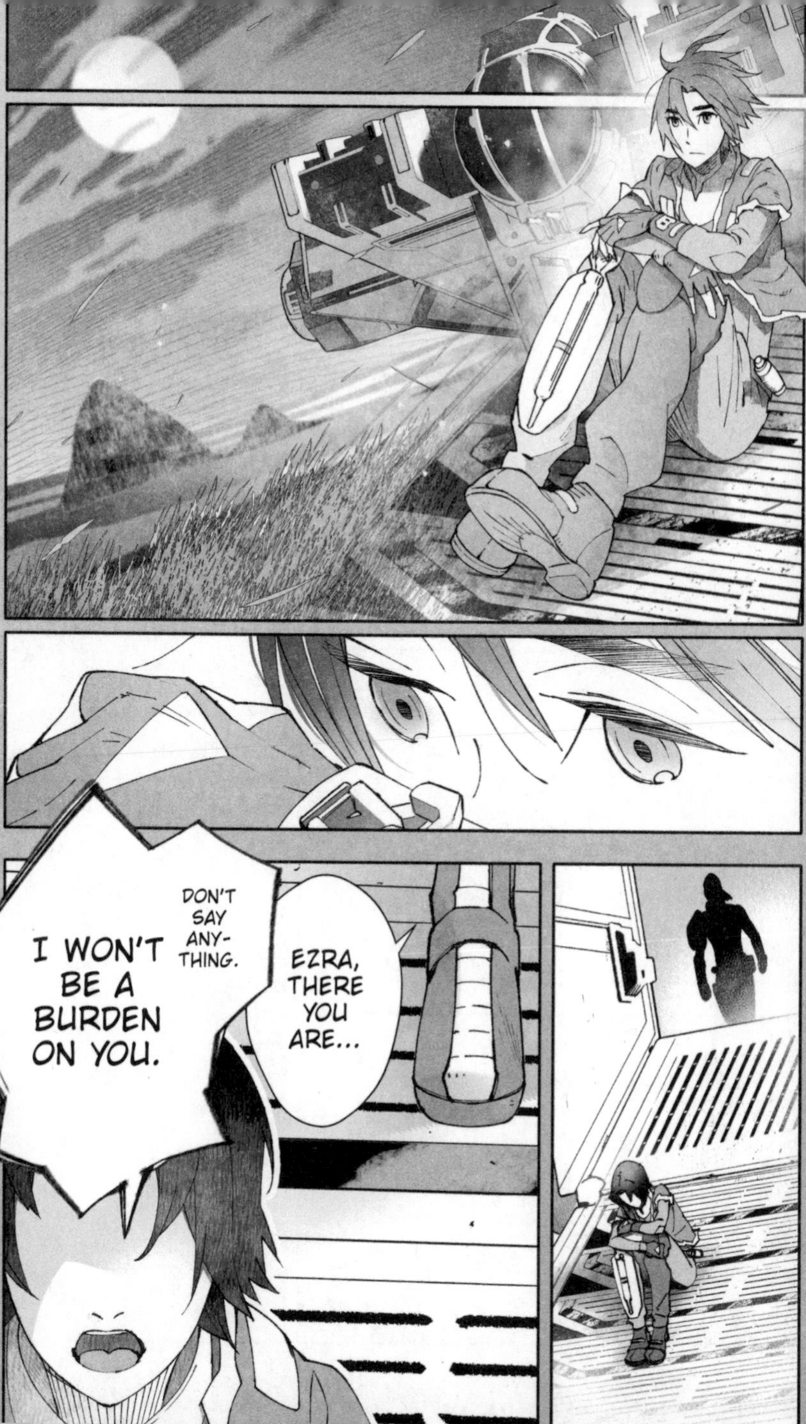
EZRA, THERE YOU ARE...
DON'T SAY ANY-THING.
I WON'T BE A BURDEN ON YOU.

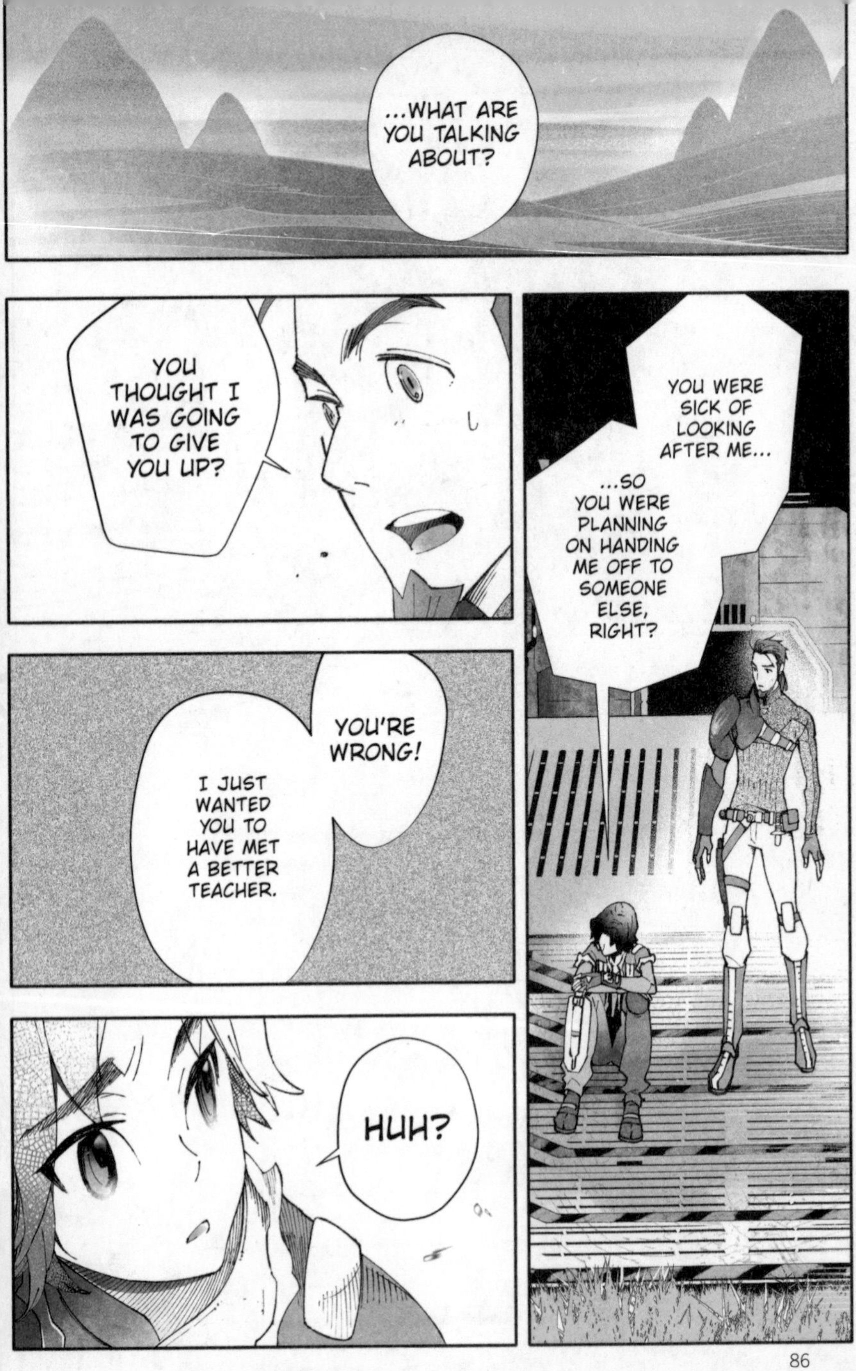
...WHAT ARE YOU TALKING ABOUT?
YOU WERE SICK OF LOOKING AFTER ME...
...SO YOU WERE PLANNING ON HANDING ME OFF TO SOMEONE ELSE, RIGHT?
YOU THOUGHT I WAS GOING TO GIVE YOU UP?
YOU'RE WRONG!
I JUST WANTED YOU TO HAVE MET A BETTER TEACHER.
HUH?

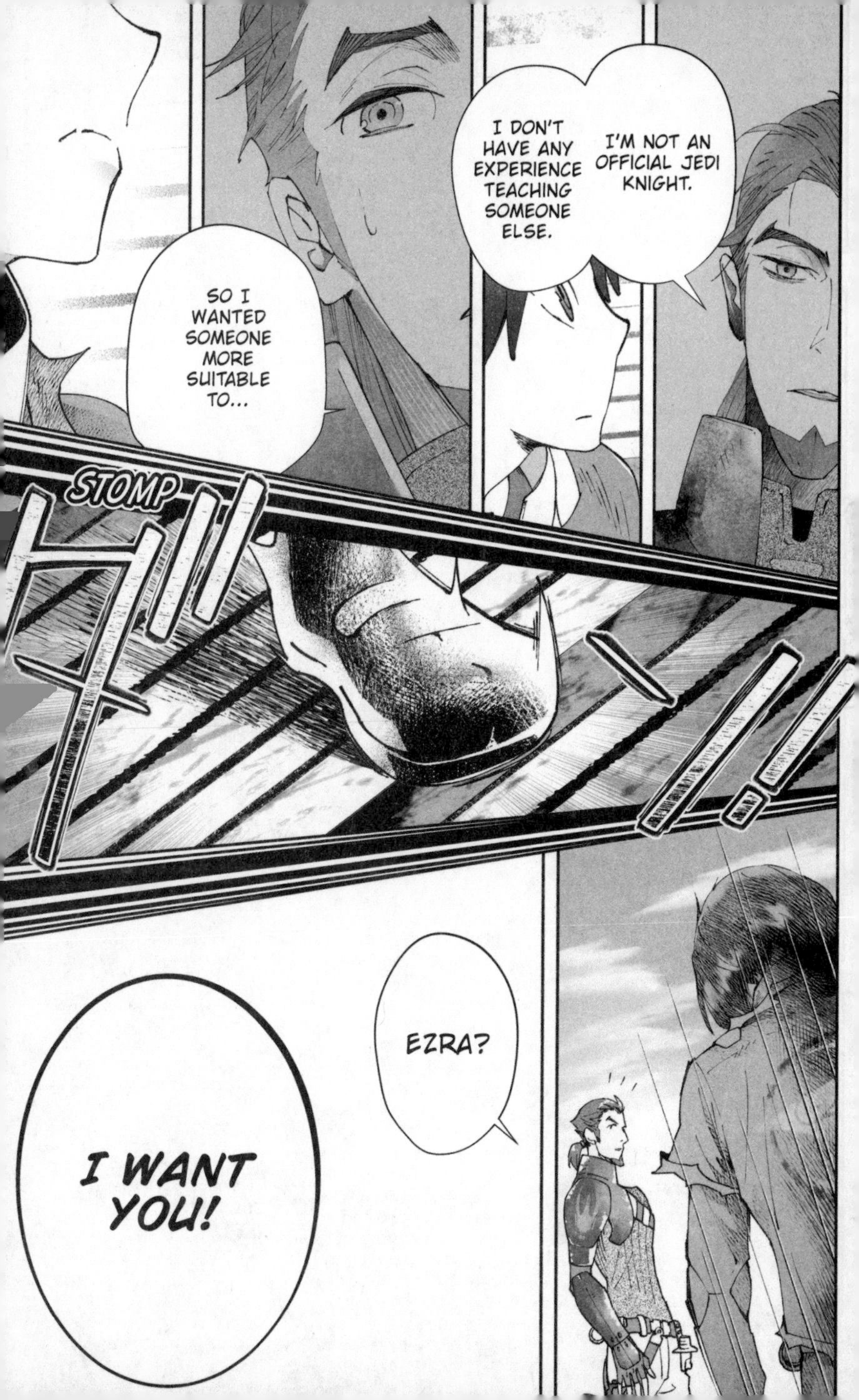
I'M NOT AN OFFICIAL JEDI KNIGHT.
I DON'T HAVE ANY EXPERIENCE TEACHING SOMEONE ELSE.
SO I WANTED SOMEONE MORE SUITABLE TO...
STOMP
EZRA?
I WANT YOU!

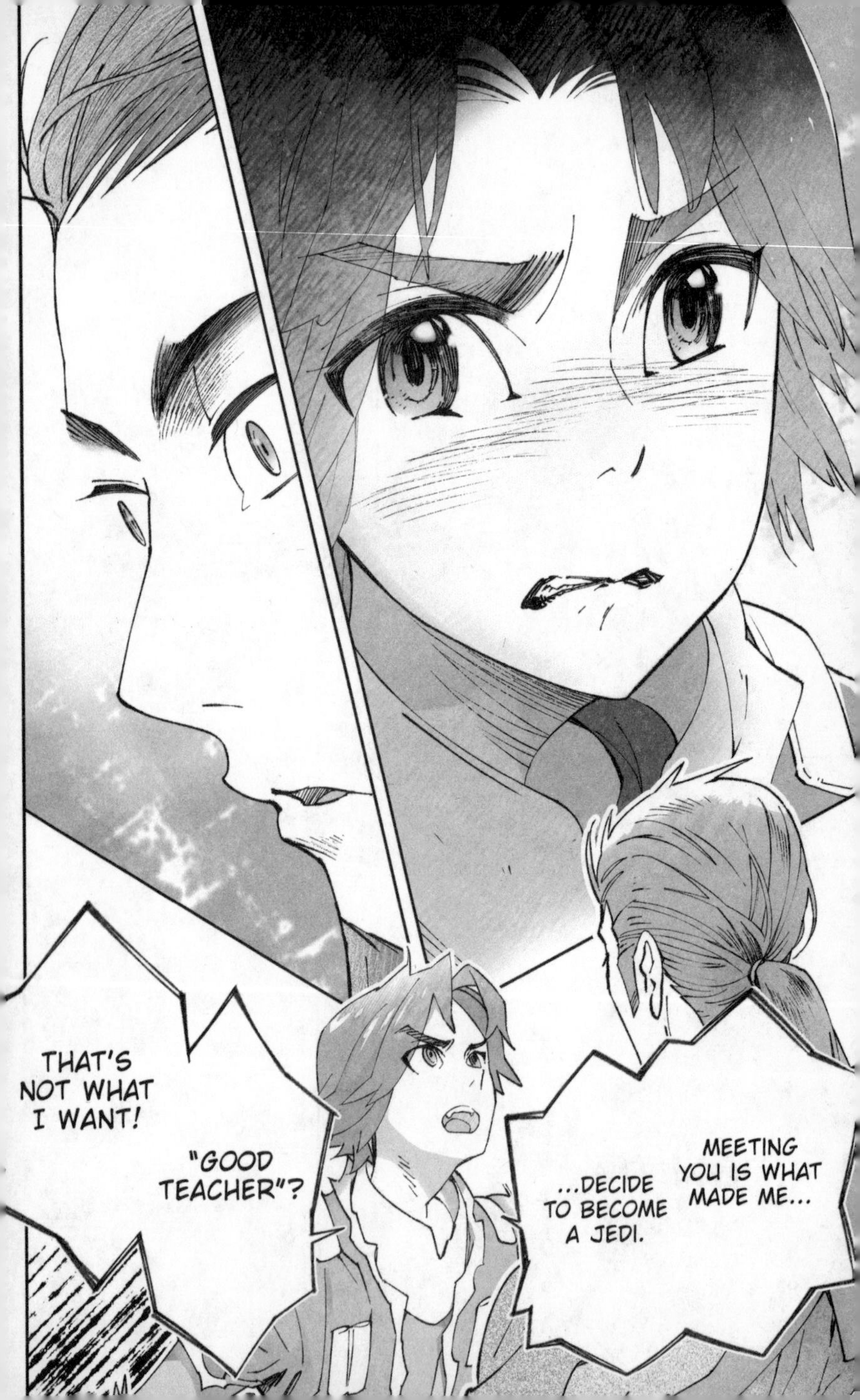
MEETING YOU IS WHAT MADE ME...
...DECIDE TO BECOME A JEDI.
"GOOD TEACHER"?
THAT'S NOT WHAT I WANT!

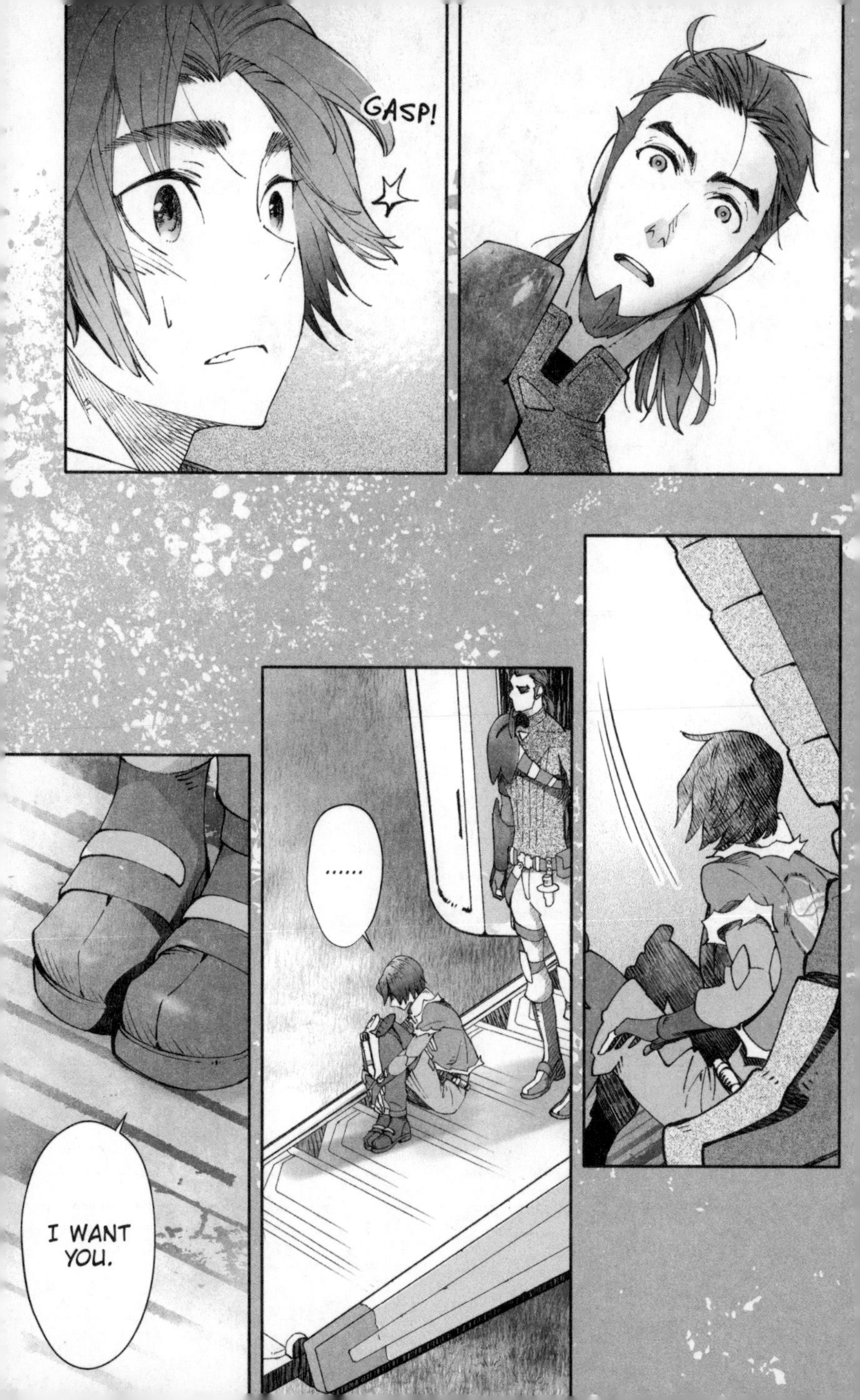
GASP!
......
I WANT YOU.

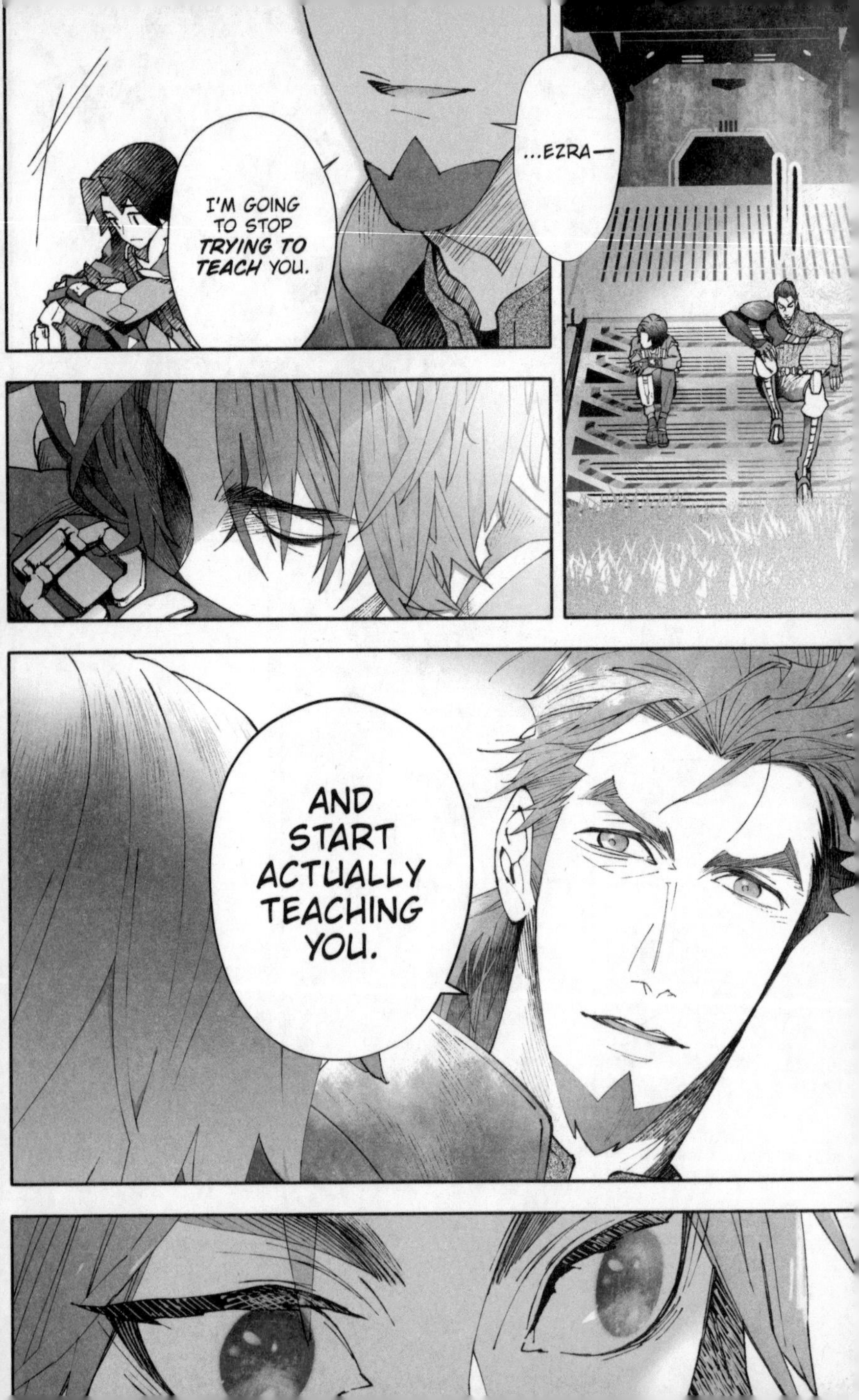
...EZRA—
I'M GOING TO STOP *TRYING TO TEACH* YOU.
AND START ACTUALLY TEACHING YOU.

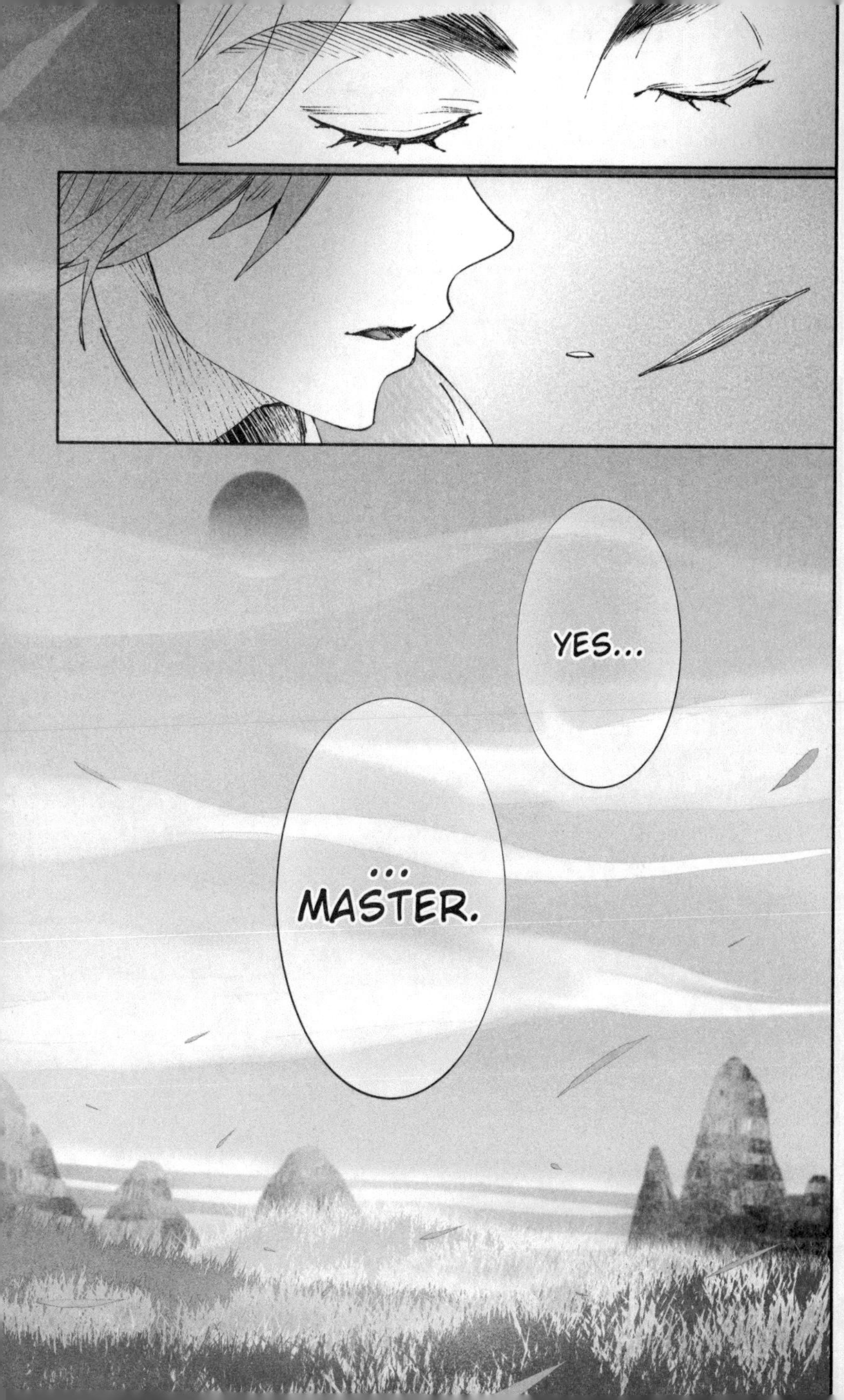
YES...
...MASTER.

STAR WARS
REBELS

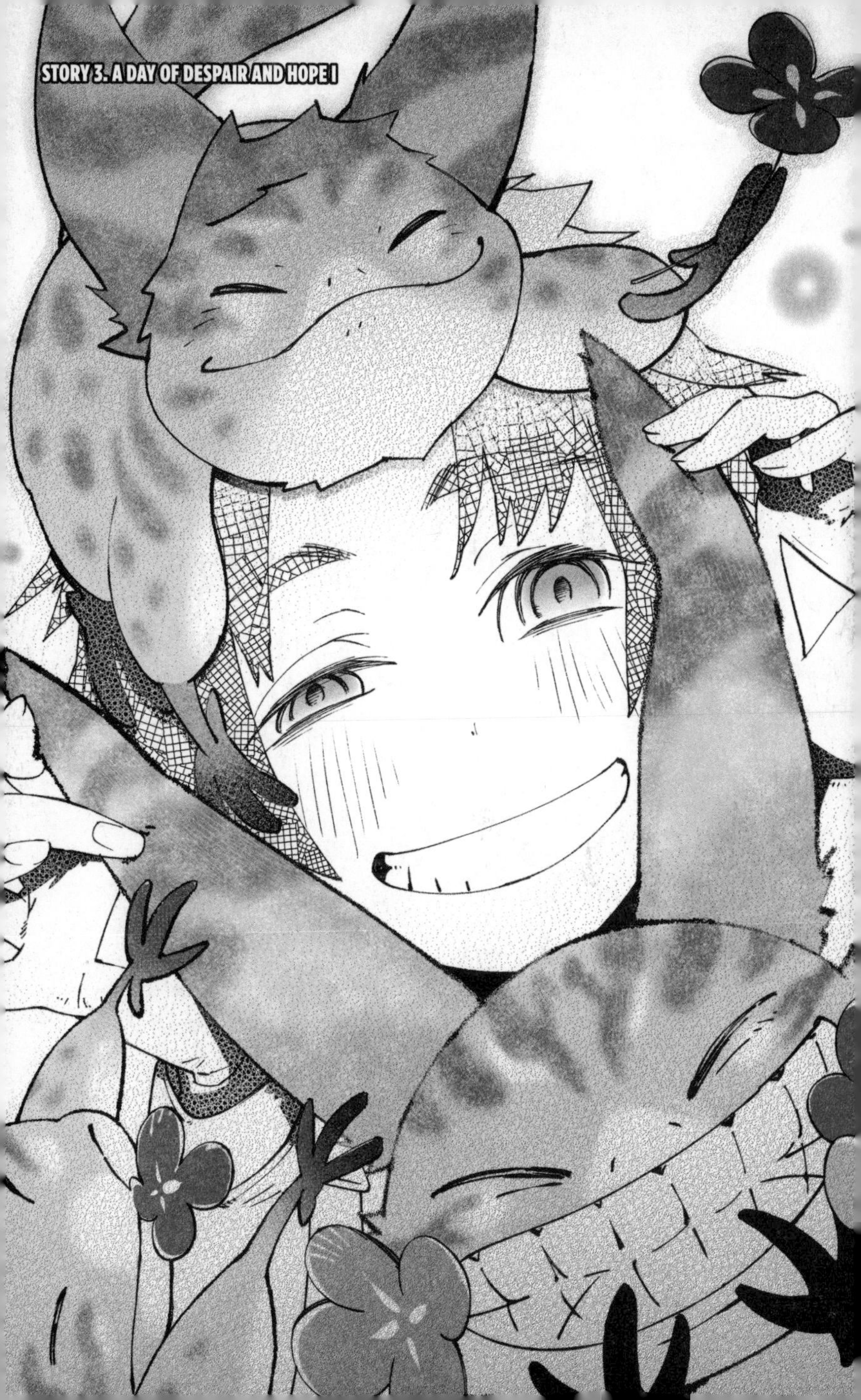
STORY 3. A DAY OF DESPAIR AND HOPE I

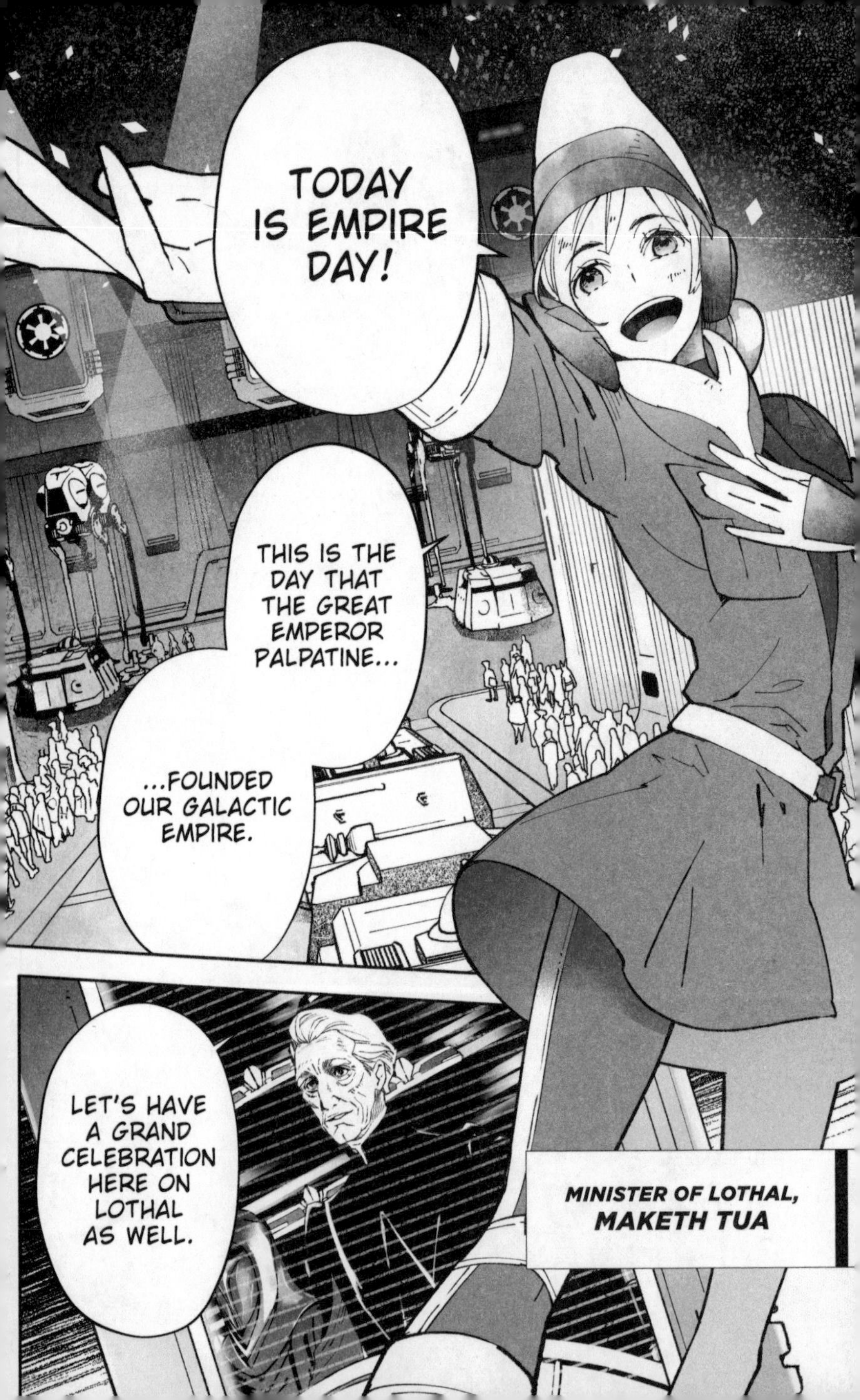

TODAY IS EMPIRE DAY!
THIS IS THE DAY THAT THE GREAT EMPEROR PALPATINE...
...FOUNDED OUR GALACTIC EMPIRE.
MINISTER OF LOTHAL, MAKETH TUA
LET'S HAVE A GRAND CELEBRATION HERE ON LOTHAL AS WELL.

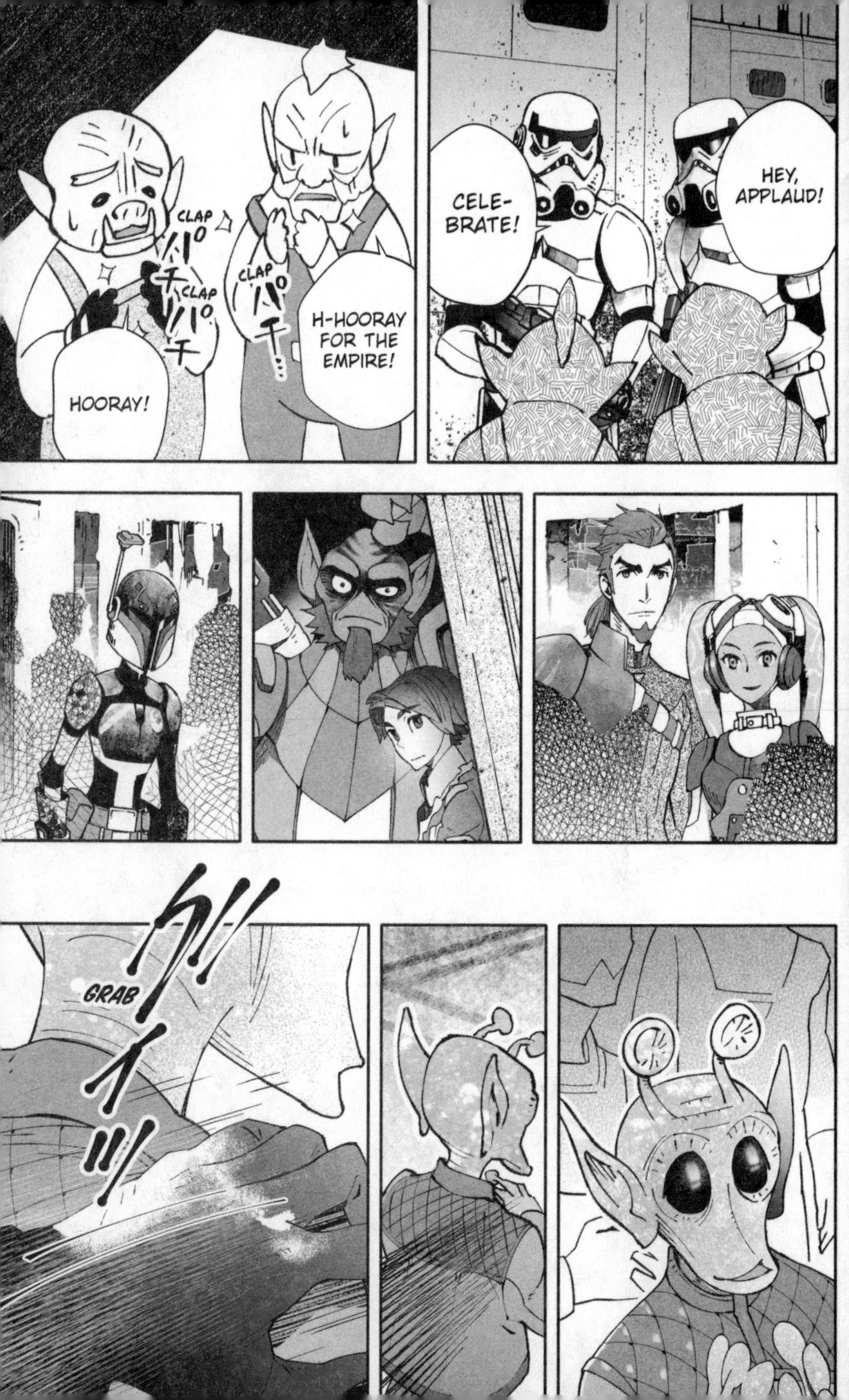
HEY, APPLAUD!
CELE-BRATE!
H-HOORAY FOR THE EMPIRE!
CLAP
CLAP
CLAP
HOORAY!
GRAB

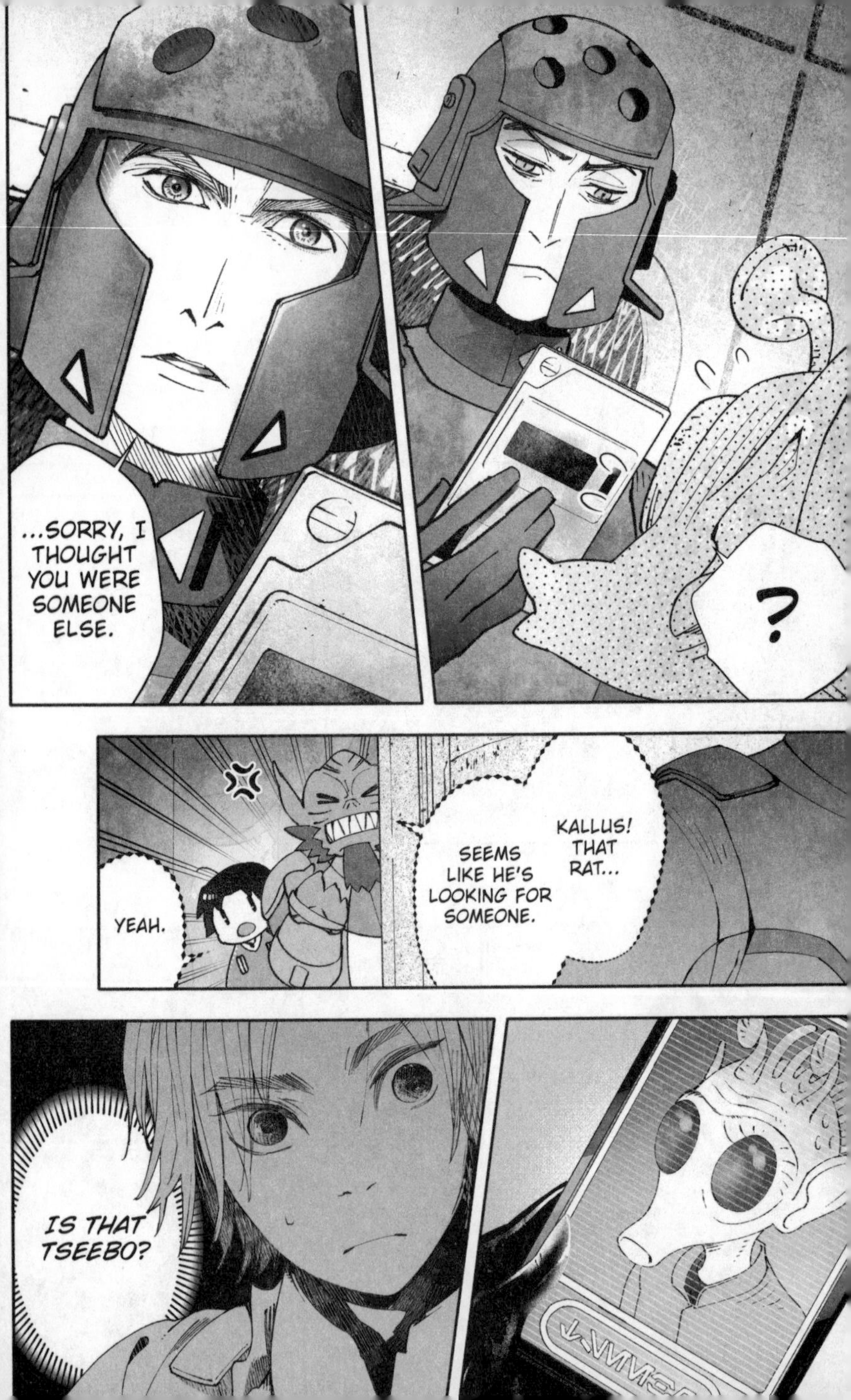
?
...SORRY, I THOUGHT YOU WERE SOMEONE ELSE.
KALLUS! THAT RAT...
SEEMS LIKE HE'S LOOKING FOR SOMEONE.
YEAH.
IS THAT TSEEBO?

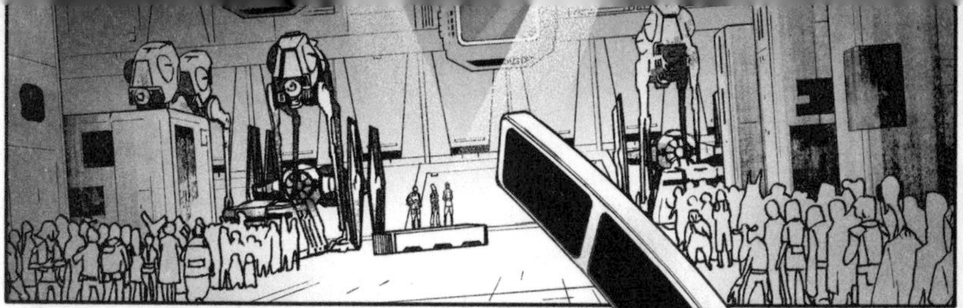

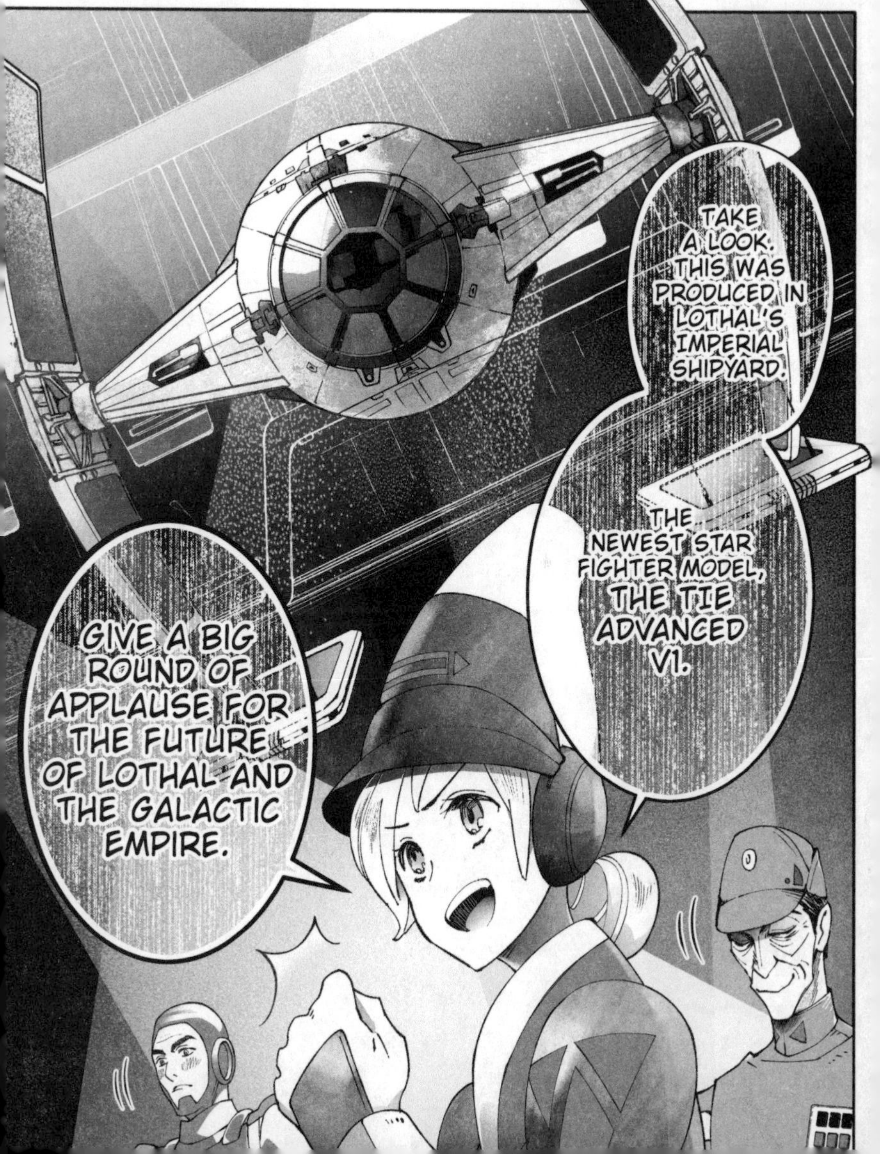
TAKE A LOOK. THIS WAS PRODUCED IN LOTHAL'S IMPERIAL SHIPYARD.
THE NEWEST STAR FIGHTER MODEL, THE TIE ADVANCED V1.
GIVE A BIG ROUND OF APPLAUSE FOR THE FUTURE OF LOTHAL AND THE GALACTIC EMPIRE.

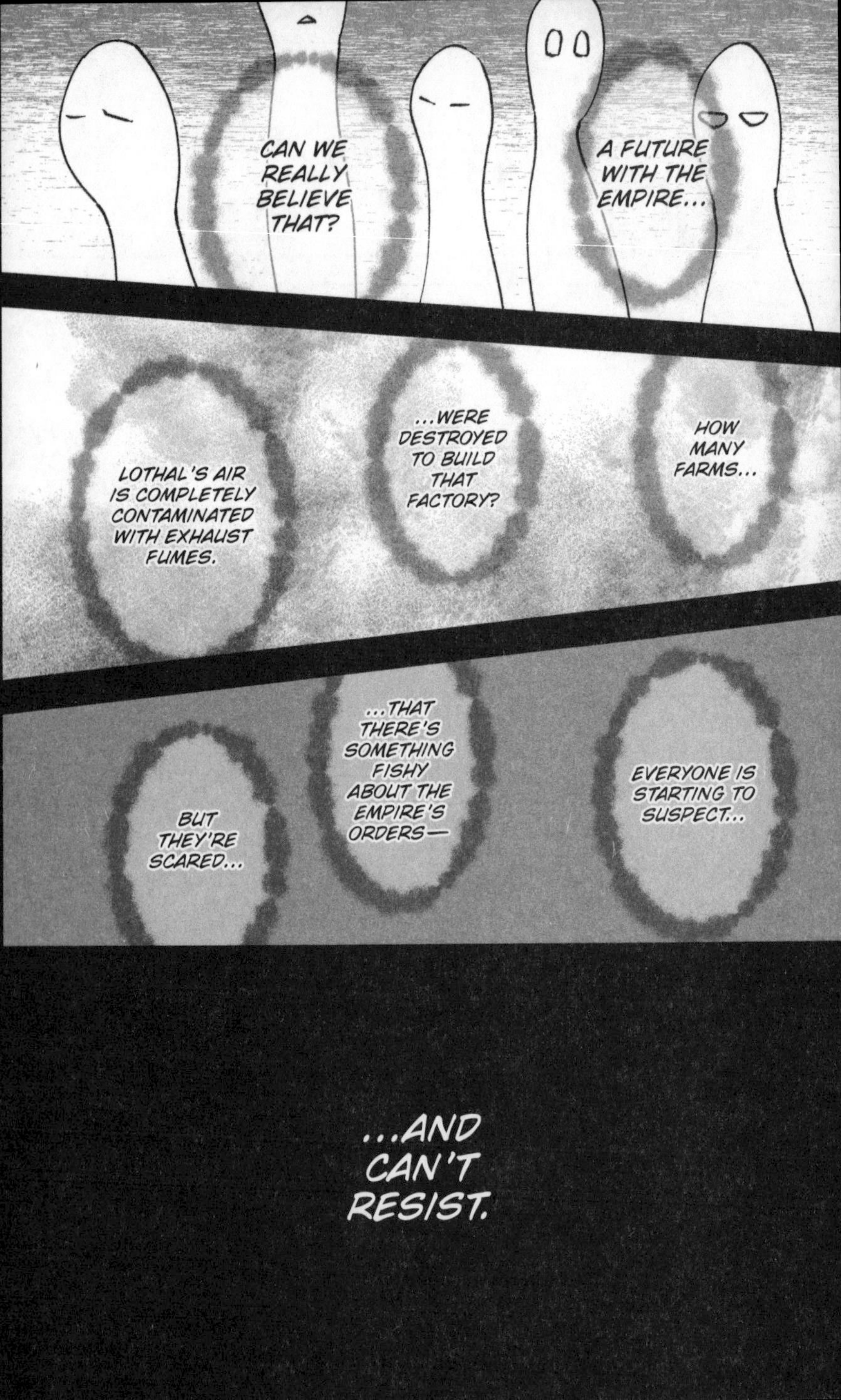
A FUTURE WITH THE EMPIRE...
CAN WE REALLY BELIEVE THAT?
HOW MANY FARMS...
...WERE DESTROYED TO BUILD THAT FACTORY?
LOTHAL'S AIR IS COMPLETELY CONTAMINATED WITH EXHAUST FUMES.
EVERYONE IS STARTING TO SUSPECT...
...THAT THERE'S SOMETHING FISHY ABOUT THE EMPIRE'S ORDERS—
BUT THEY'RE SCARED...
...AND CAN'T RESIST.

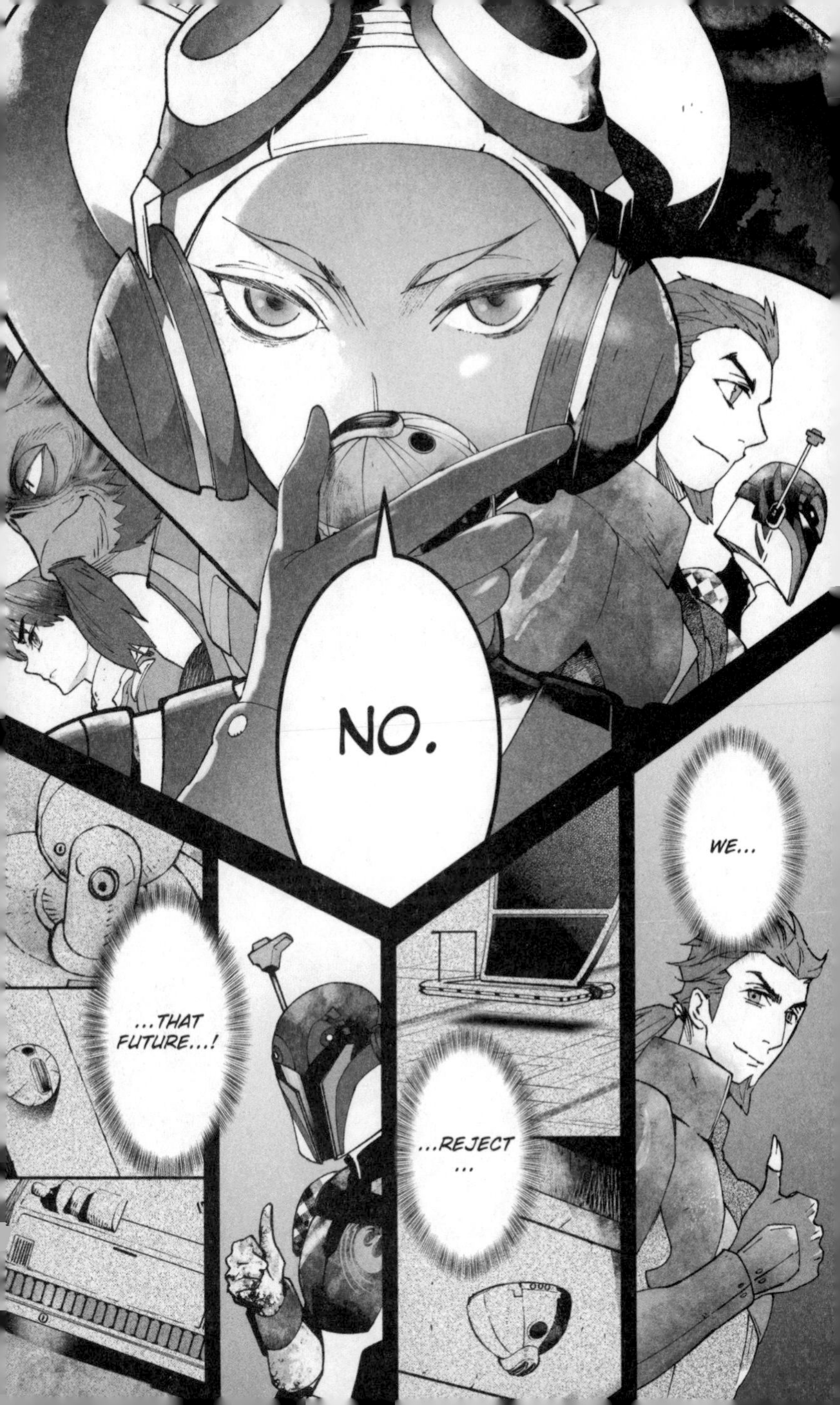
NO.
WE...
...REJECT ...
...THAT FUTURE...!

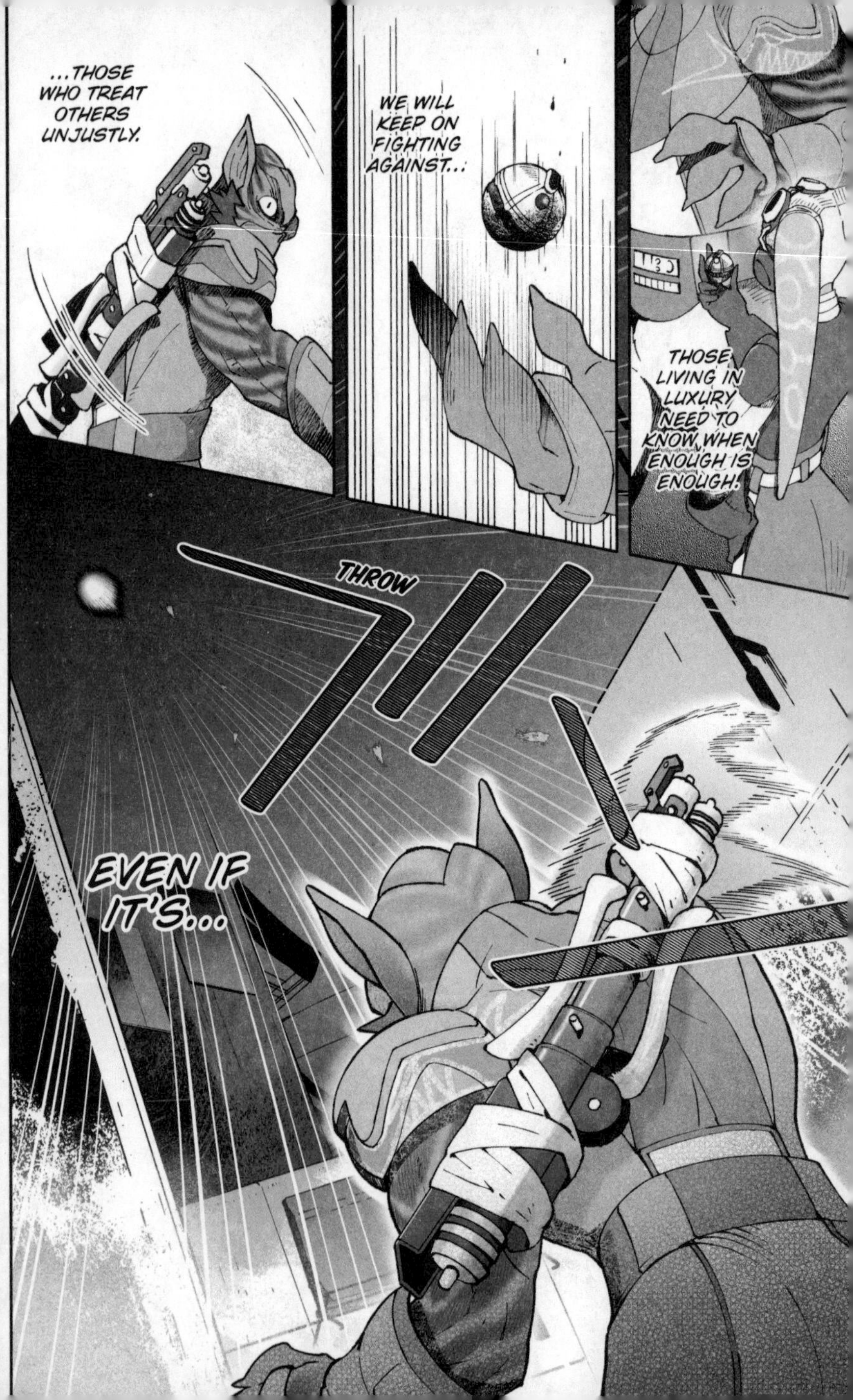
THOSE LIVING IN LUXURY NEED TO KNOW WHEN ENOUGH IS ENOUGH!
WE WILL KEEP ON FIGHTING AGAINST...
...THOSE WHO TREAT OTHERS UNJUSTLY.
THROW
EVEN IF IT'S...

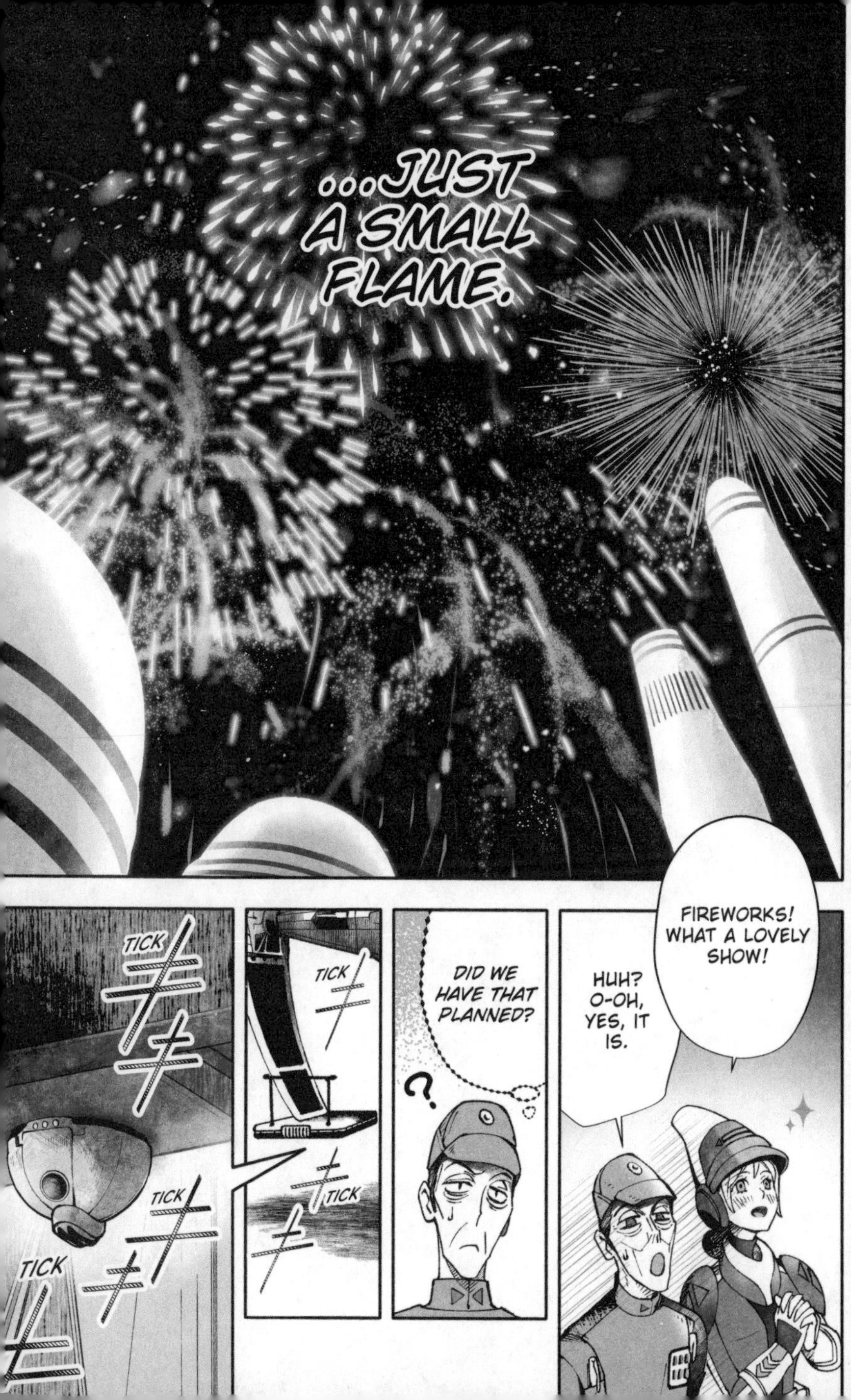
...JUST A SMALL FLAME.
FIREWORKS! WHAT A LOVELY SHOW!
HUH? O-OH, YES, IT IS.
DID WE HAVE THAT PLANNED?
TICK
TICK
TICK
TICK
TICK

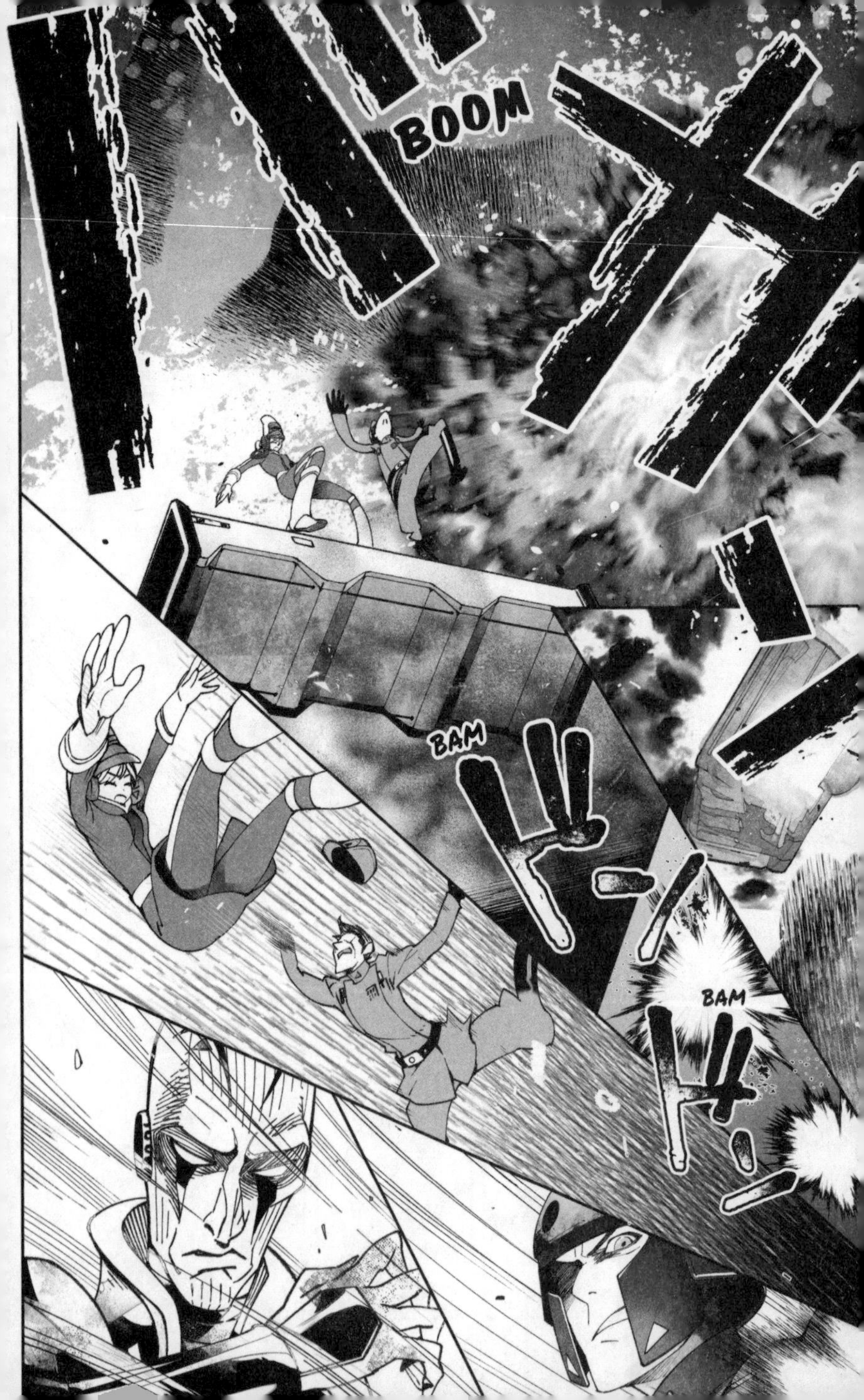
BOOM
BAM
BAM

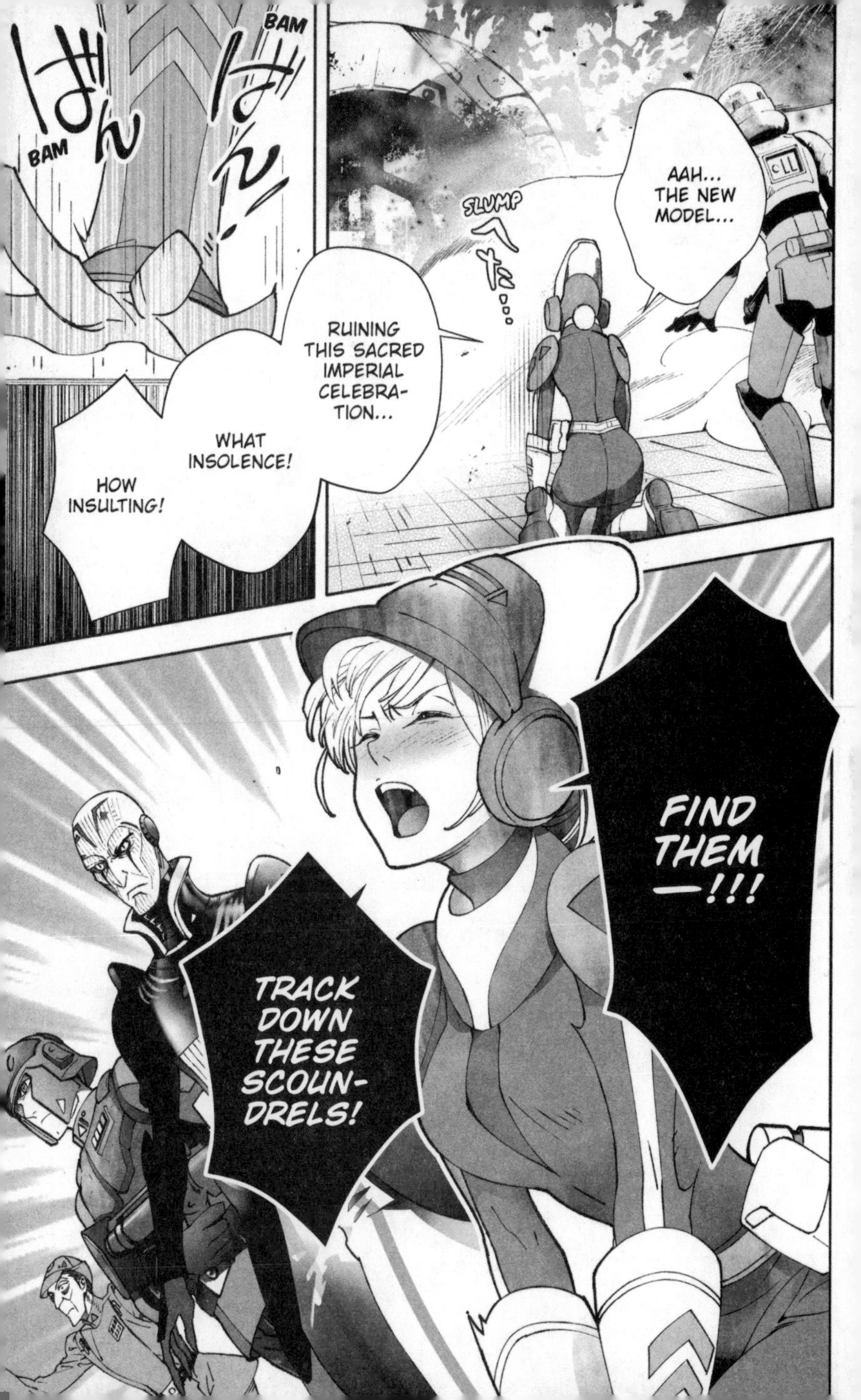
AAH... THE NEW MODEL...
SLUMP
BAM
BAM
RUINING THIS SACRED IMPERIAL CELEBRATION...
WHAT INSOLENCE!
HOW INSULTING!
FIND THEM—!!!
TRACK DOWN THESE SCOUNDRELS!

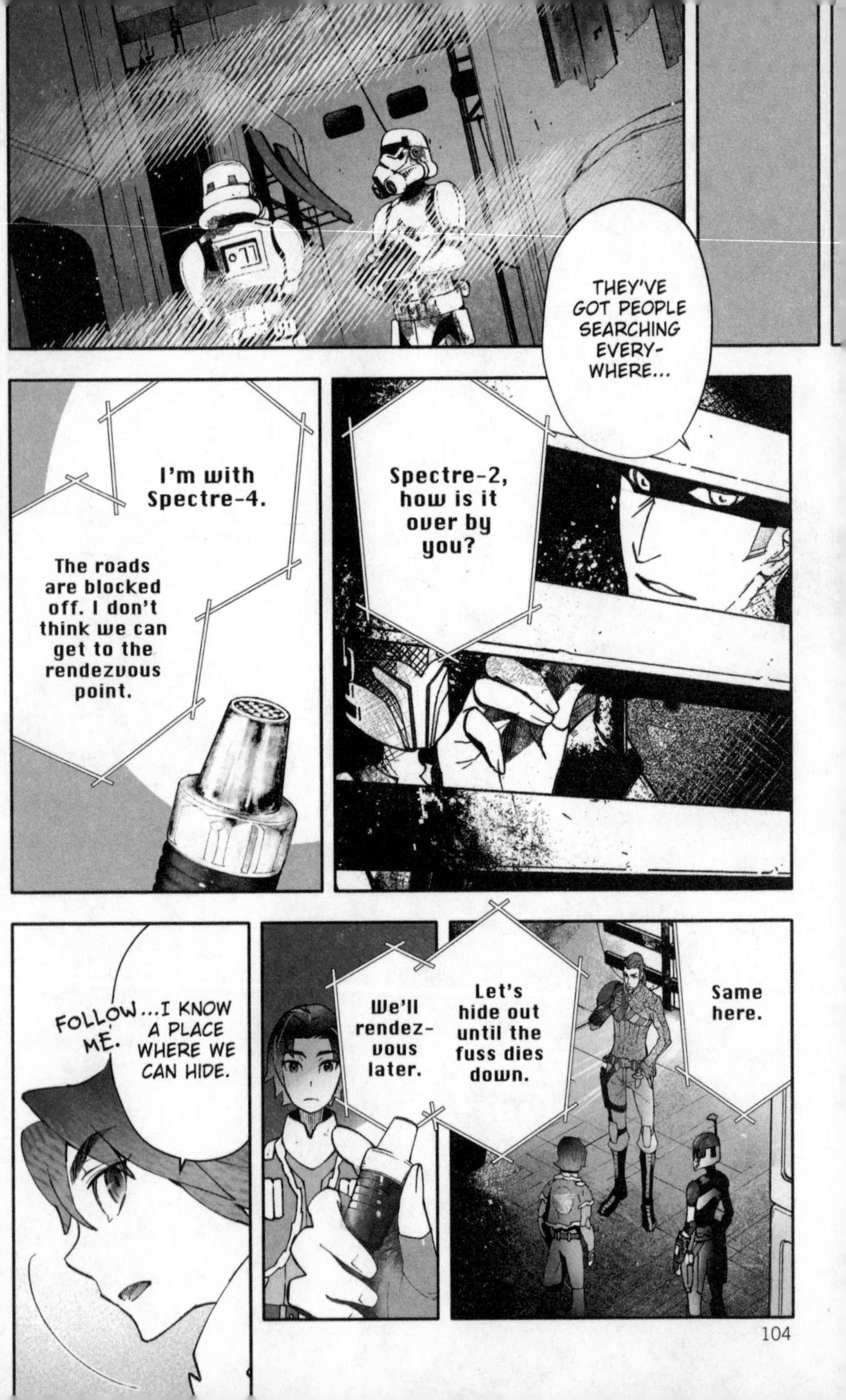
THEY'VE GOT PEOPLE SEARCHING EVERY-WHERE...
Spectre-2, how is it over by you?
I'm with Spectre-4.
The roads are blocked off. I don't think we can get to the rendezvous point.
Same here.
Let's hide out until the fuss dies down.
We'll rendez-vous later.
...I KNOW A PLACE WHERE WE CAN HIDE.
FOLLOW ME.

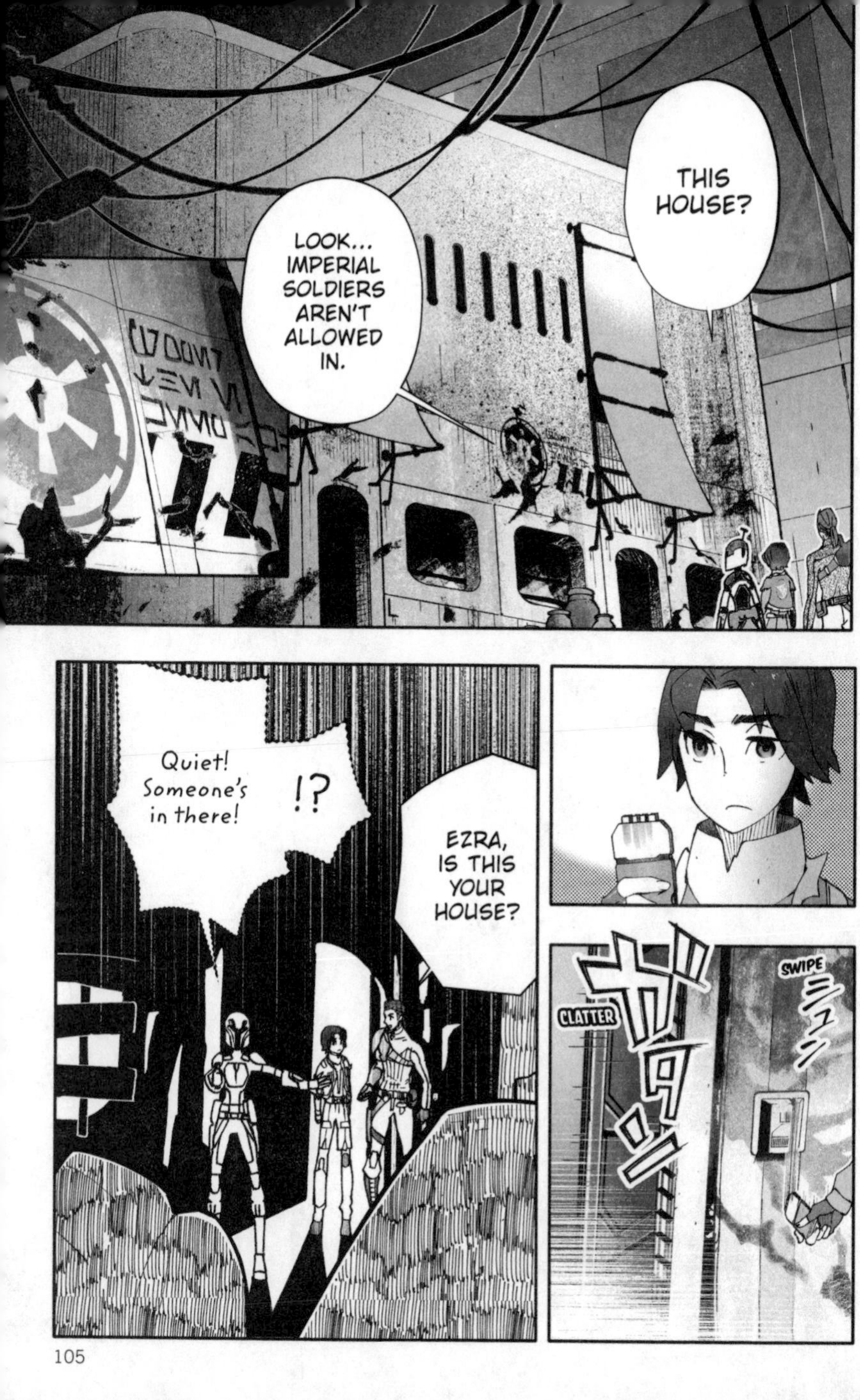
THIS HOUSE?
LOOK... IMPERIAL SOLDIERS AREN'T ALLOWED IN.
SWIPE
CLATTER
EZRA, IS THIS YOUR HOUSE?
!?
Quiet! Someone's in there!

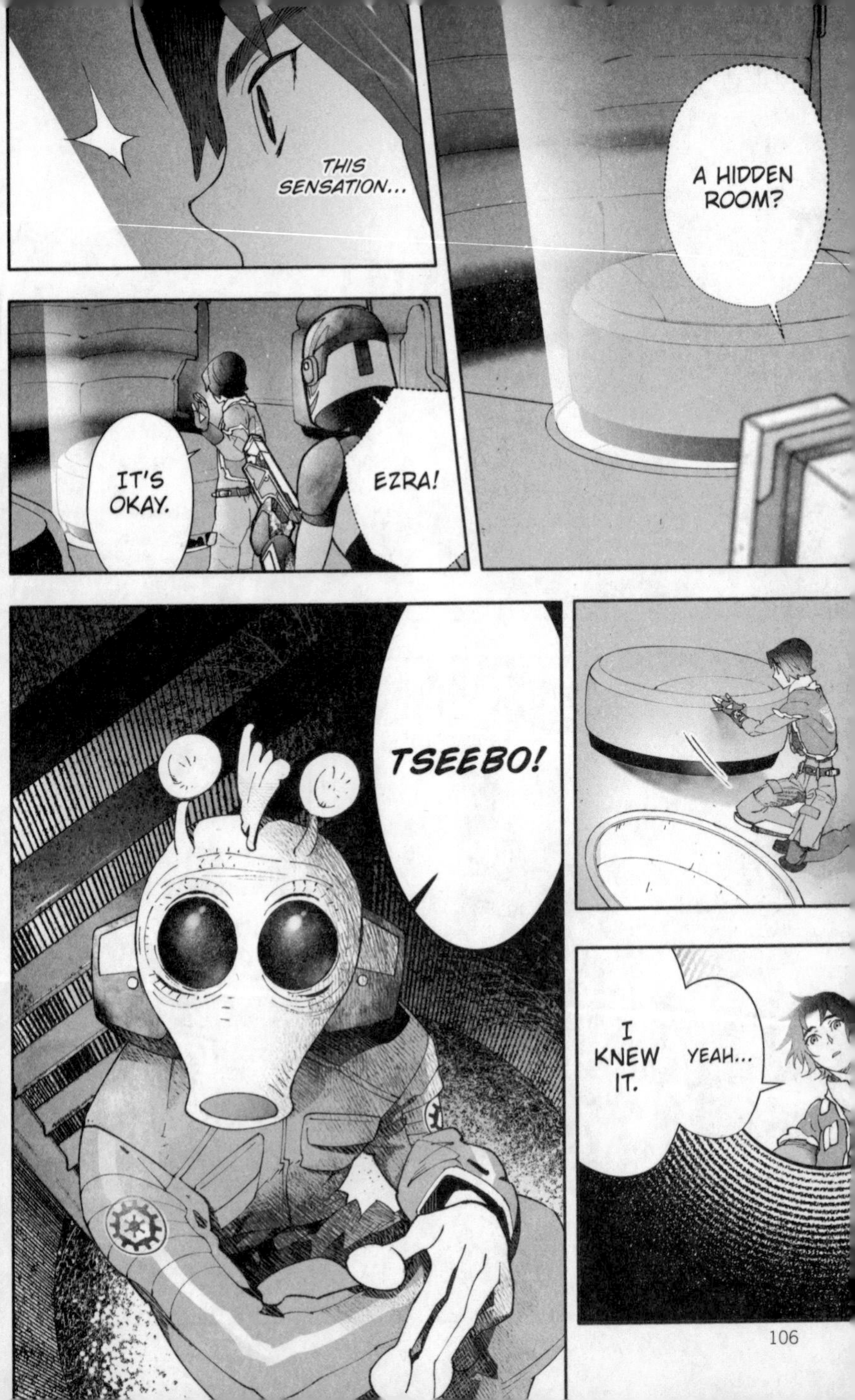
A HIDDEN ROOM?
THIS SENSATION...
EZRA!
IT'S OKAY.
YEAH...
I KNEW IT.
TSEEBO!

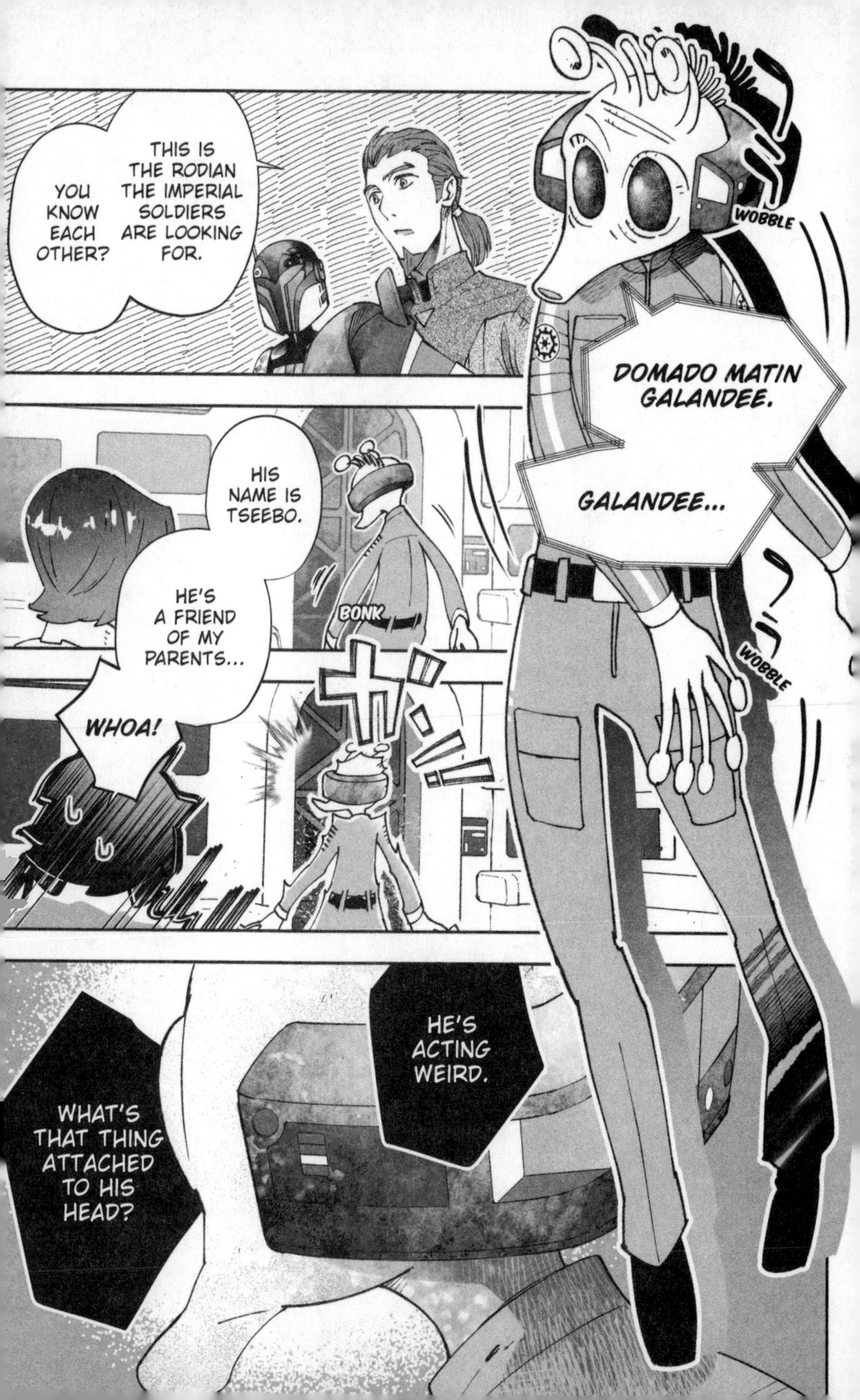
WOBBLE
DOMADO MATIN GALANDEE.
GALANDEE...
WOBBLE
THIS IS THE RODIAN THE IMPERIAL SOLDIERS ARE LOOKING FOR.
YOU KNOW EACH OTHER?
HIS NAME IS TSEEBO.
HE'S A FRIEND OF MY PARENTS...
BONK
WHOA!
HE'S ACTING WEIRD.
WHAT'S THAT THING ATTACHED TO HIS HEAD?

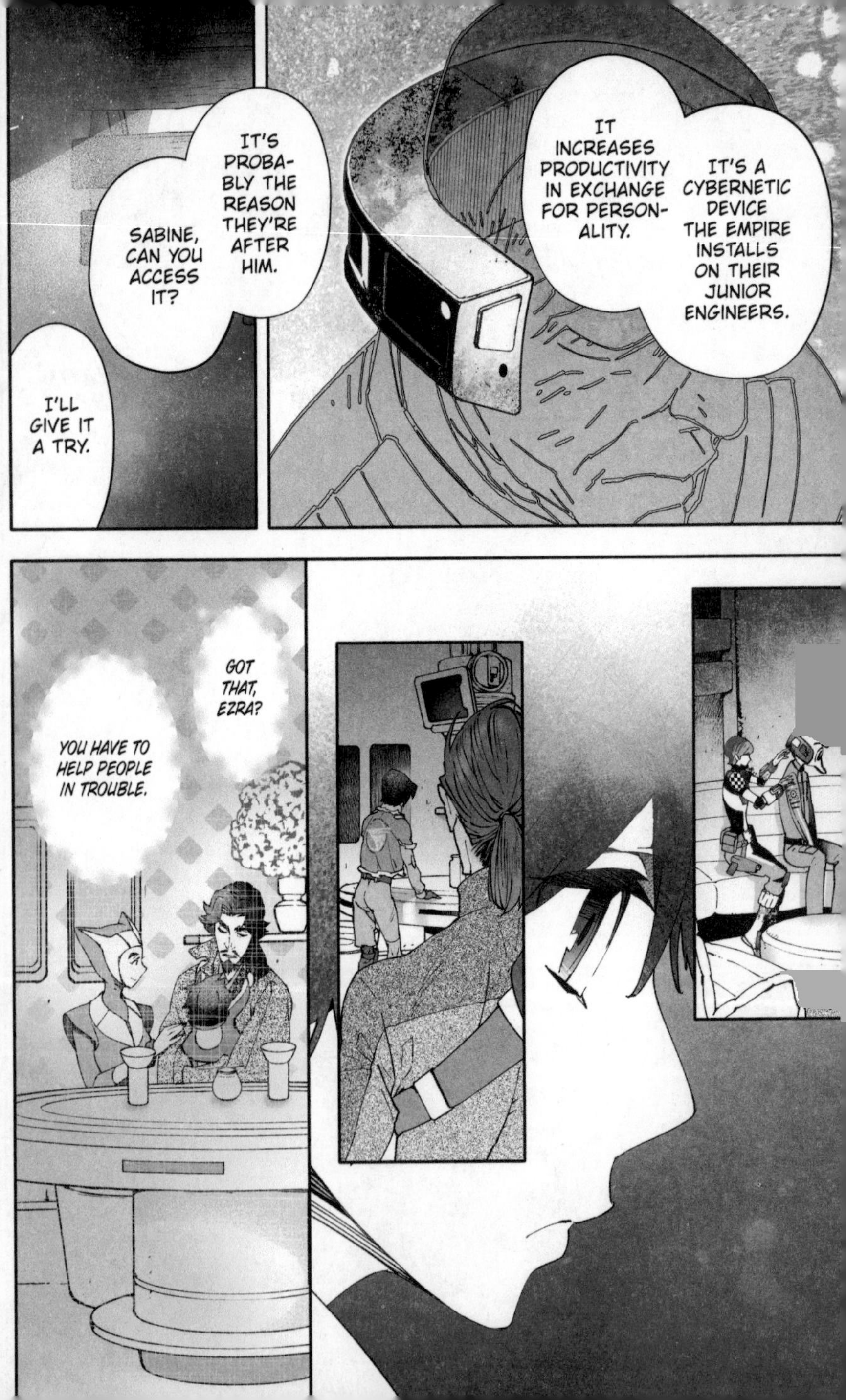
IT'S A CYBERNETIC DEVICE THE EMPIRE INSTALLS ON THEIR JUNIOR ENGINEERS.
IT INCREASES PRODUCTIVITY IN EXCHANGE FOR PERSON-ALITY.
IT'S PROBA-BLY THE REASON THEY'RE AFTER HIM.
SABINE, CAN YOU ACCESS IT?
I'LL GIVE IT A TRY.
GOT THAT, EZRA?
YOU HAVE TO HELP PEOPLE IN TROUBLE.

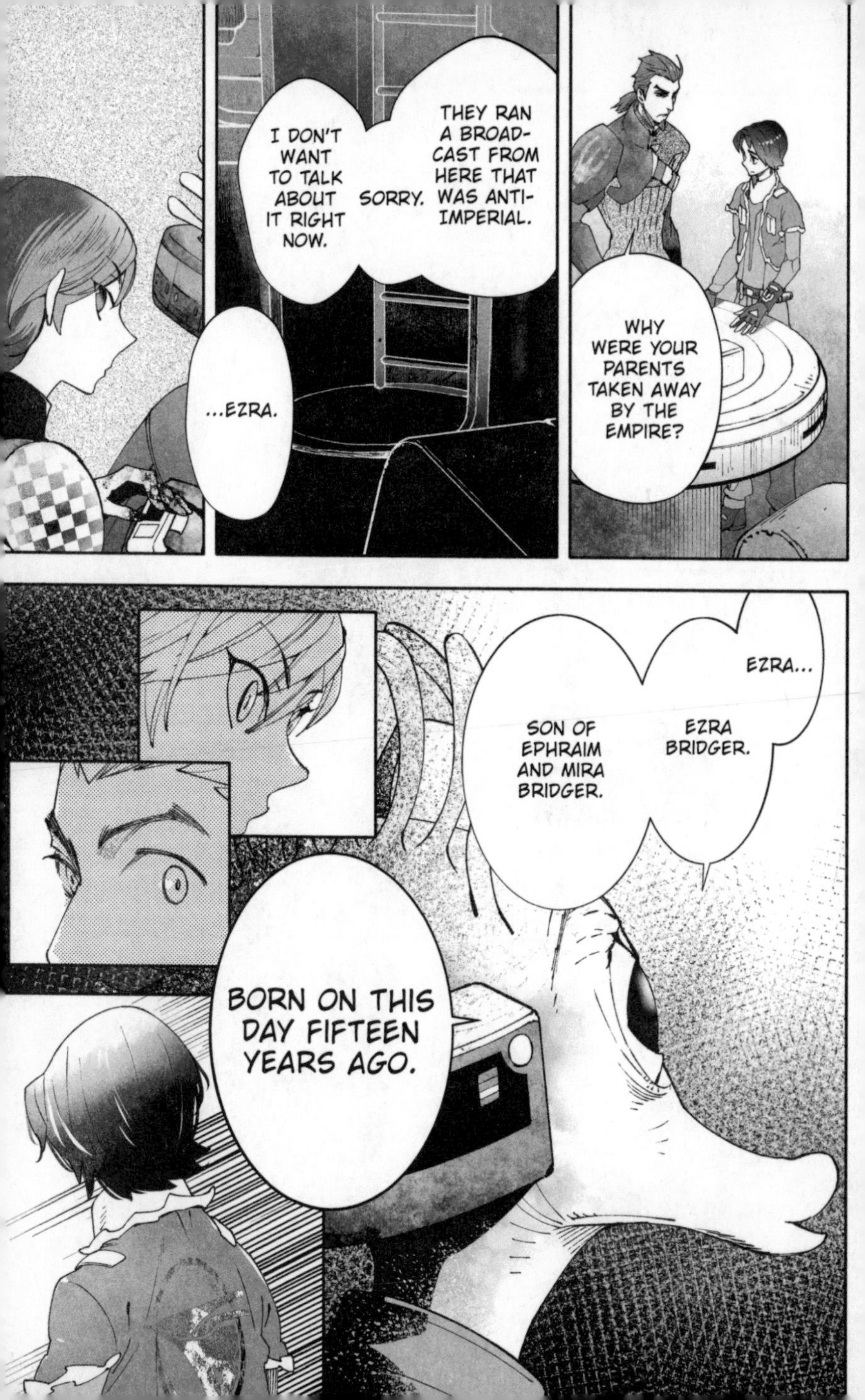
WHY WERE YOUR PARENTS TAKEN AWAY BY THE EMPIRE?
THEY RAN A BROADCAST FROM HERE THAT WAS ANTI-IMPERIAL.
SORRY.
I DON'T WANT TO TALK ABOUT IT RIGHT NOW.
...EZRA.
EZRA...
EZRA BRIDGER.
SON OF EPHRAIM AND MIRA BRIDGER.
BORN ON THIS DAY FIFTEEN YEARS AGO.

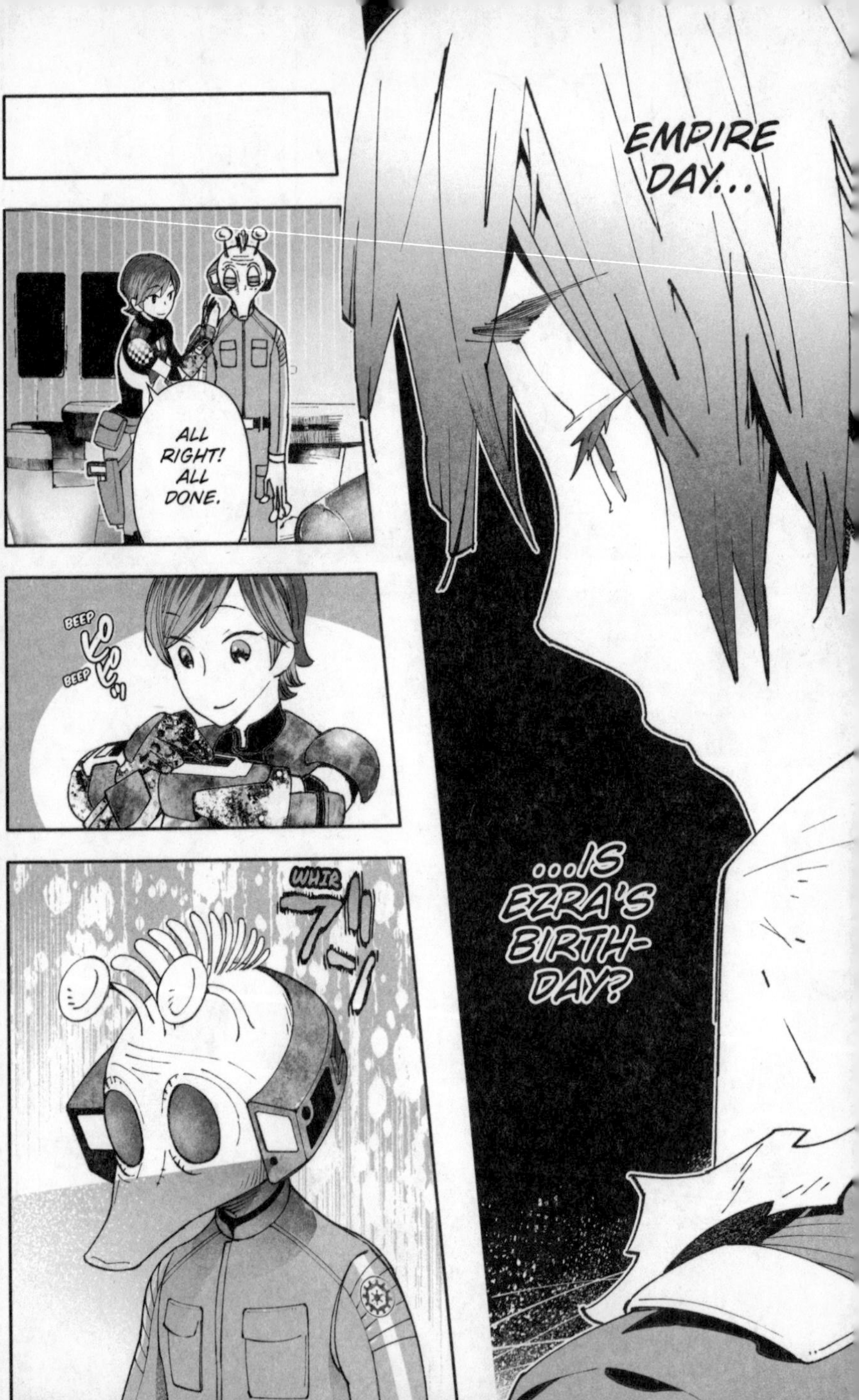
EMPIRE DAY...
...IS EZRA'S BIRTH-DAY?
ALL RIGHT! ALL DONE.
BEEP
BEEP
WHIR

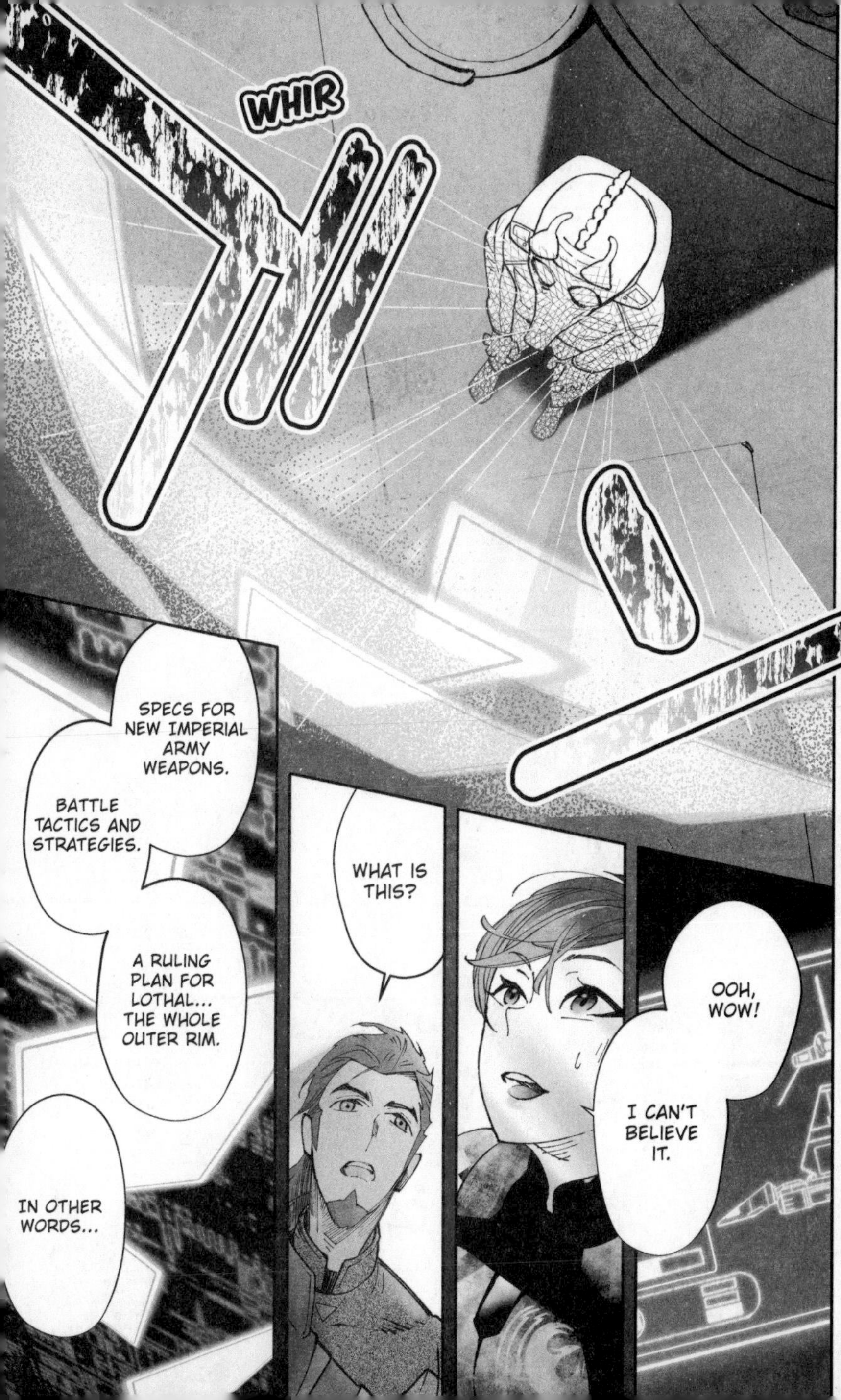
WHIR
OOH, WOW!
I CAN'T BELIEVE IT.
WHAT IS THIS?
SPECS FOR NEW IMPERIAL ARMY WEAPONS.
BATTLE TACTICS AND STRATEGIES.
A RULING PLAN FOR LOTHAL... THE WHOLE OUTER RIM.
IN OTHER WORDS...

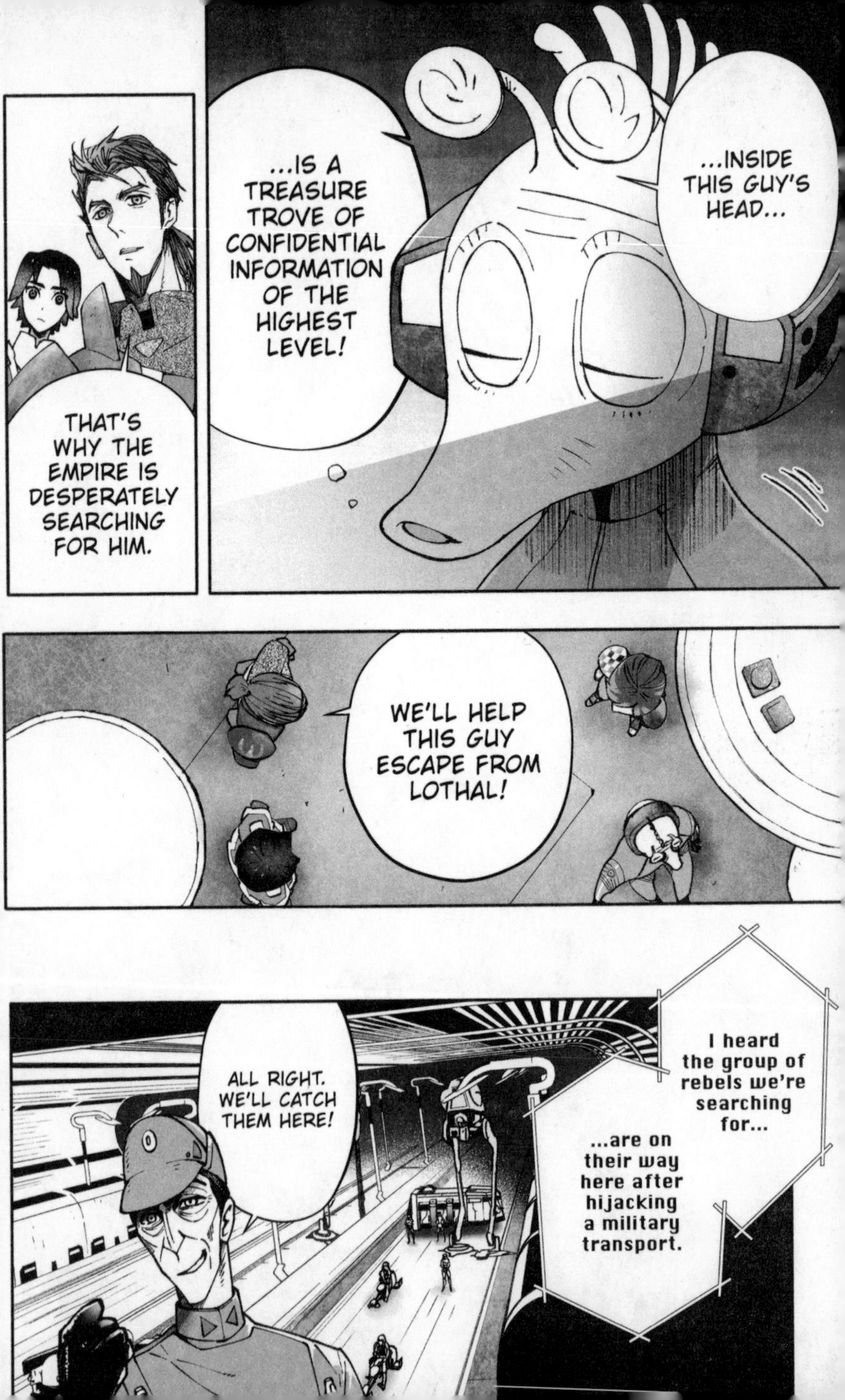
...INSIDE THIS GUY'S HEAD...
...IS A TREASURE TROVE OF CONFIDENTIAL INFORMATION OF THE HIGHEST LEVEL!
THAT'S WHY THE EMPIRE IS DESPERATELY SEARCHING FOR HIM.
WE'LL HELP THIS GUY ESCAPE FROM LOTHAL!
I heard the group of rebels we're searching for...
...are on their way here after hijacking a military transport.
ALL RIGHT. WE'LL CATCH THEM HERE!

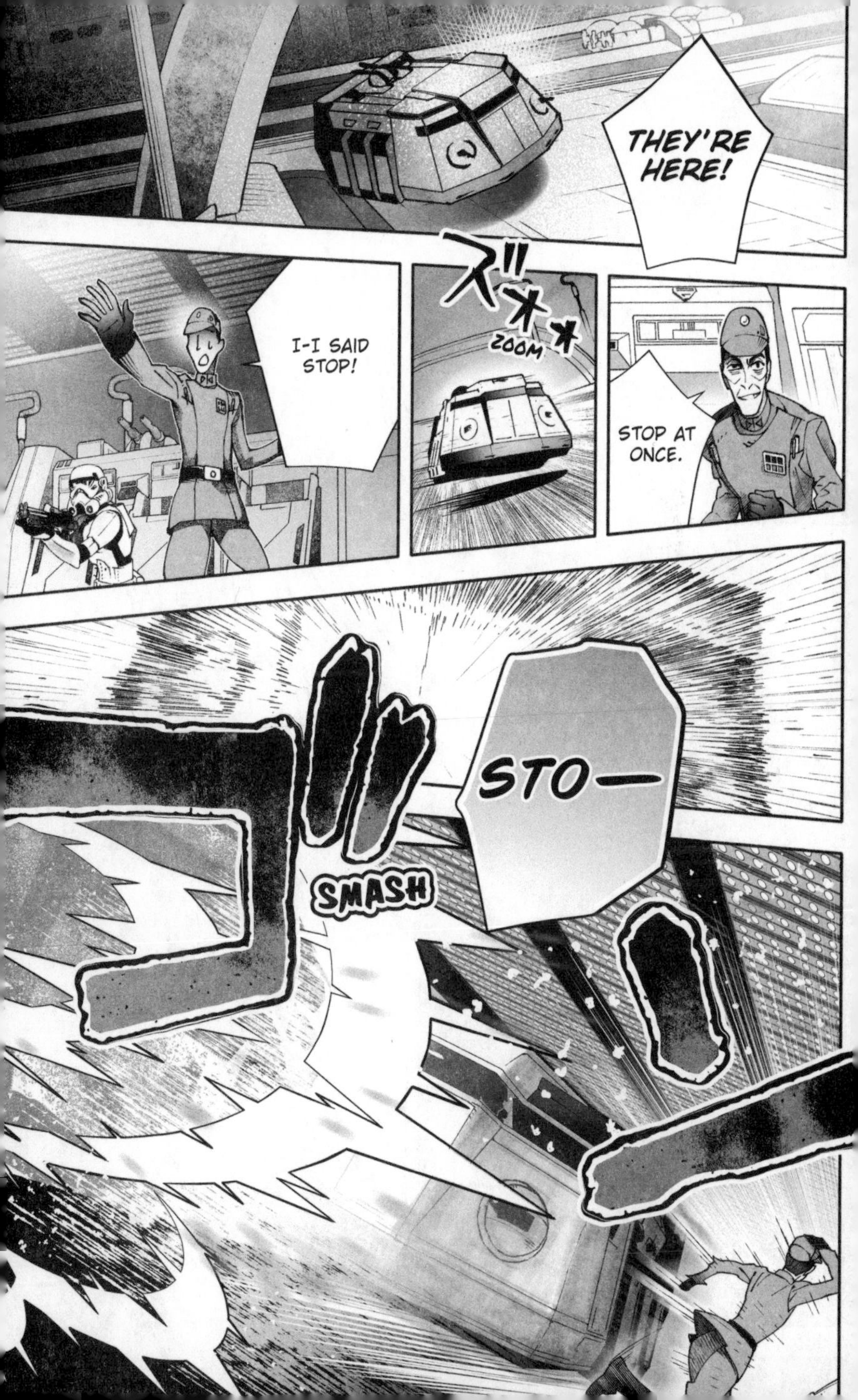
THEY'RE HERE!
STOP AT ONCE.
ZOOM
I-I SAID STOP!
STO—
SMASH

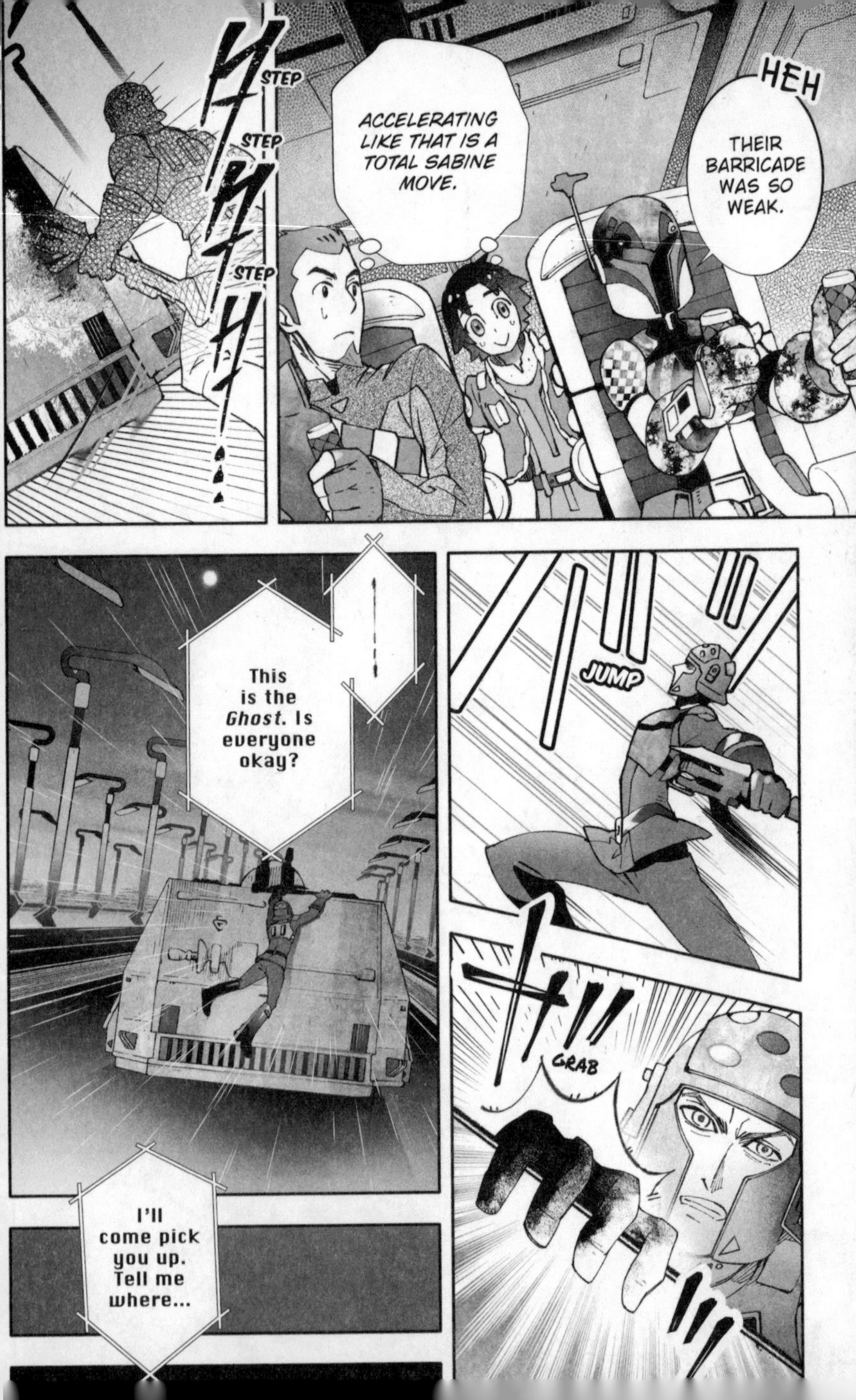
HEH
THEIR BARRICADE WAS SO WEAK.
ACCELERATING LIKE THAT IS A TOTAL SABINE MOVE.
STEP
STEP
STEP
JUMP
GRAB
!
This is the *Ghost*. Is everyone okay?
I'll come pick you up. Tell me where...

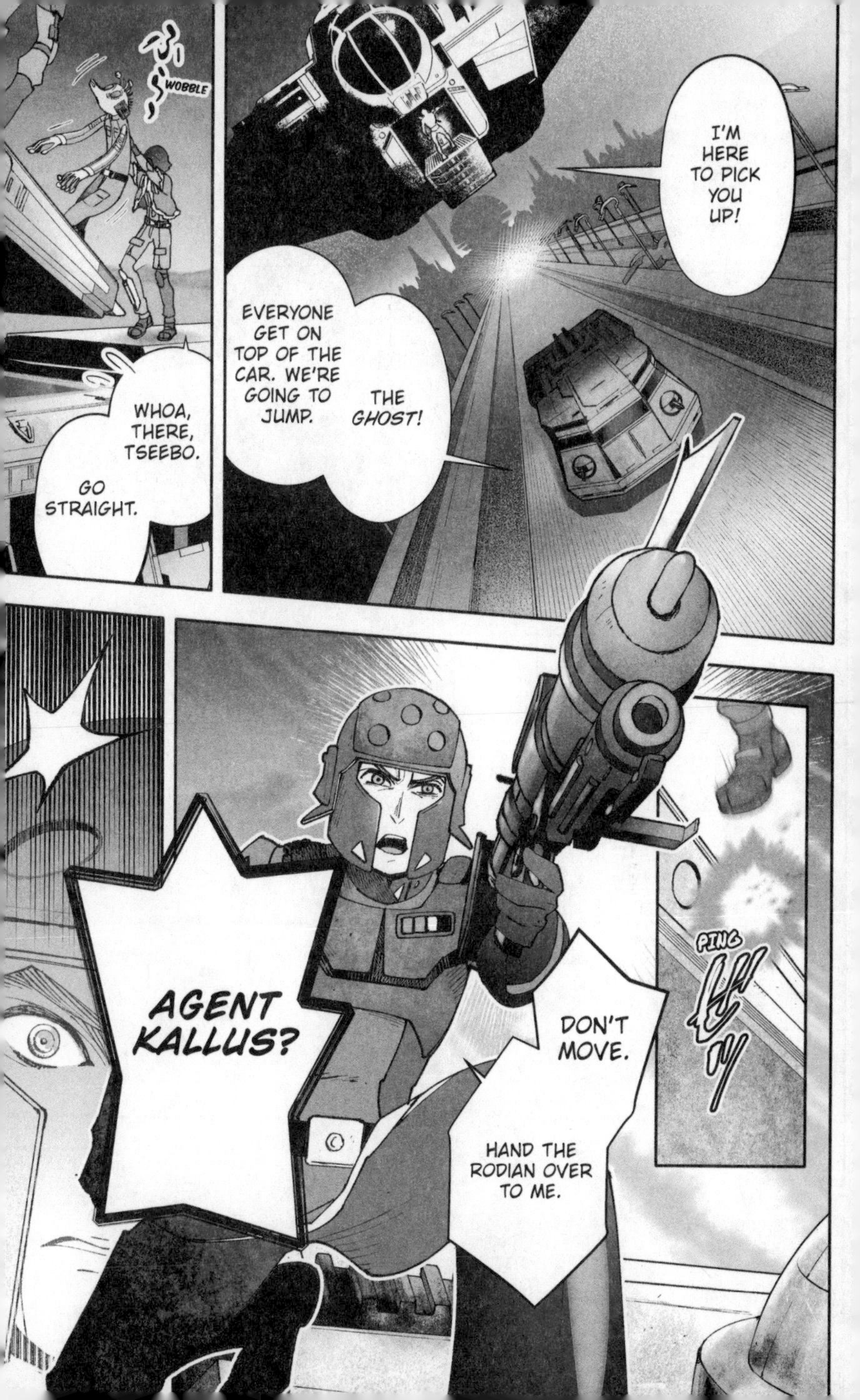
I'M HERE TO PICK YOU UP!
THE GHOST!
EVERYONE GET ON TOP OF THE CAR. WE'RE GOING TO JUMP.
WOBBLE
WHOA, THERE, TSEEBO.
GO STRAIGHT.
PING
DON'T MOVE.
HAND THE RODIAN OVER TO ME.
AGENT KALLUS?

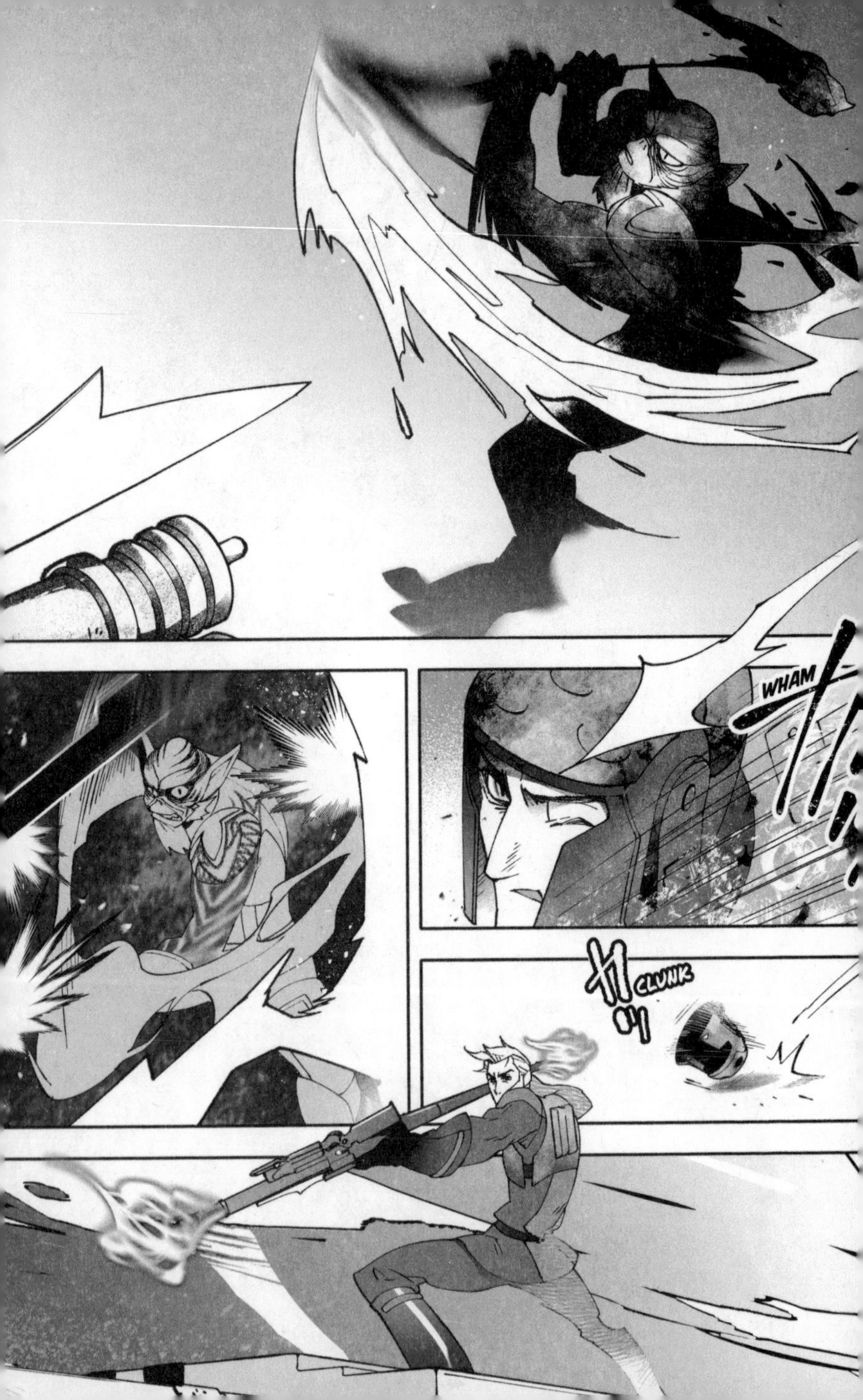
WHAM
CLUNK

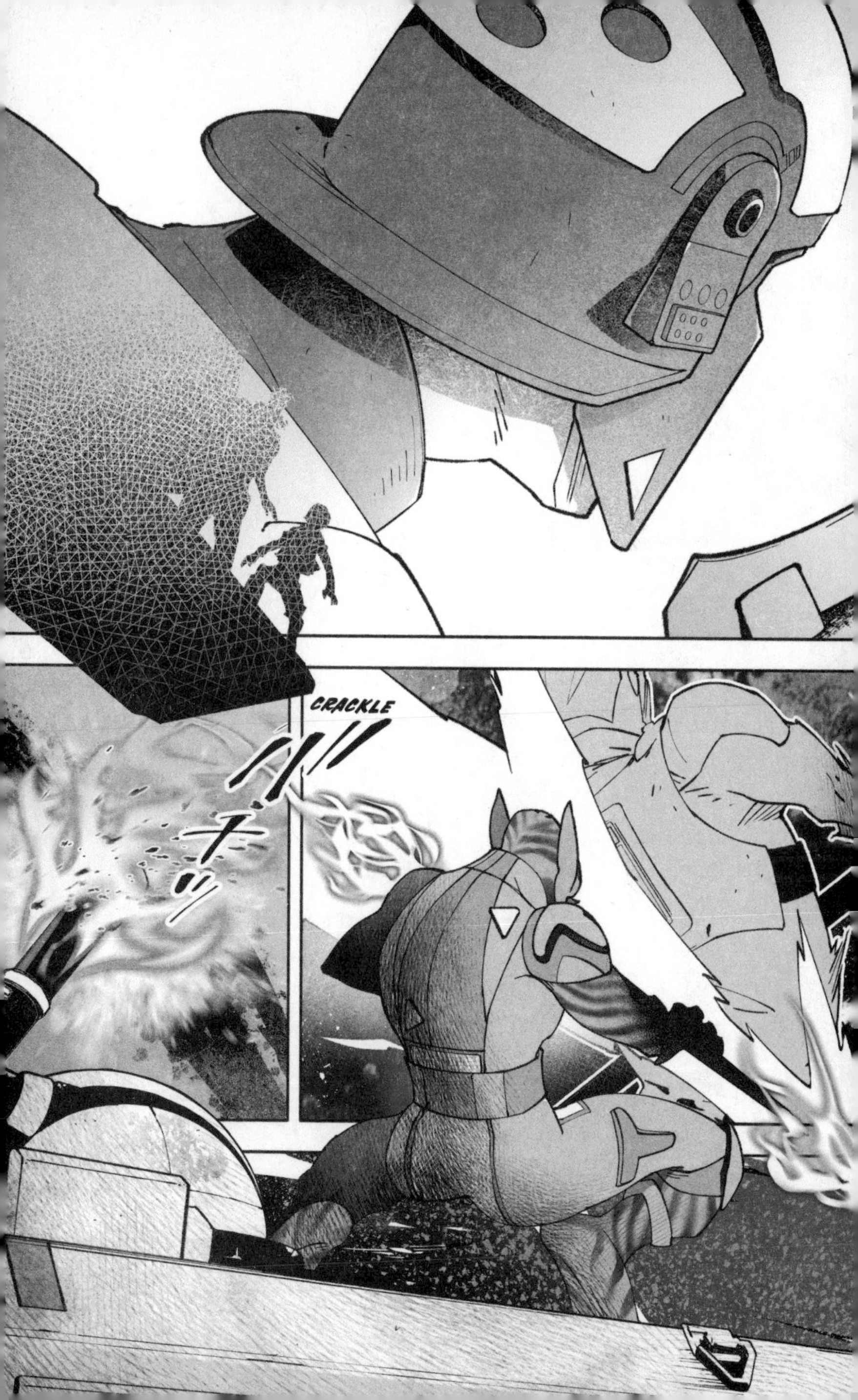
CRACKLE
バチッ

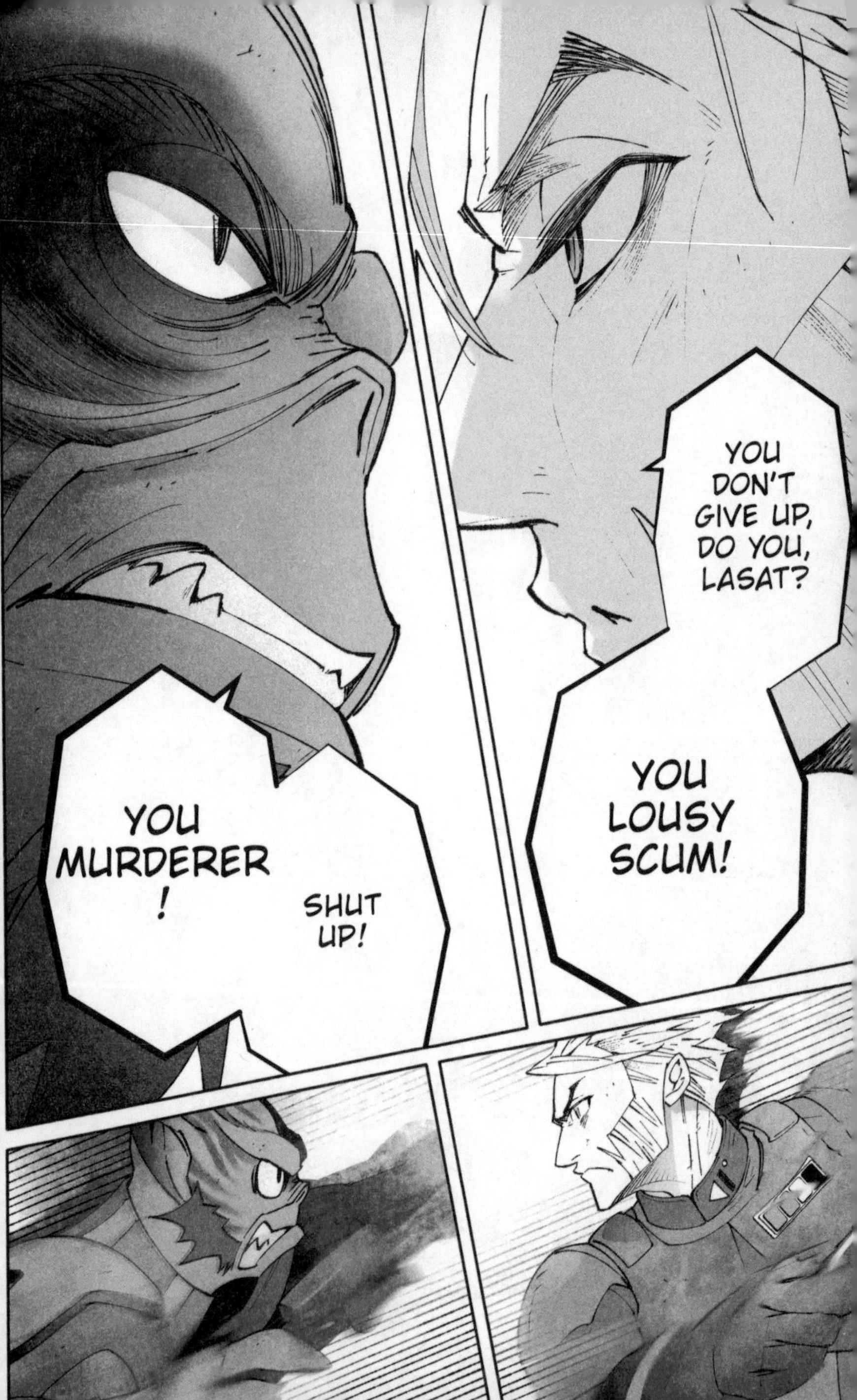
YOU DON'T GIVE UP, DO YOU, LASAT?
YOU LOUSY SCUM!
YOU MURDERER!
SHUT UP!

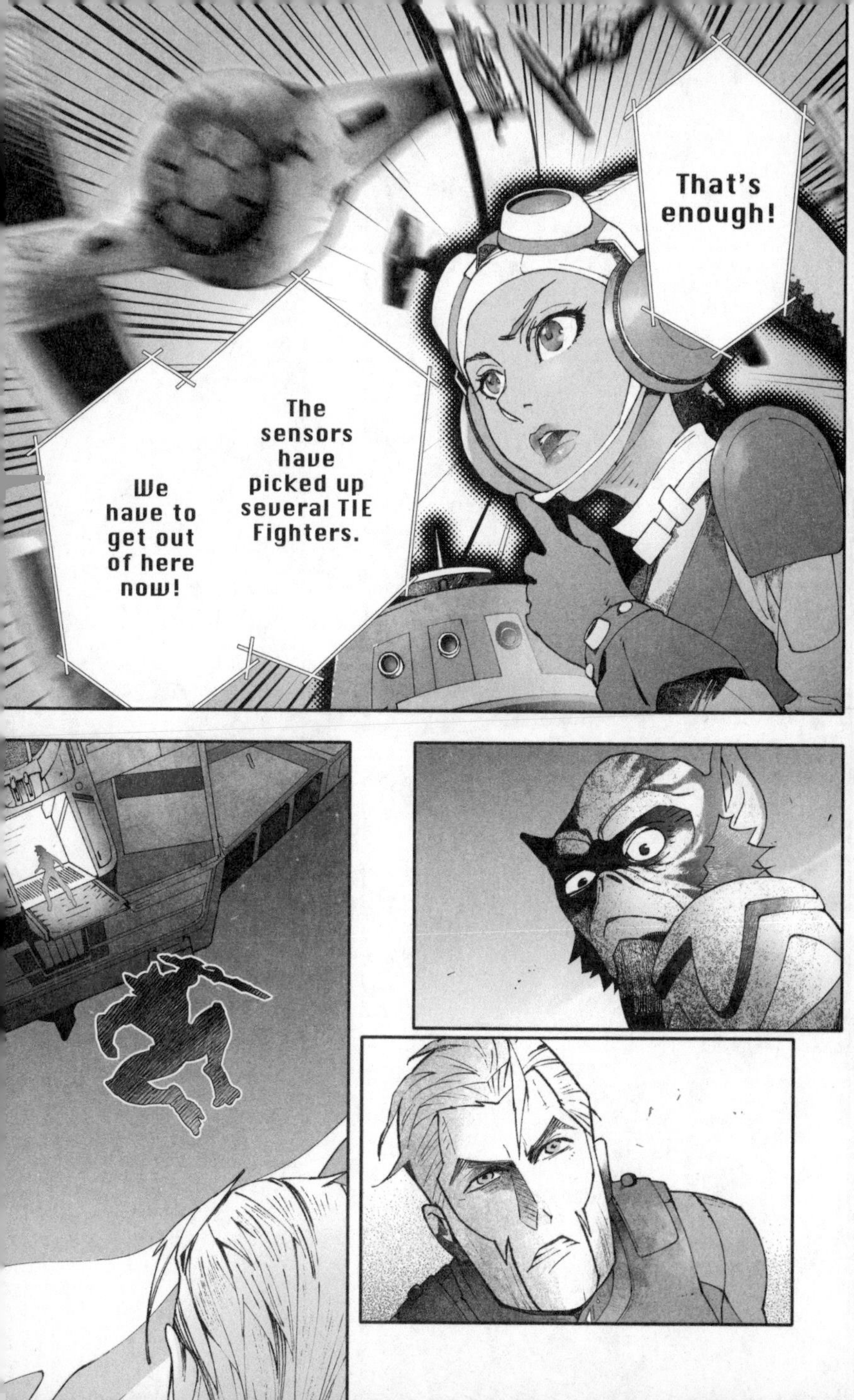
That's enough!
The sensors have picked up several TIE Fighters.
We have to get out of here now!

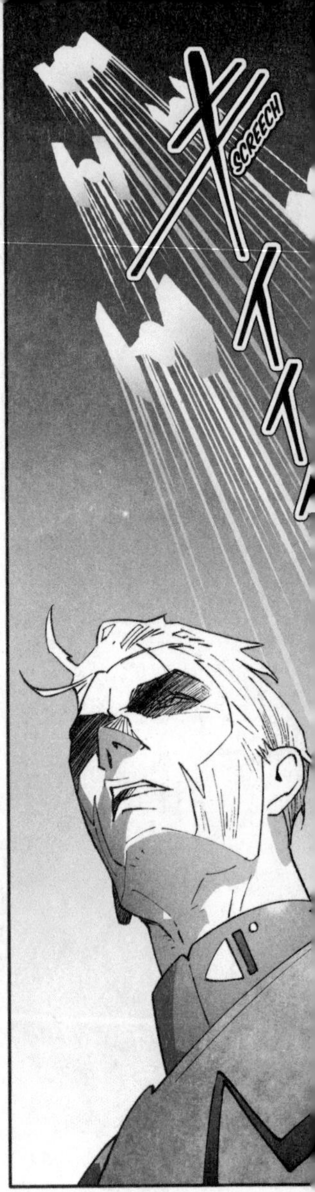
SCREECH
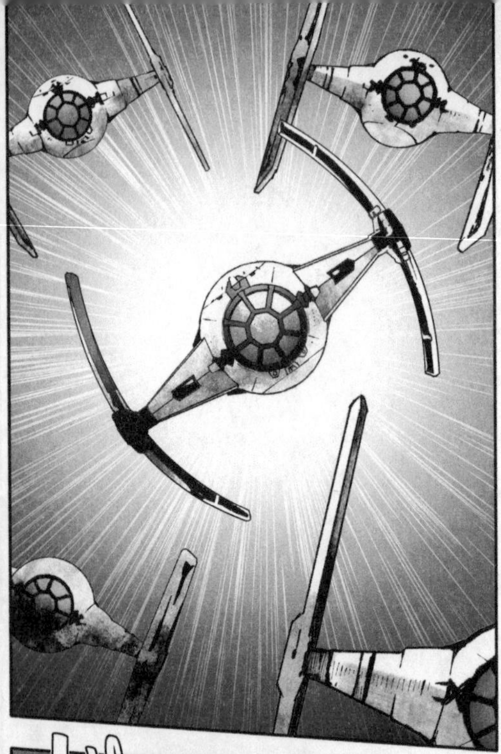
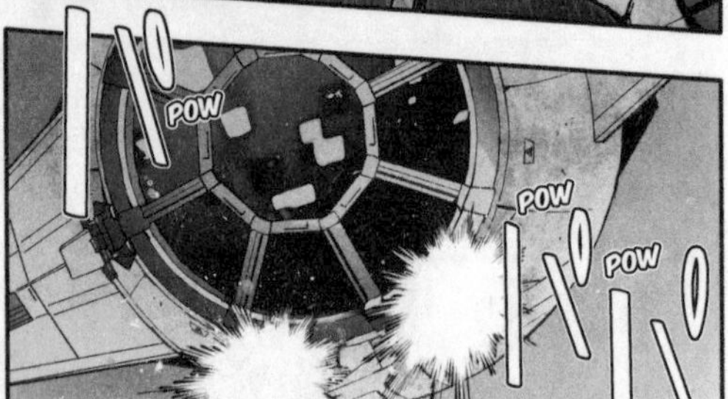
POW
POW
POW
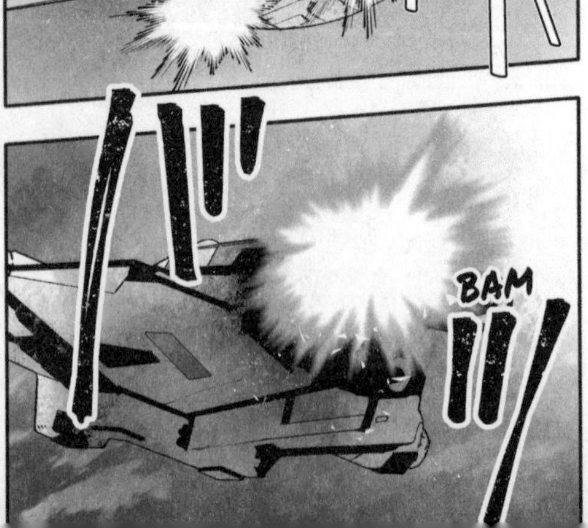
BAM

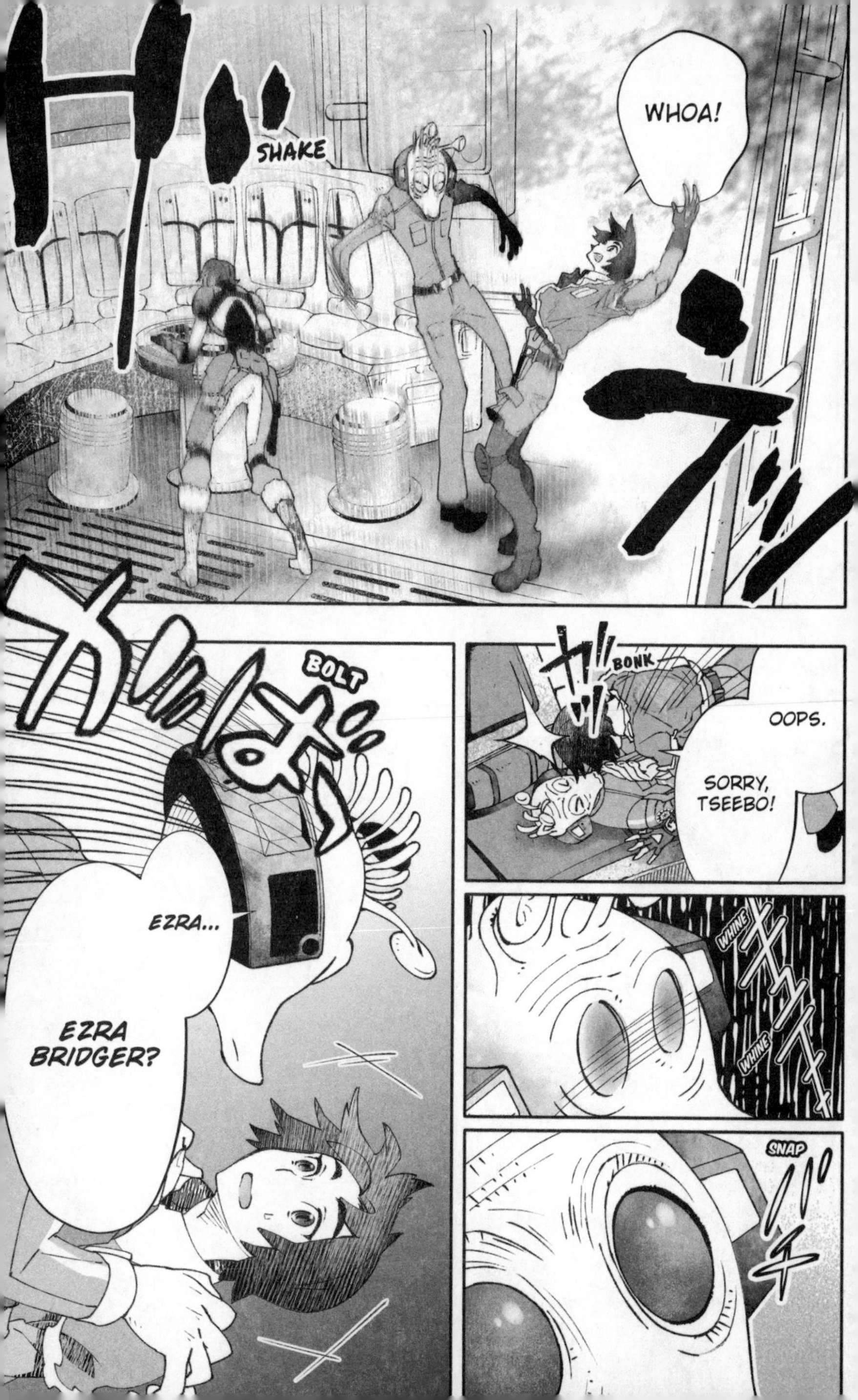
SHAKE
WHOA!
BOLT
EZRA...
EZRA BRIDGER?
BONK
OOPS.
SORRY, TSEEBO!
WHINE
WHINE
SNAP

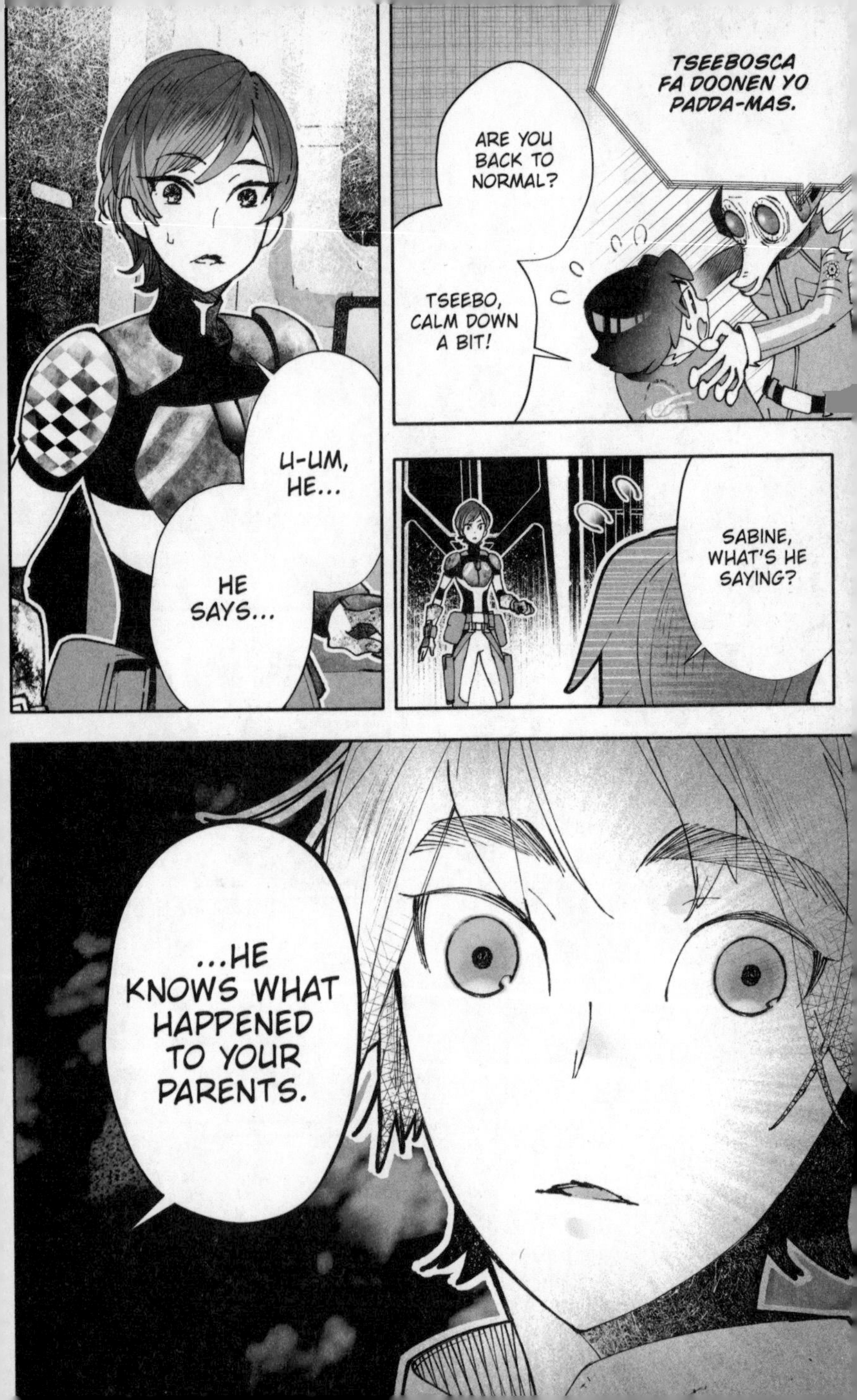
TSEEBOSCA FA DOONEN YO PADDA-MAS.
ARE YOU BACK TO NORMAL?
TSEEBO, CALM DOWN A BIT!
SABINE, WHAT'S HE SAYING?
U-UM, HE...
HE SAYS...
...HE KNOWS WHAT HAPPENED TO YOUR PARENTS.

STAR WARS
REBELS

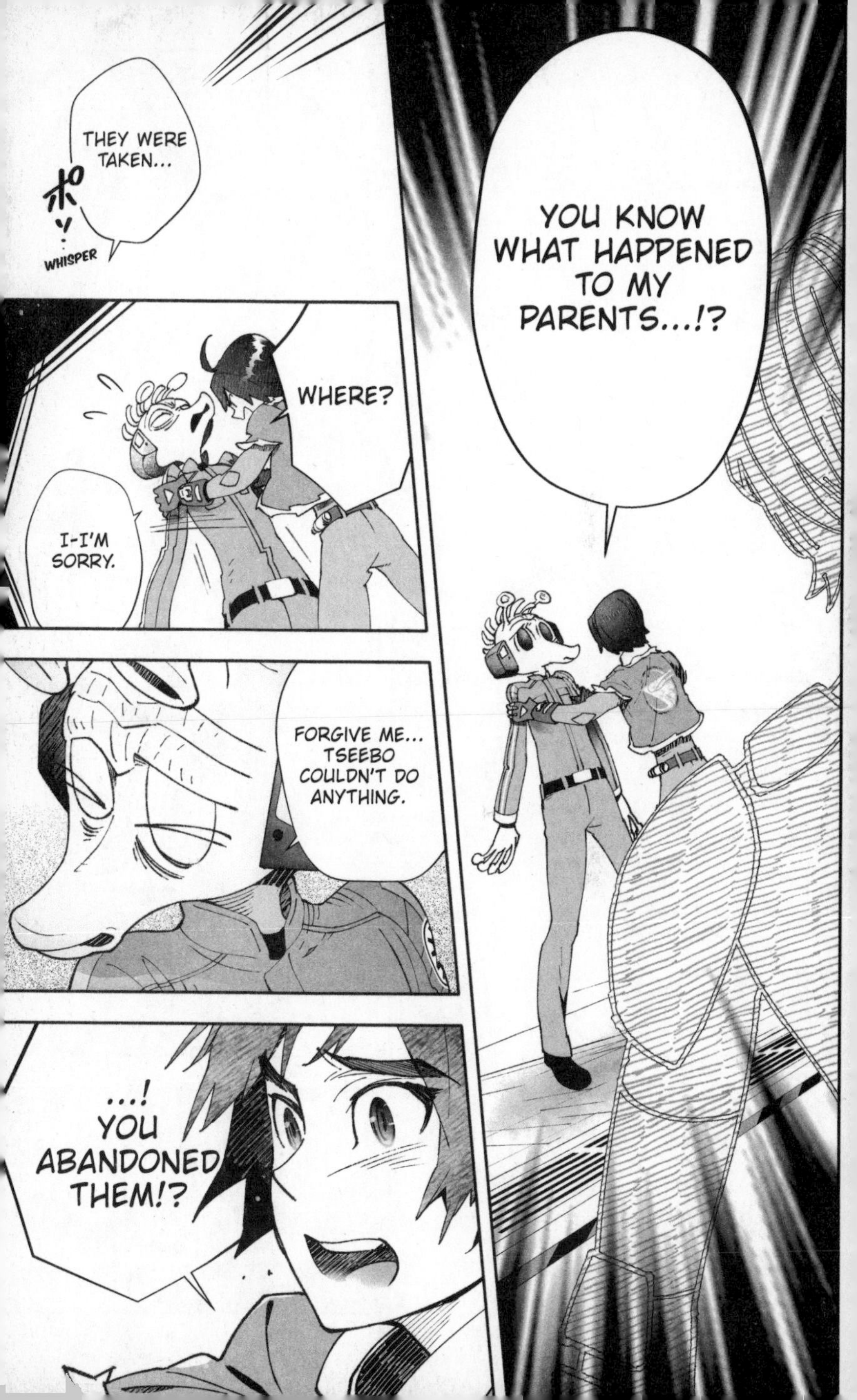
YOU KNOW WHAT HAPPENED TO MY PARENTS...!?
THEY WERE TAKEN...
ポソ
WHISPER
WHERE?
I-I'M SORRY.
FORGIVE ME... TSEEBO COULDN'T DO ANYTHING.
...! YOU ABANDONED THEM!?

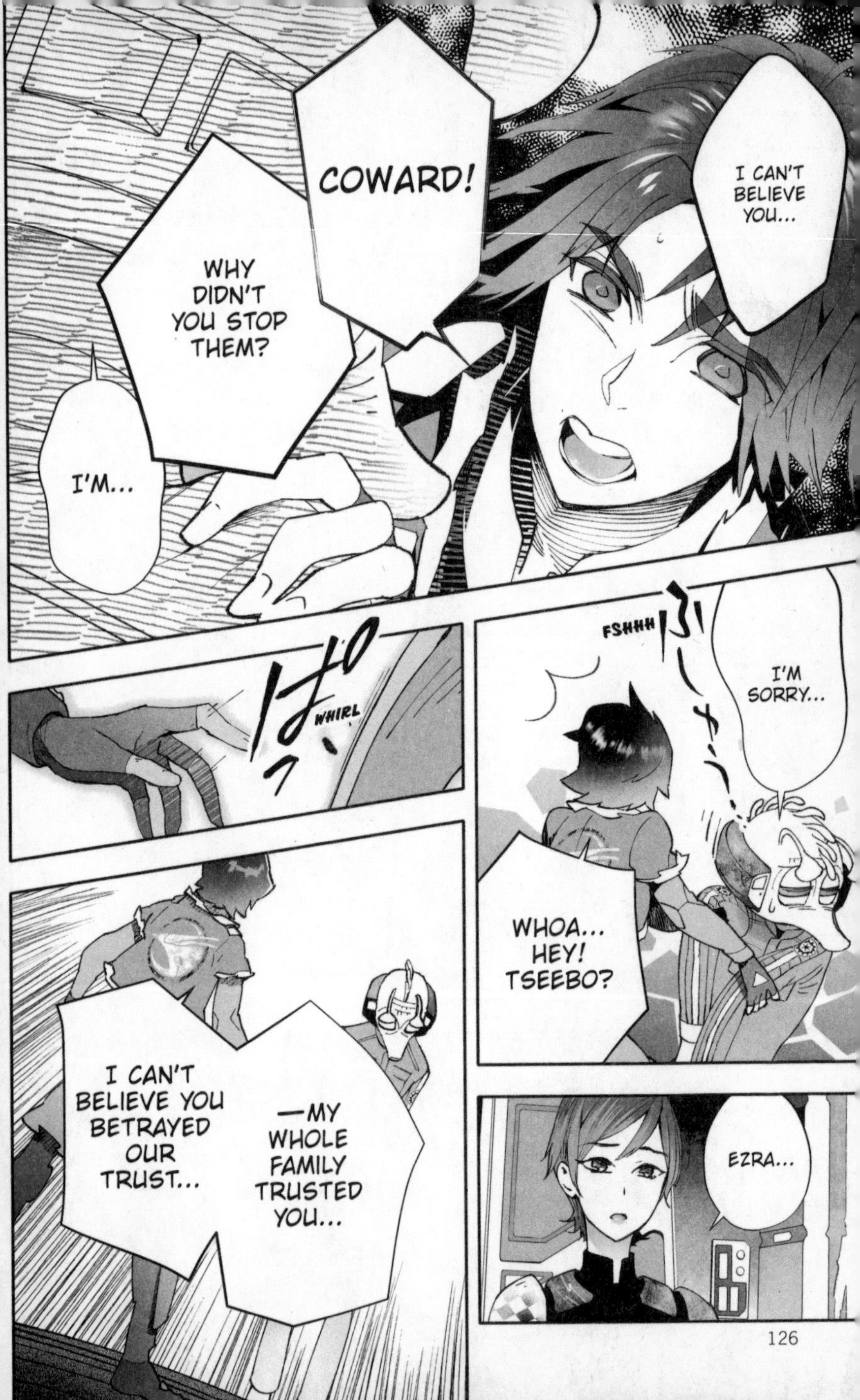
I CAN'T BELIEVE YOU...
COWARD!
WHY DIDN'T YOU STOP THEM?
I'M...
FSHHH
I'M SORRY...
WHOA... HEY! TSEEBO?
WHIRL
EZRA...
I CAN'T BELIEVE YOU BETRAYED OUR TRUST...
—MY WHOLE FAMILY TRUSTED YOU...

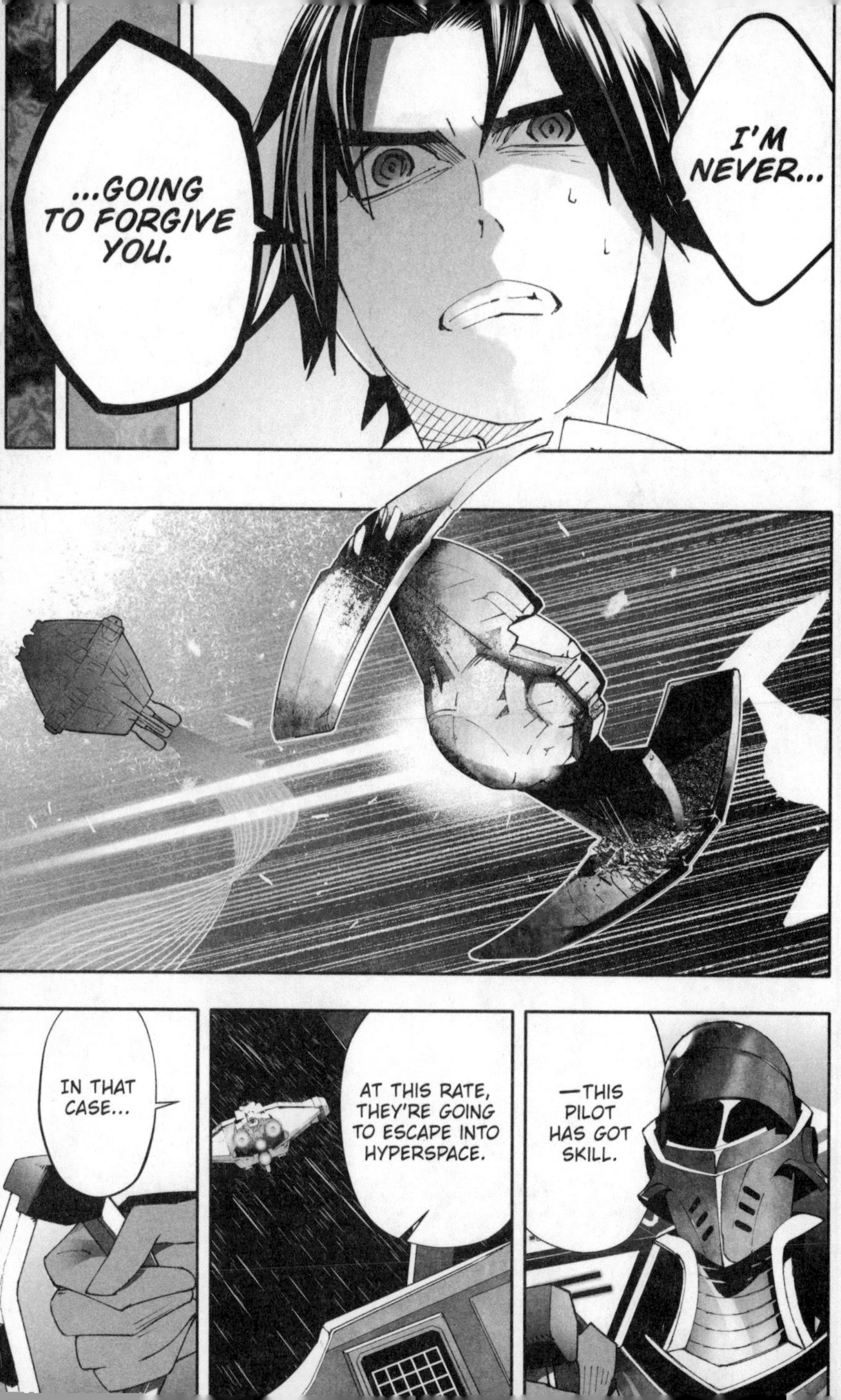
I'M NEVER...
...GOING TO FORGIVE YOU.
—THIS PILOT HAS GOT SKILL.
AT THIS RATE, THEY'RE GOING TO ESCAPE INTO HYPERSPACE.
IN THAT CASE...

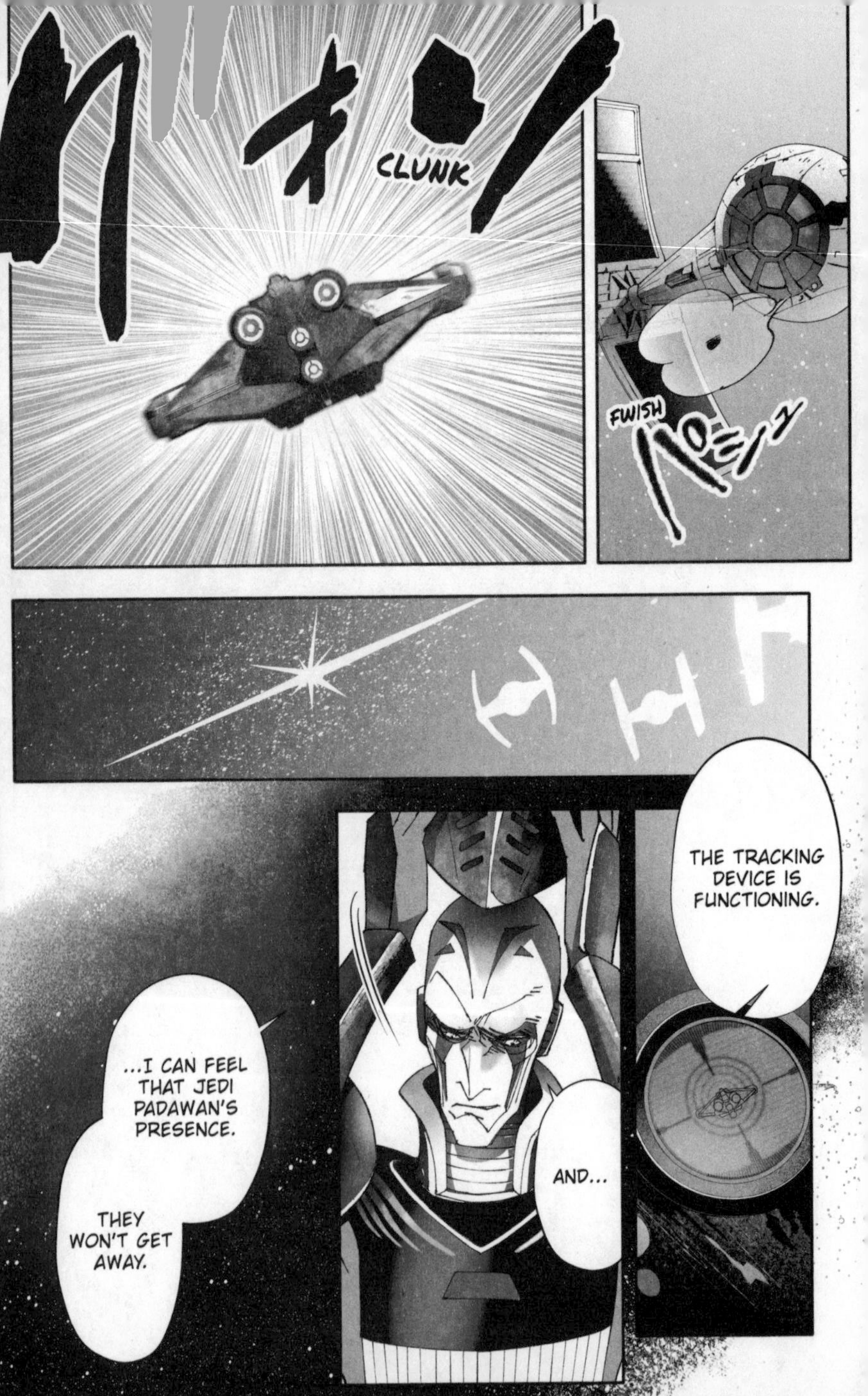
FWISH
CLUNK
THE TRACKING DEVICE IS FUNCTIONING.
...I CAN FEEL THAT JEDI PADAWAN'S PRESENCE.
AND...
THEY WON'T GET AWAY.

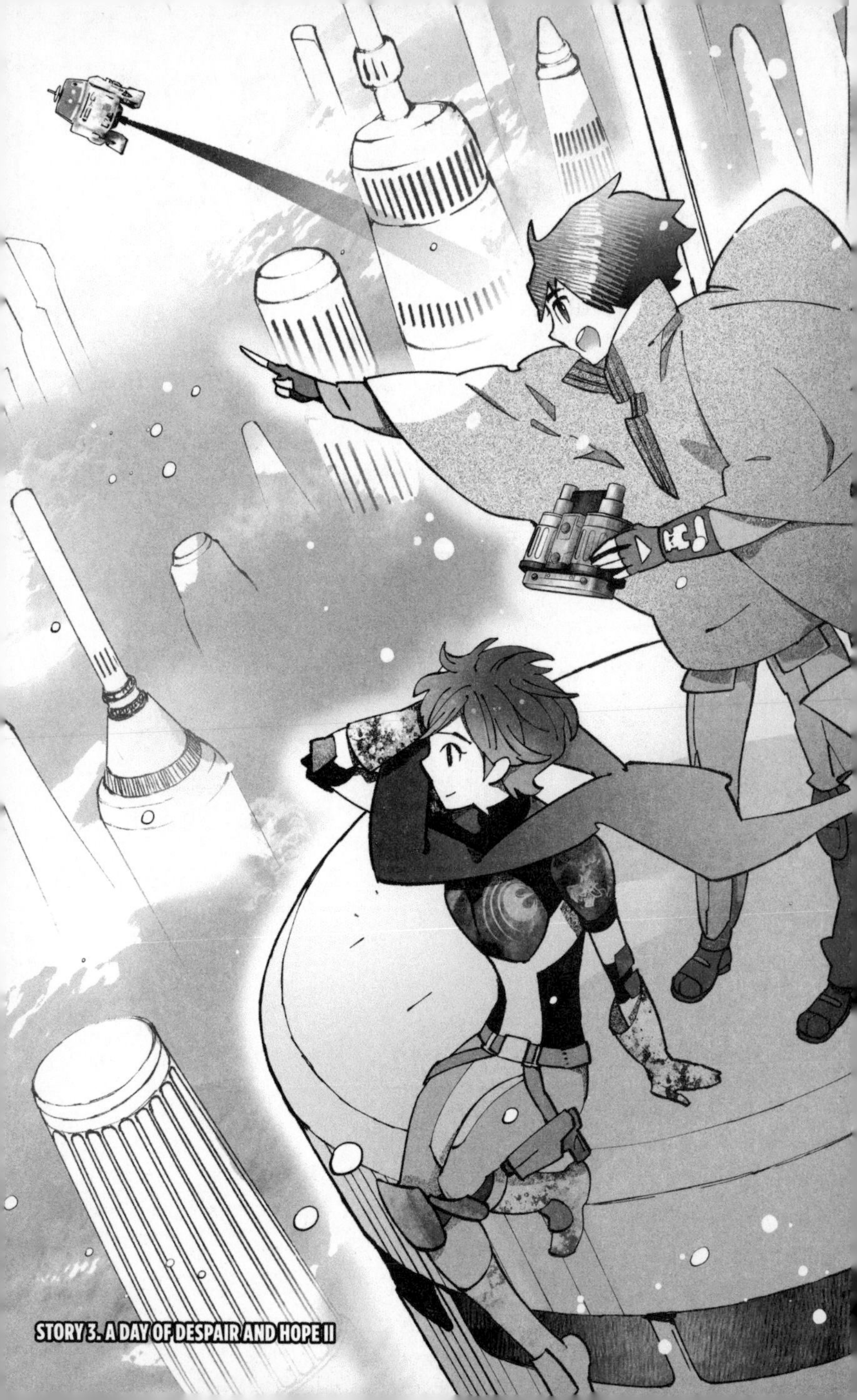
STORY 3. A DAY OF DESPAIR AND HOPE II

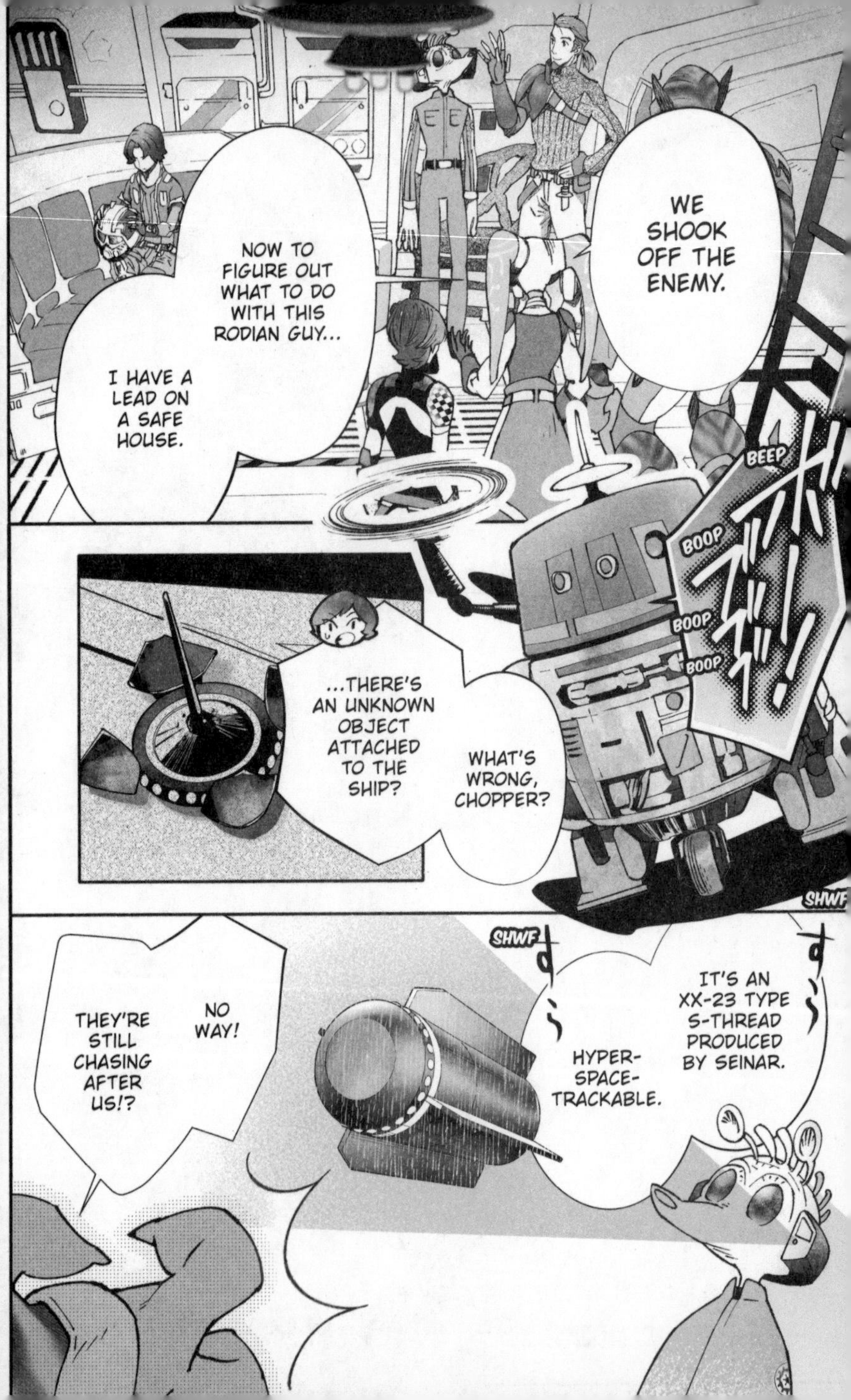
WE SHOOK OFF THE ENEMY.
NOW TO FIGURE OUT WHAT TO DO WITH THIS RODIAN GUY...
I HAVE A LEAD ON A SAFE HOUSE.
BEEP
BOOP
BOOP
BOOP
WHAT'S WRONG, CHOPPER?
...THERE'S AN UNKNOWN OBJECT ATTACHED TO THE SHIP?
SHWF
IT'S AN XX-23 TYPE S-THREAD PRODUCED BY SEINAR.
HYPER-SPACE-TRACKABLE.
SHWF
NO WAY!
THEY'RE STILL CHASING AFTER US!?

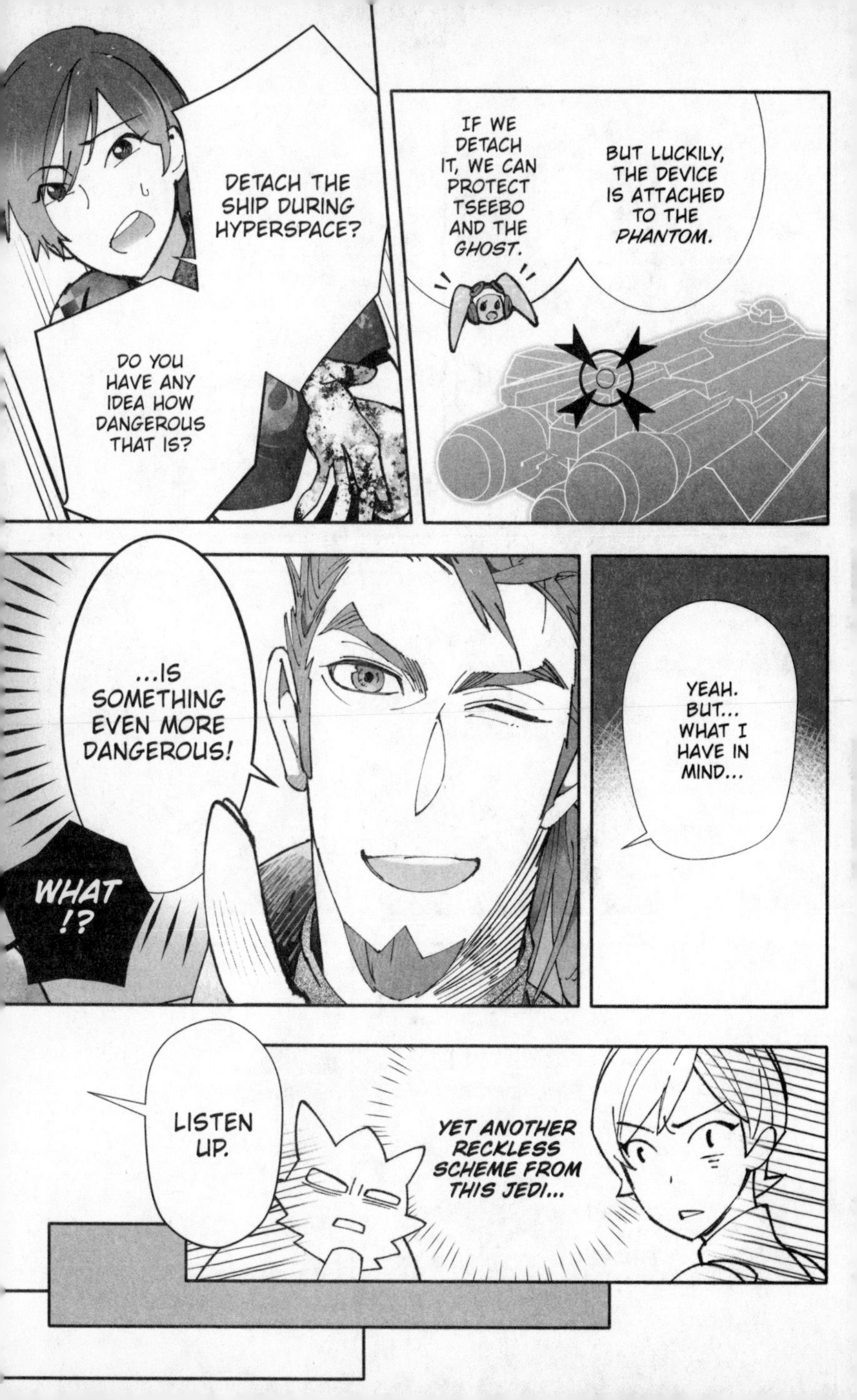
BUT LUCKILY, THE DEVICE IS ATTACHED TO THE *PHANTOM*.
IF WE DETACH IT, WE CAN PROTECT TSEEBO AND THE *GHOST*.
DETACH THE SHIP DURING HYPERSPACE?
DO YOU HAVE ANY IDEA HOW DANGEROUS THAT IS?
YEAH. BUT... WHAT I HAVE IN MIND...
...IS SOMETHING EVEN MORE DANGEROUS!
WHAT !?
YET ANOTHER RECKLESS SCHEME FROM THIS JEDI...
LISTEN UP.

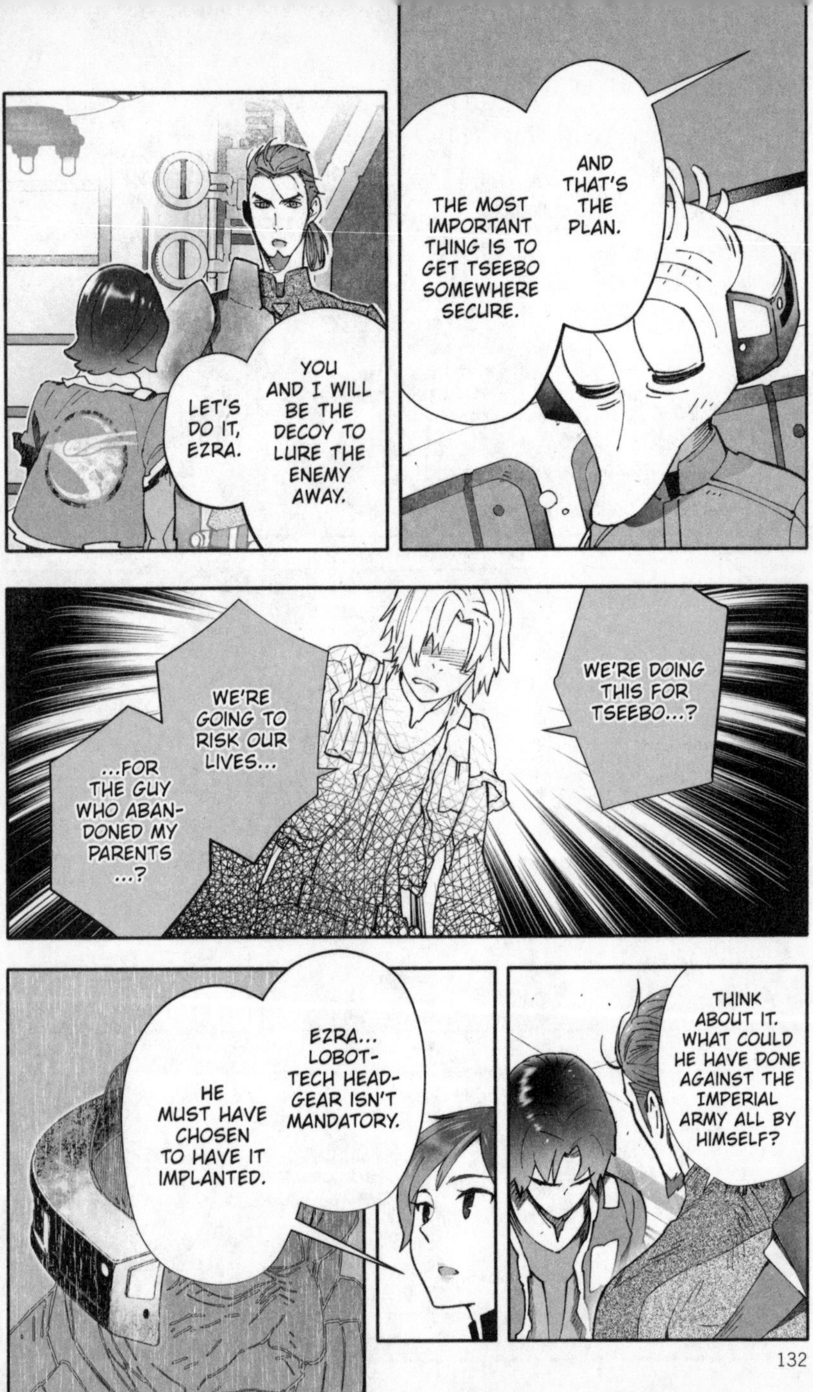
THE MOST IMPORTANT THING IS TO GET TSEEBO SOMEWHERE SECURE.
AND THAT'S THE PLAN.
YOU AND I WILL BE THE DECOY TO LURE THE ENEMY AWAY.
LET'S DO IT, EZRA.
WE'RE DOING THIS FOR TSEEBO...?
WE'RE GOING TO RISK OUR LIVES...
...FOR THE GUY WHO ABAN-DONED MY PARENTS ...?
THINK ABOUT IT. WHAT COULD HE HAVE DONE AGAINST THE IMPERIAL ARMY ALL BY HIMSELF?
EZRA... LOBOT-TECH HEAD-GEAR ISN'T MANDATORY.
HE MUST HAVE CHOSEN TO HAVE IT IMPLANTED.

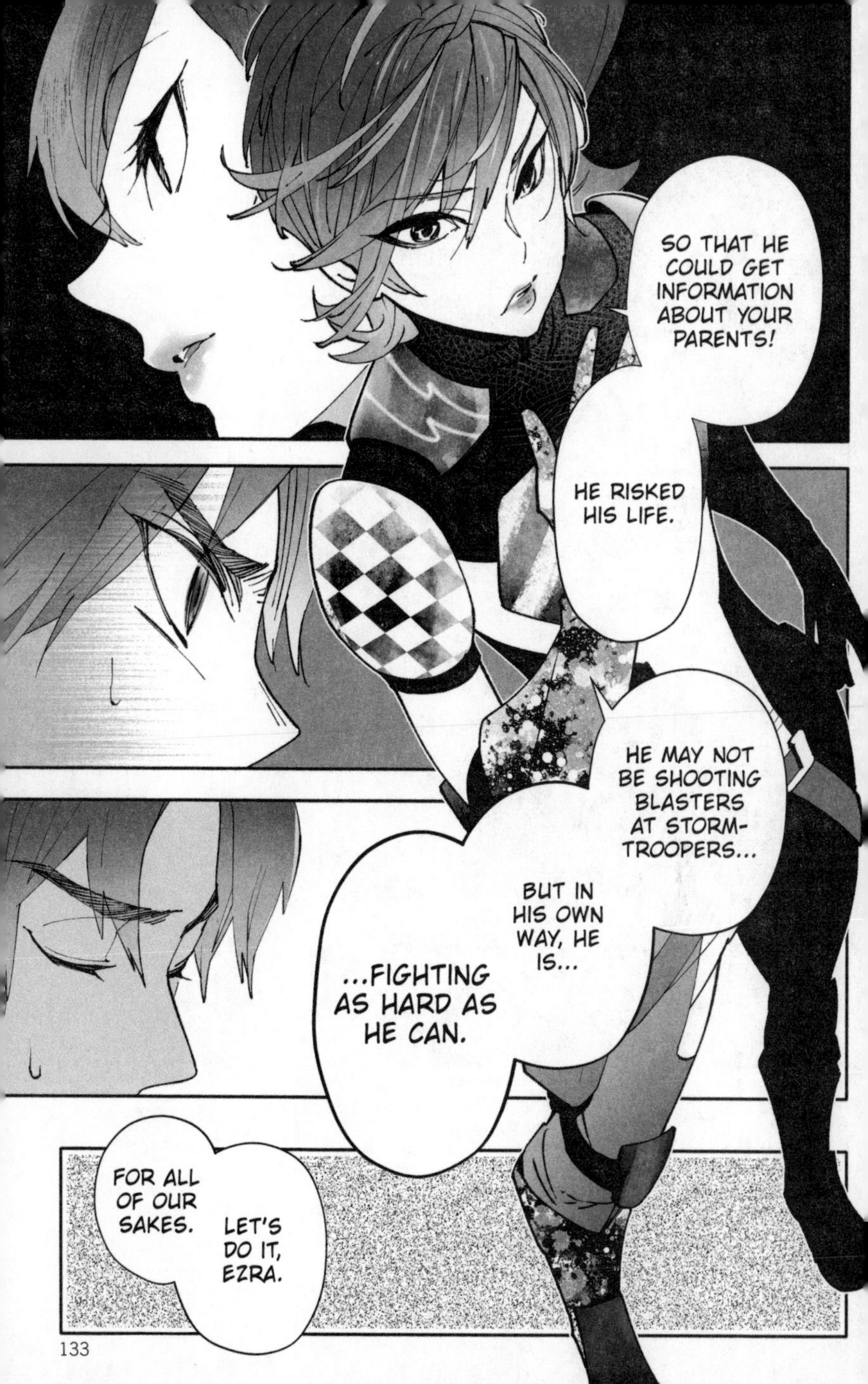
SO THAT HE COULD GET INFORMATION ABOUT YOUR PARENTS!
HE RISKED HIS LIFE.
HE MAY NOT BE SHOOTING BLASTERS AT STORM-TROOPERS...
BUT IN HIS OWN WAY, HE IS...
...FIGHTING AS HARD AS HE CAN.
FOR ALL OF OUR SAKES.
LET'S DO IT, EZRA.

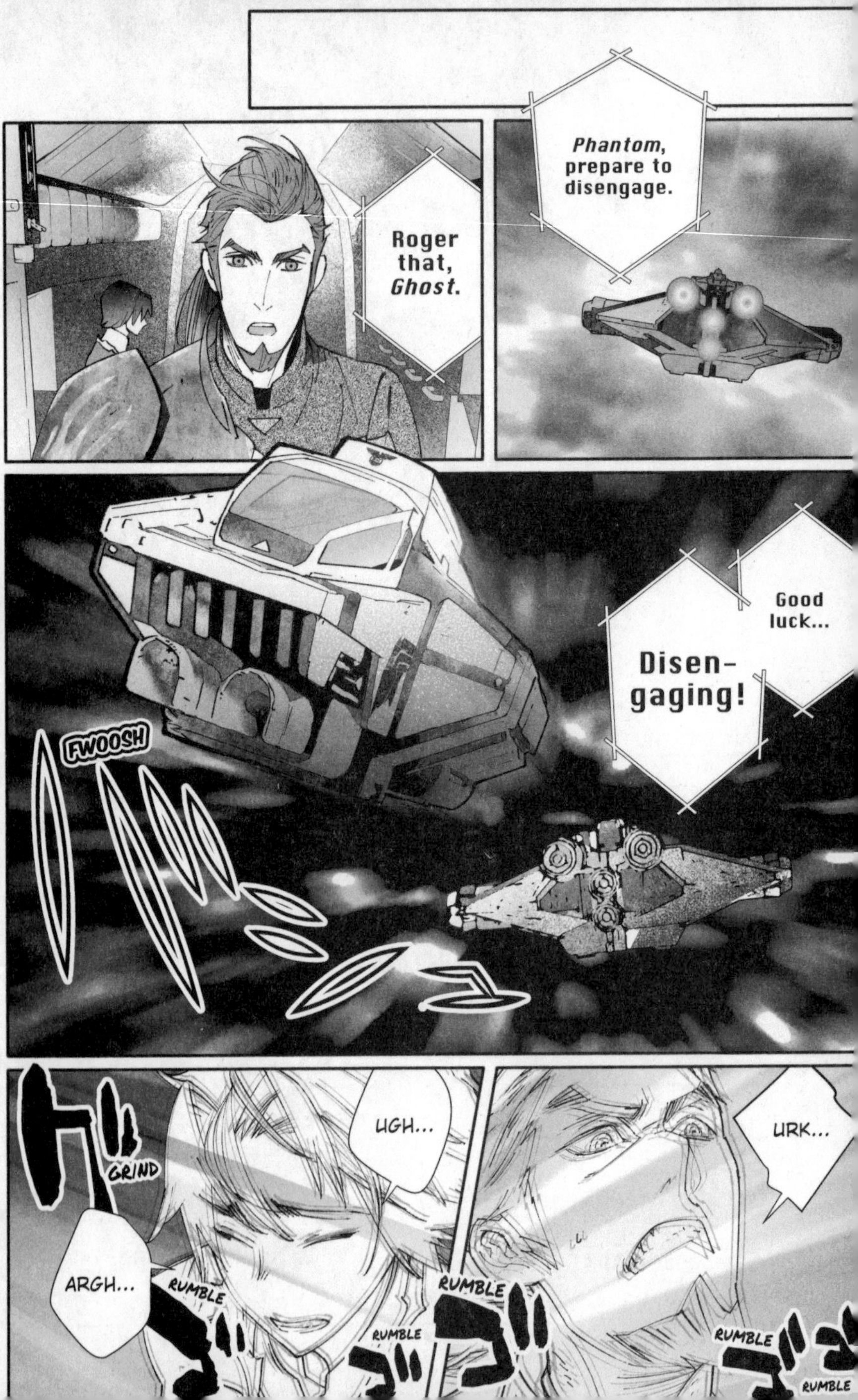

Phantom, prepare to disengage.
Roger that, *Ghost*.
Good luck...
Disengaging!
FWOOSH
URK...
RUMBLE
RUMBLE
UGH...
GRIND
ARGH...
RUMBLE
RUMBLE
RUMBLE

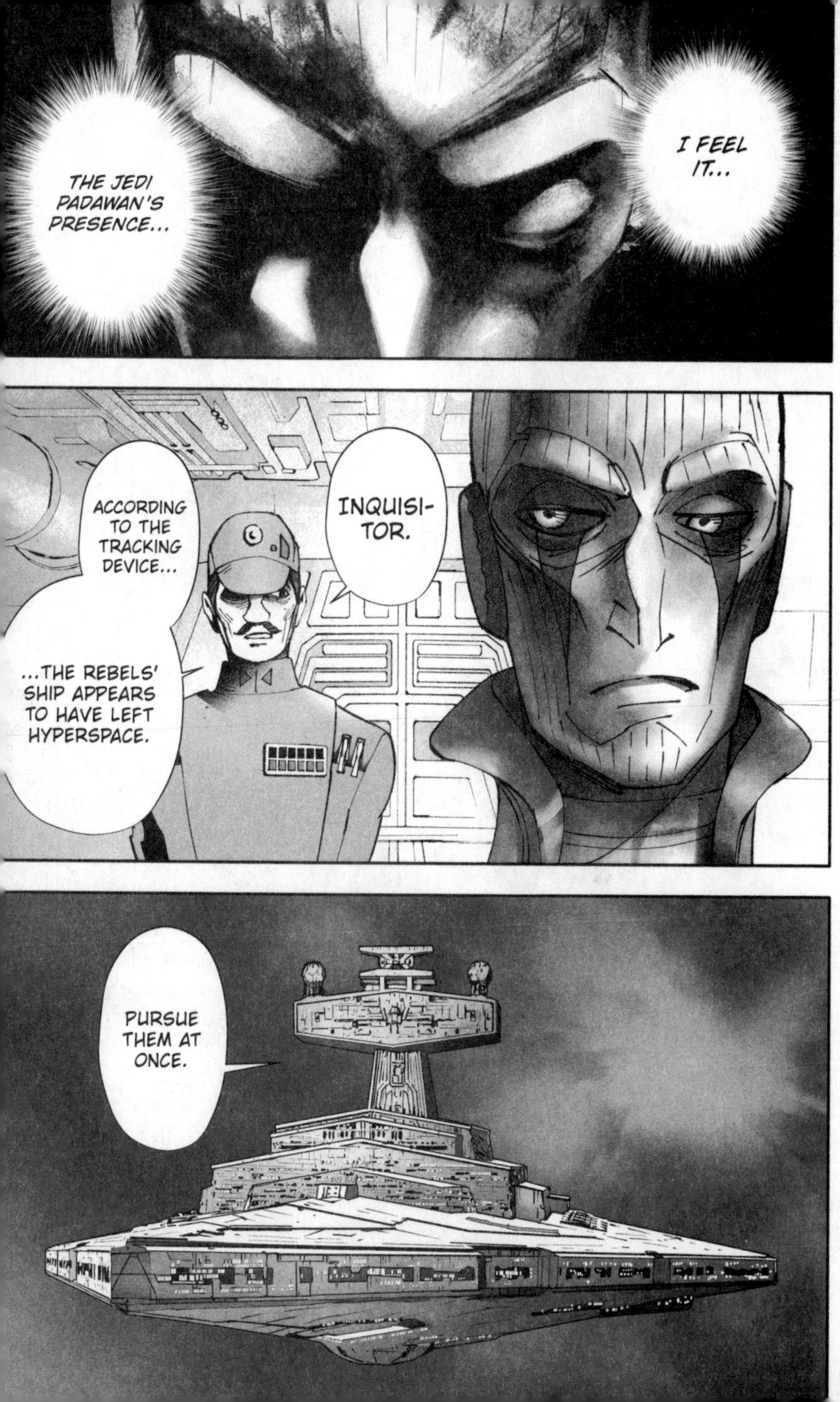
I FEEL IT...
THE JEDI PADAWAN'S PRESENCE...
INQUISITOR.
ACCORDING TO THE TRACKING DEVICE...
...THE REBELS' SHIP APPEARS TO HAVE LEFT HYPERSPACE.
PURSUE THEM AT ONCE.

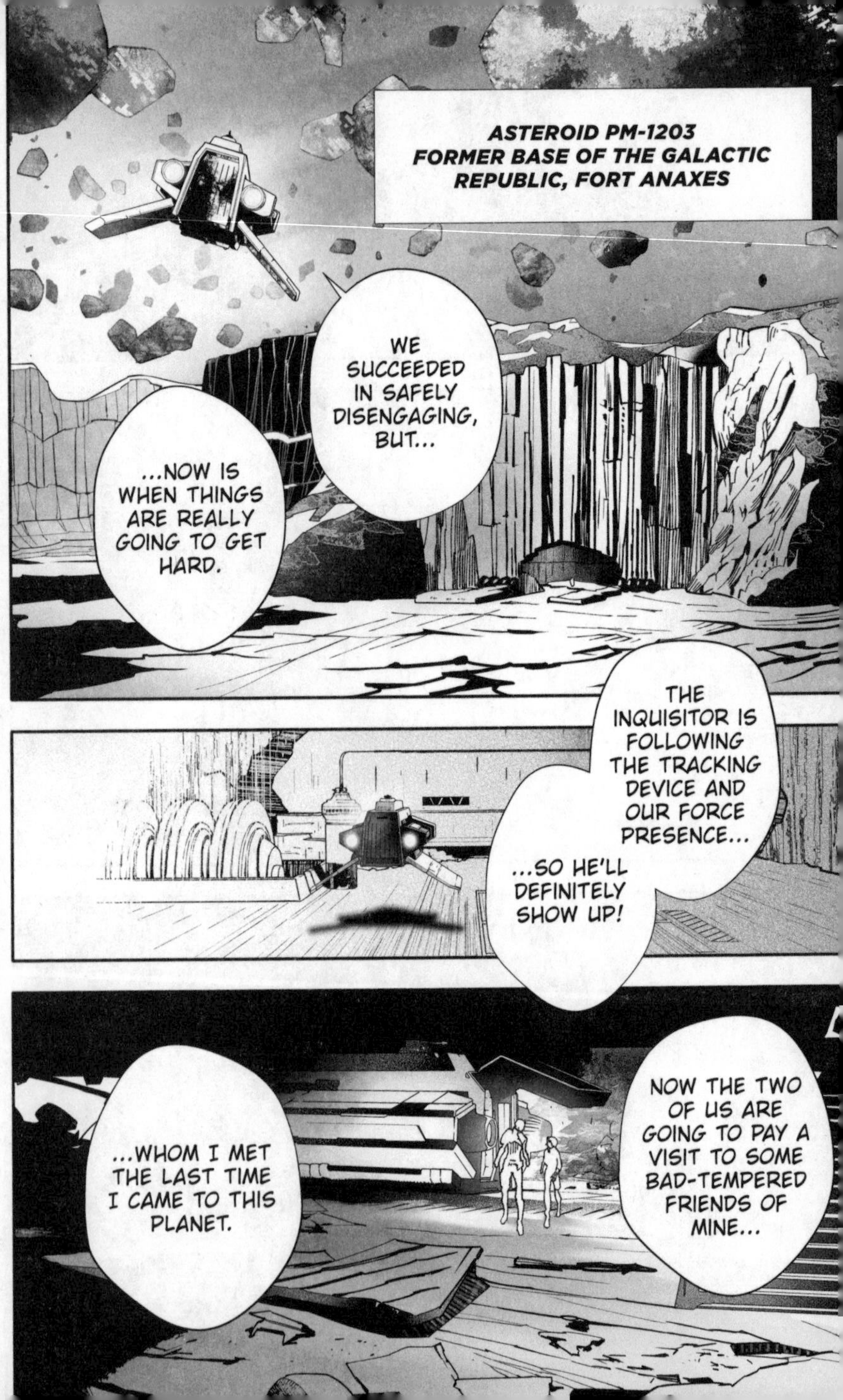
ASTEROID PM-1203 FORMER BASE OF THE GALACTIC REPUBLIC, FORT ANAXES
WE SUCCEEDED IN SAFELY DISENGAGING, BUT...
...NOW IS WHEN THINGS ARE REALLY GOING TO GET HARD.
THE INQUISITOR IS FOLLOWING THE TRACKING DEVICE AND OUR FORCE PRESENCE...
...SO HE'LL DEFINITELY SHOW UP!
NOW THE TWO OF US ARE GOING TO PAY A VISIT TO SOME BAD-TEMPERED FRIENDS OF MINE...
...WHOM I MET THE LAST TIME I CAME TO THIS PLANET.

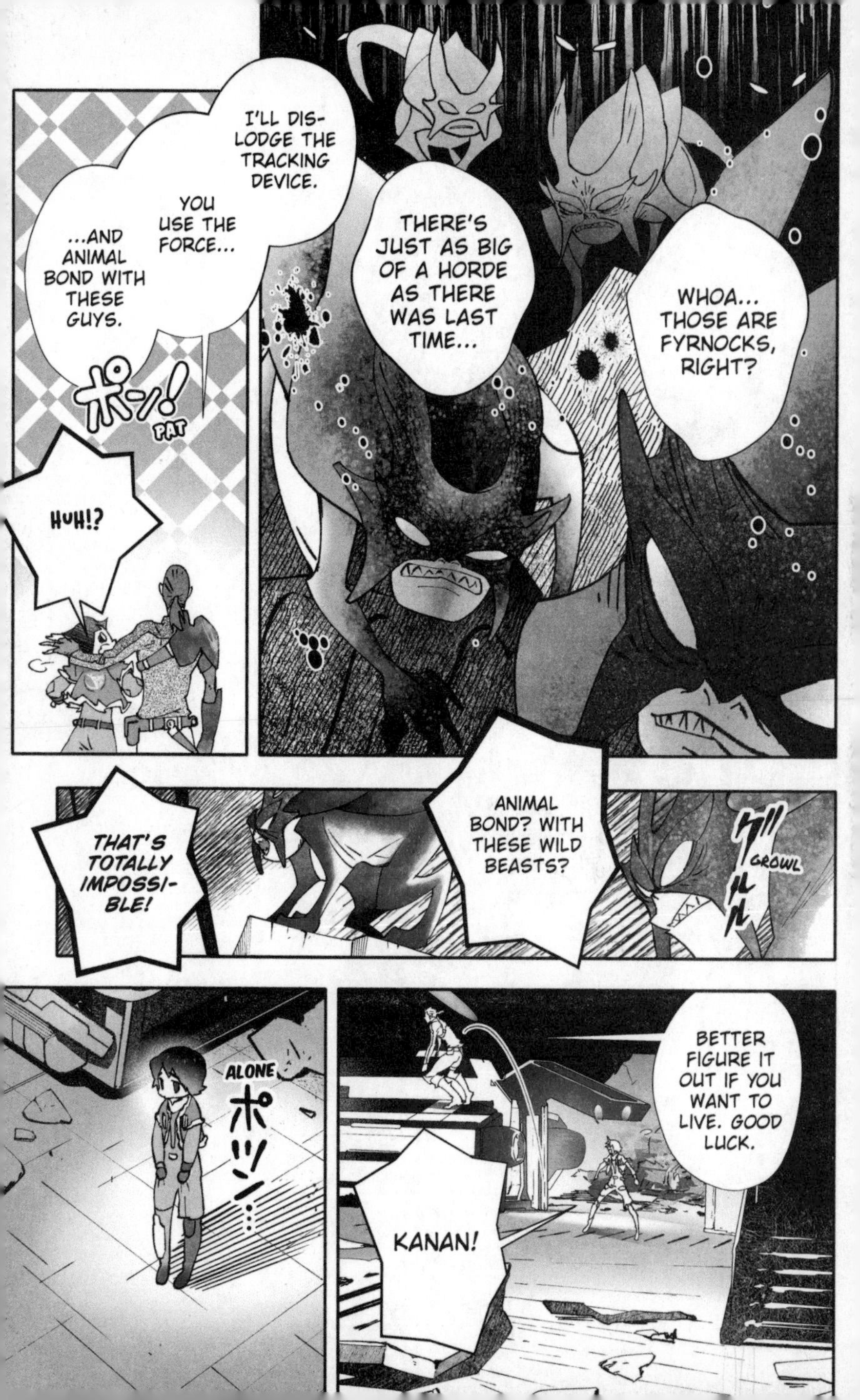
WHOA... THOSE ARE FYRNOCKS, RIGHT?
THERE'S JUST AS BIG OF A HORDE AS THERE WAS LAST TIME...
I'LL DIS-LODGE THE TRACKING DEVICE.
YOU USE THE FORCE...
...AND ANIMAL BOND WITH THESE GUYS.
PAT
HUH!?
GROWL
ANIMAL BOND? WITH THESE WILD BEASTS?
THAT'S TOTALLY IMPOSSI-BLE!
BETTER FIGURE IT OUT IF YOU WANT TO LIVE. GOOD LUCK.
KANAN!
ALONE

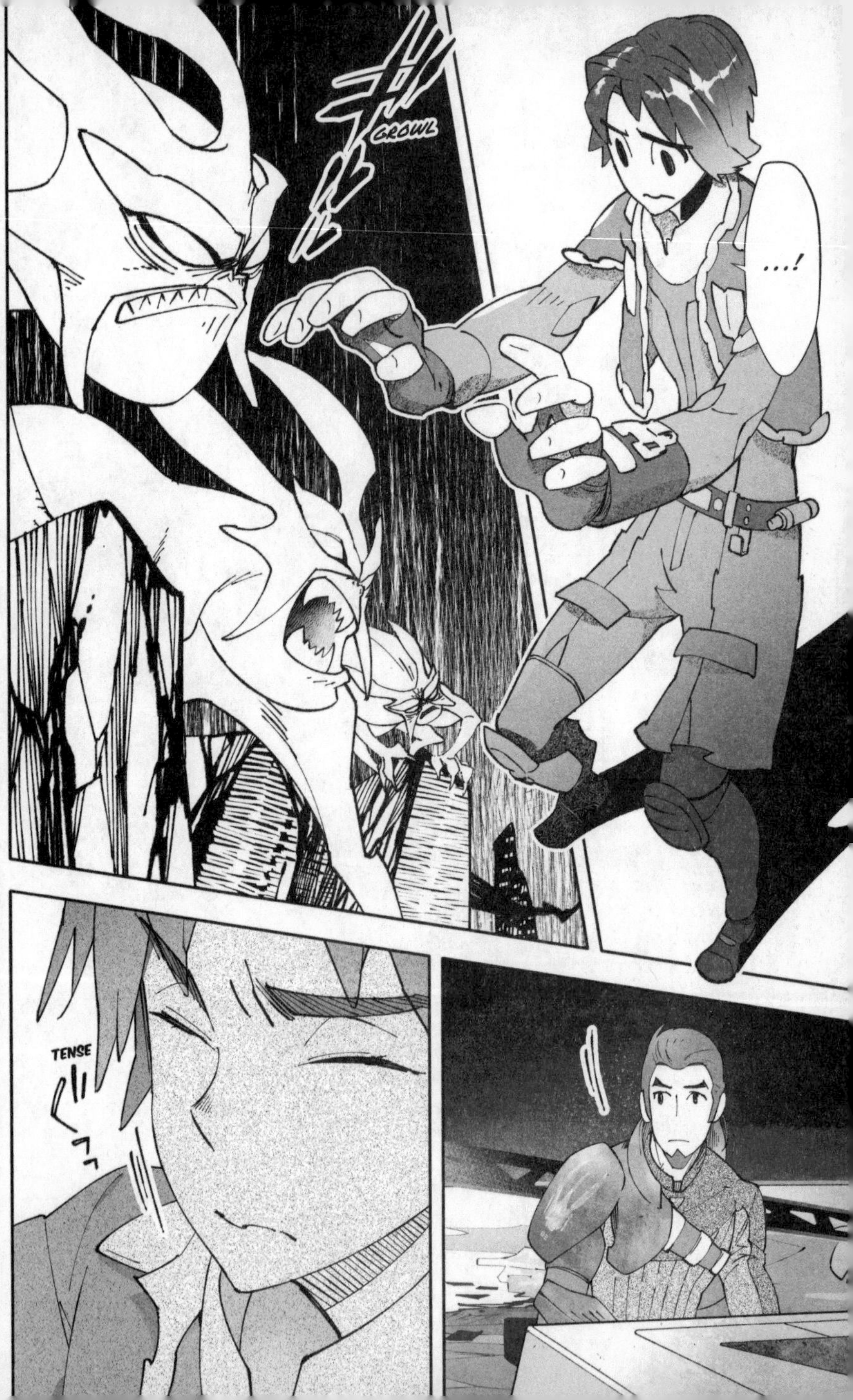
...!
GROWL
TENSE

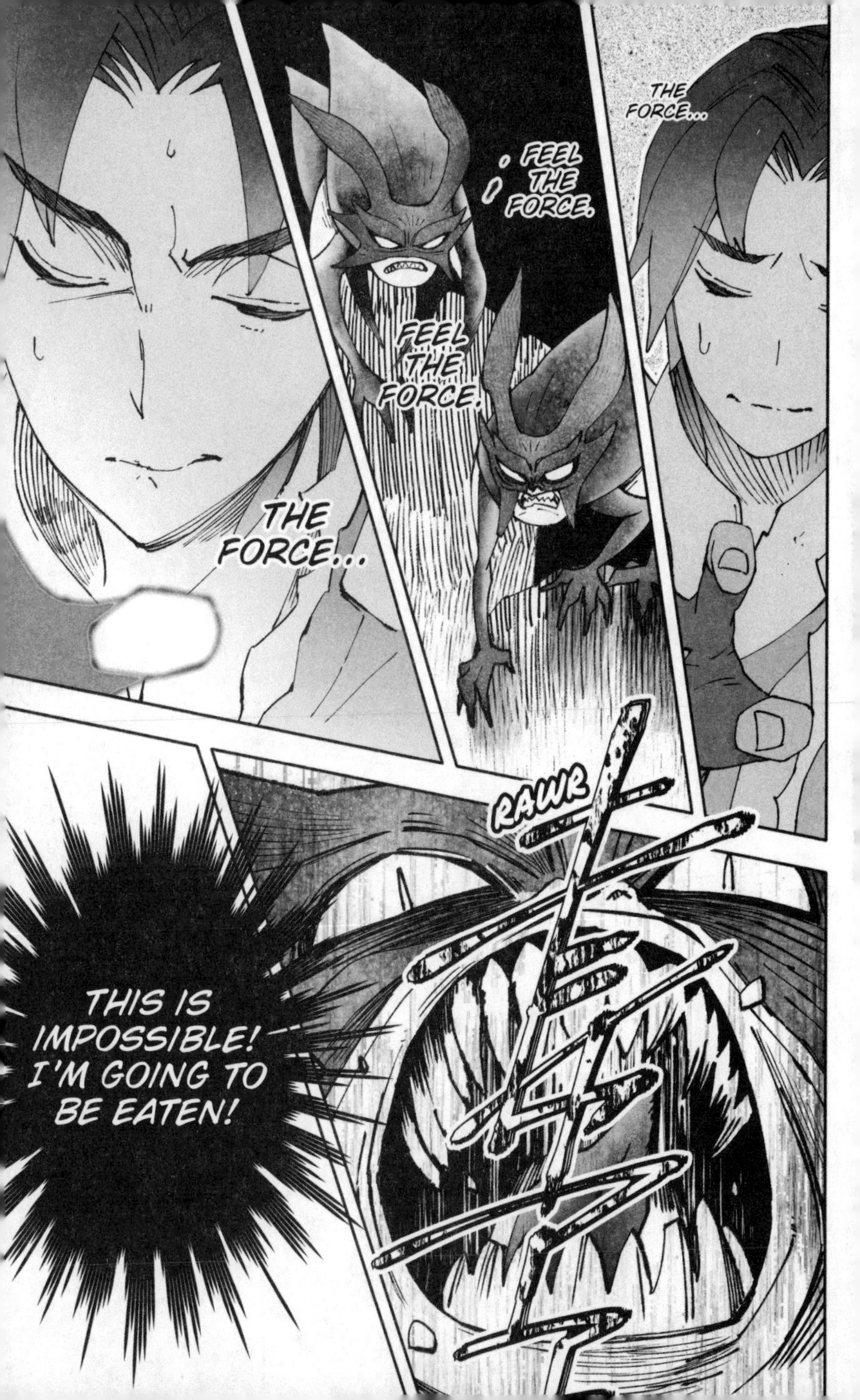
THE FORCE...
FEEL THE FORCE.
FEEL THE FORCE.
THE FORCE...
RAWR
THIS IS IMPOSSIBLE! I'M GOING TO BE EATEN!

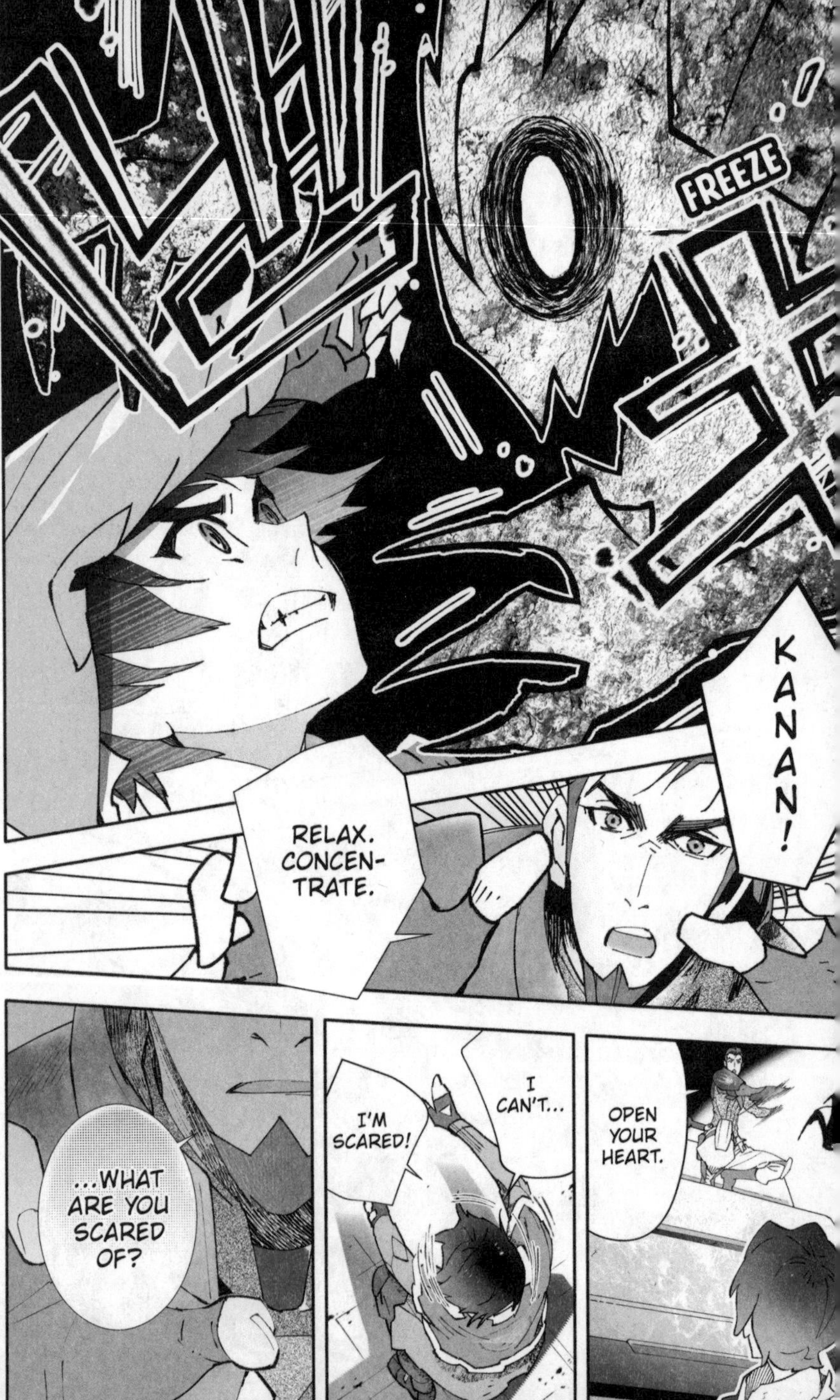
FREEZE
KANAN!
RELAX. CONCENTRATE.
OPEN YOUR HEART.
I CAN'T...
I'M SCARED!
...WHAT ARE YOU SCARED OF?

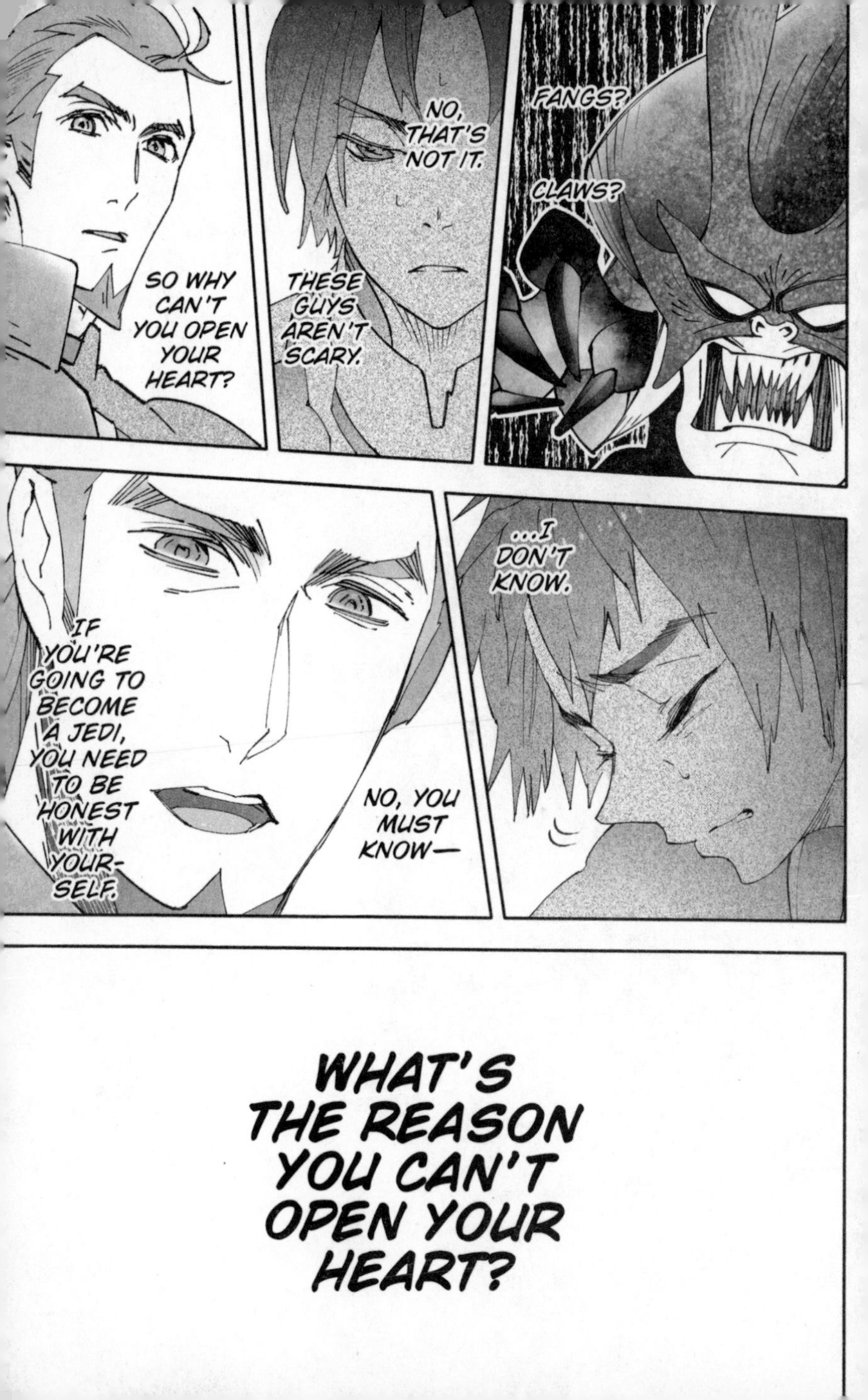
FANGS?
CLAWS?
NO, THAT'S NOT IT.
THESE GUYS AREN'T SCARY.
SO WHY CAN'T YOU OPEN YOUR HEART?
...I DON'T KNOW.
NO, YOU MUST KNOW—
IF YOU'RE GOING TO BECOME A JEDI, YOU NEED TO BE HONEST WITH YOUR-SELF.
WHAT'S THE REASON YOU CAN'T OPEN YOUR HEART?

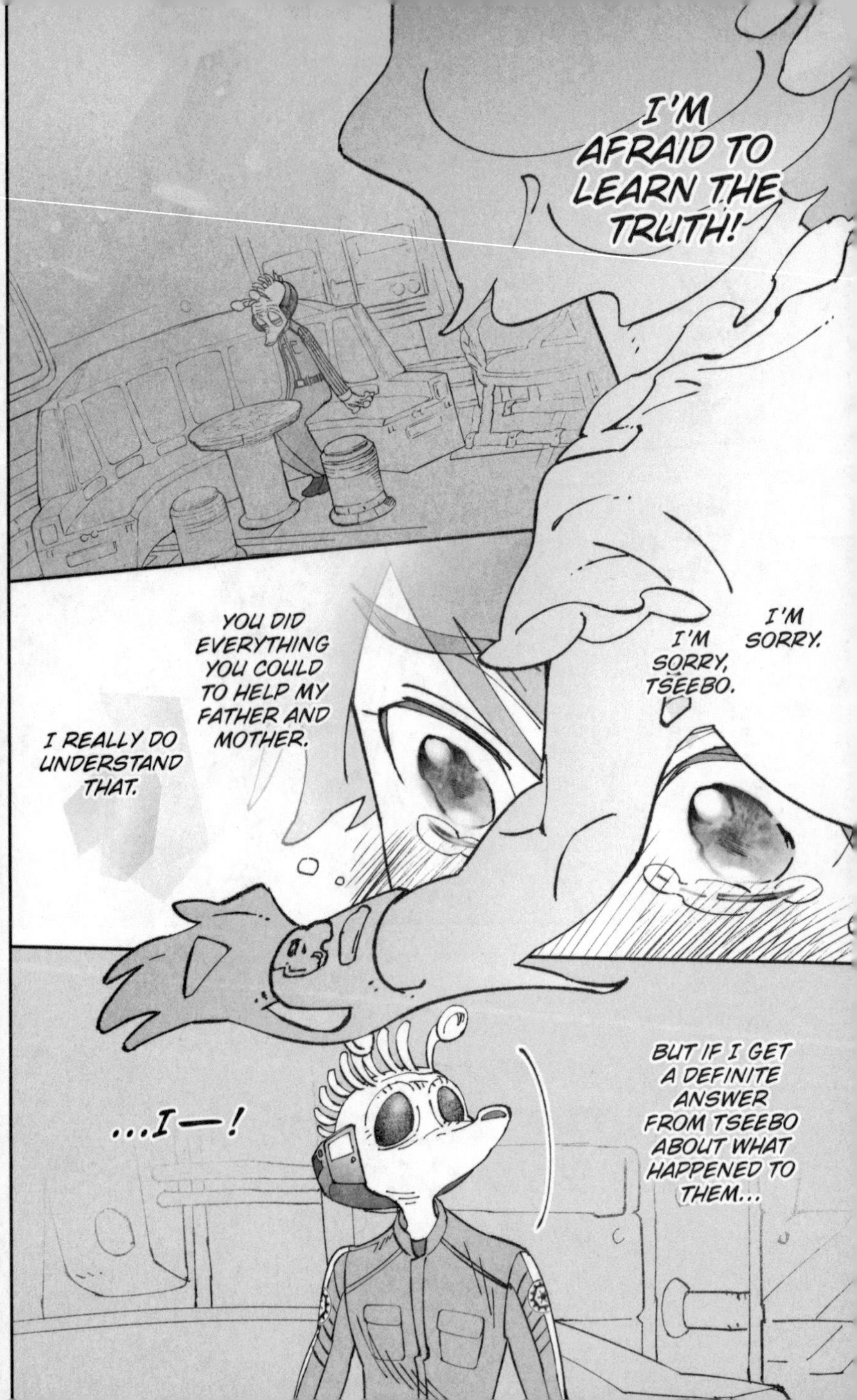
I'M AFRAID TO LEARN THE TRUTH!
I'M SORRY.
I'M SORRY, TSEEBO.
YOU DID EVERYTHING YOU COULD TO HELP MY FATHER AND MOTHER.
I REALLY DO UNDERSTAND THAT.
BUT IF I GET A DEFINITE ANSWER FROM TSEEBO ABOUT WHAT HAPPENED TO THEM...
...I—!

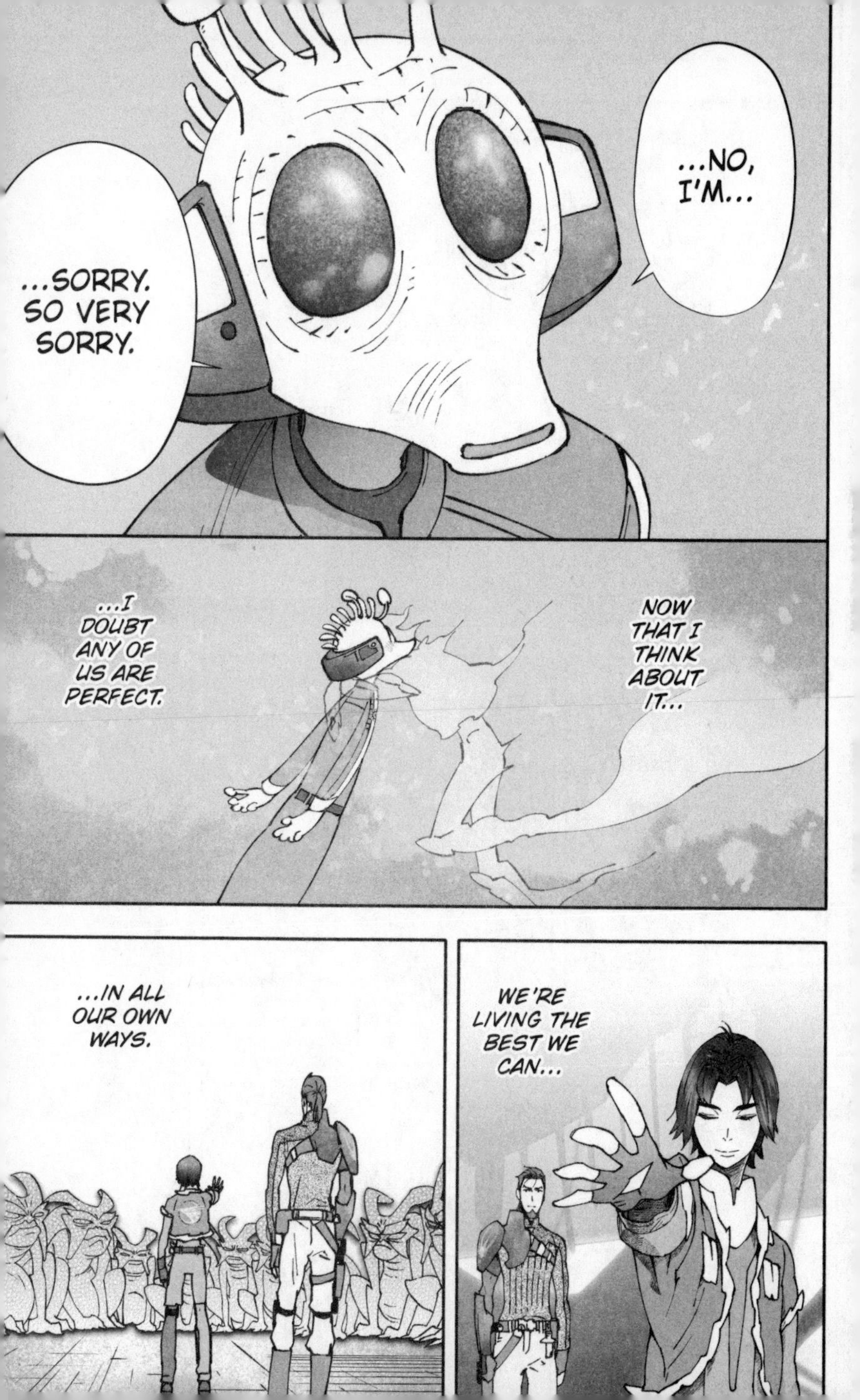
...NO, I'M...
...SORRY. SO VERY SORRY.
NOW THAT I THINK ABOUT IT...
...I DOUBT ANY OF US ARE PERFECT.
WE'RE LIVING THE BEST WE CAN...
...IN ALL OUR OWN WAYS.

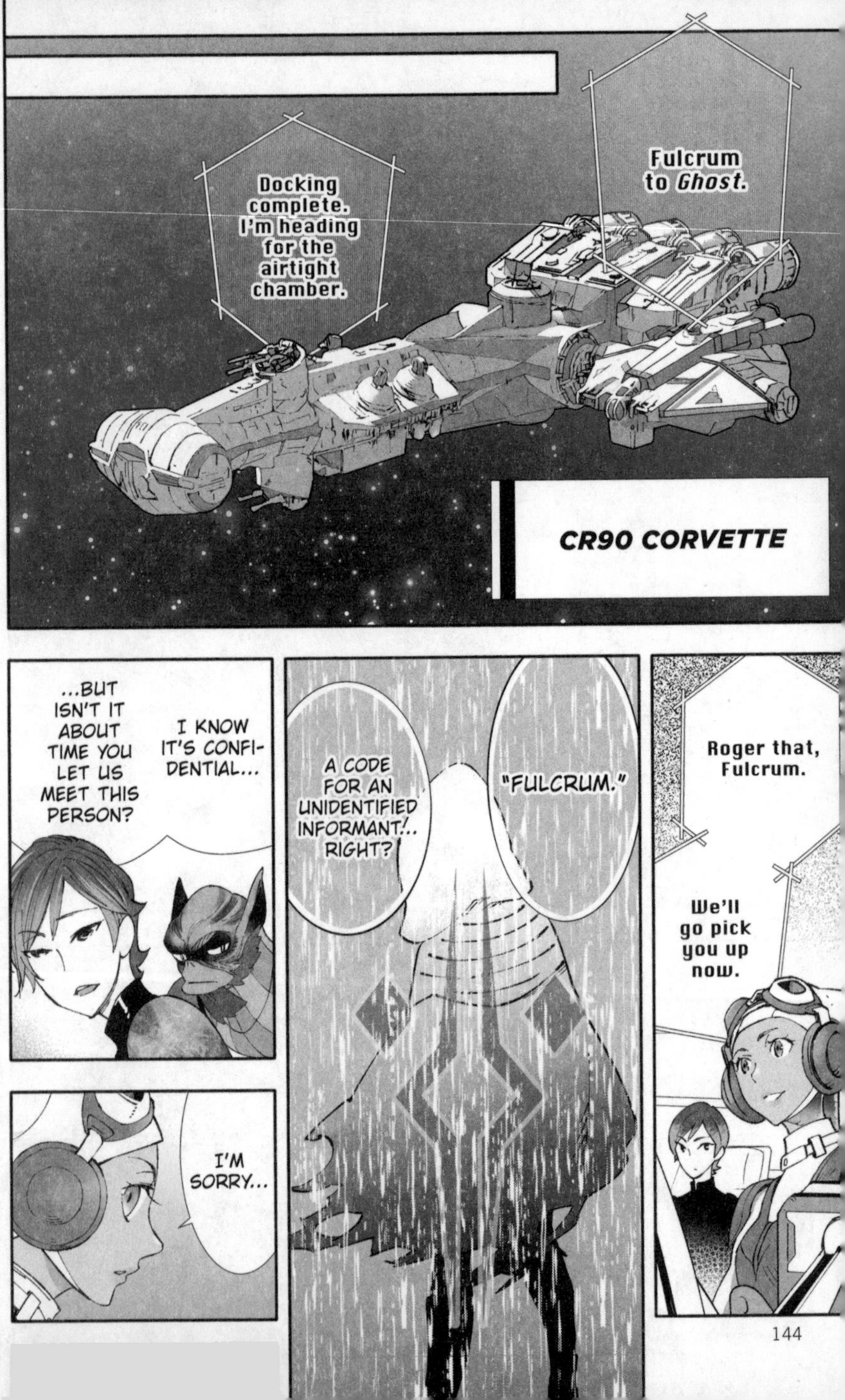
Fulcrum to Ghost.
Docking complete. I'm heading for the airtight chamber.
CR90 CORVETTE
Roger that, Fulcrum.
We'll go pick you up now.
"FULCRUM."
A CODE FOR AN UNIDENTIFIED INFORMANT!... RIGHT?
I KNOW IT'S CONFI-DENTIAL...
...BUT ISN'T IT ABOUT TIME YOU LET US MEET THIS PERSON?
I'M SORRY...

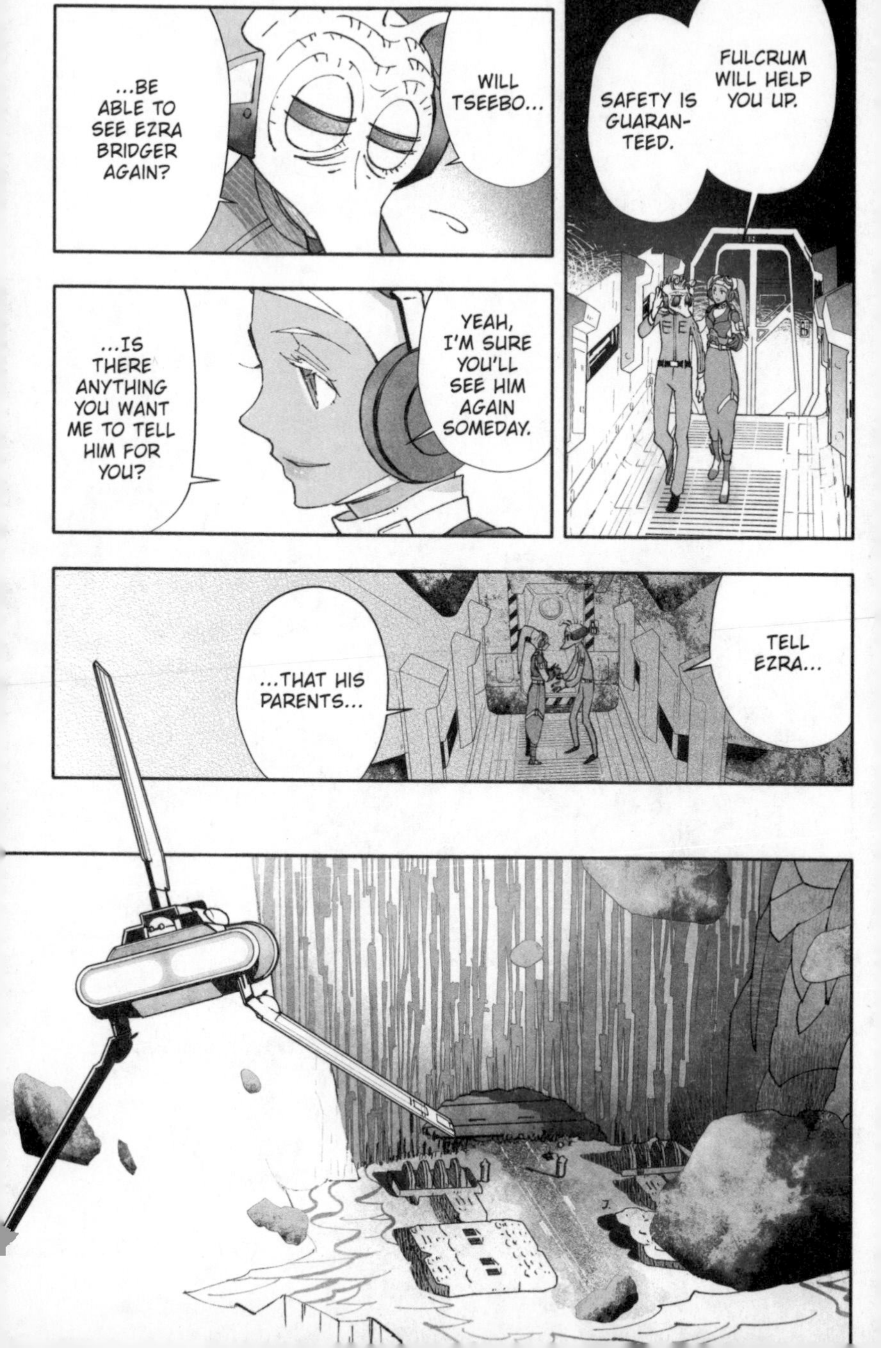
FULCRUM WILL HELP YOU UP.
SAFETY IS GUARAN-TEED.
WILL TSEEBO...
...BE ABLE TO SEE EZRA BRIDGER AGAIN?
YEAH, I'M SURE YOU'LL SEE HIM AGAIN SOMEDAY.
...IS THERE ANYTHING YOU WANT ME TO TELL HIM FOR YOU?
TELL EZRA...
...THAT HIS PARENTS...

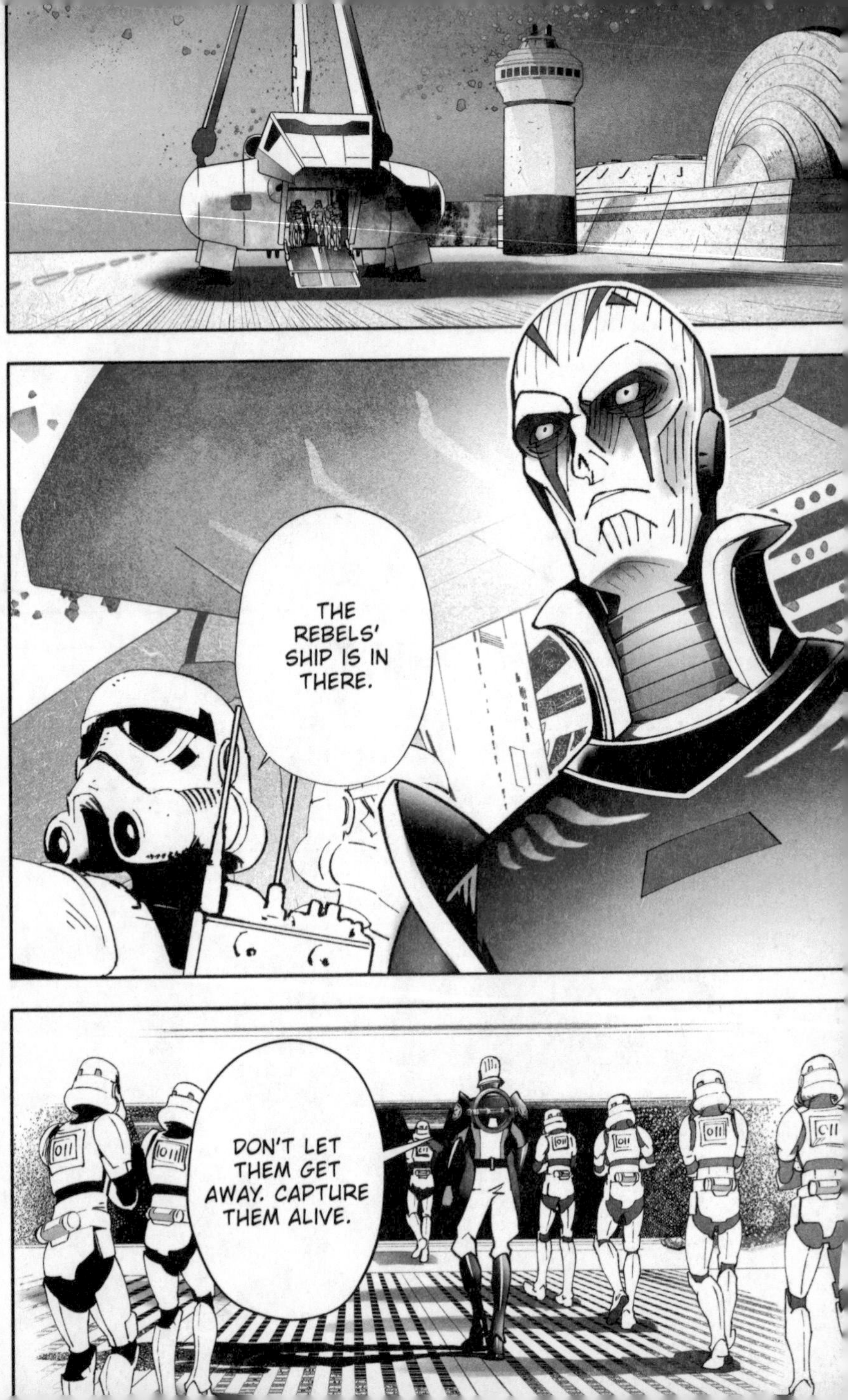
THE REBELS' SHIP IS IN THERE.
DON'T LET THEM GET AWAY. CAPTURE THEM ALIVE.

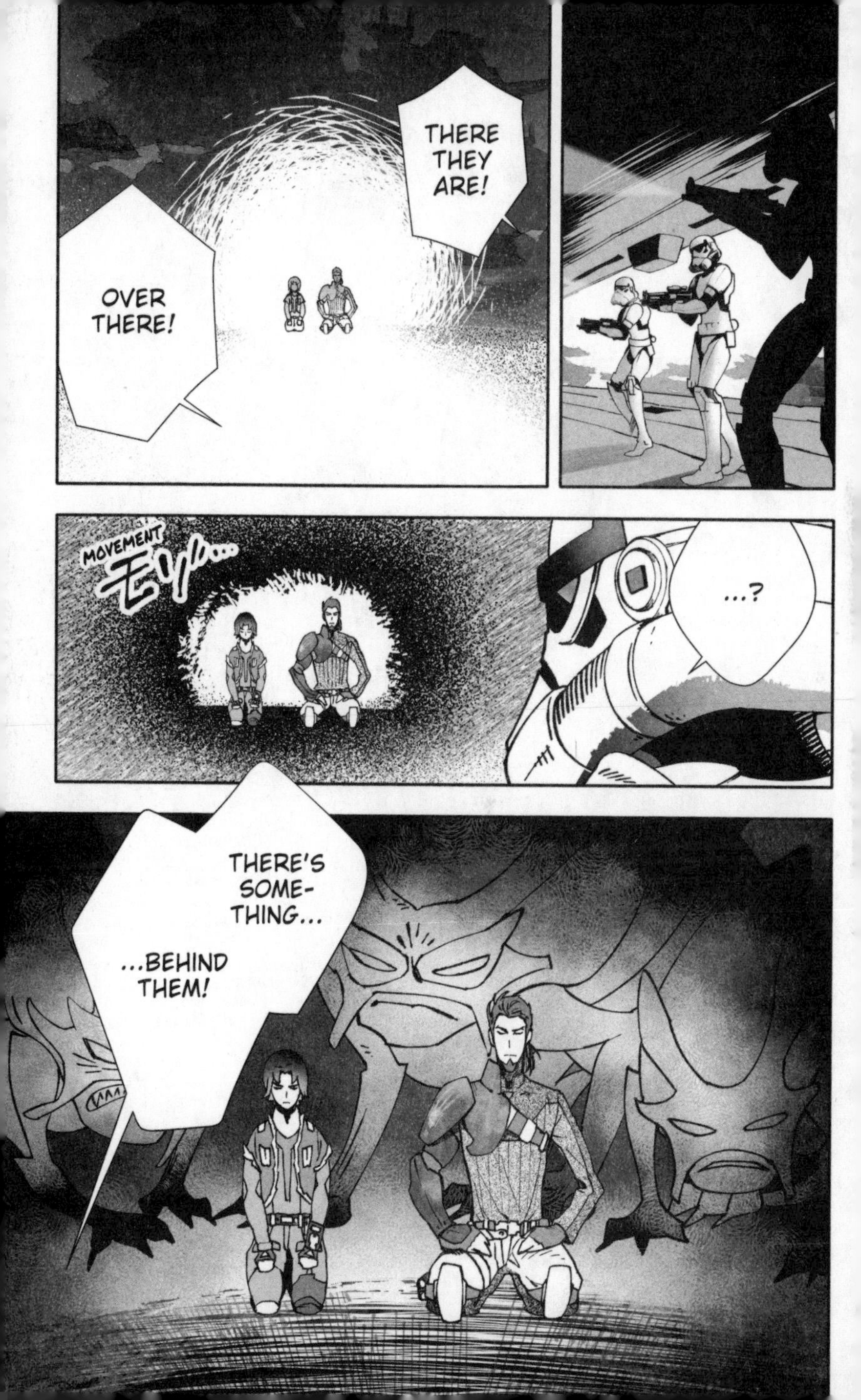
THERE THEY ARE!
OVER THERE!
...?
MOVEMENT
THERE'S SOME-THING...
...BEHIND THEM!

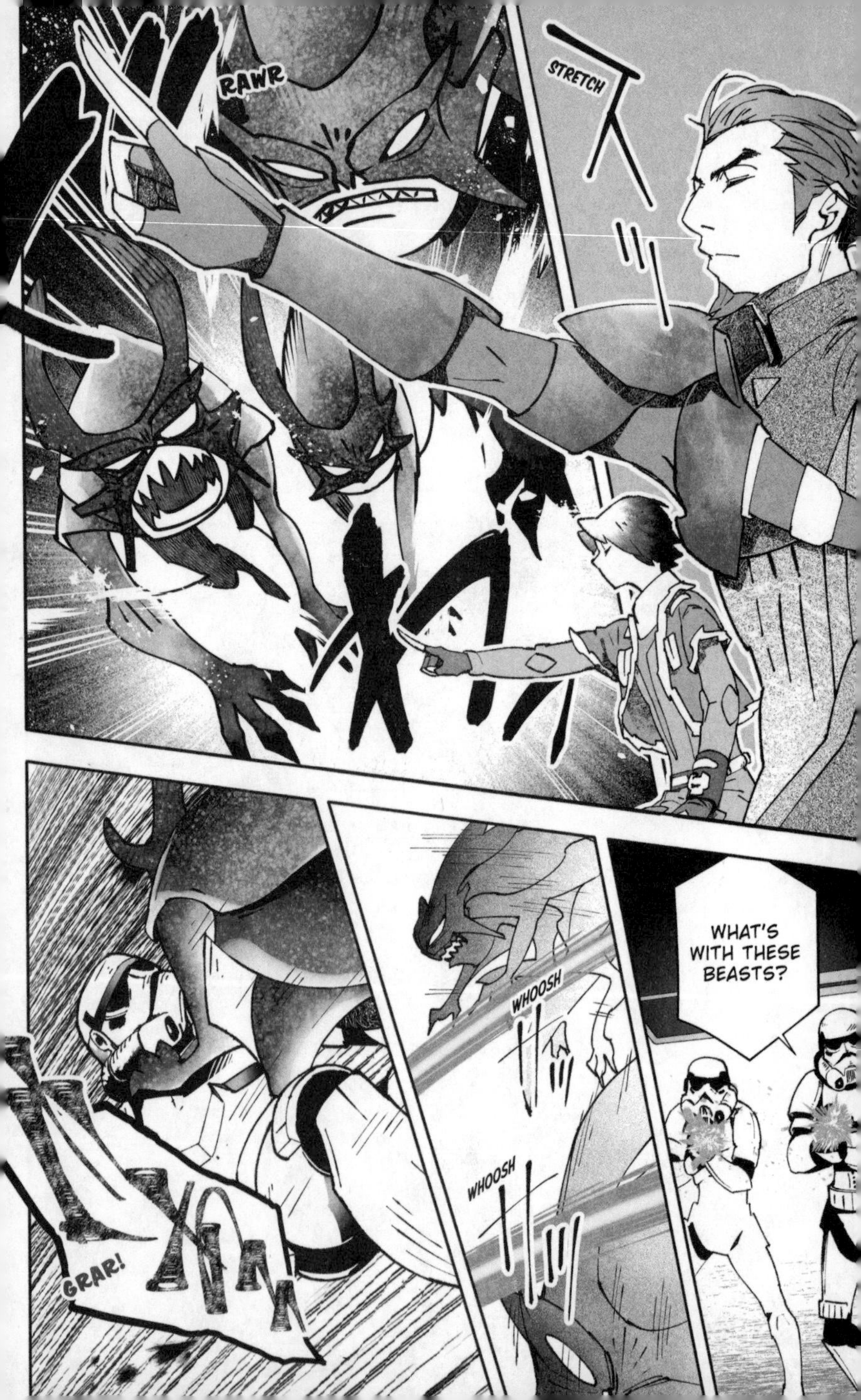
STRETCH
RAWR
WHAT'S WITH THESE BEASTS?
WHOOSH
WHOOSH
GRAR!

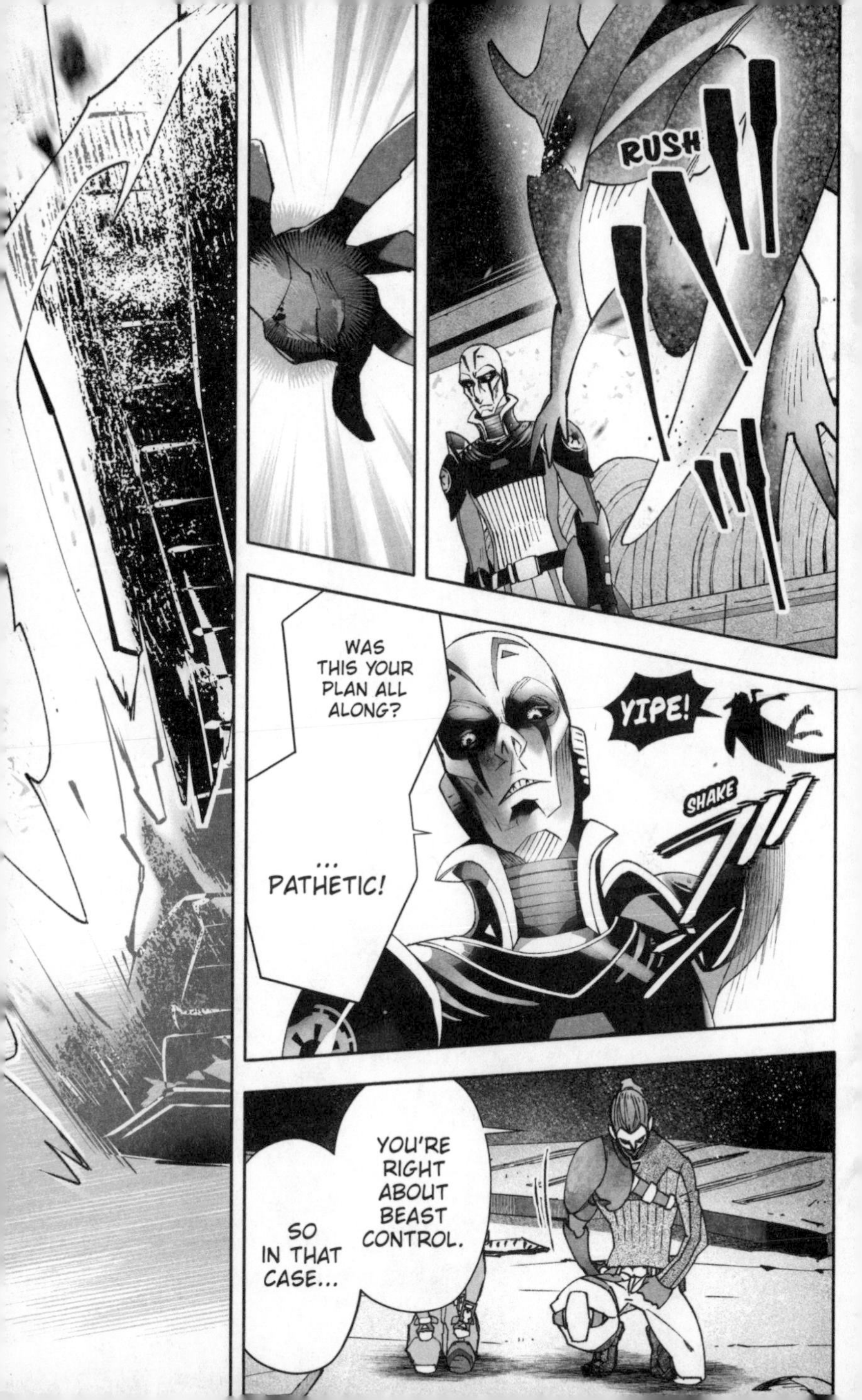
RUSH
YIPE!
WAS THIS YOUR PLAN ALL ALONG?
SHAKE
... PATHETIC!
YOU'RE RIGHT ABOUT BEAST CONTROL.
SO IN THAT CASE...

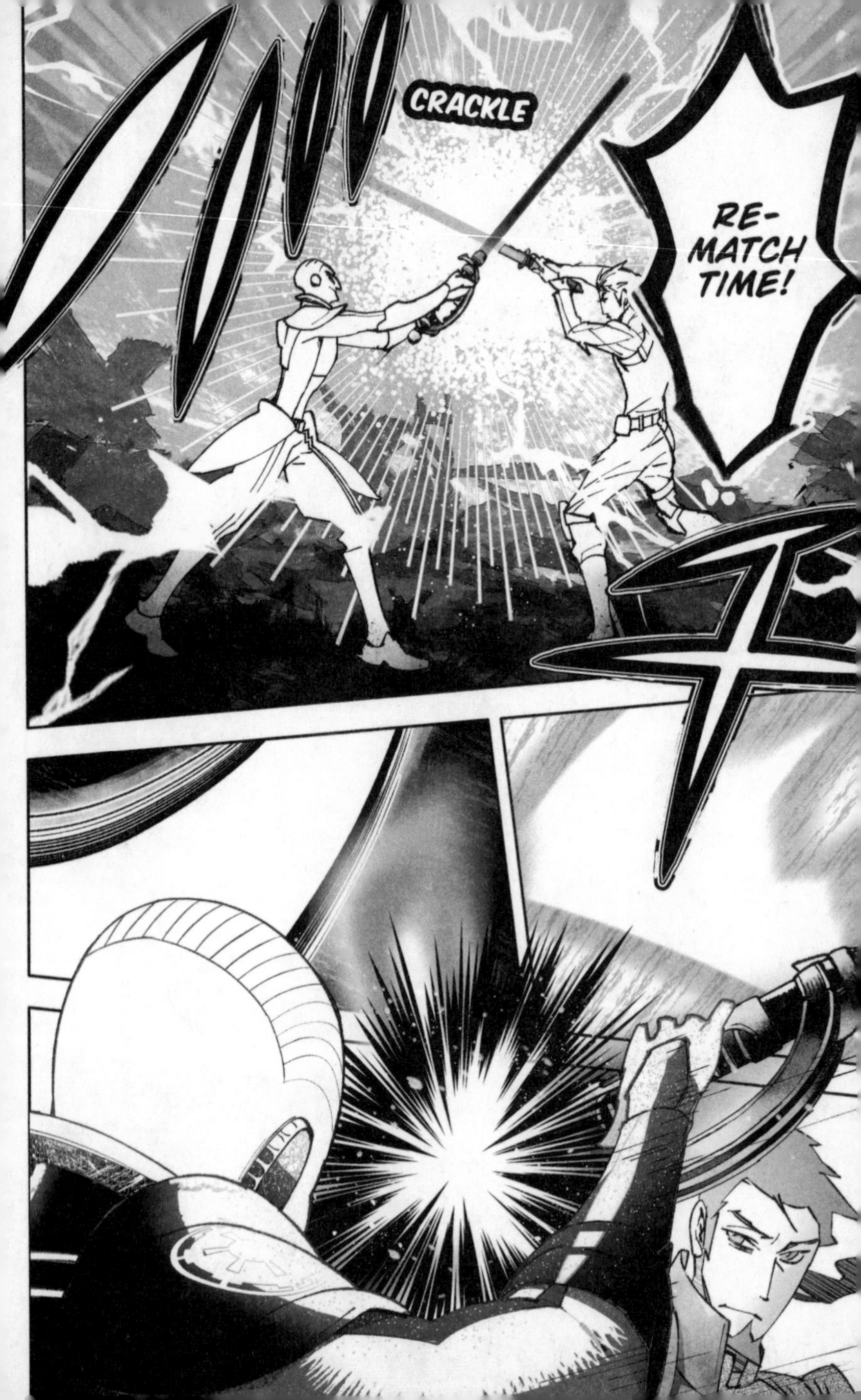
RE-MATCH TIME!
CRACKLE

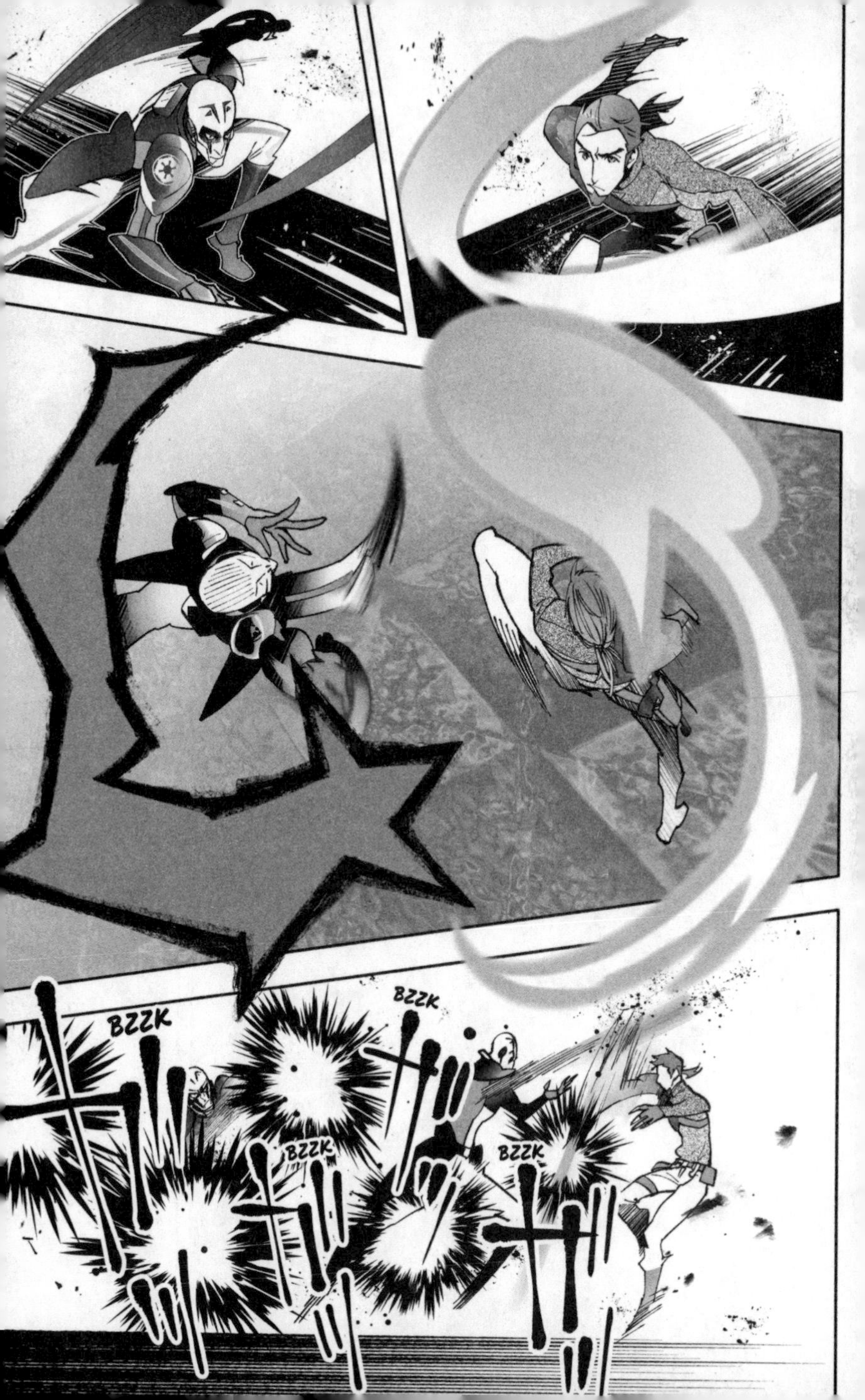
BZZK
BZZK
BZZK
BZZK

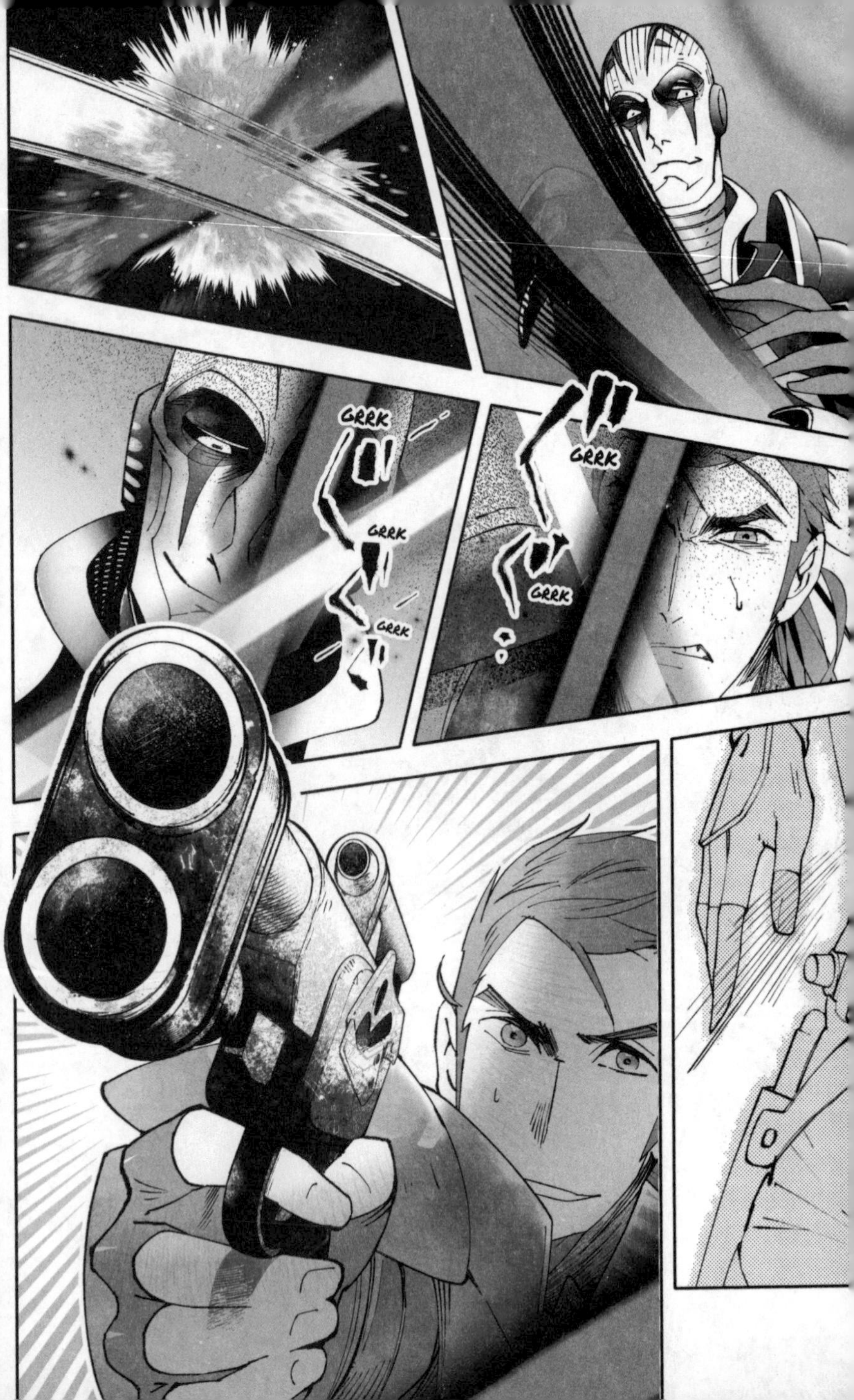
GRRK
GRRK
GRRK
GRRK
GRRK

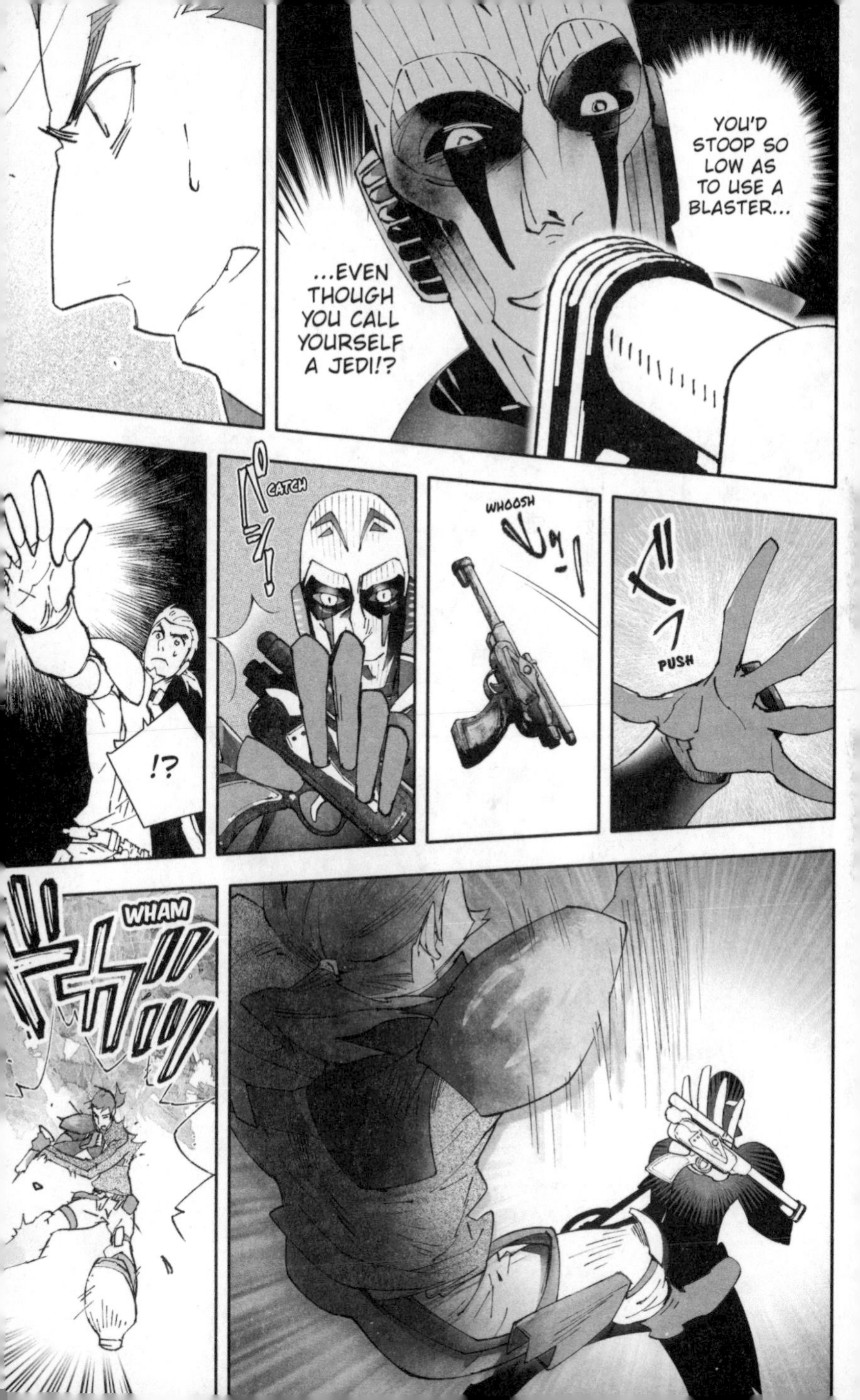
YOU'D STOOP SO LOW AS TO USE A BLASTER...
...EVEN THOUGH YOU CALL YOURSELF A JEDI!?
PUSH
WHOOSH
CATCH
!?
WHAM

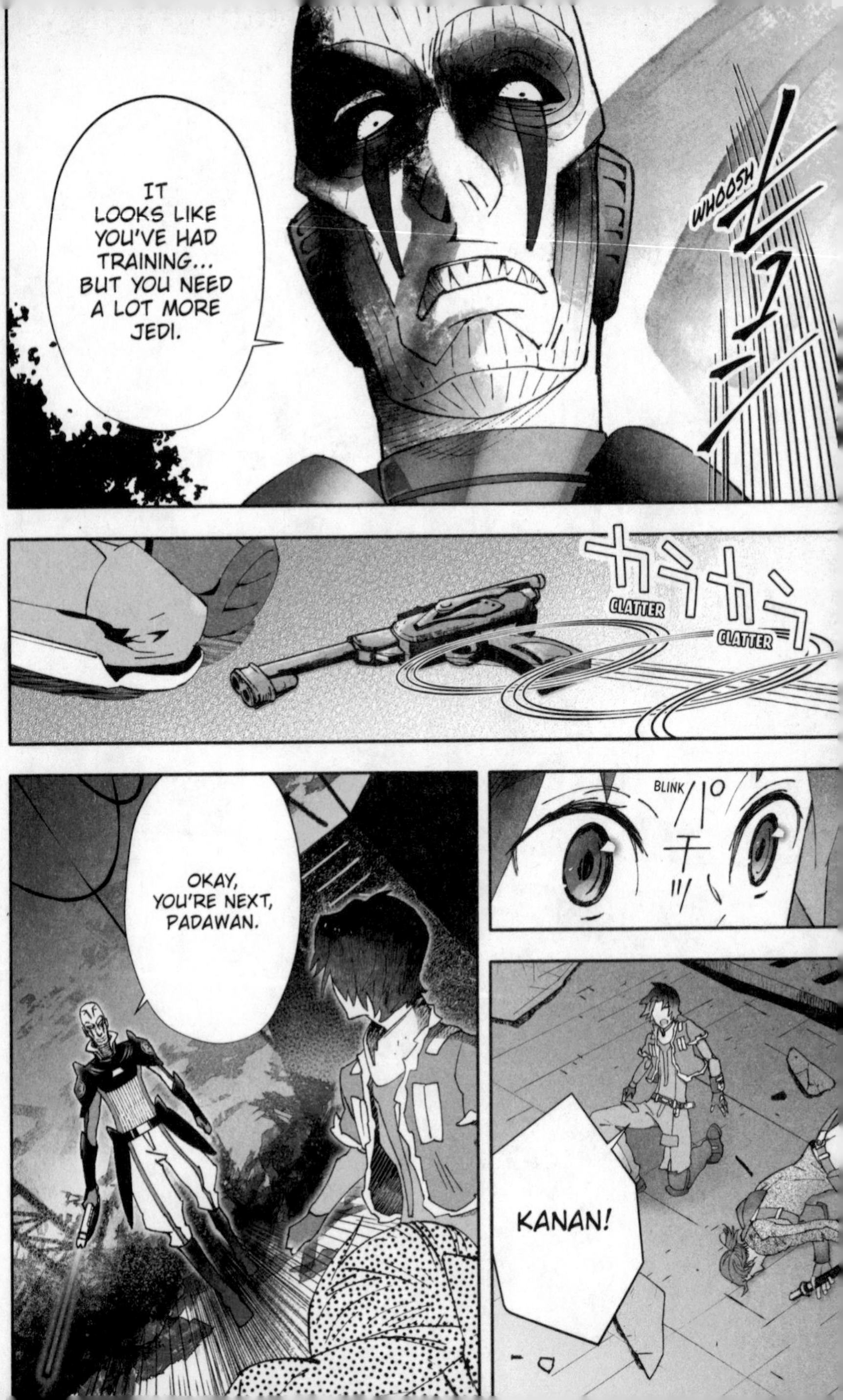
WHOOSH
IT LOOKS LIKE YOU'VE HAD TRAINING... BUT YOU NEED A LOT MORE JEDI.
CLATTER
CLATTER
BLINK
KANAN!
OKAY, YOU'RE NEXT, PADAWAN.

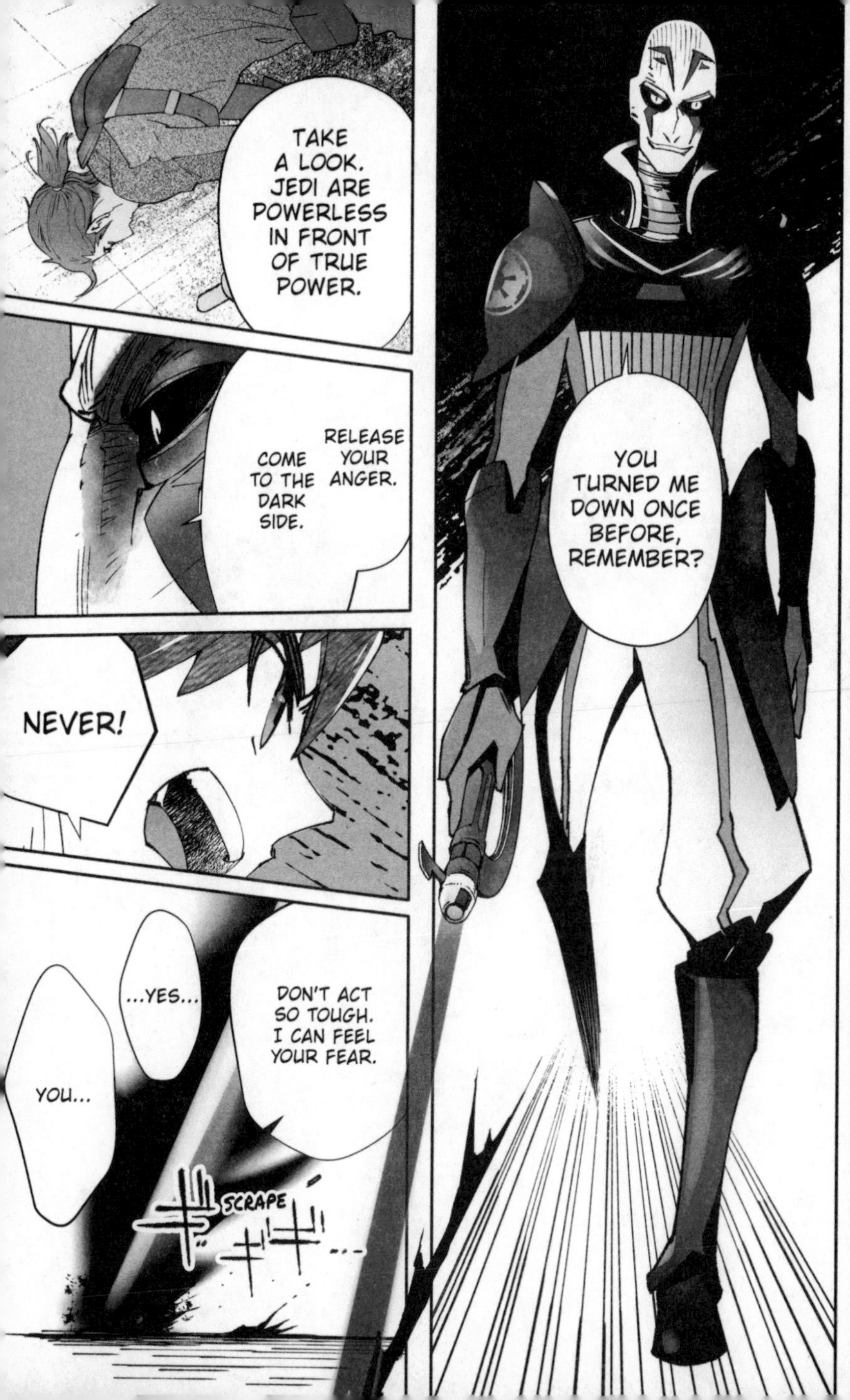
YOU TURNED ME DOWN ONCE BEFORE, REMEMBER?
TAKE A LOOK. JEDI ARE POWERLESS IN FRONT OF TRUE POWER.
RELEASE YOUR ANGER.
COME TO THE DARK SIDE.
NEVER!
DON'T ACT SO TOUGH. I CAN FEEL YOUR FEAR.
...YES...
YOU...
SCRAPE

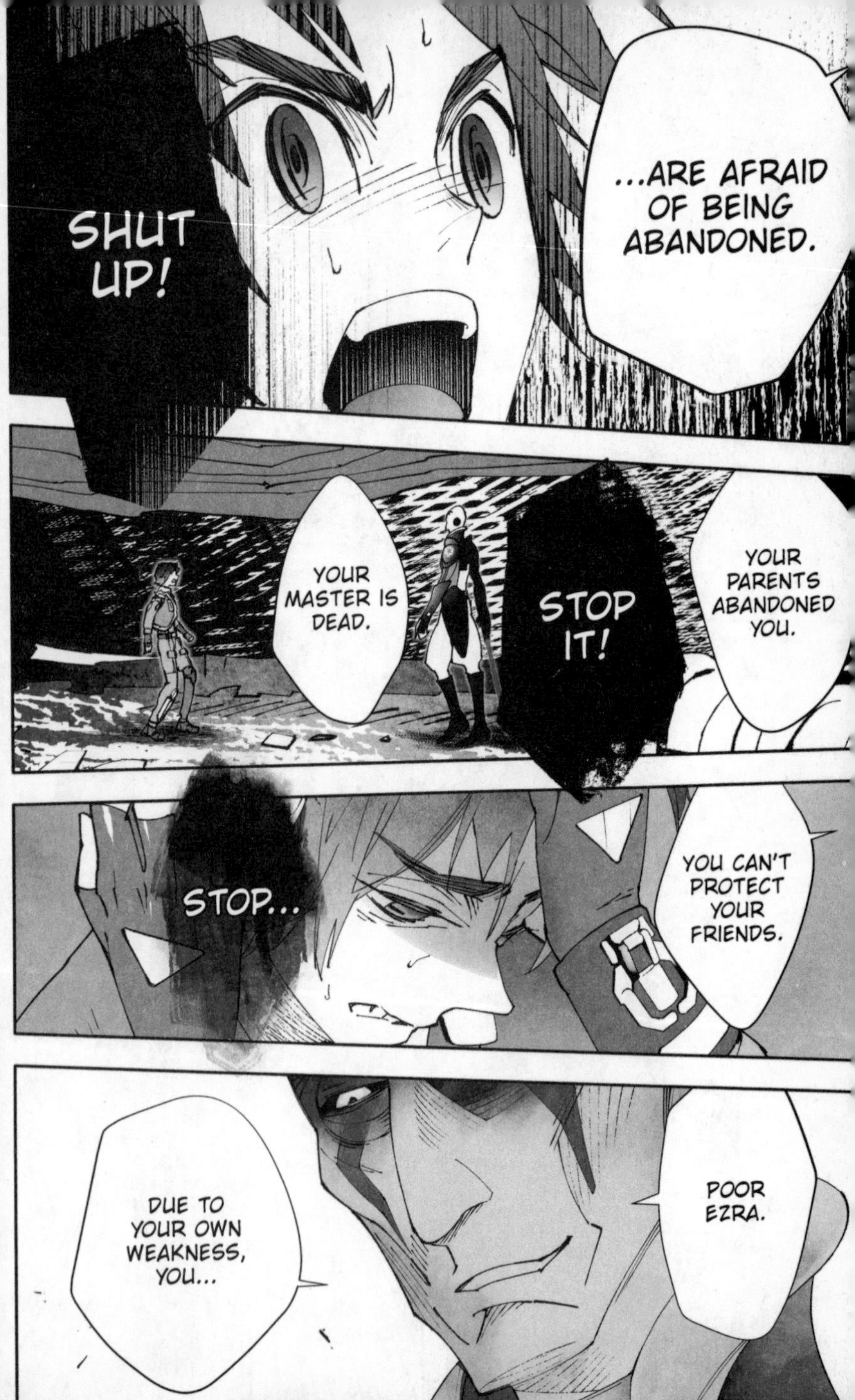
...ARE AFRAID OF BEING ABANDONED.
SHUT UP!
YOUR PARENTS ABANDONED YOU.
STOP IT!
YOUR MASTER IS DEAD.
YOU CAN'T PROTECT YOUR FRIENDS.
STOP...
POOR EZRA.
DUE TO YOUR OWN WEAKNESS, YOU...

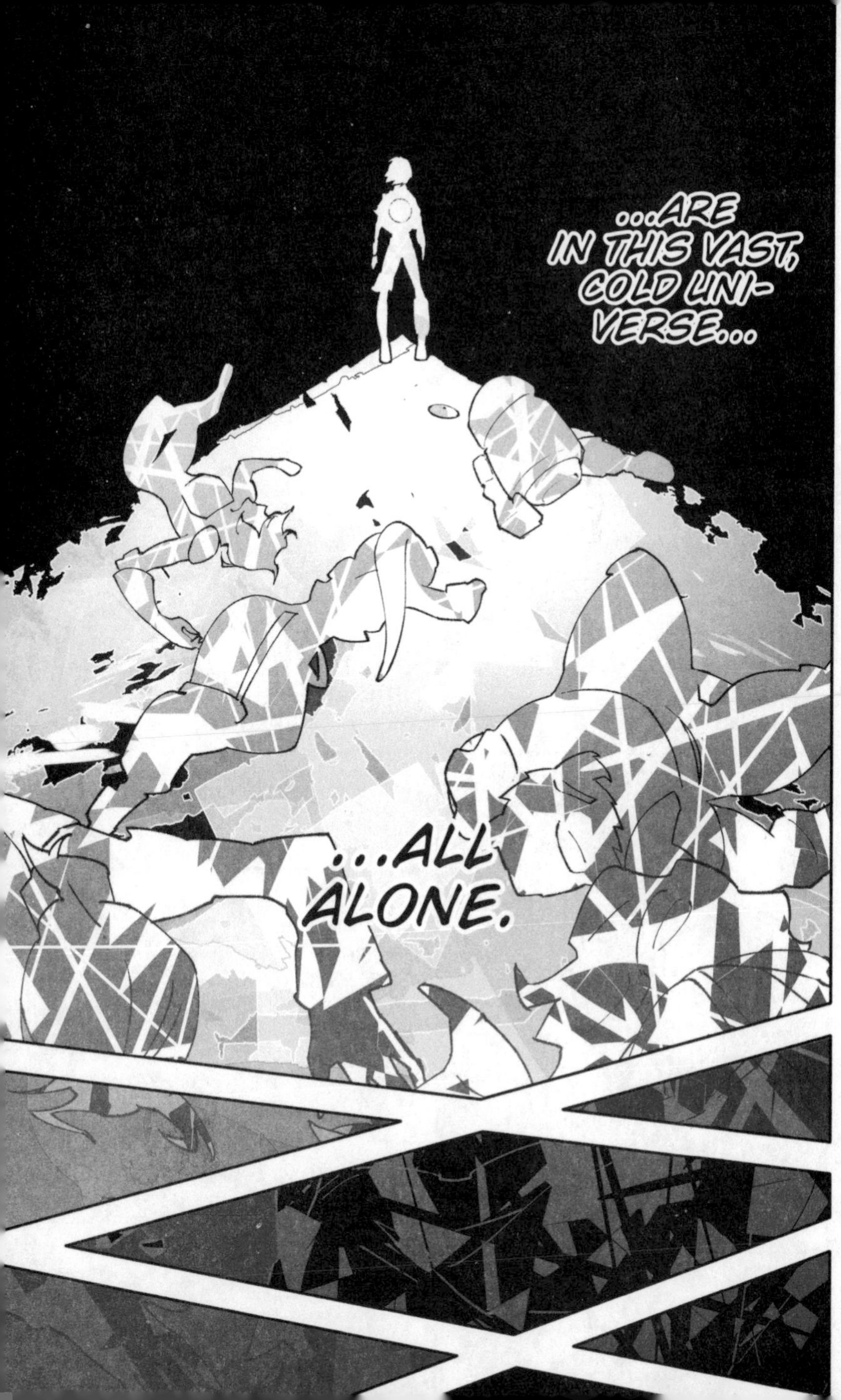
...ARE IN THIS VAST, COLD UNI-VERSE...
...ALL ALONE.

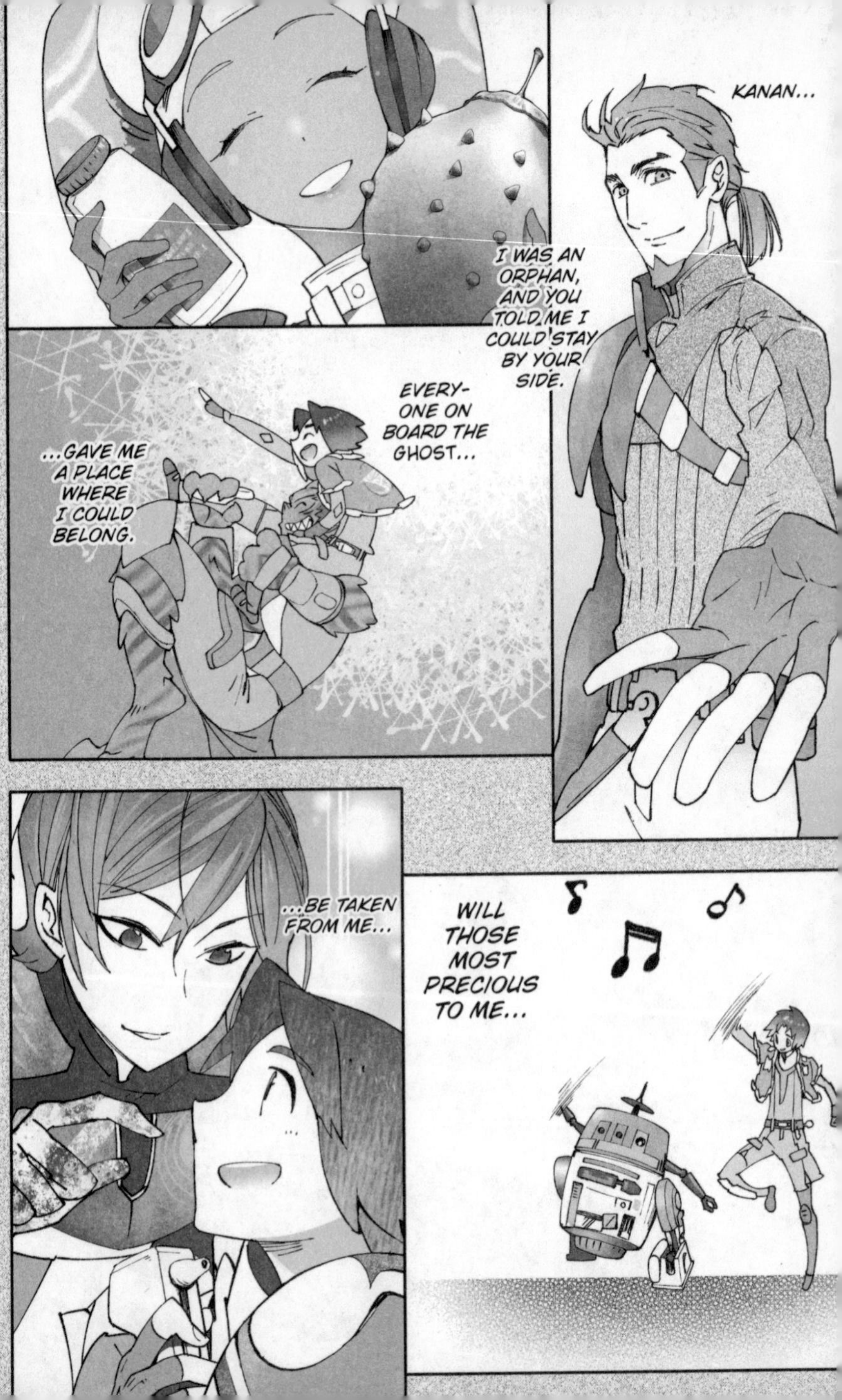
KANAN...
I WAS AN ORPHAN, AND YOU TOLD ME I COULD STAY BY YOUR SIDE.
EVERY-ONE ON BOARD THE GHOST...
...GAVE ME A PLACE WHERE I COULD BELONG.
WILL THOSE MOST PRECIOUS TO ME...
...BE TAKEN FROM ME...

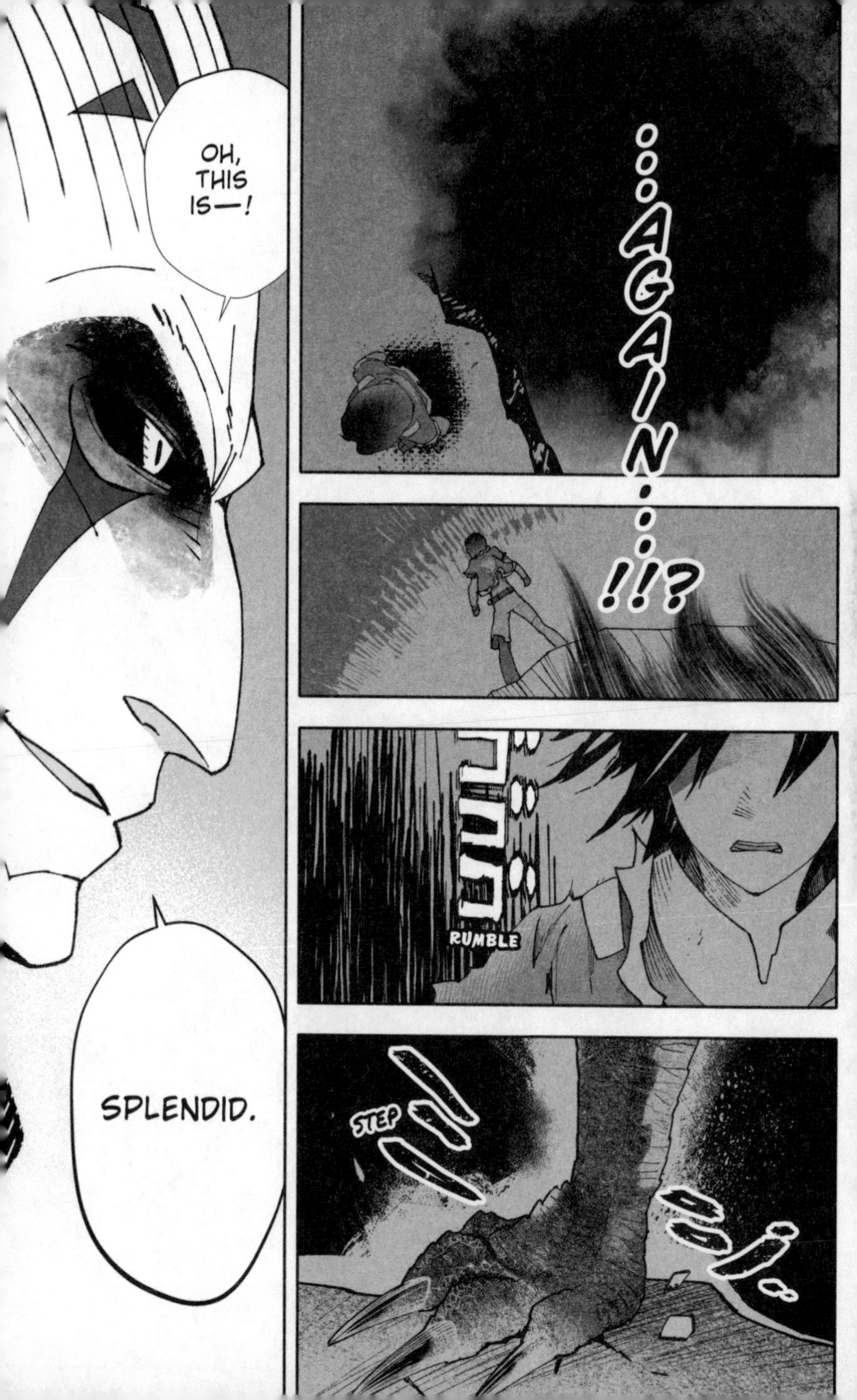
...AGAIN...!!?
RUMBLE
STEP
OH, THIS IS—!
SPLENDID.

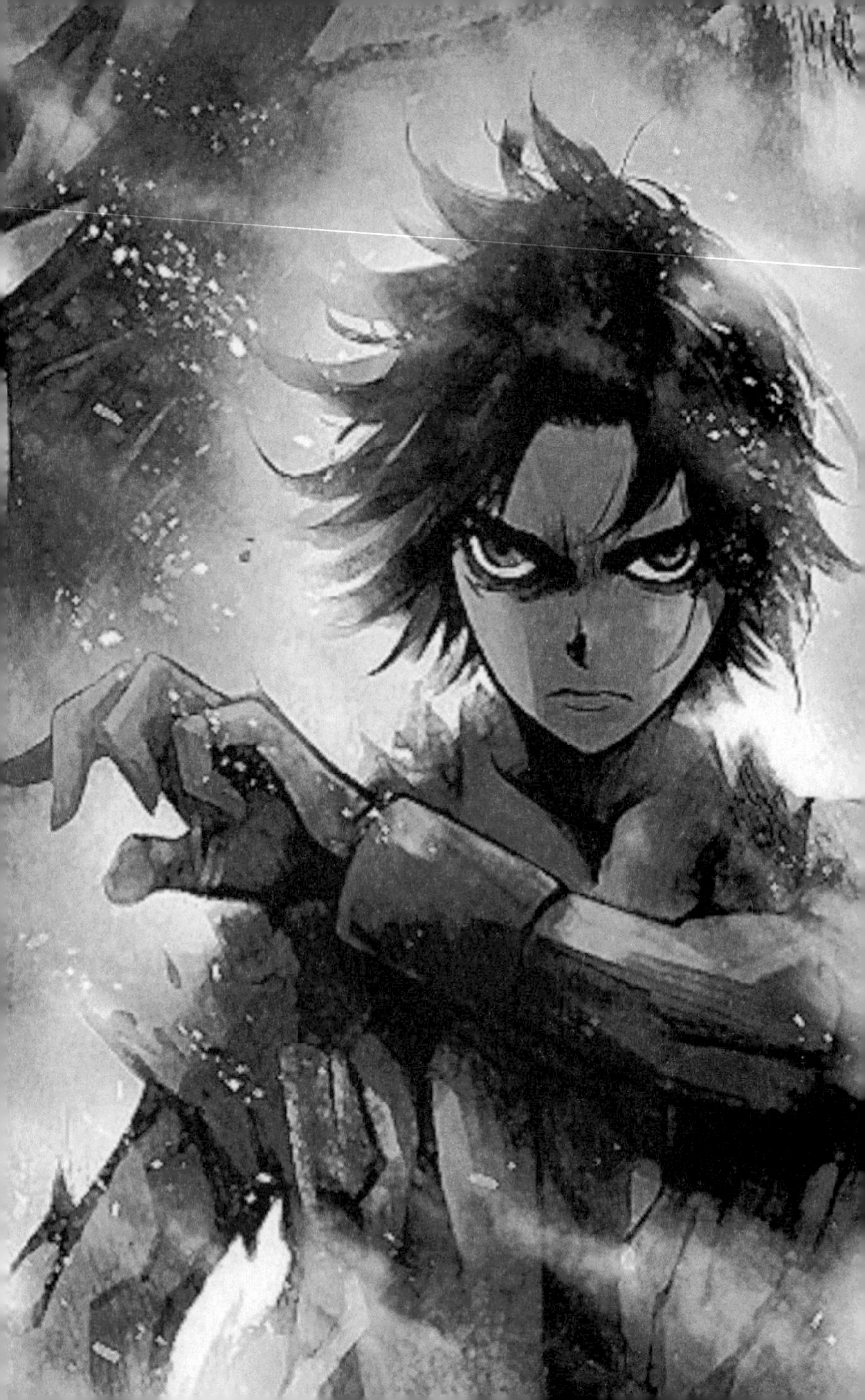

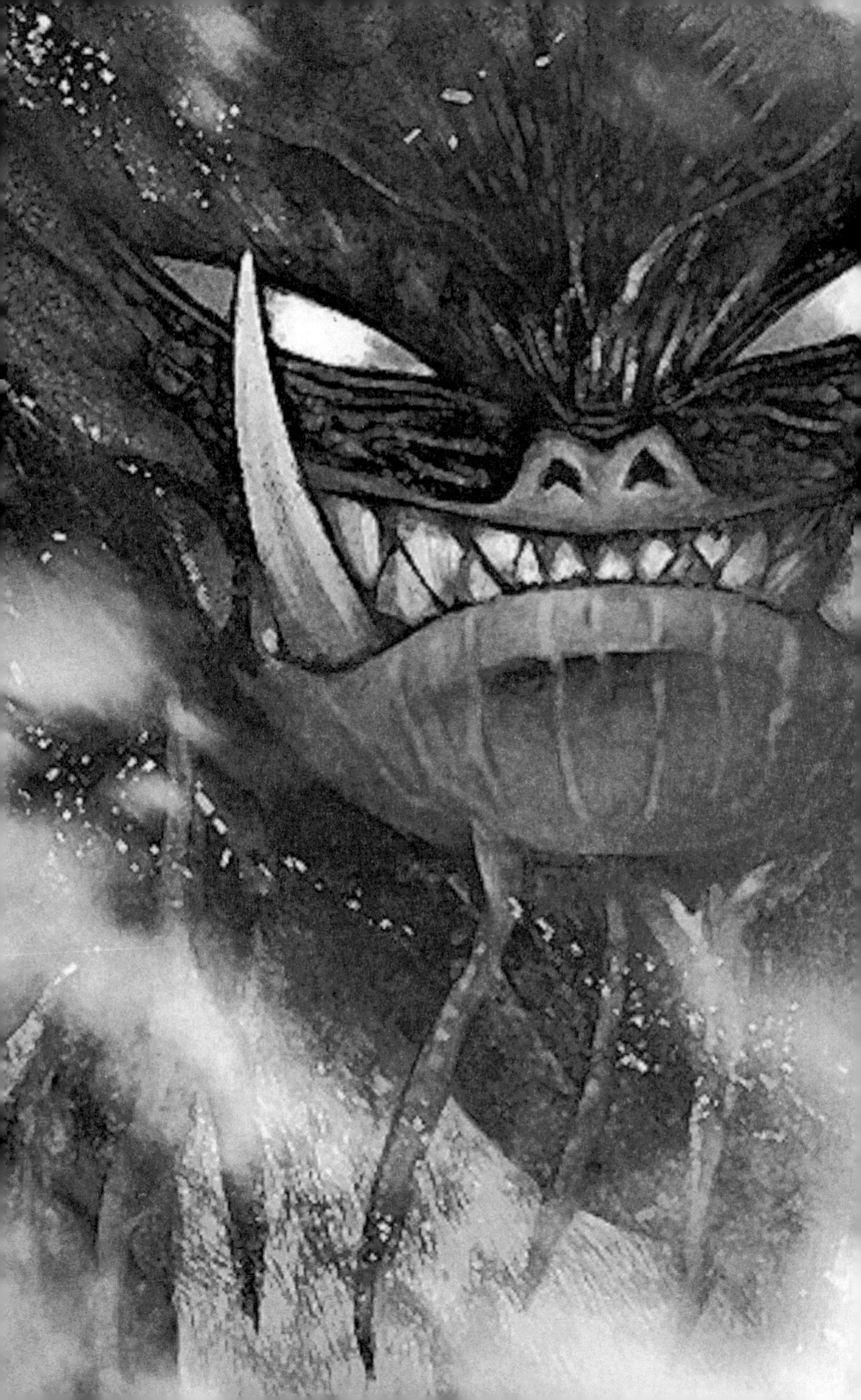

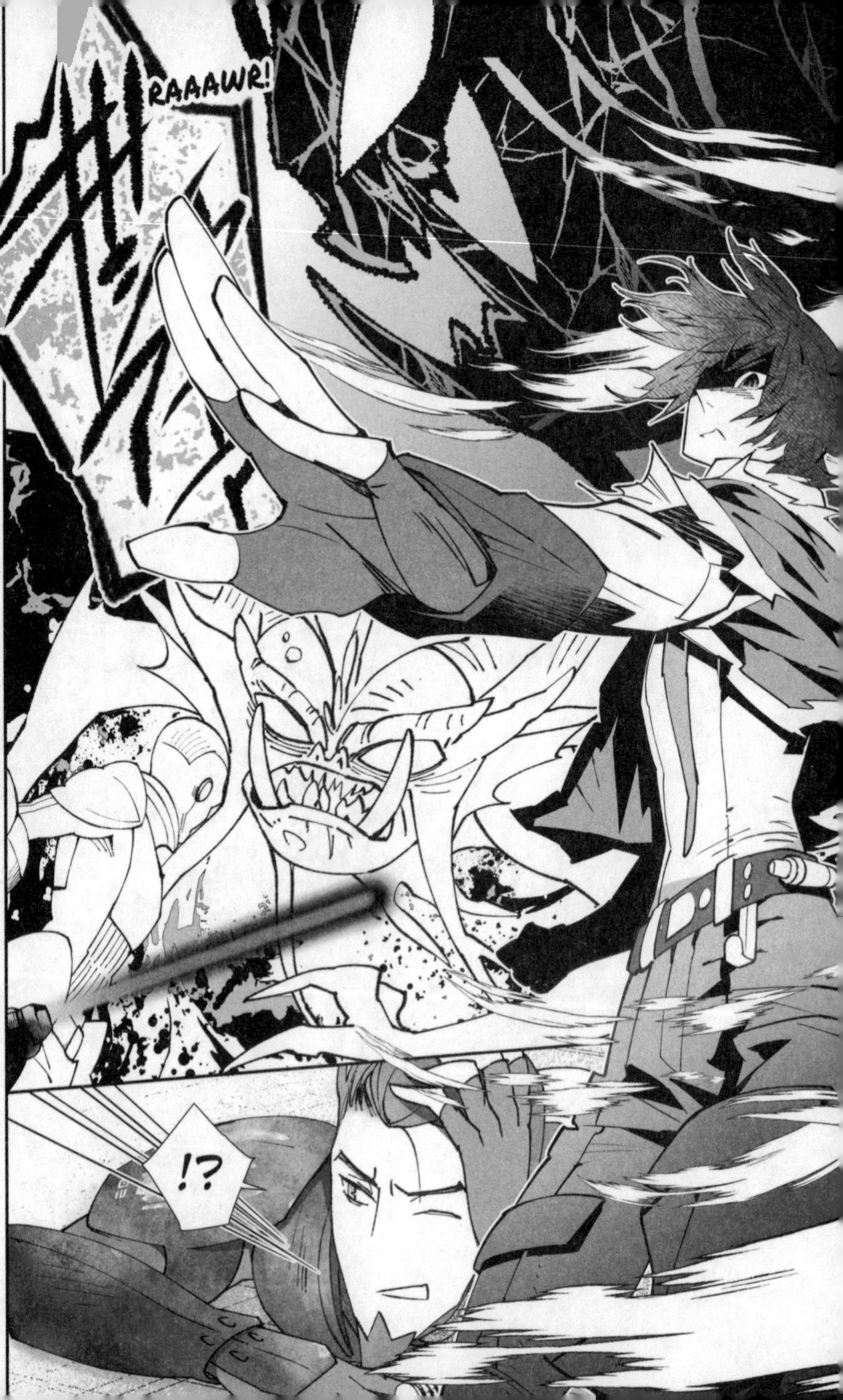
RAAAWR!
!?

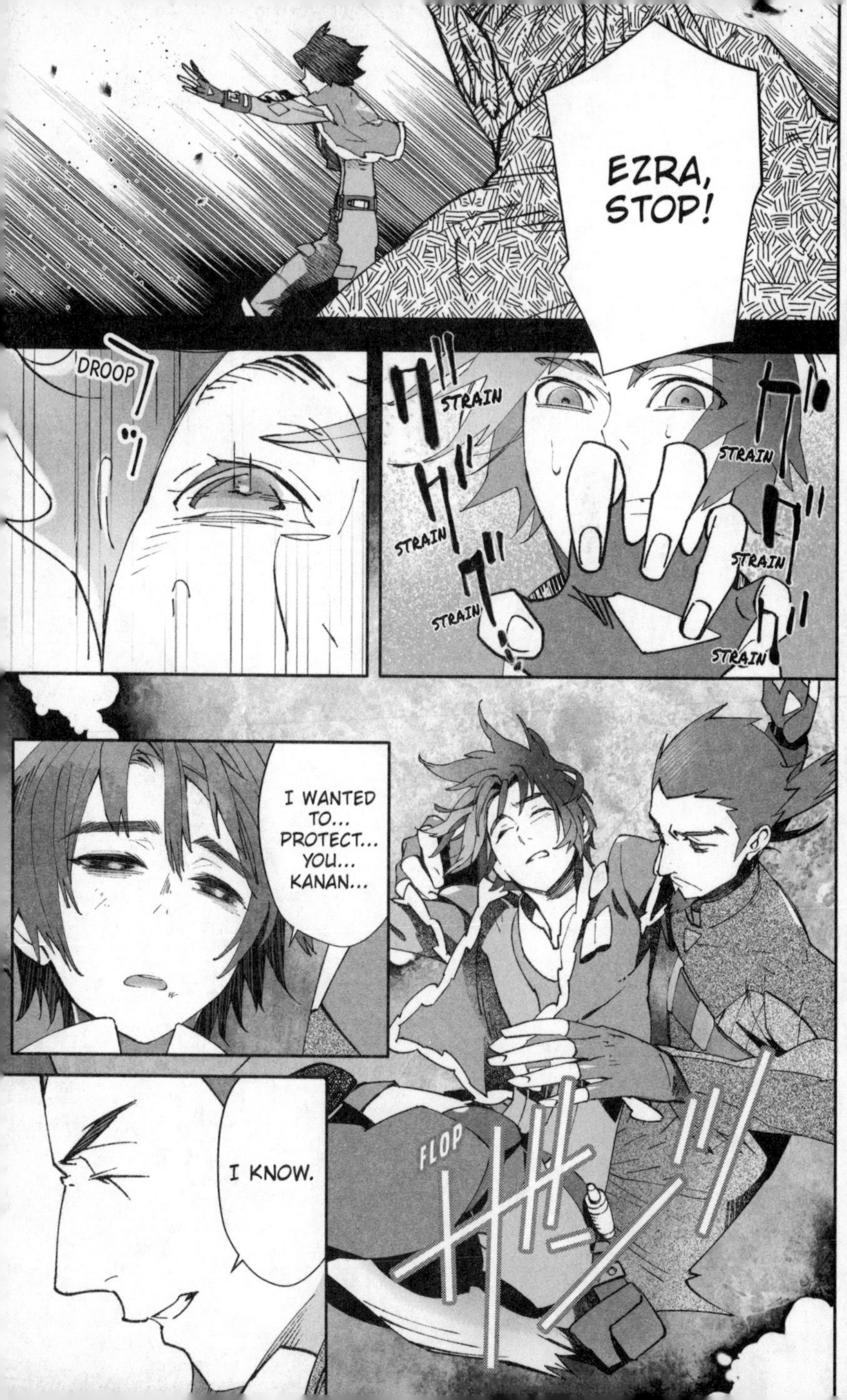
EZRA, STOP!
STRAIN
STRAIN
STRAIN
STRAIN
STRAIN
STRAIN
DROOP
FLOP
I WANTED TO... PROTECT... YOU... KANAN...
I KNOW.

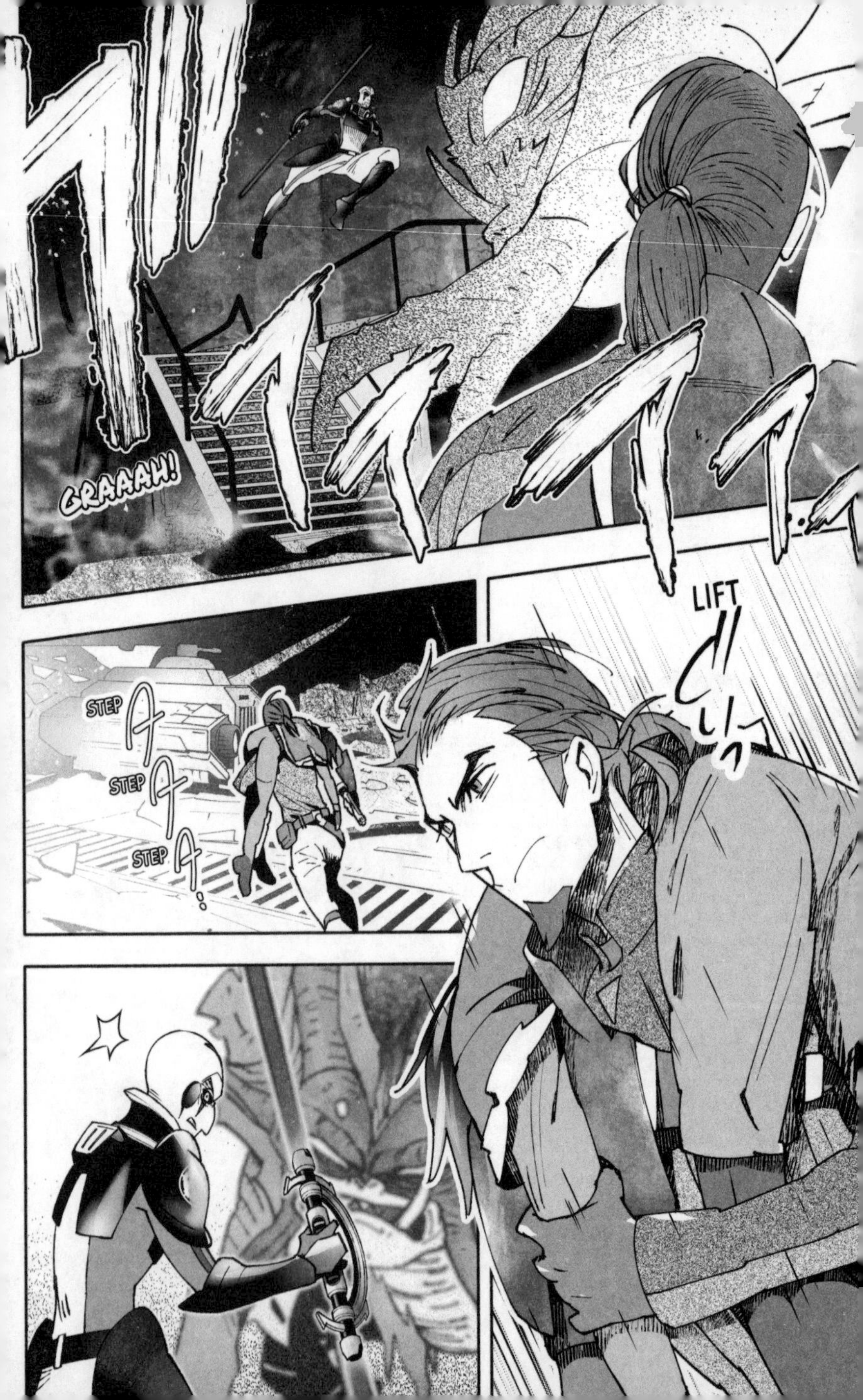
GRAAAH!
LIFT
STEP
STEP
STEP

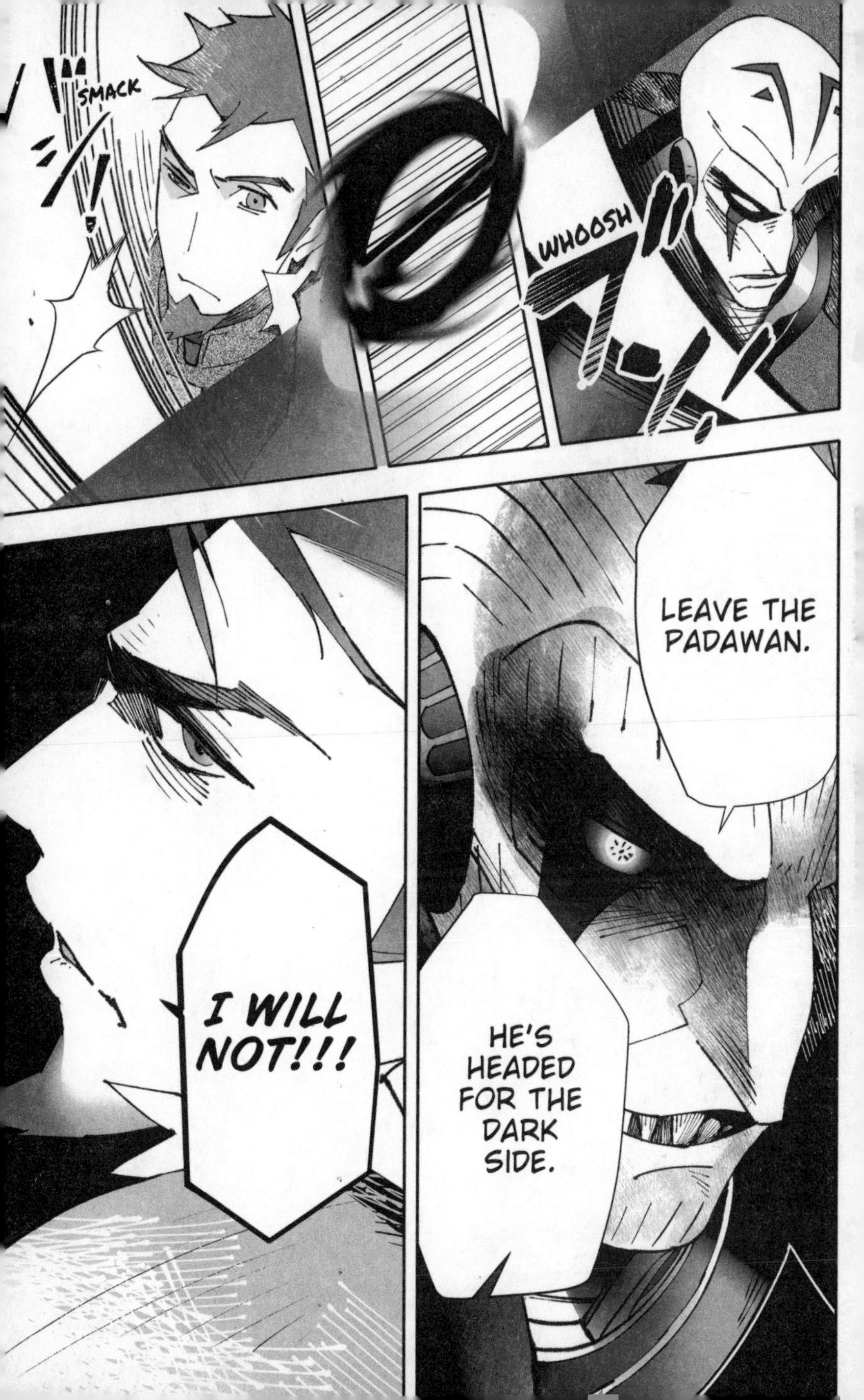
WHOOSH
SMACK
LEAVE THE PADAWAN.
HE'S HEADED FOR THE DARK SIDE.
I WILL NOT!!!

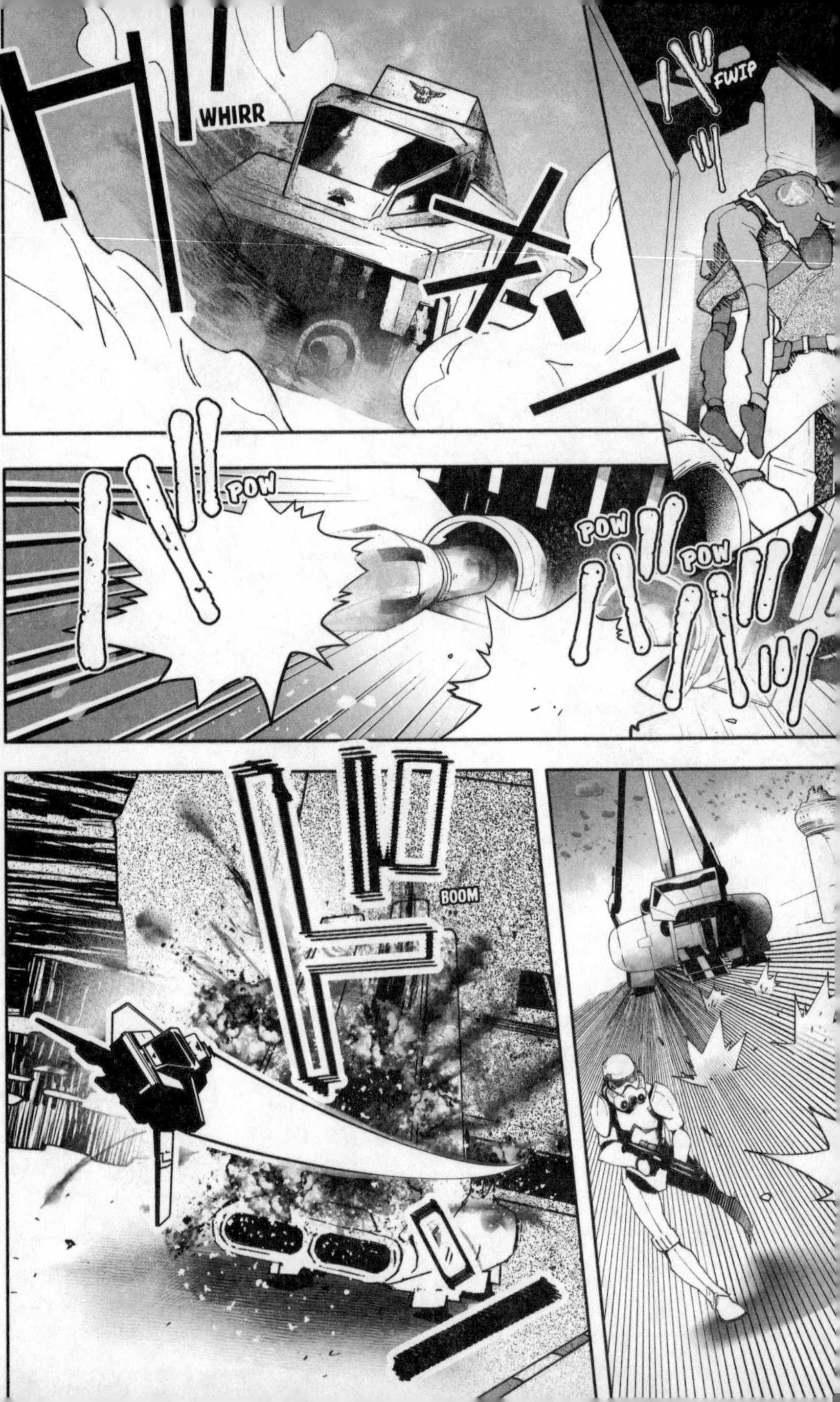
FWIP
WHIRR
POW
POW
POW
BOOM

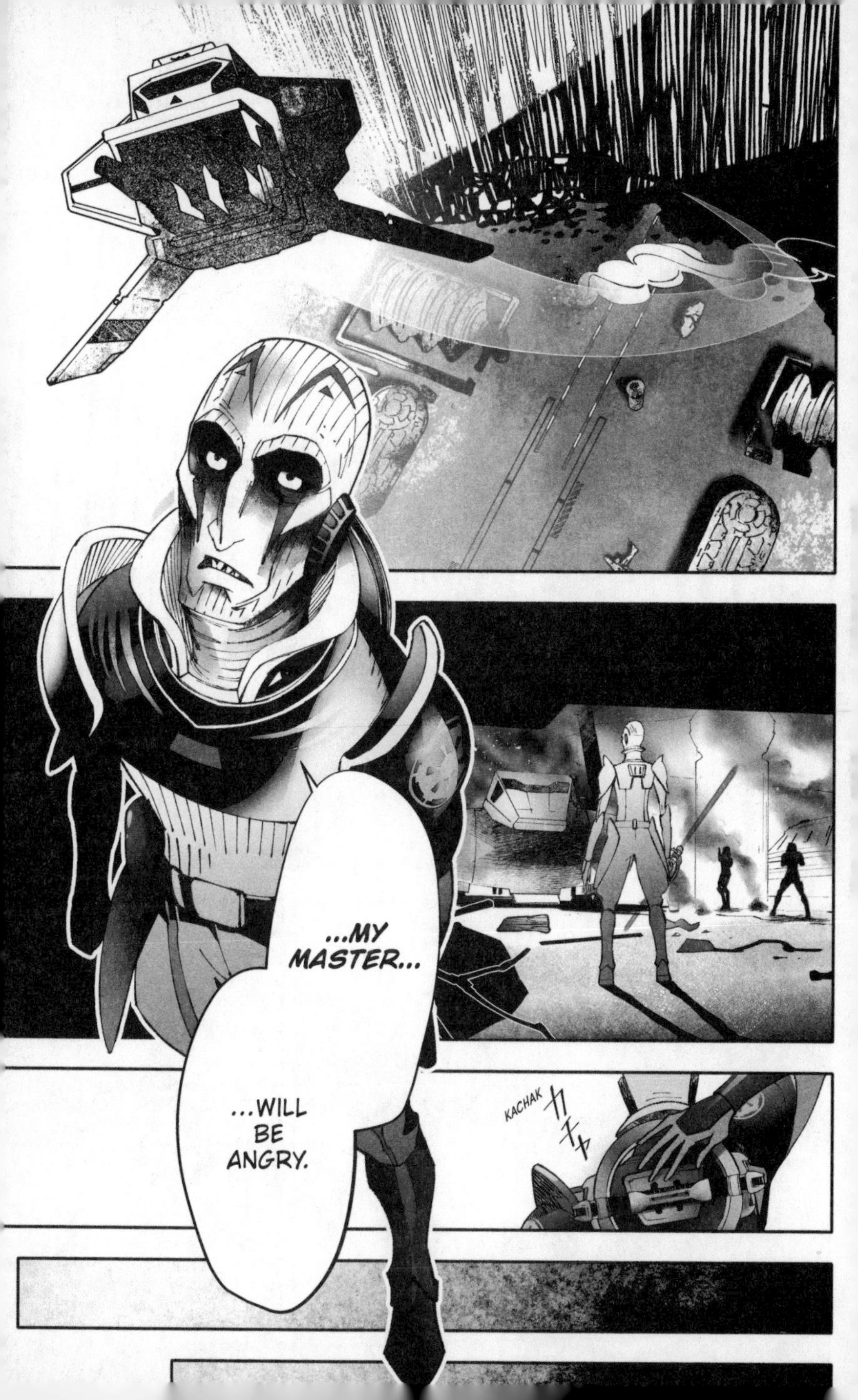
...MY MASTER...
...WILL BE ANGRY.
KACHAK

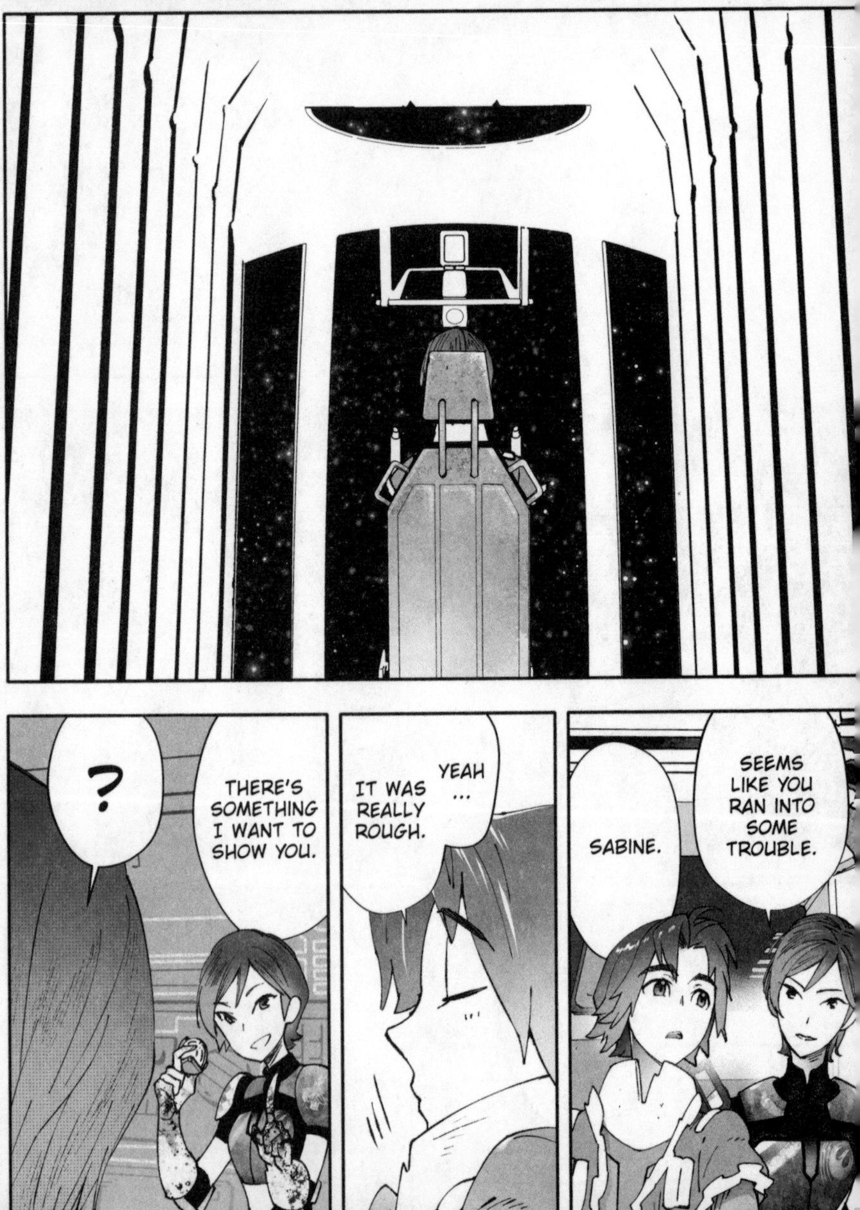
SEEMS LIKE YOU RAN INTO SOME TROUBLE.
SABINE.
YEAH ...
IT WAS REALLY ROUGH.
THERE'S SOMETHING I WANT TO SHOW YOU.
?

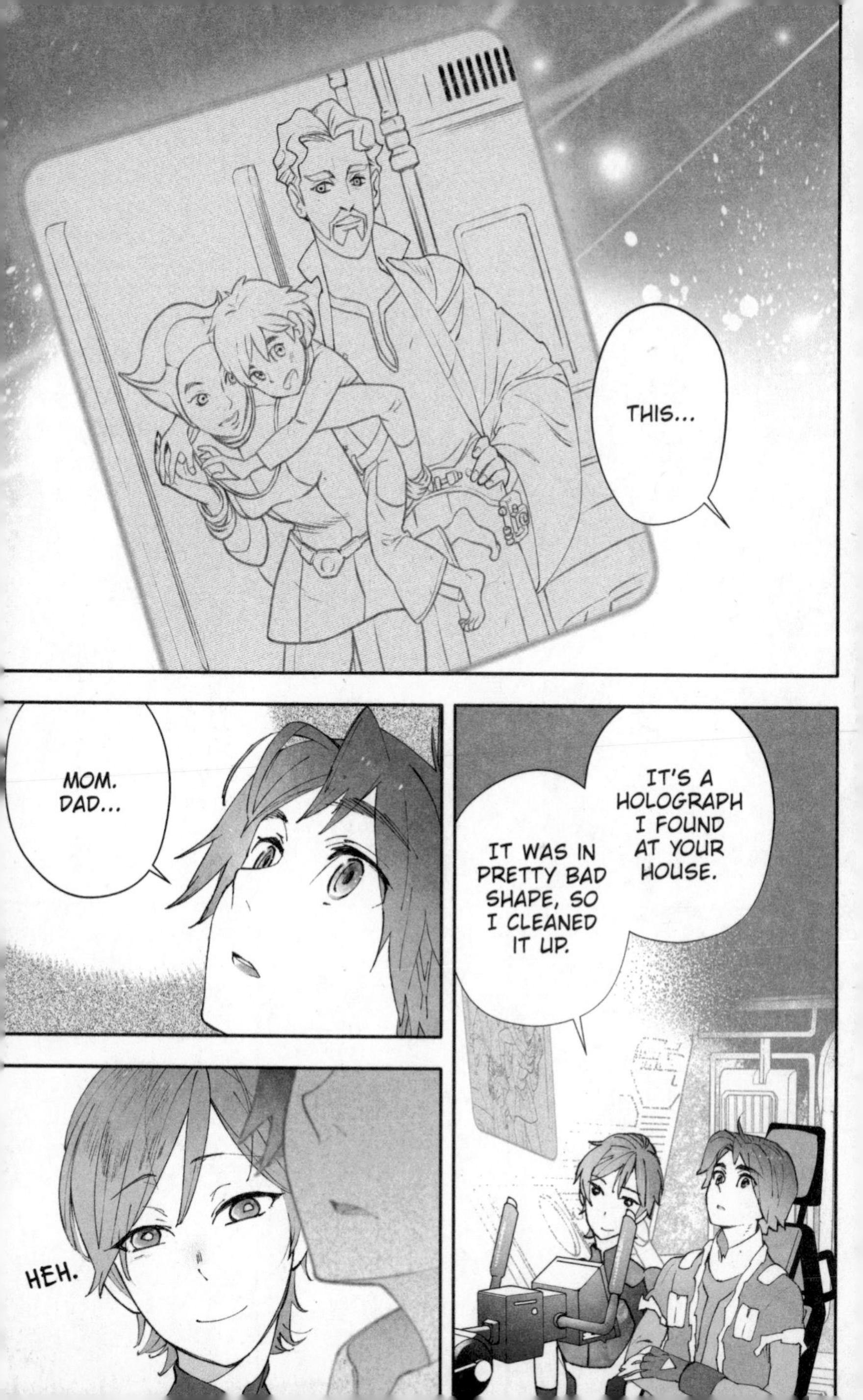
THIS...
IT'S A HOLOGRAPH I FOUND AT YOUR HOUSE.
IT WAS IN PRETTY BAD SHAPE, SO I CLEANED IT UP.
MOM. DAD...
HEH.

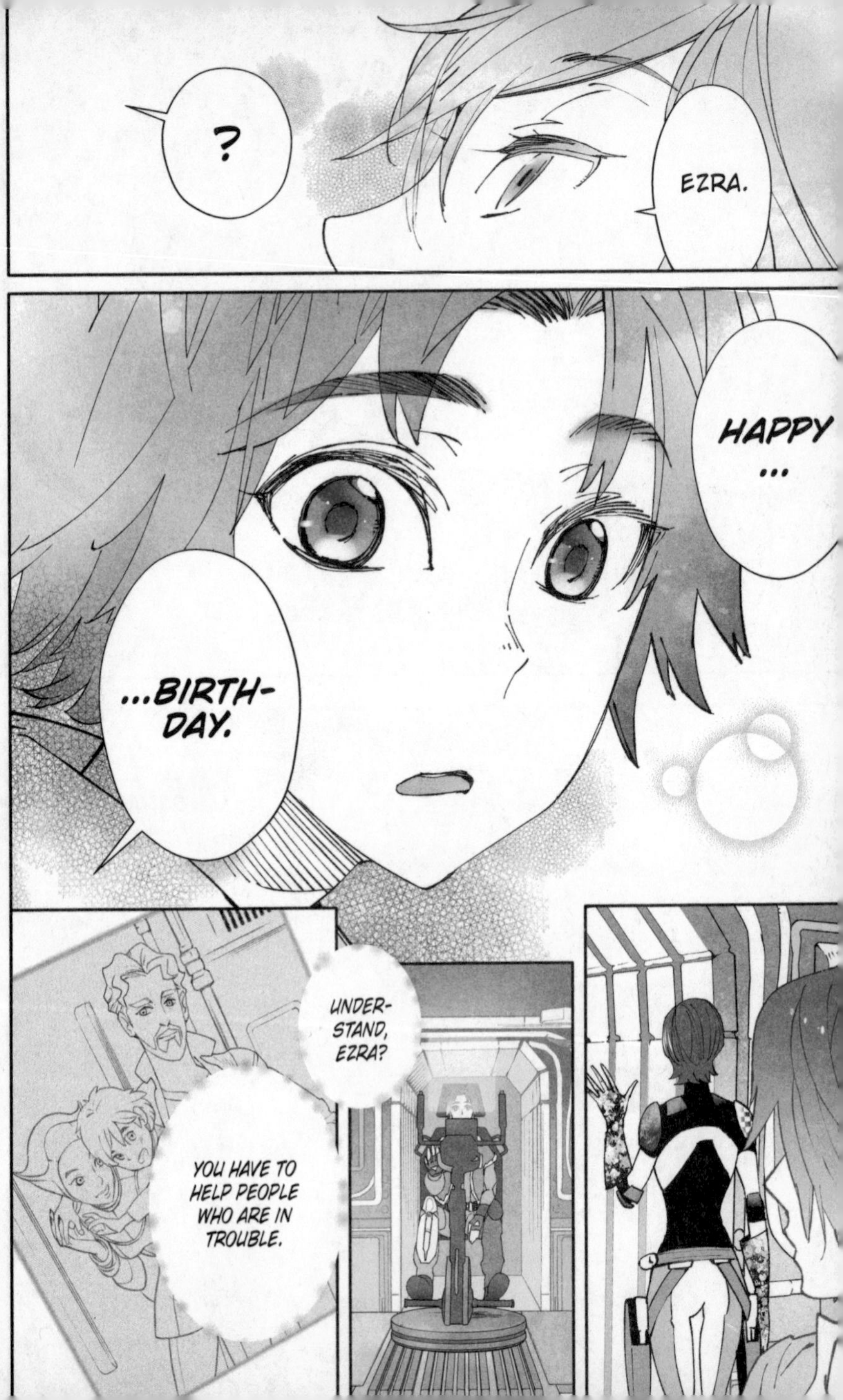
EZRA.
?
HAPPY ...
...BIRTH-DAY.
UNDER-STAND, EZRA?
YOU HAVE TO HELP PEOPLE WHO ARE IN TROUBLE.

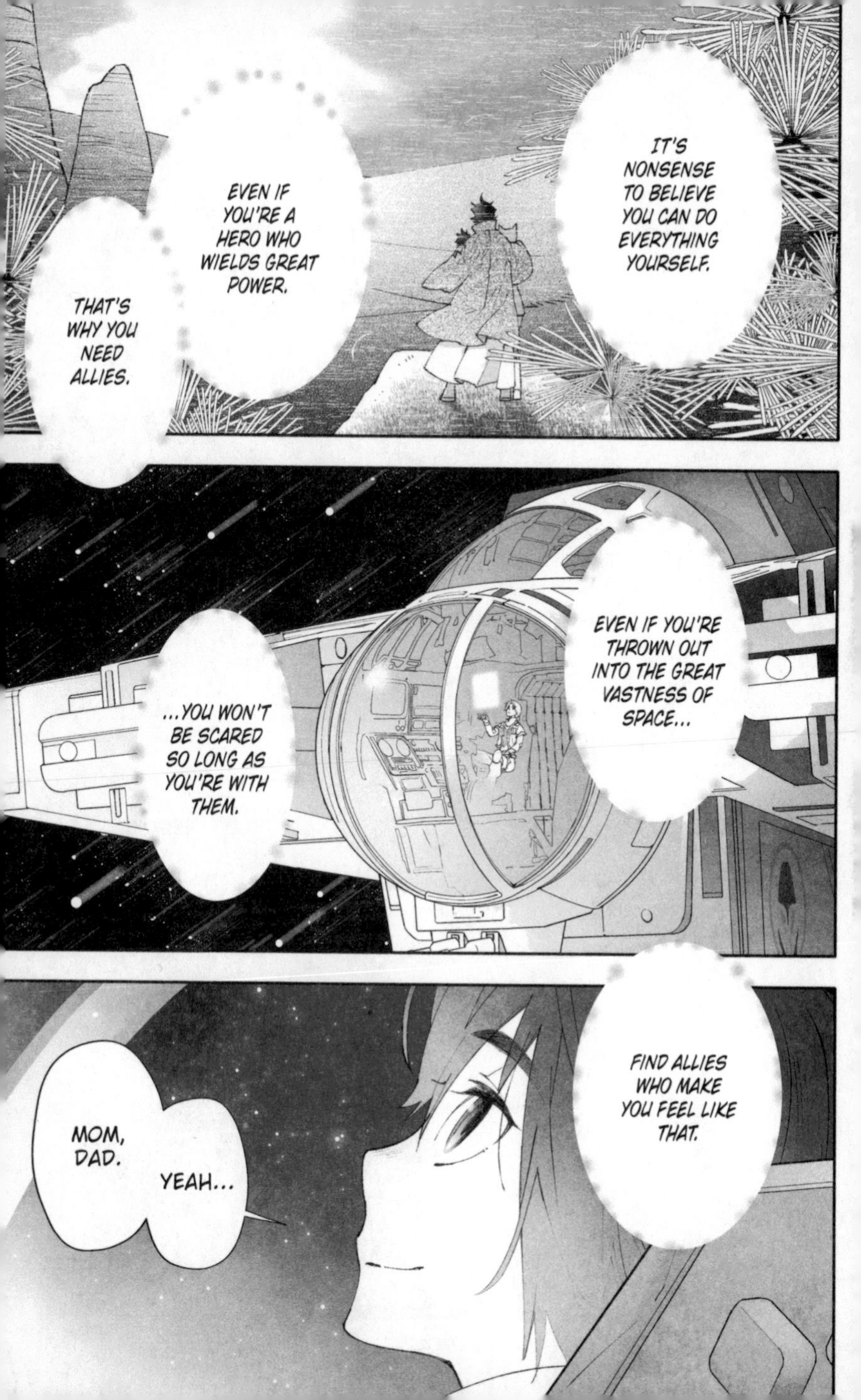
IT'S NONSENSE TO BELIEVE YOU CAN DO EVERYTHING YOURSELF.
EVEN IF YOU'RE A HERO WHO WIELDS GREAT POWER.
THAT'S WHY YOU NEED ALLIES.
EVEN IF YOU'RE THROWN OUT INTO THE GREAT VASTNESS OF SPACE...
...YOU WON'T BE SCARED SO LONG AS YOU'RE WITH THEM.
FIND ALLIES WHO MAKE YOU FEEL LIKE THAT.
MOM, DAD.
YEAH...

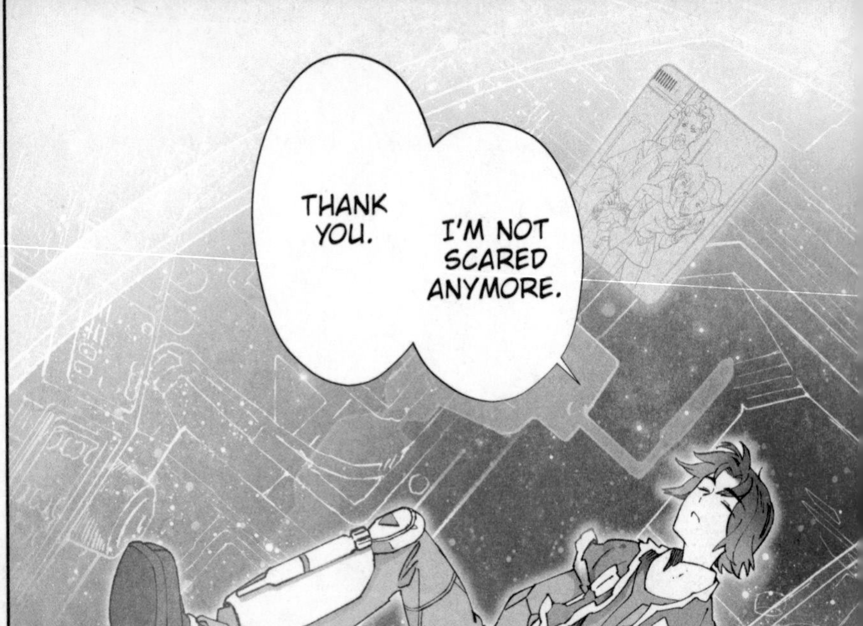
THANK YOU.
I'M NOT SCARED ANYMORE.
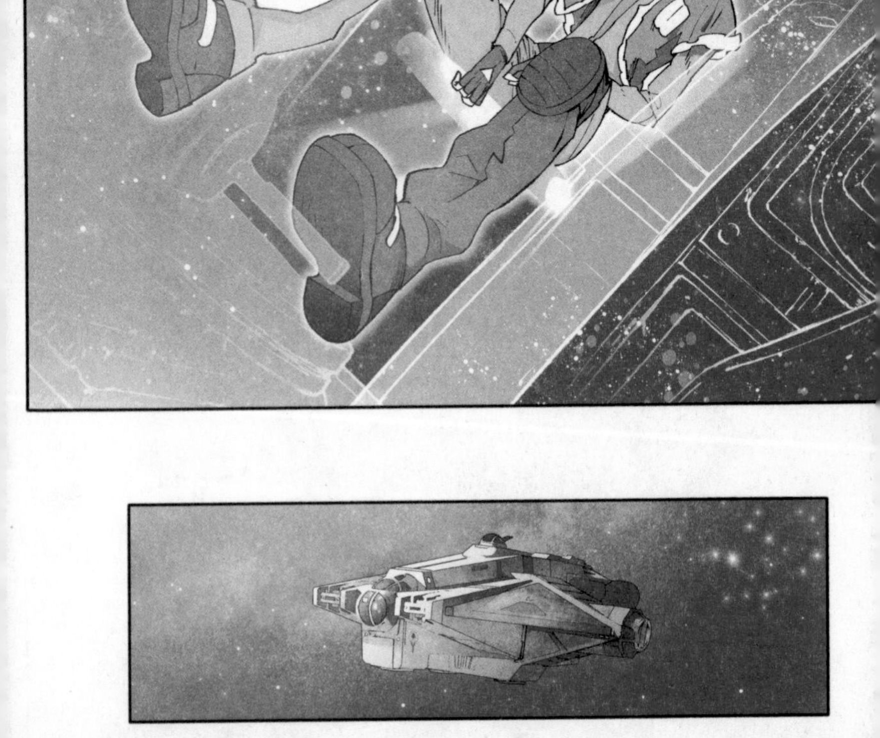

STAR WARS
REBELS
VOLUME **2 — END**

STAR WARS
REBELS